Praise for Prior Editions of *The Complete Idiot's Guide to Starting Your Own Business*

"As a novice entrepreneur, *The Compete Idiot's Guide to Starting Your Own Business* has provided me with easy-to-follow, detailed step-by-step procedures required to establish and maintain a successful small business. It was very helpful to read the experiences of other entrepreneurs as well, which enlightened me to the opportunities and pitfalls of owning my own business. It's really the only book you'll need to start a small business."

—Bonnie Neroda, ASID, owner, Bonnie's Creations

"About two years ago, I was considering purchasing an existing business … I prepared a business plan using your book as a guide [and] realized the business was not profitable and decided not to purchase it. I found out later the business was purchased by someone else, and closed down about a year later! Your book saved me $100,000! Thank you!"

—Jan Magree, vice president, Image Pro Services & Supplies, Inc.

"I have recommended *The Complete Idiot's Guide to Starting Your Own Business* to numerous clients who are contemplating or have already embarked on their own commercial venture. This guide serves as an outstanding introduction and subsequent desk reference that puts to rest myths and points out realities so that the new entrepreneur is aptly prepped to go forward."

—Kenneth G. Daemicke, CPA, principal, Mulcahy, Pauritsch, Salvador & Co., Ltd. (mpscpa.com)

"This book answers your business questions and is a great resource for anyone who's starting up their dream. The price of the book is saved on what you now won't have to spend on accounting and lawyer advice."

—Frank Warner, founder and president, Electronic Script Prompting

"*The Complete Idiot's Guide to Starting Your Own Business* is a treasure trove of valuable information for the beginner to the seasoned entrepreneur. I had a business idea but no understanding of where to start, and Ed gave me that understanding. He seemed to know what questions I needed answers to. I highly recommend his guide as your new business bible."

—Richard Foster, CEO, SuperF111

"When I graduated from school I believe that I received about 45 minutes on the business aspects of practice. *The Complete Idiot's Guide to Starting Your Own Business* is what is needed and wanted. At the very least, it should be used as a referral to help make those tough early decisions."

—Richard C. Gelband, owner and chiropractor, Gelband Natural Health and Chiropractic

"Managing the legal and financial aspects of a company is complicated. Thanks for making it easy to understand so that I can spend more time building my business."

—Joe Pipal, builder

"Anyone starting a business must read this book first. It is a concise, easy-to-understand guide that will save time and money. I recommend it to my business clients."

—Geraldine J. Tucker, attorney and consultant, Law Office of Geraldine J. Tucker

"The first day on the job of your new business should be spent reading this one-of-a-kind guide to launching your new venture. Paulson's advice provides practical, relevant strategies to the most important issues facing every small business founder."

—Dan McManus, founder and president, Team Floral and McManus Group

"Paulson's guide is an invaluable tool. As a small business owner it helped me with everything from accounting and knowing how to interview potential employees to being in touch with my truest motivation for being in business in the first place."

—Anne Heaton, singer-songwriter, business owner (anneheaton.com)

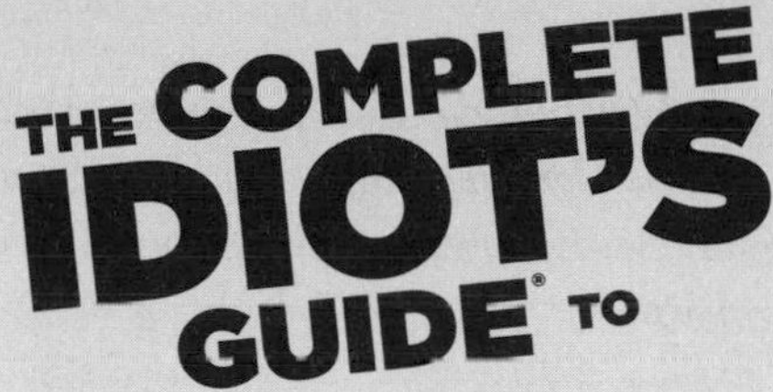

Starting Your Own Business

Sixth Edition

by Ed Paulson

A member of Penguin Group (USA) Inc.

Dedicated to the many readers, clients, and students who continue to teach me, and for whom I hope this returns the favor.

ALPHA BOOKS

Published by the Penguin Group

Penguin Group (USA) Inc., 375 Hudson Street, New York, New York 10014, USA • Penguin Group (Canada), 90 Eglinton Avenue East, Suite 700, Toronto, Ontario M4P 2Y3, Canada (a division of Pearson Penguin Canada Inc.) • Penguin Books Ltd., 80 Strand, London WC2R 0RL, England • Penguin Ireland, 25 St. Stephen's Green, Dublin 2, Ireland (a division of Penguin Books Ltd.) • Penguin Group (Australia), 250 Camberwell Road, Camberwell, Victoria 3124, Australia (a division of Pearson Australia Group Pty. Ltd.) • Penguin Books India Pvt. Ltd., 11 Community Centre, Panchsheel Park, New Delhi—110 017, India • Penguin Group (NZ), 67 Apollo Drive, Rosedale, North Shore, Auckland 1311, New Zealand (a division of Pearson New Zealand Ltd.) • Penguin Books (South Africa) (Pty.) Ltd., 24 Sturdee Avenue, Rosebank, Johannesburg 2196, South Africa • Penguin Books Ltd., Registered Offices: 80 Strand, London WC2R 0RL, England

International Standard Book Number: 978-1-61564-151-2
Library of Congress Catalog Card Number: 2011936775

14 13 12 8 7 6 5 4 3 2 1

Interpretation of the printing code: The rightmost number of the first series of numbers is the year of the book's printing; the rightmost number of the second series of numbers is the number of the book's printing. For example, a printing code of 12-1 shows that the first printing occurred in 2012.

Printed in the United States of America

Publisher: *Marie Butler-Knight*
Associate Publisher: *Mike Sanders*
Executive Managing Editor: *Billy Fields*
Senior Acquisitions Editor: *Brook Farling*
Development Editor: *Nancy D. Lewis*
Senior Production Editor: *Kayla Dugger*

Copy Editor: *Amy Borrelli*
Cover Designer: *Rebecca Batchelor*
Book Designers: *William Thomas, Rebecca Batchelor*
Indexer: *Julie Bess*
Layout: *Ayanna Lacey*
Senior Proofreader: *Laura Caddell*

Contents

Appendixes

Introduction

Becoming your own boss makes a lot of personal and financial sense. Personally, you have more control over your destiny and can better plan your future because you call your own shots. Financially, your future income is dependent on how hard and smart you work instead of on the whim of an employer. Many of us have worked hard for an employer, sacrificing weekends with family or vacations, only to receive a small salary increase at the end of the year and *maybe* a thank-you. I worked at a couple of jobs where my sales activities made the company boatloads of money, only to have executives become unavailable when it came time for them to pay the commissions that they contractually owed me. One day I got fed up with working for people who were interested in making short-term money for themselves (totally okay with me) while demonstrating little interest in doing right by the employees who were making them rich (not okay). On that day I started taking steps toward becoming my own boss. It took some time, but eventually I made it happen.

If you are someone with a great boss and someone who enjoys his or her job, then I am happy for you. But I am starting to believe that happy employees who trust their employers are becoming a rarity. It is common for me to meet people who are dissatisfied with their job, who don't trust their employer, who don't feel like they are being rewarded for working harder, and who want more control over their financial future. For these folks, starting a business is the obvious next step, and my fervent intent with this book is to put the odds of startup success on their side.

Some people start a business without a lot of introspection or planning; these businesses often earn minimal income, if they survive at all. Unfortunately, when these businesses close down they take dreams, aspirations, investment capital, and reputations with them, returning the founders to corporate employment—if they can even find a job. It is my belief that wrapping their passion and money around a unique business idea validated with a smart plan would have helped them avoid their later travails. I applaud their willingness to take a chance and their resolve; I also want to see them achieve the business outcome they envision instead of discouragement.

A lot is involved with turning a new business idea into a financially successful venture, and much of what happens is inside of you. Typical questions you might find yourself asking are: "What type of business should I start?" "Should I buy a franchise or an established business instead of starting my own?" "I have kids going to college in a few years. Am I being selfish to risk their tuition money on my new business idea?" "My spouse would have to carry the brunt of the family and financial responsibilities for a while after I start the business. Is this asking too much?" "Can I really afford to give up my current job with its salary, insurance, and social benefits?"

These questions are some of the toughest questions we have to answer in our lives because many of them have no simple "right" answers. I hear them frequently from people interested in starting a business, and I assume you have a lot of them, too, which is why most of Part 1 is dedicated to helping you answer them.

Let's complicate it even more by adding that selecting the right business for you is not as easy as it sounds. Questions come up such as: "Who will use my services?" "How much can I charge?" "How many will I be able to sell?" "How much will it cost me to build the product?" "How much will it cost me to keep the lights on?" "Will I need an office?" "How much will I take home in pay at the end of the year?" "How much will it cost me to get the business started?" And many, many, more. It helps to have someone experienced working with you as you answer these questions, and I hope that the experiences presented on these pages serve that purpose.

Hundreds of thousands of people have purchased the five earlier editions of this book, and many have let me know how the book contributed to their startup success. A sampling of these businesses would include a home entertainment system design and installation service, a dog health-food retail store, a real estate inspection service, a home and business environmental testing service, an antique doll refurbishing eBay home business, a very successful independent musician, a therapeutic massage practice, several chiropractic practices, and many others. The approach presented is based on a lifetime of my experiences and those of my colleagues, friends, and students. Using the presented method will put the odds of success in your favor.

I ask you to push yourself one level beyond simply making a living as your own boss. I am going to ask you to accept that work can be something you do as an expression of who you are and your personal passion. That's right! I contend that you can have fun working at something you love, and make a lot of money as you do it. Try to imagine a world where you look forward to going to work, where you feel that your work makes a real difference, where you enjoy working with customers, where you are making more money than you have ever made before, and where you control your own destiny. All of this is possible when you own the right business for *you*. I have seen clients start businesses from scratch and a few years later take home nearly half a million dollars in annual personal income while their business continued to grow at double-digit rates. Yes. It is possible, but only if you are dedicated and smart about making it happen.

When you have finished the book you will have: 1) evaluated yourself as a business owner; 2) picked the type of business that is right for you; 3) created a plan that simulates whether your idea makes business sense or not; and 4) be on your way to successfully making it through your first year of operation. If you love your business idea and believe it can make you a decent living, take the time to evaluate it objectively before taking the plunge. Any good idea deserves at least that, and so do you.

The approach in this sixth edition is different from earlier editions based in large part on feedback from readers, colleagues, and my adult DePaul University entrepreneurship students. Yes. My students are typically in the 30- to 55-year-old range and are taking my classes to learn how to start their own business. They are probably a lot like you, and their feedback helped me revise this edition to make it a more valuable tool *for* you.

- Important chapters were added to help you assess yourself regarding your business and personal interests, along with your tolerance for risk and uncertainty. Special emphasis is placed in evaluating your current job in light of starting your own business, addressing the common issues that pop up.
- Special chapters were added that cover using technology and information to uncover new online businesses ideas, along with an approach to using social networking as a powerful new business marketing tool.
- Editable versions of most of the business legal forms you will need to start and run your business are included for free at the website. I use many of these forms myself, and using only one form will pay for the book in the legal savings. Readers who do not check out the website are ignoring a huge benefit. Don't be one of them.
- Special emphasis was placed on not only writing a great business plan but also understanding how it will be read, interpreted, and used by investors, key employees, and other stakeholders. You are not writing just a plan, but writing a plan that will achieve a specific result from key people.
- Part 4 was put together to help you focus on the issues that are critical to surviving your first year in operation. A special chapter was included, based on reader feedback, that covers recognizing if your new venture is in trouble and should be shut down before it takes you with it. A sad topic, for sure, but an important one.
- You will find additional content at the website that complements what's included in the book. Again, not checking out the website is a huge mistake.

I have incorporated the key points from prior editions while adding material that keeps the book current, comprehensive, and useful for you. I continually learn from my clients, students, and readers, and these important and sometimes painful lessons are included here for you to understand and apply. This isn't reality television. This is the real world where people have invested real time, real money, had real success, experienced real disappointment, and shared real stories.

I have been in one form or another of entrepreneurship for over 30 years, and I can tell you without question that there is nothing more exciting than seeing your idea become a thriving reality—and there are few things more painful than seeing it die. You don't have to go through a windshield before learning to wear a seat belt. I and my colleagues have already been through the "windshields." The thoughts, ideas, and stories in this book are your seat belt. I hope you will take the time to share your stories with me so I can pass them onto future readers.

You are on the verge of a wonderful roller-coaster ride where you decide the direction of the track and the speed of the cart. Use this book to pick the optimal track layout, and then apply the tools to successfully steer the cart. A simulation of your business idea will unfold as you work your way through this book, and as that idea develops, you will feel it become more "real." Don't let uncertainty about the future stop you from controlling your professional destiny. If you are creative, smart, diligent, and lucky, you will put your plan to work and never have to worry about financial freedom again. Success will be yours in abundance, and well deserved. There is nothing idiotic about that in my book.

How This Book Is Organized

The book is divided into four parts. The sequence is designed to lead you through finding the right business idea for you, evaluating the marketing environment, creating an effective sales plan, writing a solid business plan including realistic financial projections, and managing your business through its first year.

Part 1, Matching You to Your New Business, is designed to help you learn about yourself as a potential entrepreneur, understand the types of businesses that would be a good fit for you, and investigate the various ways you could get into business. Chapter 1 is a detailed look at your interests, your experiences, and your motivations, because in reality your business starts with you. Chapter 2 addresses questions you might have about the right level of risk to take on, the attraction of your current job, reasons why you have not yet started a business, and how to use planning as a tool for evaluating the future. Chapter 3 gives you an overview of various business types so that you can have a better idea of what you will getting yourself into by selecting a business type or industry. Technology and information present amazing business opportunities the likes of which have never been previously possible, and reading Chapter 4 will give you a solid understanding of how to turn this incredible combination into a new business. Chapter 5 will help you determine if buying a business or franchise is a better approach for you than starting a business from scratch. Chapter 6 is included especially for those of you who have become a licensed professional and now want to set up your own practice. Check out this chapter to develop an understanding about the key and critical issues that you must address to handle the business side of your own practice. Chapter 7 lays the foundation for business plan writing by explaining the value of planning, how plans are used, and the ingredients that should be part of any well-developed business plan.

Part 2, Evaluating Your Idea's Sales Potential, is dedicated to helping you create success in the critical, and often underdeveloped, areas of marketing and sales. Many plans are not well received because the readers simply do not believe the sales projections. The approach presented in this part will help you create the credibility needed to move investors toward believing your plan. Chapter 8 presents a method for estimating the prospective market for your offering using scraps of information from readily obtainable sources. Chapter 9 shows you how to determine your competition and then how to use them to refine your plan toward competitive success. Chapter 10 is dedicated to creating a realistic understanding of how your customers will buy your offering and how you should set up your business to address their sales needs. Chapter 11 presents a way of using social networking and media as a powerful tool for creating marketing awareness and sales. Those of you interested in creating some type of online business should read this chapter in conjunction with Chapter 4 to see how technology can be put to best use in creating your success.

Part 3, Finalizing Your Plan and Making a Decision, is intended to help you evaluate critical aspects of your business that must work properly for you to capitalize on your sales success. Chapter 12 presents the operational aspects of your business as the way your company keeps its sales commitments. Completing this chapter will help you better understand the difference between running a product or service company and how to put the right people into the right jobs. Chapter 13 is the financial analysis chapter, and much of the rest of the book helped to develop the numbers that will be entered into the cash flow analysis presented here. By the time you finish this chapter you should know your sales projections, your costs, how much money you can expect to make, and how much money you will need to get your business up and running. The approach outlined in Chapter 14 will help you find the money you will need as determined in Chapter 13. Chapter 15 covers a sort of boring but really important topic—protecting yourself legally from unexpected business troubles. It also presents important tax implications associated with choosing one legal business form over another. Chapter 16 is included to help you interpret your idea, market evaluation, sales projections, financial analysis, and operational plans with the intent of answering one question: are you going to start this business or not? At some point all of the analysis comes down to this simple and yet often complicated decision. Reading this chapter after completing the rest of the planning work will help you determine if the business idea you came up with is the right one for you.

Part 4, Surviving the First Year, is included to help you make it through your critical first year in business. The first year is not like any others, and your business will need to adapt to unexpected events that surely will come up. How you deal with the unexpected good and bad will affect your success not only in the first year but in the years to come. Chapter 17 presents a detailed and valuable discussion about how to manage cash, your business's air supply. If you don't read anything else in this part of the book, read this chapter. Chapter 18 will help you understand the good and challenging aspects of hiring employees. It is tough to grow without adding employees, but you can do yourself harm by not managing the employment process properly. Chapter 19 will help you deal with the many unexpected events and opportunities that will come your way as you and your business start to gain recognition and success. Managing yourself and your business in a flexible yet focused way is important to surviving your first year, so take this chapter seriously. Chapter 20 was included at the suggestion of others who asked for the warning signs of a business in trouble. I hope that you never have to deal with a failed business. Heck—the intent of this entire book is for you to succeed! But if your new business does not perform up to expectations, this chapter may help you recognize trouble's warning signs and protect yourself or, better yet, even find a way to turn your struggling business into a second-chance success.

At the very back, I included several appendixes to give you further sources of insight and information. Appendix A gives you definitions for oodles of terms used not only in this book, but in the industry as well. Appendix B contains a complete business plan for a retail dog grooming business. This plan is not as detailed as the Kwik Chek plan, which is included in Appendix C and offers an alternate plan concept. Appendix D gives you resources to use when you want more information than is provided in this book. It also gives you a listing of books and other printed matter you can use to further round out your background in key areas.

More About the Business Plans

Almost anything is easier to do when you have a picture of how it's supposed to look when it's done. It's kind of like trying to assemble a jigsaw puzzle without the picture showing what it will look like when it's completed. It's one thing to read about how a business plan is created, but something completely different to read an actual plan. For this reason, I have included a business plan for a retail dog grooming service in Appendix B, and a second plan in Appendix C evaluates a mobile used car inspection service named Kwik Chek. I wrote this plan to see if Kwik Chek would work as a national franchise operation.

The dog grooming plan was added to this edition because many of the plans I have seen lately are for locally run and owned businesses, many of which are services. These plans do not require as much detail as a nationally oriented business such as Kwik Chek, and I thought a simpler sample plan would be helpful. In writing this plan I almost convinced myself to start it, being the dog lover I am.

As I stated earlier, my goal with Kwik Chek was to find out if the idea would fly as a national franchise or whether I should go back to the drawing board. Unfortunately, the Kwik Chek business concept didn't work for me because the financials really only work out for an owner-operator as opposed to the absentee owner setup I was hoping for. Fortunately, by writing the business plan I found out that Kwik Chek wasn't right for me. Should you decide to pursue the idea using this business plan, good luck! If you succeed with the idea, please let me know; send me a dozen free car inspection certificates, and buy me dinner some time when you're passing through the Chicagoland area. Or a new Lexus would be nice!

You might, early on, want to read through both of the plans to give you an idea about where your plan might go. Although the format I used in preparing the plans is not the only one that works, it provides a starting place and a guide for you to follow when you start to write your own plan.

Extras

We included a few guideposts to help you along the way with tips, stories, and bits of information from those who have been there. For starters, each chapter begins with a little story based on a real occurrence. The names and locations have been changed so any similarity you might see to someone you know is highly unlikely. Read these stories because they not only help you understand where the chapter is taking you, but also because every one of them is based on something that really happened. You can learn a lot from the stories alone.

You'll also find words of street wisdom, cautions, terminology, and helpful tips in these additional sidebars:

AT THE WEBSITE

This sidebar lets you know that the book's website (idiotsguides.com/startingyourownbusiness) has a legal form or additional chapters and content on it that directly applies to the topic under discussion. This information is invaluable and can save you hours of frustration and potentially loads of money in professional fees. And it is free with the book!

ED'S LESSONS LEARNED

This sidebar gives you perspectives from businesspeople who have gone through the same situation you're going through now. Use their advice to help you make the right decisions.

WATCH OUT!

This sidebar provides warnings to let you know about major, potentially business-threatening pitfalls.

STREET SMARTS

This sidebar shows you street-smart information, shortcuts, and helpful advice.

DEFINITION

This sidebar defines technical business terms for you. These are usually also included in the glossary.

But Wait! There's More!

Have you logged on to idiotsguides.com lately? If you haven't, go there now! As a bonus to the book, we've included tons of additional forms and a bonus chapter, "Understanding Corporation Realities," you'll want to check out, all online. Point your browser to idiotsguides.com/startingyourownbusiness, and enjoy!

Acknowledgments

There are numerous people to acknowledge and thank for their contributions to prior editions as well as this sixth edition. Up front, let me thank all those who contributed to the earlier editions. Thank you, Alpha Books and Penguin Group (USA) Inc., for your continued success with the *Complete Idiot's Guide* series and for your commitment to this sixth edition. Thank you to Marie Butler-Knight for keeping this book available as a valuable tool for our readers; to Brook Farling for his professionalism, enthusiasm, and vision; to Nancy Lewis for making this book better by her constructive development editing; to Amy Borrelli for her detailed review and feedback on the draft; to Kayla Dugger, who continues to teach me how to tell stories in under 150 words; and to the other members of the production staff for adding the final touches that make this product special. Thank you, Marcia Layton, for your contributions to the first and second editions. Thank you, Stephen Maple, for the incredibly valuable legal content included at the website.

The following is a partial listing of people who provided vision, comment, inspiration, talent, and information that kept this book current, realistic, and valuable: Mike Borch, Dan McManus, Mark Hallam, Frank Warner, Uday Om Pabrai, Bill Cartmill, Henry Wong, Benito Suero Jr., Rick Richie, and my many students from DePaul University. How-to-do, and not-do, insight was provided by colleagues from GenRad, Plantronics, Seagate, NuTech Testing Services, DAVID Systems (DSI ExpressNet), Telenova, IBM, Wang Laboratories, AT&T, and hundreds of clients and customers. Please accept my thank-you for the contribution you know that you made.

The Morton Arboretum in Lisle, Illinois, deserves a special acknowledgment for being one of the loveliest and most inspiring places to write. Thank you to Joe Pipal for your thoughts on Chapter 20 and to Laura Pesek for your enthusiasm and feedback along the way. As always, a thank-you goes to my mother, Jean, who once again put her professional secretary skills to work, and to Beth Hemzacek for reviewing many of the early drafts. A very special thank-you goes to my wife, Loree, who not only tolerated my writing schedule and offered moral support when needed, but also acted as a sounding board even when she would have rather been watching HGTV. Maybe someday we will get to go camping, when I am not on a writing deadline.

Special Thanks to the Technical Reviewer

The Complete Idiot's Guide to Starting Your Own Business, Sixth Edition, was reviewed by an expert who double-checked the accuracy of what you'll learn here, to help us ensure that this book gives you everything you need to know about starting your own business. Special thanks are extended to Stephen Maple.

Stephen Maple is the Fitzwater Chair of Business for the University of Indianapolis School of Business, where he has taught since 1975. He is a graduate of the Indiana University School of Law and the Southern Methodist University School of Law. A member of the American Bar Association and a member of the Indiana bar since 1969, he is the author of *The Complete Idiot's Guide to Law for Small Business Owners* (Alpha, 2000) and *The Complete Idiot's Guide to Wills and Estates* (Alpha, 2009).

Trademarks

Part 1

Matching You to Your New Business

Some people have a clear idea of the business that they are destined to start, but the majority of people that I meet aren't lucky enough to have this clarity. Most people interested in starting a business have a strong belief that they should run their own show but have serious questions about the type of business to start and the level of risk they are willing to take.

I've had the privilege of working with many clients, colleagues, friends, and adult students to help sort through the mix of excitement, angst, enthusiasm, and uncertainty that clouds decision making in the early days. Some decided to stay with their corporate job, accepting that this is the best course. Others convince themselves that when they find the right business with the right level of income they will take the plunge. The chapters in Part 1 will help you determine the group that you are in and the possible business opportunity that is right for you.

In this part, we look at the relationship between you and your new business, take a detailed look at the important role that risk and uncertainty play in the business startup decision, offer an approach to finding the right business type for you, and take a look at the special issues presented to professional practice business owners. We wind up by presenting the reasons for writing a business plan and then detail the process involved in bringing the plan into existence. The material covered in this part is arguably the most powerful because it will help you realize the most possible value out of your most valuable asset—you!

Chapter 1

Creating Your Own Business Future

In This Chapter

- Discovering why you may be better off with your own business
- Understanding the relationship between you and your new business
- Determining whether your current job is the right one
- Deciding when you are ready to start
- Transitioning from employee to business owner

"Aren't you supposed to go into the office today?" asked Judy's husband Mike, nudging her shoulder from his side of the bed.

"Just let me sleep a little while longer. It's Saturday and I've had a long week," grumbled Judy.

Mike sat for a moment waiting to see if she would say more. She didn't.

"Okay. What's up? You have a big contract proposal due on Monday, and I think you said that it will take you all day to prepare it. So what's the deal?"

Judy rolled over to face him. He was right, and she knew it. But she just wanted a day off, even if it was a Saturday. On the other hand, she stood a reasonable shot at winning this proposal, and it would set her up for at least three months of work. Not a bad deal in a slow economy.

"I'm just missing being home with you and the kids," she said. "I get tired of working alone all the time, and the thought of working all day on a weekend by myself while you guys are off playing bums me out."

Mike had seen her like this before and had a proposal for her.

"Tell you what. You get your butt out of bed and head into the office for the morning. Get as much done as you can by 1 o'clock, and the kids and I will bring you in some sandwiches. We'll do a picnic at work on that little lawn area."

Judy looked resolute in her lethargy, so Mike pulled out the big negotiation guns. He knew that once she started she would finish.

"Okay. I'll sweeten the pot a little. If you win this job, we'll plan a vacation to spend some of the money you'll earn. How does a week in Paris sound?"

Judy brightened up with the thought of a vacation. It had been well over a year since they took some time off, and she would need it if she won this project.

"Throw in lunch today with Paris and you have a deal," she replied, already heading toward the shower.

When you work as an employee, you always have one eye watching your boss to make sure that he or she is happy with your work. The boss and your peers are always an external motivator that helps to get you into work on those days when you would rather stay in bed. When you start your own business, you are the boss. As your own boss, there is nobody to put pressure on you but you, and if you do not perform, nobody inherits the problems more than you. You are fully responsible for and to you.

It turns out that some people are not meant to run their own business. There are plenty of people who prefer working for someone else. In reality, some people are better off working for someone else. Understanding your own motivations is critical to deciding whether starting your own business will bring you happiness or grief. It's really easy to start a business. All you have to do is sell something or fill out a few forms, and you're in business. However, starting a business that will generate adequate and consistent income while providing personal reward is much more difficult. It is actually more of a business science than a hard-charging, high-energy game of chance.

Every journey has its beginning, and your journey to becoming a successful small business owner starts right here. In this chapter, we will discuss your interests, your personality traits, and the realities of leaving a job to start your own business. This chapter will help you make decisions that will enable you to understand what is needed for you to create the right business future for you.

Making Your Next Job Your Own Business

If you are like most people I meet, you do not believe that you will be working for your current employer when you retire. It may be that you have seen your fellow employees be "right sized," and you are wondering when your turn will come. It may be that you now don't trust corporate life as the secure lifetime investment you previously assumed it to be and want to have more control over your employment destiny. Perhaps you think management isn't very bright and believe that you can do a better job running a business than they do. Or maybe you already work for a small business and simply want to go off on your own. No matter your reasons, at some point in the future you will almost surely change employers.

You work for your employer by choice, and if a better job offer comes along, you will take it. And in turn, companies lay people off even if they have enough cash on hand to suffer a sales downturn. Work might start feeling like a contracting relationship: The contractor chooses the client and the client selects the contractor, both knowing that the relationship will end at some future date. They negotiate the financial and responsibility details that apply during the contracting period, but both know that the relationship is temporary and not one for life.

Once you realize that you are essentially a contractor, your approach to work changes. You start to manage your time differently, always looking over your shoulder for your next engagement, knowing that the steady paycheck will at some point come to an end. You start to increase your savings, knowing that you might have a period of no income between engagements. You start to set up your medical and other personal benefits so that you, and not an employer, have primary control over them.

Here are a few steps you can start taking now to provide yourself with more freedom, either as an employee or as a new business owner:

- Start building your savings today so that you have a minimum of 6 months of living expenses (12 months preferred) on hand to weather an unexpected job termination or the new business startup period. But don't stop there—keep saving. More cash will always pay off.
- Start the personal evaluation and business planning process while you are still employed to give yourself a running start should you be terminated or quit.
- Knowing that you have employment options may make you more effective in your current job.

- Increase your business knowledge by taking business classes. This will help you with your current job and also with your own business, and your employer may pay the tuition to boot!
- Keep it to yourself that you are considering going off on your own. You may never take the *entrepreneurship* plunge, and nothing is gained in letting your co-workers or your employer know about your aspirations at this stage.

DEFINITION

An **entrepreneur** is an individual who starts and runs his or her own business rather than remain an employee of someone else's company. You can open an antique store or start an at-home accounting business, and you are considered an entrepreneur.

- If applicable, look for ways that your employer could become your first startup customer. Only bring it up after you have a clear plan in place, money in the bank, and the willingness to start the business. If they think you have business ownership aspirations, they may let you go on the spot. It does happen.

Be honest with yourself about your current job. If it is one that allows you to do what you enjoy, to do what you are good at, to make a good income with solid benefits, and provides a sense of personal satisfaction, why would you want to leave? There is little in professional life more satisfying than working with a group of dedicated people doing what they love while making a positive difference in the world. Larger companies can provide this opportunity where, by contrast, starting your own business is usually a very solitary experience, especially in the early days. Just know that a shifting of the economic environment at your company could cost you your job through no fault of your own. At that point, you want to have taken the steps outlined in this chapter to make sure that you are ready for the change, perhaps using it as a starting point for becoming a successful entrepreneur.

STREET SMARTS

Just as you might occasionally envy the entrepreneurial lifestyle, the entrepreneur occasionally envies people who love their job working for someone else. More than one entrepreneur has returned to corporate life after selling his or her own business simply to end the headaches that come with running one's own business.

The Positives of Starting Your Own Business

In an uncertain job market, it only makes sense to do what any solid professional should be doing—looking for your next working opportunity. You picked up this book to see if owning your own business *is* that next opportunity. Let's find out by presenting some realities of being your own boss.

Much of the uncertainty that comes with being an employee goes away when you are the business owner. For example:

- You will know before anyone else if your company is having trouble.
- You will control your own benefits such as health insurance, life insurance, and pension.
- If the company does well, you will have an opportunity to make more money from the success instead of staying with the same old salary.
- You have direct control over what you do instead of having to answer to someone else whose agenda might not put you at the top of their priority list.
- If you are having problems with your boss, you can always have a heart-to-heart to get the problem resolved. Hopefully you will have better results than with your current boss.

The benefits associated with running your own successful business are great, and the rate at which new businesses are being created indicates that many have already figured that out. Maybe now it is your turn.

STREET SMARTS

Startups are usually cash poor and must make do with as few employees as possible to stretch out the initial funding as long as possible. Keeping the employee overhead low is best accomplished with the founders doing as much of the work as possible until the cash flow becomes predictable enough to justify adding employees—along with their associated expenses.

The Negatives of Starting Your Own Business

The previous section presented some of the pros associated with running your own business, but there are also drawbacks that don't always get talked about. For example:

- The buck starts and stops with you—if you don't think it up, do it, or pay for it, it won't get done.

- You are financially liable for all of the company's obligations to vendors, employees, and investors.
- When you first start your business, there will likely be long hours and lots of uncertainty that can take a toll on you, your family, and your close relationships.
- As your business becomes more successful, the level of financial obligation you will inherit will grow as well.
- As the business owner, it is not easy to leave because you will likely have to close down the business or sell it, both of which are complicated options. As an employee, if you get fed up with your current job, you can always find another one.
- Working for yourself can get pretty lonely; you will spend long hours working solo, especially when first starting out.
- When you start out, you will likely be the sales, accounting, procurement, and operations departments as well as executive management. In other words, it will just be you, and you will have to do it all until you are successful enough to pay someone else to do it.

When you are accustomed to working for a larger company, you learn to depend on the other employees and departments to handle much of the daily activity of business. There is a tacit security in being part of a larger organization. You take it for granted that these services will be done by someone else. The good news is that as you become more successful, you will be able to hire people to do many of these jobs. The operational approach presented in Chapter 12 will help you figure out the positions that will most likely be filled first so you can keep an eye out for people who might be your first new employees. More about hiring employees is included in Chapter 18.

Creative People Create Their Own Opportunities

Now that we have looked briefly at the pros and cons, let me ask you an honest question: *Is your current employer someone with whom you are willing to trust your professional destiny and the financial security of your family?* At the time of this writing, unemployment is running at high levels where roughly 1 out of every 10 people you meet on the street is unemployed. Just remember that you and many other fine people have been caught in the squeeze of these tough economic times through no fault of your own.

But also remember that there is hope. The United States has a $14 trillion economy, which means that a whole lot of money is passing between hands every business day. You only need a tiny piece of that to make a decent living. Sure, there is high unemployment, but the vast majority of people are still employed, which means that they are earning a wage and still spending money. There has always been promise for those creative enough to see an opportunity and resourceful enough to take advantage of it. If you want to make your own business work, you can. You are at least as resourceful as those who came before, aren't you? Let's take a closer look at the personality traits of entrepreneurs.

Your Business Starts with You

Perhaps the one characteristic that differentiates a small business from all others is the dramatic impact that the founders/owners have on the operation of the company. There is simply no way to separate the owners from the company in the early stages. Customers write checks to the company name, but they think of themselves as doing business with the founder/owner. After all, when a company is small, there is really only one major decision maker: you, the owner. Owners set the direction, ethics, quality, and values of their company, and those who think otherwise are kidding themselves. You will create the public reputation and internal framework by which your future, larger company will function. I believe that you should create a framework that makes you money while also being one you can happily live with. Doing otherwise makes no sense to me.

STREET SMARTS

The founders should have a clear handle on their own personality strengths and weaknesses, along with a comprehensive inventory of each founder's specific skills. In this way, they can use themselves to best advantage while keeping employee expenses low.

Do You Have What It Takes?

It is often difficult to separate fact from fantasy when evaluating founders, their startups, and their successes or failures. Mythology ranges from the boisterous and flamboyant sales guy who never shuts it off to the poorly dressed engineer with Coke bottle–thick glasses who changes the world from his basement. Sure there have been successful startup instances involving both personality types, but most of the rest of us fall somewhere in the middle and are pretty normal people … whatever normal means.

Here are a few things that I have learned from entrepreneurs, about entrepreneurs. Many have started multiple businesses with a common thread being that the first few attempts did not do very well. Most resent bureaucracy and tend to fall behind in maintaining the administrative sides of their businesses. Most get restless when things are going smoothly and are always looking for that next growth opportunity.

Most have a passion for whatever is the core competence of their successful business. They may treat the business like it is a child to be nurtured at first, and treated differently later as a family member. Don't laugh. It will likely happen to you as well. Think about it: you will likely spend more time with your business than with your family, all the while working to improve your family's financial security.

Most will complain about the level of personal risk they live with, and then risk it all again on what they believe is their next great idea. Many simply enjoy the process of turning ideas into successful businesses and then selling them. The challenge is what they value more than the particular industry or type of work.

Most earn a decent income, but very few earn the Bill Gates billions that make such great publicity. Again, depending on which statistics you believe, the average small business owner has a salary of somewhere between $50,000 and $100,000 annually, varying on the industry, size of the company, location, and years in business.

In general, entrepreneurs are normal people with a strong work ethic and commitment to providing the best quality to their customers. They enjoy the freedom that comes with running their own show and paying their own bills, and are willing to accept the responsibilities that come with having that freedom.

It is common for an entrepreneur to run his own businesses for a few years and then return to work as an employee of another company, no longer wanting to have the headaches associated with running their own shops. These people often make great employees, as they have a more senior-level perspective of what is required to make a business run.

STREET SMARTS

A lot of people are tired of working for "The Man." And in today's reality, "The Man" might be a woman. Around two out of every five businesses in the United States is owned by women, with the number growing at a faster rate than the national average for all businesses.

If many of these points ring true for you, then you might have the right stuff for becoming a successful entrepreneur. Now it is time to see if you have the personality traits and skills needed to turn your business passion and idea into a profitable reality.

What Makes a Great Entrepreneur?

Whether an entrepreneur is born or made is a topic for scholars and philosophers. Suffice it to say that entrepreneurs come in all shapes, sizes, races, genders, and nationalities, and that they have a few common characteristics that tend to differentiate them from those who work as employees. These differences are not themselves criteria for success. They are valuable when dealing with the typical demands of the entrepreneurial life.

To most effectively deal with typical startup situations, entrepreneurs must ...

- Have the ability to move forward in the face of large uncertainty.
- Be willing to start—to get going when others might wait.
- Be highly self-motivated.
- Be willing to adapt along the way as things change from the expected.
- Believe in their ability to do what must be done to fulfill their customer commitments and business obligations.
- Make the image of success secondary to functioning on a financial shoestring.
- Have faith in their idea when others are not sure, while also not holding on too long to a bad idea that jeopardizes the financial health of the company or their family.
- Be able to sell their products or services to prospective customers, and be perceptive enough to determine how to create a fit between the customer's needs and their company's offering.

- Be able to quickly understand the important aspects of a situation, and then act appropriately to those important aspects.

STREET SMARTS

Always look for what your customer cares about the most. If your customer is primarily interested in the color of product X, you have to be perceptive enough to see that and talk about the color of product X (not another color, or product Y and Z). Avoid focusing on what you think is important at the expense of hearing the customer's feedback. After all, he or she is the one who will write the check to buy your product. You might as well listen.

What Are Your Strengths and Abilities?

You may now be wondering how you personally size up against the traits exhibited by successful entrepreneurs. The following quick assessment should not be treated as an absolute barometer of a "good" or "bad" entrepreneur temperament, but it will give you a general idea of how ready you are to go off on your own.

Answer the following questions as honestly as possible by placing a number between 1 and 10 in the blank. Use a 1 when you feel that the statement *least* applies to you and a 10 when it *very strongly* applies to you.

This is important: don't look at the paragraphs following this table *before* completing the personal assessment. Answer as honestly as you can.

Personal Assessment Procedure

Assessment	Statement
(1 = LOW, 10 = HIGH)	
________	I am comfortable with moving forward and making decisions when I don't have all the answers to important questions.
________	I am typically the one initiating things for my family and friends or at work.
________	I can keep myself on track even when nobody else is watching or monitoring my performance or activities.

Assessment	Statement
(1 = LOW, 10 = HIGH)	
________	I can adapt my thinking and focus along the way as events change.
________	I trust my current capability level, and also believe that I can learn what is needed to meet future demands.
________	I care more about getting the job done than how good I look doing the job. Performance is more important than image.
________	I trust my business judgment and am willing to move forward on what I believe to be a good business idea, even if others are not supportive of that idea.
________	I trust my sales ability and know that I can sell my business along with its products and/or services as well as anyone.
________	I tend to see the truth of a situation before others and can take the most effective actions for a given situation.
________	I have enough money in savings, or access to enough money, to pay my personal and business bills for at least six months.
________	**Sum Total of All Rows**

Add up all the table rows and write that total on the Sum Total line. Your total number should be between 10 and 100.

No doubt you will score yourself higher in some areas and lower in others. That is normal for all people, including entrepreneurs. The following discussion will give you a general idea as to where you fit on the overall successful entrepreneurship scale. Notice that the assessment tool also tells you something about your areas of strength, as well as areas where you could use some improvement.

If you scored less than 50, you may not be ready *today* for starting your own business. You may be better suited as an employee for now instead of being the person responsible for all of the pressure and uncertainty of running your own show. Many very successful larger company employees fit happily into this category, so there is no negative connotation associated with being here. If you believe your answers and you have already started your own business, then I think you should look to surround yourself with people who are strong in the areas where you scored lower.

If you scored between 51 and 70, you show some entrepreneurship tendencies, but might be better off first working for a small business to see how you like it. These are people who like the excitement of starting something new, but are not the people to get it started. Many people in this group will follow the lead entrepreneur from one new company to the next, making good money along the way and occasionally hitting it big with a startup that skyrockets.

If you scored over 70, you are likely chomping at the bit to get started on your own business. You are probably beyond thinking about whether you should or shouldn't, and are on to when, how, how many, and for how much. This will be particularly true for those who score higher and have fairly routine jobs with little excitement or uncertainty. This group should beware jumping on the first idea that comes along and should definitely spend the time finishing this book and writing a plan.

No simple test like this can possibly evaluate all of the skill and personality aspects that make you who you are. And no generalization could possibly tell you *with absolute certainty* whether you will or won't make it starting your own business. Always remember that ultimately your decision and your fate are in your hands.

Do yourself a favor. Don't skimp or delude yourself on this portion of your evaluation process. All small business entrepreneurs quickly learn that they are their company's most important asset. They also learn that they will spend an immense amount of time doing what is required to make their businesses succeed. Doing what you enjoy improves your chances of success because you will likely be better at something you enjoy than at something you do "for the money." Doing what you like also improves the quality of your life and gives customers a reason to use you over someone else. Not ensuring a match in both of these important areas plants the seeds of failure before you even start. Before you commit money, energy, and time to your venture, make sure that it is something you really want to do. I cover this topic in detail in Chapter 3.

ED'S LESSONS LEARNED

A few years ago, when things were on a downturn with my business, I was talking with a fellow entrepreneur. When she asked how things were going, I said, "They are pretty bad right now, and I think some radical changes are due." She asked, "Are you thinking of getting a job?" I smiled and said, "No," to which she replied, "Then things aren't that bad."

What Is Your Personal Bottom Line?

I have covered a lot of important ground in this chapter, and you might be feeling a little overwhelmed wondering where to start. Answer the following questions to give you a solid starting point for determining where you are today and where you would like to go. Just remember, you should not start a business because anyone else thinks you should. Ultimately, it all comes down to you. Consider the following:

- What do you want, and why do you want it?
- Do you think that running your own business will give you the fulfillment that's been missing in your current job?
- Are you willing to earn less money for a while as you try to establish your company?
- How far are you willing to go to make your business work?
- Are you willing to get up and go to work even when nobody is going to yell at you if you stay home and watch talking dogs on YouTube?

If you like the stability of working 9 to 5, wake up! Owning your own business means that you won't have set hours. Expect to work long hours in the early stages. If this chapter alone is enough to talk you out of pursuing your own business, then send me a thank-you card. You are not ready yet to make that kind of commitment. It doesn't mean that you never will, just that right now is not your time.

On the other hand, if after reading this chapter you not only feel that starting your own business is the right thing to do but also have a better idea of what you personally bring to its success, then congratulations! You have just crossed the first major hurdle toward not only thinking and acting like an entrepreneur, but also trusting that you are the right person to start your business. Some feel that these may be the most important decisions you will ever make in creating a successful business.

The Least You Need to Know

- Accept that lifelong employment is a myth and that it is up to you to protect your working future.
- Understanding your personal needs, goals, skills, and personality before you start your own business is critical to later success.

- There are positive and negative aspects to owning your own business, and as the owner you inherit both.
- Understand that your customers will see you as the face of your business at first; it will expand to include others as you succeed and grow.
- You will be committing your family in your new business journey, so include them in your decision process.
- Planning to start your own business while still employed is a good move that protects you and your family from an unexpected job termination.

We All Treat Risk in Our Own Way

Chapter 2

In This Chapter

- Learning how opportunities change with life stages
- Separating risk and uncertainty for better understanding
- Appreciating a person's risk tolerance level
- Understanding that all business decisions combine risk, uncertainty, and opportunity
- Relating business planning to risk and uncertainty management

Kim and Justin sat across the table from each other in silence. Kim had pulled out an expensive bottle of Justin's favorite wine for the conversation, but so far it wasn't working.

"Come on, honey, this idea is a great one. Everyone I've showed it to has said that they would buy one. We can make a fortune off of it," said Kim. Justin actually believed what Kim was saying, but he had reservations that he just couldn't shake.

"Okay. I'll buy all that for now. But think about what you're asking me to go along with. A second mortgage on the house, plus we borrow money from the kids' college fund. That is a lot to put up, and I am not as sure as you are about getting it all back. Oh, and did I mention that I would now be the sole bread winner for the family because you would quit your job to run this business? This all seems like pretty big stuff to me."

Kim knew that he was right, but she just believed that this was a great idea and could not let it go. There had to be some way to figure out how they all could win.

"I sort of agree with you, except think about this—we are getting like 1 percent on the money in the college fund, and this idea could make us 20 times that in just a few years. Wouldn't that be nice to see in the fund?" Justin nodded in agreement.

"Plus, you know that I hate my job, and with the cutbacks I will probably not be getting any type of promotion or pay increase. Heck, in a year I might not even have a job." Justin nodded again and Kim poured him some more wine.

"We can still get the medical benefits from your job, so that is handled. We are only 30, so if it doesn't work out we still have time to rebuild the fund before the kids start college." She could tell that Justin was thinking about it all and not just digging in his "no" heels. "And there is nothing else out there like this on the market. In a few years the chance to get it out there could be gone." Justin took a long drink and then poured himself and Kim some more wine.

"Okay. Tell you what—You convince me that this idea of yours has a reasonable chance of succeeding, and I will be willing to go along with it." Kim liked what she was hearing, but a knot formed in her stomach as she realized that Justin might be talking about a business plan. "After all, I could stand to go into retirement a millionaire, too, you know," he continued. Kim tried to keep a calm look on her face as her mind went into overdrive.

No two people look at the same business situation in exactly the same way. We all bring our own personal history, skills, and personality to the situation. Many people have had a variation on the conversation between Kim and Justin when one person is sold on an idea and is looking for the buy-in from a partner. Hesitation or frustration by either party is rarely something personal against the person with the idea. It is more than likely a difference in how the two perceive the situation and how much they are willing to put at stake to try it out.

This chapter presents a few powerful and interconnected concepts related to how we all evaluate business situations. These concepts have application across business in general, but have direct applicability when talking about justifying the time to prepare a business plan or when working with potential investors. We will refer to these concepts throughout the rest of the book. Strap yourself in, get a cup of coffee, and let me take you on a journey into how we all evaluate risky situations.

Your Life Situation Changes Over Time

What you bring to your life and the business table at 20 is different from what you bring when you are 60. Nothing personal to either group … that is just the way it is. When you are 20, you are full of energy, enthusiasm, and generally know very little about business or yourself as a businessperson. You likely own little, have few obligations, and have a complete future to create with plenty of possibilities and unknowns.

What I owned at 20 was a few boxes full of stuff, an old car, and a portable bed. My checking account had less than a hundred dollars in it, and I was going to college and working two jobs just to pay my rent and occasionally eat. If I had lost all that I owned, life might have done me a favor because I ended up dragging those boxes around with me for years. But I was ready to take on what life sent my way. What I did not appreciate until much later in my life was that I had 40 or more years of time on my side to create a nest egg for retirement. More on this in the "Road Not Taken" section of this chapter.

At 40, you will likely have a family, some type of education, and more than 20 years of working experience. You now have a much clearer understanding of how business works within the industry of your choosing. You likely have a job and some type of future, with benefits reasonably within reach. You might have a family with several children heading to college (along with tuition expenses) within the next few years. And, let's face it, college is no longer a minor expense that you can figure out how to pay for when the time comes. It is one of the largest expenses a family will incur, next to a house. You might have health challenges within your family, might be taking care of aging parents, and likely have a mortgage, a car payment (or two), and other obligations that extend beyond the "just you" that you had at 20. You have something to lose at this point, but also have enough knowledge about your career that you might well be itching to put to work for yourself instead of "The Man."

At 60, the situation is different again. You have 40 years or more of working experience and might be tired of the industry where you gathered that experience. You have built up some type of nest egg (hopefully) and are often looking to get out of the daily working grind within 5 to 10 years (or less). Your children's college expenses are not an issue at this point, but it might be for your grandchildren, if you feel financially responsible for them. You are, however, wondering how you are going to deal with the loss of income from the daily job. You are probably trying to determine what life will be like when you have to live off of whatever pension, Social Security, or other income you might have. If you live another 15 years, those numbers work out one way. But if you live to be 100, they could work out very differently. How do you plan, and what if you make a mistake? You don't have the 40 years to make up for a mistake that you had when you were 20.

What you know, what you have, and what you want change with age. Now that we see how things change over time, let's take a closer look at the way opportunities affect the choices we make along the way.

ED'S LESSONS LEARNED

I was joking to my 92-year-old mother one day about my plans to spend my last quarter just before I took my last breath. My mother is very healthy and aware, by the way, and has outlived many of her family and friends. She listened patiently to my story and asked a simple question with profound repercussions: "What if you don't die after spending your last quarter? Do you really want to be 128, alive, and broke?" She made a good point that drove home the realities of financial planning and getting older in today's society of medical marvels.

How the Road *Not* Taken Can Cost You

Bear with me for a few paragraphs here while I cover a somewhat abstract, but very important, concept related to making entrepreneurship choices. As presented in the earlier section, our lives change as we work our way through life. What also changes are our opportunities. But to appreciate how those opportunities affect life and career decision making, we need to talk about something that sounds very MBAish called *opportunity cost*. Why? Because it affects almost all business decisions we make, whether we consciously realize it or not.

DEFINITION

Opportunity cost is the cost of what you give up to do something else. To start your business you might have to give up your regular job. Your regular job would be the opportunity cost associated with starting your business. Opportunity cost is a consideration for almost all business (and arguably life) decision making, but often it is unconscious.

Opportunity cost sounds like what you will have to pay to follow up on an opportunity that you pursue. Actually, it is just the opposite—it is what you give up by *not* doing something. Picture yourself sitting at your kitchen table considering two business opportunities—let's call them A and B. Assume that you cannot take advantage of both opportunities: if you choose to do A, you *cannot* do B, or if you choose to do B you *cannot* do A. So far, so good?

Doing either A or B will require you to invest time or money, but will also bring you some type of reward. Assume that the costs and rewards of the two options are very different for purposes of this example. Remember that if you choose A, you must give up any opportunities associated with doing B because you cannot do both, and vice versa.

Here is where it all becomes valuable to our entrepreneurship discussions. If you are in your early 20s just starting out, you probably do not have much time invested in your job, employer, or career. You probably don't have much in the way of savings, and probably don't have kids in school; if you're married, your spouse likely has a job with income and perhaps benefits that can cover you. The locked-in expenses associated with your lifestyle may not yet be too high because you rent instead of own your home. In summary, your opportunity costs associated with starting a new business are pretty low because your investment in your current path is pretty low and what you can expect to gain from it in the near term is relatively low. It would be typical for you to assess a new startup opportunity as something along the lines of, "Why not? I can always go back and get a job if it doesn't work out." Taking the chance does not seem like that big of a deal. (Of course, if you are in your early 20s but have young children or an amazing job paying tons of money, your situation gets more complicated, and the analysis of your situation points toward the 40s scenario that follows.)

If you are in your 40s, you might have 15 or more years invested in creating a good name for yourself with your employer and within your industry. Your employer might be fine to work for and you might like your job. You may also have great benefits and be in a growing industry. Notice that all of this makes a pretty attractive package that would arguably be difficult to give up to start your own business. Why? If you have to give it up to start your new business, then the opportunity cost of starting your business is giving up all of the security of your current job. That could just be too expensive. Is opportunity cost starting to make sense?

ED'S LESSONS LEARNED

I was in a pub in Cornwall, England, a few years back and met a man from London. It turned out that he had an earlier edition of this book and asked for my advice on whether he should start a company. I asked him a few questions and then summarized my thoughts. "It sounds like you have a job that you really like, that pays you well, with great benefits, in a growing industry with wonderful future prospects." He nodded. "So why would you want to start your own business?" The wife leaned forward in her seat to hear the next part. "If not now, then when?" was his reply. What do you think I told him? What would you have told him? Look for my answer later in the chapter.

Now let's look at a person in her 60s making the decision to start her business. She might be ready to retire from her job, and be eligible for Medicare along with a company pension, so giving up the job might not be that big of a deal. But giving up a large percentage of her nest egg to fund the new business might be a problem. So here we have a person with time, but also the need to protect her savings. Her opportunity cost associated with starting a business is the security of having a certain amount of money in the bank, but not the income and benefits.

At this point you should start to see that the decision to start your own business will involve giving up something, and what you give up will be related to where you are in life. There is simply no cookie-cutter approach to determining when and if you should start a business. The answer is dependent on where you are in life, what your current opportunities offer you, and what the new business can offer you as an alternative. So the right answer to whether you should quit your job and start a business is really the standard consultant's answer to most questions: it depends. And what it depends on is unique to you.

The Background, Incentive, and Motivation Conundrum

If I were to ask you whether rich or poor people are more likely to start a business, what would you say? It turns out that the answer is neither. Most successful new businesses come from those in the middle class.

Let's start with richer people. They already have a lot. They are comfortable financially and do not have a burning need such as food, tuition, or a place to sleep as motivation to make money. They already have money. If that is enough, then there is no need for them to start a business—unless they are personally motivated. Starting the right business for them requires that they answer what I think is one of the toughest questions we will ever be asked: "What do you want to be when you grow up?" Or perhaps, "What do you want your life to stand for?" If you are one of the folks in this position, cut yourself some slack if you have not started a business. You have likely not seen the right opportunity come along. This is why a lot of charitable organizations are started or run by wealthy persons. They bring influence and resources to the organization, and don't require a salary—a pretty cool combination when you think about it.

What about people on the poorer end of the financial spectrum? They have a different set of circumstances that affect their opportunities. They do not have much money, might have limited education as a result of not having money to pay the tuition, and may have limited work experience at the management level, which means that they might not be able to recognize or take advantage of a business opportunity when it appears. To be clear, there are most definitely poorer people who are capable of starting and running a business, but their circumstances limit what they have to work with in creating the idea and getting it up and running. Isn't it interesting that rich people have the resources but don't have the built-in incentive, and poorer people have the built-in incentive but do not have the resources? Matching the resources of richer people with the motivation of those less well off is often the role of philanthropic organizations.

If you are someone in this less fortunate economic situation who knows that you have it in you to be your own boss, then do a realistic assessment of what you want to accomplish and what you have to work with in making it happen. See where the mismatches are, and then start to make contacts outside of your immediate sphere of influence to fill in the mismatches. Look for a mentor who can help steer you, as well as possibly introduce you to those who can help financially. Know that your first idea might be only the stepping stone to later ones that will be the real brass ring. Look for organizations that have been set up to help people in exactly your situation get the guidance, money, and contacts needed to get you started. They are out there. You just need to open your thinking and environment enough to find them. Make sure to check out Appendix D for more information about these helpful organizations.

You will notice a common theme throughout this book—the individual creates the entrepreneurial opportunity, not just the idea. People invest time and money in people, not just ideas or companies. There are plenty of ideas out there, but there are not a lot of people who have the ability to make an idea into a successful new business.

We have now looked at the lower and upper extremes of the economic spectrum. What about those in the middle? It turns out that this group is the most fertile ground for creating new businesses. They have motivation to make their future lives better, they have a solid level of education and experience, and they have time, money, and contact resources to bring to the startup party. They have also probably been working in a field for enough years that they've developed a solid level of expertise in an industry, have noticed a need that is not yet being filled, and have enough industry knowledge to make the idea happen. Those of you in the middle class are the new business engine.

The Powerful Influence of Uncertainty

Here is the question to ask yourself: "If I knew for sure that I could make exactly the same amount of money in my own company as I am making now (including benefits), would I start my own company?" If the answer is yes and you would even take a cut in pay to run your own show, then you are right on target with your motivation to start your own business.

If your motivation is so high, then why have you not done it? We talked earlier in the chapter about the influence of opportunity cost on your decision process. What about the unknowns associated with your future venture? Notice that the question I asked at the beginning of this section offered certainty in your ability to make what you are making today, which took a lot of the financial opportunity cost influence out of the decision. They were the same from a money perspective. The question also removed something else that most of us don't think about—*uncertainty*.

DEFINITION

Uncertainty is what you do not know about something that has influence on your situation. You can usually state what you are uncertain about. Investigating the uncertainty helps to make it more certain. High uncertainty can create inaction.

Uncertainty is what you do not know but what still has an influence on your situation. For example, you may believe that the economy will change, but you may be uncertain about whether it will be better or worse, and by how much. Investigating the opinions of economists and other credible experts may help you to come to the conclusion that the economy will improve over the next few years, and within what percentage range. Notice that the investigation reduced your uncertainty about this part of your decision. If your investigation reduced it to the point that the economic outlook has become more certain to you, it can no longer be a major worry. Keep working through each item in the same way and you keep reducing the overall uncertainty associated with the decision under investigation.

STREET SMARTS

The only time you can ever be certain about something is after it has already happened. Until it is history, it is always open to change. All you can ever do is make your best guess.

Not knowing about how the future is going to turn out has a powerful influence on our decision-making processes. It turns out that in general we are programmed to avoid uncertainty. Research has shown that we will even pay a premium to reduce uncertainty. Think about this for a minute. We are willing, perhaps, to follow courses of action that are not to our benefit only because that path is the more certain.

Taking this concept to heart may help you understand why you may have kept on a familiar course only to later chastise yourself for your inaction. Don't be so hard on yourself. Dealing properly with uncertainty helped our ancestors survive the saber-toothed tiger—it's just part of our DNA. Once you understand uncertainty and your reaction to it, you put yourself into a position of being able to effectively manage it.

To summarize, as humans we naturally avoid uncertainty and will strongly tend toward the certain; when faced with much uncertainty we have a natural tendency to want to maintain the status quo. Opportunity cost involves choosing between two options, and for purposes of our discussion one of the options is a new business idea that is full of uncertainty. It is new. It has no history. It is substantially unknown. The current path is certainly more certain and the one with the greatest natural attraction. Now, remember your answer to my earlier question about whether you would start the business if you knew you would make the same amount of money as you make now? If you said yes, then what is probably keeping you from going off on your own is the uncertainty that making the same amount will really happen.

What Are You Really Willing to Risk?

How many times have you heard someone say that something is too risky? Or that something isn't worth the risk? How did you interpret what they said? What were they talking about as being really at risk? It turns out that it is pretty difficult to define something related to risk without referring to risk itself. Try it and you will see. We all know something about risk, but we have a hard time getting a handle on how it works. So what is risk?

I am going to define *risk* as meaning everything you stand to lose should your new venture be a total bust. In this context, risk is quantifiable. It is money. It is time. It is reputation. It is important relationships. In other words, it is something that you can specifically state and also attach some type of importance to.

DEFINITION

Risk is something of importance that you could lose if something does not work out as planned. It is definable and can be measured in some way. Risk does not have a likelihood associated with it. That is uncertainty's role. If you invest $100, then you have $100 at risk.

For example, should a business that you funded with $200,000 fail, then you would have your $200,000 at risk. If a new business is going to take two years of your time working for the company to see if it will work, then you risk two years of your time. If you are putting up both the two years of time and the $200,000, then both are at risk. Now add in the two years of income at $60,000 per year from your current job that you would have to give up to work for the new company, and you can add $120,000 in salary to the risk list. So to start this venture you risk: two years of time, $120,000 in salary opportunity cost, and $200,000 in cash that you invested in the idea ... assuming that the idea never earns you a nickel. But what if you are going to be putting your hard-earned credibility in an industry at stake for your new business idea? And what if that idea doesn't work? Have you also risked your reputation such that it could take you years to recover it, if ever?

The point from this example is that what you risk is fairly objectively determined. There isn't a lot of unknown with respect to what is at risk. Coming back to our earlier statement about an opportunity being too risky, most people use this phrase to mean a combination of what is at risk and the uncertainty associated with it ever working out as projected. They are blending risk and uncertainty into a single statement, and by doing so hamper their ability to objectively evaluate an opportunity. This blending hampers their ability to understand what would need to be changed about the opportunity to transform it into something acceptable.

How Risk Tolerant Are You?

There are people who are uncomfortable with any level of uncertainty. There are also people who will try anything once. How we react to uncertainty is in many ways intrinsic to our personalities, and in my opinion not likely to change very much. I have seen people take on opportunities with more uncertainty than they were comfortable with, only to drive themselves nuts worrying about things over which they had no control. On the other hand, I have seen entrepreneurs risk all that they have gained on a new idea about which little was known but that they felt was worth trying. Where would you put yourself in the space between totally uncertainty-averse to willing to risk it all? This is very important to know about yourself.

Remember earlier when I said that you will only know for certain about how something will turn out after it becomes history? The problem with this approach in business is that the opportunity will have already passed at this point. Business risk and reward are related to each other, and little in business involves no risk; if the risk is very low, then the opportunity for reward is also very low. A new business is full of uncertainty. How much uncertainty is too much? That depends on the idea, its level of development, and the uncertainty tolerance of the person considering the idea.

It turns out that risk and uncertainty tolerance are related in a blend of the amount that the person is being asked to risk and the level of uncertainty associated with the idea. The impact associated with a $200,000 loss will be different for a 60-year-old with $300,000 in savings than for a 30-year-old millionaire. The millionaire could lose the $200,000 and be upset, but not necessarily impacted in a major way with respect to his eventual retirement. Plus, he has at least 30 years to recover the loss before retiring. The 60-year-old would have a different view. The amount of the investment is the same—$200,000—but the amount being risked by the two different people is very different in relation to what they have in total and what they can stand to lose before being negatively impacted. Under these circumstances, it would be completely understandable for the 60-year-old to be more conservative in terms of the amount being risked and the level of uncertainty he or she would be willing to accept with respect to getting the money back.

Combining Risk, Uncertainty, and Opportunity

Is there a way to convince the 60-year-old to make an investment in your new venture? What if you found out that he was willing to take a chance with $75,000 of his $300,000 nest egg? All we have left to deal with is uncertainty and opportunity cost. Assume that you presented him with a business plan that spelled out in detail all of your ideas for his money such that he believed it had a high likelihood of success. That helps to handle uncertainty. Now you have to deal with opportunity cost. Assume that your new company investment offered him a 12 percent annual return for at least five years. Assume that he could put the money in the bank and get 3 percent per year over that same five years. Your investment is four times more rewarding over the same period of time than the risk-free CD opportunity. Notice how you have now presented him with an investment opportunity that is at a dollar level within his personal risk threshold; the idea is of low enough uncertainty that he believes it could work, meanwhile offering him an investment four times the level of his risk-free bank CD. What was before a risky venture has become an idea worth his serious consideration, all because you separately and responsibly addressed risk, uncertainty, and opportunity cost. Pretty cool, no?

You should use this same approach on yourself as the time and money investor of your own company. Why not? It worked for this hypothetical investor. It should work for you and it will help get buy-in from a less risk-tolerant person whose support you will need. If you do this analysis as the investor and find that you are still uncomfortable, then look for what needs to be answered to reduce the discomfort. Keep doing that until you are at your comfort level or until there is nothing left to resolve. See Chapter 16 for more about how to make your go or no-go decision with your idea.

What Is Your Personal Bottom Line?

At this point we have covered a lot of conceptual ground; now it is time to start applying it to your own situation. After all, you are the one reading this book and considering a new business for yourself. Take some time to answer the following questions to help you evaluate your own reality.

What is your current situation? How good is your job and salary? How does your salary level compare to your expenses? How good are the benefits? How good are your future job prospects and potential future salary? How much do you like what you are currently doing or expect to be doing in the future?

How much are you *really* willing to risk to start your own business? How much time can you invest? How much money can you invest? Would starting the business jeopardize important personal relationships? What else could be lost if the business idea did not work out as you expected and you ended up shutting down? What if the idea succeeded? What would be the impact on you, your family, and others important to you?

ED'S LESSONS LEARNED

What did you come up with as a response to the man from the Cornwall pub? Here is what I told him. "A new business is going to cost you money and time to get started and it might be a year or two before you get back to the income level you are at right now if at all. It sounds to me like you have a great deal going right now. I just don't see anything that you would get out of starting your own business that you don't already have." The wife started to breathe again.

To me, his decision and hesitation was all about opportunity cost. Giving up his current opportunity for all of the risk and uncertainty of his own business just did not make business sense. I think at some level he knew it, too, but could not put it into words. He was happy where he was and liked his future prospects. That is a pretty good deal in my book.

How much do you know about the business that you want to start? I don't mean in general—I mean specifically. The business planning process presented in Parts 2 and 3 of this book will help you reduce uncertainty in this regard.

How much of a risk taker are you, really? Are you someone who needs to have all the answers before starting something? Are you willing to move forward if you don't know the answers to important questions? Can you pick the important questions from those that are not?

Notice that you can start most of this self-evaluation process even if you do not yet have your business idea firmly in mind. The more you know about yourself, your situation, and what you bring to the startup table, and with a realistic understanding of others from whom you need support, the more effective you will be in navigating future conversations related to the business opportunity you choose. As always, your business success starts with you. Now you have some powerful concepts to put to work in helping you make a more informed decision about a future that is right for you.

The Least You Need to Know

- Our view of opportunities differs as we move from our 20s, through our 40s, and into our 60s.
- We all evaluate options in light of available opportunities, and doing it consciously is more powerful.
- Uncertainty is what we don't know, and we are naturally averse to uncertainty. The more we know about something, typically the more certain and comfortable with it we become.
- Risk is objectively measured and something we can assess with some clarity.
- Risk tolerance is our natural ability to deal with what is being risked and the uncertainty associated with its success.
- Business planning is a method for reducing uncertainty related to a business idea to the point that it can be compared against the risk tolerance level of stakeholders.

Finding the Right Business for You

Chapter **3**

In This Chapter

- Understanding your personal needs as well as your financial needs
- Knowing what customers will pay for
- Learning about the daily reality of various business types
- Appreciating the relationship between creativity process and your business idea
- Appreciating that uniquely creative business ideas show up on their own schedule and cannot be forced to happen

Jason looked around the coffee shop and saw Naomi sitting by the far window. She almost jumped out of her chair with excitement when she saw Jason at the door. He was relieved to see her happy. The last year had been difficult for her since her employer closed up shop and she lost her job. Money was tight for Naomi and she was having a tough time finding a new job. Sadness was starting to turn into depression, but this was the first time that he had seen her genuinely smile in a long time.

"So, what's up, smiley?" he asked. Naomi grabbed his hand and led him to their table. His coffee was already there—two sugars and one cream—just as he liked it.

"I found a job," she pronounced.

"All right! Doing what?"

"I'm going to buy in to a beauty shop franchise," she said. Jason, for the first time, noticed that her hair was a little lighter and that she had a new cut. For tomboy Naomi, this was really rare.

"Wow! Your own business. That's a pretty big deal. What brought this on?" he asked.

"I met this woman who owns it now. She needs to move out of town and is looking for someone to buy her out. She's even willing to let me take out a loan from her that I can pay off over 5 years instead of having to pay her $30,000 today. She figured out pretty quickly that I'm broke," she said with some of the old sadness returning to her face.

"I can't tell you how great it is to see you happy about something. Would I be a wet blanket if I asked you a couple of questions?" asked Jason hesitantly.

"Not at all. That's part of why I wanted you here. What do you think?" Jason felt that she meant it so he started in.

"I've never, ever heard you talk about wanting to go to the beauty shop to get your hair done except for prom, and we both know how long ago that was. And how many times have you made fun of those women who plan all week to go and get their hair done? And now you want to own a beauty shop? I am just a little concerned that in a few years you are going to hate the business and not be able to get out of it. Plus, how good are you going to be running a business that you don't like?"

"Hmmm. All good points," she responded, clearly thinking about his comments. "Here is the real deal, Jason. When I do dress up, I actually look pretty good, and it can sort of be fun. And as you know, I'm broke and need some money, not to mention something to do. Right now I sort of don't care about the long term as long as it keeps me busy and can make me some money. I figure that I can play 'dress up' for a while and will worry about being happy at work later on once I have some money in the bank."

He took a long drink of his coffee and then a deep breath. She was going to give this a try, and he might as well help her get started on a positive note. Raising his mug he proposed a toast. "To the newest shop owner in town. Hey, does this mean I can get a discount on haircuts? Even more important—are you dangerous with a pair of scissors?"

Willingly marrying someone you didn't like would make little sense. I am not so sure that starting a business about which you are not passionate is any different. Money is important, but how long will the money be enough to keep you working long hours and taking the risks needed to grow a business that does not reward you personally or spiritually as well as financially? Not very long; soon enough you will start to resent the business.

This chapter takes a detailed look at the combination of personal, financial, and professional rewards that we all hope to gain from starting our own business. I will help you look at the unique aspects of the intersection of your interests and what your customers will be willing to pay for. You will also find a summary of the characteristics intrinsic to businesses in various industries. My intent here is to briefly give you a starting point for understanding yourself, your professional skills, your professional and personal goals, what customers will pay you for—and how to go about finding the right mix for you. A special section on creativity is included to guide you in uncovering the unique business idea that is right for you.

What Can You Do That People Will Pay For?

It is one thing to be good at something; it is another to be good at something that others will pay you to do. Your opinions and beliefs are hugely important to the success of a new business, but never lose sight of the fact that ultimately it is the opinion of your customers that will determine your success.

This means that you should be evaluating any new business idea from the viewpoint of the prospective customer. Look for those ideas that not only make sense to you but will also make sense, and will be valuable, to others, too. Be cautious of taking the opinion of a few people who have nothing to lose if your venture fails. Make sure that you get an objective read on your idea before committing major time and resources to its implementation. This is where the planning process becomes so valuable. Taking the time to prepare the plan, even if it is not too detailed, forces you to take a step back from your passion to see the idea in a more objective way.

After completing the plan, you will have a much better idea about who is most likely to buy your product, what they will be willing to pay, why they should buy from you instead of your competition, and the benefits they will gain from using your product or service. Until you have a clear understanding of these points, your success will be based more on luck and energy instead of filling a real void in the marketplace that people can't wait to have filled.

STREET SMARTS

Your hobby might be a great place to start investigating a new business idea. We choose our hobbies because we like them and are usually pretty good at them, and rarely because we intend for it to make money. Sometimes people feel a little guilty charging money for helping out others with their hobby skills. In reality, others would probably pay for the help. Why? Because they need something done, they trust you to do it, and they know that with you they have someone who cares about doing a good job. Isn't that what any of us would want from one of our vendors? It might be that the only reason you are not getting paid for helping people out with your hobby is because you haven't asked for money. They might be very willing to pay you, which could lead to your hobby becoming your next job.

The later sections of this book will help you understand the marketing and sales aspects of your business, the financial realities of daily operation, and a projection of how much money you can expect to make and by when. At this point just be aware that these realities will have to be dealt with eventually, and the process detailed in this book will help you better appreciate what you are getting into.

What Are Your Needs?

When determining the viability of a startup *business*, you must consider how well it fits with your financial, family, and personal (spiritual) requirements. Otherwise, a few years down the road you may find yourself resenting the business right at the point when it is poised to become the financial success you intended it to be. If your business does not make any money, it is a *hobby*. It helps to know how much you need to make ends meet.

This section prompts you to evaluate your own needs so that you can later map them against the requirements of your intended business. The overall intention is to best ensure that what your intended business will ask of you will be what you are willing to give. Now *that* is business success if I have ever heard it.

DEFINITION

A **business** exists to make money. A **hobby** is something you do for the fun of it. **Wealth** comes from consistently having money left over after you pay all of your bills.

Financial Needs and Goals

How much money do you *want* to make, and how much money do you *need* to make? Understand that these two amounts are not the same. I've never met anyone who makes as much money as he or she wants, but most people make as much money as they need. It all comes down to how well they manage the money they make.

Wealth is a relative term. If you make $100,000 per year and spend $110,000, you are living beyond your means. Most people would consider you poor. However, if you make $65,000 and spend $50,000, then you're saving or investing $15,000 a year. Over the course of just a few years, you would be considered wealthy.

In short, don't just calculate how much money you want to bring in; look also at what it costs to live your current lifestyle. Calculate how much money you need to cover all your living expenses. You'll also have to account for the expenses associated with your business—federal taxes, state taxes, health insurance, life insurance, vacation time, and other benefits. Don't guess at these amounts. Find out what you've actually spent in each area over the last 12 months and use that as your baseline measurement for monthly financial survival. Let's face this issue head on: if your business idea does not have a reasonable chance of making this required amount of money in a reasonable period of time, you should likely not start the business. You simply cannot support yourself for a long period of time if the business does not have the realistic prospect of earning enough to cover your monthly living expenses.

The business must earn at least enough to cover its fixed expenses (including your reasonable salary) to stay afloat without your needing to loan it more money. If the business does not generate at least this amount of money, one or a combination of the following three things must happen:

1. You decrease your personal expenses so you need less to live on.
2. You figure out a way to make more money from your new business which means increasing sales, decreasing expenses, or both.
3. You stay with your current job until your savings is high and your debt low—and perhaps lower your personal expenses along the way. This gives you more breathing room once started.

Look at your finances both on a short-term (12 months) and long-term (2 to 5 years) basis. Remember, you need to get through the short term to make it to the long term. If you do not have the money to support yourself for at least 12 months (some say 18 to 24 months), then you should hold off starting your venture until you have the needed savings. Or you can look for outside sources to provide the money you need, such as family members, friends, or banks and government agencies. You need to be able to support yourself during those initial lean months when your business probably will not be making enough to pay your rent or your mortgage. So start saving those quarters now.

You should also consider how much money you're willing to spend before you pull the plug on a struggling business that is a cash drain. Often, people go to Las Vegas determined to stop gambling after they lose a set amount, like $500. Likewise, you should set a limit on how much you're willing to invest in a new business before it must pay for itself. Your odds of success at entrepreneurship are much better than at the gambling tables, but it is still a risk and must be treated as such.

Setting your limits in writing up front can help you make the decision to shut your business down if and when the time comes. That is one great reason for writing a business plan. It's hard to set limits, but doing it up front can save you a lot of time and money. The "Funding Needs" section of your business plan should detail these up-front needs with a high degree of confidence, or you have done yourself a *huge* disservice.

STREET SMARTS

Most people dream of running their own businesses because they believe that it's the only way they'll become wealthy. In truth, most of the extremely wealthy members of our society obtained their money by owning a business. In many cases, they saw an opportunity to introduce a new product or service to the market and jumped in quickly. Some have succeeded and made millions—even billions. How about Larry Ellison of Oracle, Debbie Fields of Mrs. Fields' cookies, or even Henry Ford?

Not everyone who starts a business becomes wealthy, however. Statistics suggest that 50 percent of all new businesses will be around in five years. Not all of the other 50 percent of businesses failed. Some of them will have been sold, some simply closed down … but many of them will fail. When a business fails, the owner rarely makes money on the deal. Some statistics indicate that the average salary of a business owner after five years is around $65,000, and that it might go up to around $100,000 after 10 years or so. And owners might work 80 hours a week for the privilege. Remember that this is an average, meaning some are higher and some lower. Because most of these businesses are privately owned, getting accurate data in this area is hard to do.

That may not sound bad to some of you, but take a look at the number of hours entrepreneurs have to put in to make that money. It's hard work! If you are already making that amount of money at a job you like, why would you take the chance? Many won't.

ED'S LESSONS LEARNED

People often don't understand that your startup business is like your boss. You might have to work after hours in a "normal" job. Why should you not need to do the same for your own business? You will have to, and your family must understand this. Working for yourself doesn't mean that you take off whenever you, or they, like.

Family Motivations and Goals

If you are the type of person who cannot leave your family alone for the evening or weekend without having intense feelings of guilt, then you should examine your startup intentions and your family's needs before you begin a new business venture. There will be times when you will need to work at night, on weekends, and on holidays. At these times, you will have to choose between family involvement and business commitments. Your family needs to accept your commitment to your business without being hurt or angry. They need to understand that it is in *all* of their best interests for the business to succeed.

Communicate openly with your spouse, children, parents, and friends about what you want to do and what kind of a time and energy commitment it will take. If you sense from initial discussions that your family may resent your attention moving away from them and toward a business, think about ways that you can involve them in the company. Instead of having to choose between business and family, talk with them about what you can all do together to run a business. Putting your children on the payroll may be a savvy tax strategy to consider, as long as they are actually doing something productive for the business. Making your spouse an employee may enable you to pay for your family's health insurance through a company group plan. The more they have invested in the success of the business, the more they will support you to do the work needed to make it succeed.

Many divorces have resulted from the feeling that the business is more important than everything else in the business owner's life. Be sure your family knows that this is not the case. Typically, just telling them won't do it; you have to show them by setting aside time to be with them.

Spend the time to get your family involved from the beginning. Set their expectations properly to best avoid having recurring ugly scenes later. Your family can become a source of strength if they understand the importance of their support in your and the business's success. Nobody is an island, and you may end up alone snuggling with your checkbook if you don't handle your family situation with respect.

What Are Your Spiritual Goals?

Spirituality in the context of this section has more to do with what makes us feel good as human beings than with a formal religion. For some of us, a business helps us achieve spiritual goals through the belief that by providing a valued product or service to our clients, we are improving their lives. Spiritual goals can also be reached by creating an organization to perform social service work, such as a food kitchen or a halfway house. The *social entrepreneurship* movement is geared toward people who want to make money while also creating a business that makes a difference. Some entrepreneurs want to create an organization where their employees can realize their full potential. In a world of compromised corporate ethics, some people start their own business to ensure that they can always work in an ethical environment of their own creation. This is motivation enough for them.

DEFINITION

Social entrepreneurship refers to a startup business designed from the beginning to make money but to also make social difference in some way. This may include work-training programs for those needing work skills, or selling products where a portion of the proceeds go back to the community. These businesses are not nonprofits but instead are for-profit businesses with a social mission.

One of my clients is determined to start her own business, but not for any of the personal financial reasons we've discussed so far. She has enough money to support herself and has started businesses before. But she now wants to start one to bring new attention to the plight of people in recovery for alcohol or substance abuse. Her belief is that by creating products to better meet the needs of this group, she can draw attention to and help support them, donating the bulk of the profits to related charities and human service agencies. Like many other entrepreneurs, she is dedicated to her business idea; she just happens to be doing it for spiritual reasons.

In essence, don't neglect the nonbusiness side of your soul when deciding to start your own business. In fact, there are many people who believe that you should look here first.

General Business Types and Their Requirements

Business types come in all kinds of shapes and sizes. Your business will take on your personality after it is started, but it will also be shaped by the conventions of your industry.

STREET SMARTS

Nobody will be more committed to the success of your business than you. Know that when others do not show up or don't do a good job, you will be the one to pick up the pieces.

What follows is a partial listing of some general business types. My intent is to give you some guidelines as to what you can expect from these variations so that you can better assess the type that is right for you.

Manufacturing Businesses

A manufacturing business is one that converts raw materials such as plastic, wood, or electronic components into a finished product that can be sold. As the manufacturer you provide the labor, equipment, energy, and knowledge required for the conversion process. In the end, a product is produced that will either be incorporated into someone else's product, making you an *original equipment manufacturer (OEM)*, or it will eventually be purchased as-is directly by the end user. This product may go through several levels of sales distribution on its way to the customer. In either case, whoever purchases your products will expect them to be produced to specification, on time, and within agreed cost guidelines.

Think of it this way: if you produce a hard drive that will be included in a computer, then you are an OEM; if you combine the OEM's product into a final product that will be used by the end user, you are an *integrator.* The integrator will set up his manufacturing line expecting that all products received from your company meet certain specifications. If those specifications are not met, the final product may not function as intended, causing the end user to send it back. Returns are bad news for everyone, including the OEM.

DEFINITION

Original equipment manufacturers (OEM) produce the subcomponents that are used by **integrators** to manufacture the final product that will be purchased by the end user.

When you think about manufacturing, you should think about using equipment, materials, and labor to efficiently and reliably make a physical product. How all of these ingredients are combined to make a product is what differentiates one manufacturer from another. The best ones do it all well and for a reasonable price. Those of you interested in starting a manufacturing firm should be prepared to handle schedules, deadlines, people of various education and skill levels, vendors, and technology in what is often a high-pressure environment where precision is important. There are often high capital expenditures needed for setup, production line personnel training, and often long delays between when you spend money and when you receive payment from your customers. There is an art to successful manufacturing, and I would recommend getting experience on a production floor before going off on your own.

Service Organizations

Manufacturing organizations are dependent upon processes and procedures rather than on people. A service organization, on the other hand, is heavily dependent on its people. Typical service organizations would include consulting, medical, legal, accounting, massage, physical therapy, home health care, and similar types of businesses. Notice that these businesses are paid based on the number of hours worked and not based on how many of something they manufactured on an assembly line. The quality of a product will be determined by how it performs in the customer's environment immediately after purchased, and perhaps for many years into the future. The quality of a service is heavily dependent upon the quality of the person providing that service. This is what I mean when I say that a service organization is heavily people dependent. Another major difference is that a person can only provide a certain number of hours of work in a day, whereas a manufacturing line may produce hundreds of items one day and zero the next, adjusting to demand. Just as an airline never gets back an empty seat from a flown plane, a service organization never gets back an unbilled day from earlier in the week.

STREET SMARTS

No matter the type of business you start, always be looking for those companies and people who could be your first customers. It is not uncommon for you to notice an opportunity at your current job that your employer does not want to pursue. This does not mean that the idea is a bad one in general, just that it's not a good fit for your employer. It could be a great idea for you to start with the intent of turning around and offering your current employer the benefits of the product or service without having to invest in a new business. Your employer might be your first customer, so keep an eye out for an opportunity that allows you to start your business while simultaneously helping your employer. Heck, he or she might even help you fund it!

The implications of all of this to those of you looking to start a service business is that you must be continually focused on finding the best possible people, cultivating the best possible customer relationships (true for all businesses but particularly true for service organizations), and making sure that you build enough margin into your pricing models to cover the slow times when you will not be able to generate revenue. Product customers have limited contact with manufacturing personnel; however, service business customers will regularly work with the contracted personnel, making that relationship very important.

To effectively run a service organization, you must be service-oriented yourself, be clear on the benefit your customers gain from using your services, place value on that benefit, and also be respectful of the personnel development aspect of your employees.

Restaurant Businesses

It is common for people to want to start a restaurant business, and as someone who eats out a lot I am grateful to them for their initiative. But if you are one of those people, there are a few realities that you should be aware of before taking the plunge, no matter how great your mother's recipe for pasta sauce may be. I cover restaurants in a little more detail simply because this question comes my way a lot.

Restaurants are pretty expensive to start. They require a retail type of space which is far more expensive than office or warehouse space. There is a lot of equipment required to make a restaurant function (although you can help yourself here by purchasing used or liquidated equipment at a much reduced price), the unique marketing and sales aspects of a restaurant are critical, and it may take a very long time after starting before you can take a reasonable salary from the business.

WATCH OUT!

Some people say that you should plan to work for free for up to three years after starting your new restaurant. By some estimates, a quarter of all new restaurants will close or change hands in the first year of operation, with that number cumulatively growing to around 60 percent by year three. Compare this with SBA statistics from a few years ago that indicated half of businesses would still be operating five years after starting. My point is that the average restaurant business has lower likelihood of being in business five years in the future than an average nonrestaurant business.

Here are a few recommendations for those of you looking to start a restaurant. Keep your menu simple and excellent and have a concept for your restaurant that you reinforce to customers every chance you get. Whatever you offer on your menu, make it the best you can. You are looking to create the idea in the customers' minds that they not only will want to come back, but will want all of their friends to come back with them. Make it easy to define what your restaurant offers. Make it easy for customers to differentiate your restaurant from the hundreds of others in the area. Expect that your gross margins will be around 50 percent, and your net income will be around 18 percent. If your gross margin and net income are higher than that, hallelujah! Use these as starting points for your analysis. Oh, yeah—expect to work 80 hours per week, to put a lot of emphasis on employee training, and to build a trusting relationship with a great chef. If possible, create a buzz about your business months before you open your doors—something like, "Be one of the first 50 people to eat in our new restaurant and eat for 50 percent off for one year."

I love restaurants and sincerely hope that you succeed in starting yours. Just be aware of the special realities associated with starting a new restaurant business. Become friends with someone who knows the industry well, who will not view you as a competitor, and who will help you learn the ropes without hanging yourself.

Sales Representation and Agency Businesses

When you represent someone else, you take on the responsibility to do the best you can to promote their success; your success is created as a secondary result. This is typical of a sales representation business or a talent agency such as those that represent athletes, actors, or writers. Doing this well requires that you understand the industry norms, understand your clients, understand prospective users of the client's talents, and understand yourself enough to revel in their success. In my opinion, it is the rare person who works hard to help others succeed while playing a nearly invisible role in the background.

This is also a people business with sales success sitting front and center. If you are not willing to make new contacts, promote new products or services, and work on behalf of others while protecting your own business interests, this is not the right industry for you. As a sales representative you may travel quite a lot and may have to work with many different clients while making each one feel as if he or she has 100 percent of your time and effort, while representing everyone's policies, products, pricing, and commitments. This is a business that involves influencing transaction stakeholders while having no direct authority. If you are not a politically oriented, people-oriented, sales-oriented, and relatively selfless person, this may not be the right business model for you.

Intellectual Property–Oriented Businesses

Many businesses successfully start and are maintained based on a good idea that is somehow protected and that is needed by the marketplace. The idea is referred to as intellectual property (IP) because it may not have any tangible form beyond that of the paper on which it is printed or the computer image displayed on a computer. Examples of intellectual property include books, songs, software code, business processes, photos, paintings, records, patents, trademarks, and copyrights.

The legal protection of IP is very important, and you should spend time with experts to ensure that you have offered yourself as much legal protection as is reasonable. You should also learn the rules associated with legally protecting your IP once it is in the marketplace, and you may have to sue others who infringe on your IP to ensure that it remains protected. This is an industry where the piece of paper or jump disk on which the IP exists could be worth large amounts of money, making security critically important, almost to the point of fanaticism. Knowing how to find people you can trust is very important, as is a willingness to legally prosecute those who infringe on your IP protections. Really great ideas are rare and valuable, and you will have to jealously guard the value of the idea if this is the basis of your company's uniqueness in the marketplace.

Mom-and-Pop Businesses

A mom-and-pop business is one that operates on a smaller basis, often keeping to one location that is run by the owners, typically a husband and wife—thus the name. These are businesses that are not started with the intention of growing into the next Microsoft. They are started to allow the owners to make a decent living doing something that they like to do. The owners are the primary employees, and they will typically spend many hours at the business.

Typical mom-and-pop businesses would include small restaurants such as taco or hot dog stands, a specialty machining shop, a small manufacturing volume plant, an auto repair shop, a house or interior painting service, or a product-assembly provider. It is quite common to find one owner working the front counter or sales process, while the other handles the bookkeeping and back-office activities. Very reasonable incomes and livings can be made from mom-and-pop operations, but understand that this type of operation is likely to remain a full-time job as long as it is in operation. The good news about these types of businesses is that they are relatively easy to start, may not require a lot of startup money, and will allow the owners to fully express themselves while creating deep and lasting relationships with customers.

Major Startup-Type Businesses

Some of you might picture yourself as the next Michael Dell of Dell computers or Mrs. Fields, the cookie lady. If so, you have aspirations for starting a major startup company. I applaud your vision and drive and know that what is presented in this book will get you a long way toward making your dream a reality.

If you are one of these folks, get used to creating something with the intention of having it grow beyond your control. Any business venture with this type of growth potential is one that will need help from other talented people who will all feel as though they own a part of the success. In fact, they might, depending upon how you structure the deal. As the idea person for a major startup, you are really the nexus or hub around which others will rally with ideas, energy, money, talent, and resources. Look at yourself as the facilitator for others to contribute, and I believe you will go a long way toward better ensuring the success of your new venture. If you are someone who must control and own everything, does not trust others, and has limited personal resources, then you should not begin a startup; on the other hand, you will be a success if you involve someone at the top who can rally others while you offer the sage guidance in the background that the company leader will need to succeed.

Using Creativity to Find the Fit

When looking to solve a problem or answer a question without an obvious solution, it is often best to "live in the question" for a while. By this I mean that you immerse yourself in the problem or question, and learn as much as possible about what relates to it, but don't look for a quick answer. Instead, you keep track of possible solutions that come up while you are learning. You keep track of new questions or problems that appear as you become more familiar with your area of interest. Do all of this, trusting that at some point a reformatted problem, solution, or answer will show up that will resonate with you as the "one" that is right for you and your situation. "Living in the question" is a lot harder than it might seem from this simple description of the process. Immersion in a problem while keeping an open mind for options is incredibly powerful and a talent one cultivates over a lifetime.

Your question going into this process is really pretty simple: What is the right new business venture for me? For many this is one of the toughest questions they will ever answer. If your first idea was the right one for you, then you would probably be into the later chapters of this book, writing the details of your plan. But if you are like most people I know, you are just not sure. That is exactly the time when this creativity process will become the most valuable. By learning as much as possible about your chosen industry while keeping an open mind about potential opportunities, you are most likely to find that fit of idea, passion, and skill that uniquely combine for you and your situation. It really does work.

The Least You Need to Know

- Your business must meet your needs on several different levels, including financial and personal.
- Different business types have different startup and ongoing operational requirements.
- The right business for you is the one that blends market needs with your needs and the needs of other business stakeholders.
- Look for the possibility that your current job could help you uncover your business idea and that your employer could become your first customer.
- By "living in the question," you increase the likelihood of finding the right business for you. This is easy to talk about but hard to do.

Creating New Ideas Using Technology and Information

Chapter

4

In This Chapter

- Learning a fundamental three-part business model
- Differentiating between data, technology, and solutions
- Familiarizing yourself with several online business models
- Training yourself to watch for creative solutions
- Understanding that technology reduces geographic limitations

Jay handed his new business cards to Devin with a strong sense of pride. "Check out the new website address listed at the bottom," he said, opening up a new browser page to display the site on his notebook computer.

Devin took a Japanese approach to looking at the card, slowly pondering the color, typesetting, title, and overall layout. It looked really good, and Jay was wise to use a website name that he owned instead of one associated with an online email service. He smiled, looked at the notebook display, and nodded, to which Jay smiled and nodded back.

"So how long have you been in business?" he asked Jay.

"About five years. Why?"

"I am just wondering why it took you so long to finally get your own website URL. What was up with that?"

"Honestly, I really don't know much about all of that technology stuff. I'm into sports equipment and clothing, and that is what my customers want from me. I put together the site because I thought I should, but I really don't know what I'm going to do with it."

"Okay. Understood. What you have done has really worked well for you, but have you ever thought that people in other parts of the country, or even the world for that matter, would be interested in what you do, too?"

"For sure, which is why I put together the website. Hey, it cost me almost a grand to get it up and running. What are you thinking? I know you. Something is up. Don't you like the site?"

"I actually like the site a lot. I also like the cards, your products, and your energy. They are all top notch, and that is my point. What you do is pretty amazing and I think if you used the internet to allow others to not only see your site, but to also learn about you and also order products, you would make a lot more money. And for not much more effort. And I know this guy who can …."

Having a website for your company is much better than not having one, but in today's networked world it's only the first step in becoming an online business. If you are a service business, your clients might appreciate being able to book an appointment online instead of having to make a phone call. If you are a product business, your clients might order more from you if they could do it on their time, in quantities they want, delivered right to their location. If you offer a specialized expertise of some kind, they might appreciate being able to take additional training from your company, on their time and on topics that they feel are valuable to them. They might even be willing to pay an additional fee to take these seminars, which means that you could have a lost revenue opportunity sitting on your computer and not even know it.

This chapter is intended to create a basic understanding of the very special opportunities and information offered by today's internet and mobile technologies. I believe that we are just at the beginning of the internet revolution. This means that new business opportunities are yet to be created by someone, and I hope that someone is you.

A High-Level Look at How Business Works

At a very basic level, business consists of a customer with a need, a company that can fulfill that need, and a way of connecting the company to the customer. The wide variety of businesses evolves from the incredible complexity of life and the ability of entrepreneurs to develop ways of addressing that complexity. To explain, let's take a look at something as basic as eating.

We all have the need to eat. The way in which we fulfill that need is dependent on many factors such as schedule, location, allergies, cooking skills, and economic condition. Assume that I want to go to a restaurant for dinner. Somehow I have to connect with a restaurant either through a coupon book, Yellow Pages, online, word of mouth, or prior experience as I choose where I will eat this evening. Oh, did I mention that my preference for tonight was Thai instead of Chinese? My need is to eat with a preference to not cook; to eat Thai; and to not be too inconvenienced by getting to the restaurant. The restaurant has already been set up to offer Thai food for a certain number of people. The connection is the process that makes me aware of a particular restaurant, that helps me get me there, and eventually allows me to eat and pay for dinner. Pretty straightforward so far, right?

What if my need to eat involves a desire to cook at home? To make this work I must have a place to cook, ingredients to cook with, the skills with which to cook, and the utensils with which to cook, combined with the time and motivation to make the meal. The delivery mechanism in this case is me in my kitchen. Notice, though, in order to complete the delivery my kitchen must already be built and adequately equipped, I must have food ingredients on hand, combined with cooking skills that I probably acquired either from my mother or from prior education. I would also need a recipe to follow. The providing companies are all of the organizations that helped me with the kitchen, groceries, skills, utensils, etc.

Now assume that I don't have much time, that I live in a fairly remote location, and that my kitchen and cooking skills are pretty basic. I still need to eat, but the circumstances surrounding my eating are very different. I might be okay microwaving a frozen dinner that I ordered on the internet that was delivered earlier to my house. The need is still to eat. The delivery mechanism was a website that offered home delivery and the company was the organization that prepared the frozen meal. The same basic need is being addressed, but in three very different ways based on the customer's need. The microwave dinner would not be adequate for the person who wanted to cook, while having to cook would not be right for the microwave person with no time or cooking skills.

Each of these ideas offers enough value to the customer for him or her to be willing to spend money. Each of these approaches to business is very different from each other. And each is right for its intended customer base and needs. Pretty cool, I think. And pretty confusing, too. There is really no right way, only the way that works for the intended customer group. Understanding the needs of a particular customer group, developing an offering that addresses that need, and then creatively matching the delivery mechanism is the amazing opportunity provided by today's technological advances.

Several General Online Business Models

The ways in which technology can be implemented to solve a business problem are infinite, so there is really no way to provide a comprehensive list. The specifics of the creativity process are really up to you, and I suggest that you refer back to the section "Using Creativity to Find the Fit" in Chapter 3 to remind yourself of how it works.

In the following sections I will present a few general approaches to online business that I hope will get your creative juices flowing as you look around for ideas. Much of what will be presented here is based loosely on models presented by Don Tapscott, David Ticoll, and Alex Lowy in their fine book *Digital Capital: Harnessing the Power of Business Webs* (Harvard Business Press, May 2000). My intent here is to distill the discussion down to give you a practical sense of how technology is used today to connect customer needs to the companies who can solve those needs.

Networked Users Who Connect to Other Networked Users

Let's start with an early idea which should be familiar to all of us. America Online (AOL) and a number of other vendors entered into the online marketplace in the late 1980s with an internet-based electronic mail system. This system also allowed you to access the internet, which was not very developed at that time. The customer need that AOL wanted to address was that of instant communication between people who were not part of a larger organization. Larger companies had been using electronic mail since the early 1980s, but this capability was not readily available to the general consumer; this was the need and opportunity that AOL as a business went after. Considering that AOL's primary function was to electronically connect people, what would be one of your foremost goals as its business manager? What made AOL valuable? Instant connections to others. What if nobody else was connected? AOL becomes useless to you, doesn't it? It would be like throwing a party to which nobody could come.

For this reason, a primary focus and goal of AOL was to generate subscribers. Does that help to explain why every time you opened up your mailbox you would find an AOL subscriber disk in the stack of envelopes? The more users AOL signed up, the more valuable it became as a connection tool between users.

Think about Skype. Isn't it in a similar situation, except with video conferencing instead of email? How can Skype get tons of people signed up so that it can provide enough consumer value? I finally signed up for Skype a few weeks back and have spent time asking friends if they are on Skype. So far, most have answered no. So here I am, a Skype subscriber with nobody to talk to. Should this problem continue for very long, Skype could find itself competing with dozens of companies with similar offerings. To make the networked connection business model work, you have to focus intently on creating the most possible network connections. Making that happen has to be a central focus of the marketing and sales section of your business plan.

Competitively Connecting Buyers and Sellers

Sellers want to sell their offerings for the highest possible price. Buyers want to purchase for the lowest possible price. This tension is always at work in commerce. If I have time and know what I am looking for, I will shop around to different stores to develop a reasonable price range for things that I intend to purchase. Sellers will check out the prices of their competition as a way of determining the right sale price for their offering. Product and service prices are set in a continually evolving balance of marketplace information and customer needs.

Now assume that you are selling an item that was once owned by President Kennedy. What is it worth? Do you have the expertise to set its sale price with confidence? And even if you did, won't the marketplace eventually set the actual sale price based on the bids offered by potential buyers? That's right. The marketplace is always adjusting prices and terms of sale based on what customers are willing to pay and the prices at which vendors are willing to sell. Helping to connect vendors with unique items to sell with buyers who would be interested in purchasing is the essential function of a conventional auction company and the primary focus of online auction sites such as eBay. The auctioneer will manage the customer bidding process until the final sale price is determined by the winning bid.

If you are the seller, you want the auctioneer to draw in as many qualified buyers as possible, efficiently manage the bidding process, and then coordinate the money collection and product delivery process. If you are the buyer, you want to have the chance to bid on unique items in an efficient and reliable way, and you would like some way of verifying the credibility of the seller. You want assurance that your payments are going to the right person and that delivery (to you) of your purchase can be expected. This is the same business challenge faced by online auction sites.

Auction sites notify subscribers of certain items being offered for auction, enable sellers to post information about items being sold, coordinate the online bidding for the items, provide a simple yet credible way of handling payments, and coordinate shipping. They will not generally take responsibility for the items being sold or manage the collections process. This type of business model gains a great reputation by offering the services needed by auction buyers and sellers in an efficient and cost-effective manner. When sellers do not have buyers bidding or buyers find nothing of interest, the auction services provider is on the road to trouble.

Offering One-Stop Online Shopping

Just as many of us are looking for a way to do all of our shopping at a single store, such as Super Target or a Walmart Supercenter, online shoppers are looking for ways to combine their purchases into a single online stop. This explains the motivations behind Amazon.com's expansion into product areas far beyond their initial book entry point. Plus, you might have the ability to consolidate your many purchases into a single shipment which will likely save you money on shipping when compared to purchasing at multiple sites.

If you are a consumer looking for this type of service, you are looking for the easiest, fastest, and least expensive way of finding the products you need. If you are the vendor of this type of service you want your customers to be exposed to as many of your products that might be of interest, you want to make the purchasing process as simple as possible, and you want to ensure that purchases are delivered as expected.

As the provider of this type of business model, you want to offer your customers the benefit of having access to a large inventory of products but without having to stock the inventory yourself. You want to customize the shopping experience so that your site visitors find the products that are of most likely interest to them specifically. Your site should offer customized product exposure, adequate information, simple purchasing, and flexible delivery of products. Does your visit to Amazon.com start to make more sense now? Remember how the Amazon screen offered you a record of products that you looked at previously, along with products others with your interests had purchased? Remember how useful the vendor quality ratings were in helping you select a seller, along with the ease with which you could select a delivery option? It might not be inaccurate to think that Amazon knows more about what you have looked at before and what you are likely to look at next than you do. If it works out that this approach makes your shopping experience more efficient and rewarding as a consumer, then Amazon is doing the right thing. Right?

Combining Forces for a More Powerful Offering

One of the most amazing and invisible aspects of the internet is its ability to seamlessly link together geographically distributed organizations. On a single page you could have a company from Chicago, another from Paris, and another from Tokyo.

As a site visitor, it is pretty difficult to determine if the links are from different companies. This seamless operation presents opportunities for cooperation never really possible in earlier days.

Imagine that you have a website that caters to the clothing needs of young children. Your primary intent could be to entice visitors to your site, where you then connect the visitors to other companies as though they are your own. One link might show shoes. Another link might show coats. A third might show pants. As far as the site visitor is concerned all of these products are yours, when the reality is that it is all being provided by third-party companies—you don't inventory any of it. Your site could handle the invoicing, credit card processing, shipping, and postsale follow-up, and as far as the customers are concerned, they purchased from you. Now, that is pretty cool! If you think about it, this seamlessness presents opportunities for business combinations that are limited only by your imagination and ability to create credible business alliances. Find a customer need, align yourself with quality partners with complementary offerings, focus on finding and maintaining excellent customer relationships, and you could find yourself running a very successful business that does not even have a warehouse or office. Now that is really cool!

Time and Space in Today's Mobile World

By this point you should understand that I am talking about using technology that goes way beyond simply creating a website. I am talking about creating a business model that offers benefits specifically because it exists on the internet. It takes full advantage of the time and geography independence of the internet. If I have a retail store in St. Louis, then the vast majority of my customers will come from St. Louis. I am geographically restricted with respect to my prospective customer base. But if my store exists on the internet, the only likely geographic restrictions I have will be related to the shipping of the purchased products. If the product can be delivered over the internet, such as with software or an e-book, then that restriction disappears completely.

But let's go one step further. What if your computer is your telephone? It knows where you are geographically located; you could tell it what you are looking to purchase, and it might be able to uncover information about other similar opportunities in the same neighborhood. As an example, assume that you are interested in seeing the hottest new movie and you are in downtown San Francisco. Wouldn't it be cool to click a movies tab on your smartphone and see a display of local theaters that are showing that movie, with times and prices listed? You might be able to purchase the ticket right from your phone, which would receive an image of the ticket that you can show to gain admittance at the theater. Pretty cool, and valuable, too.

STREET SMARTS

Try this simple trick if you are seriously interested in finding a unique problem that can be solved using technology in ways discussed in this chapter. Carry a small notebook around with you and get into the habit of writing down all of the things that you see that could be solved with technology. For example, I am sitting in a park writing while the Chicago Bears season opener football game is on. I would like to watch the game for a few minutes while taking a break from writing. I have WiFi access but cannot easily find the game in real time. Write your problem down. You just might find one of these ideas that is crying for a solution, that everyone thinks is obvious, but that nobody has yet done.

Or perhaps you are on a special diet and want to make sure that the foods you purchase at the grocery store are on the diet. Wouldn't it be great if you could scan the barcode on the box of food and have your phone tell you whether the food is approved or not? No guessing. No returns. No regrets from having gone off the diet because you bought the wrong stuff. All because you could check your diet plan from your phone wherever you were.

In this prior example, the need was determined by the customer. The information already existed in the form of foods approved by your dietitian and the food contents as provided by the manufacturer. The food's availability was determined by the grocery store, the barcode on the package enabled you to focus the database question, and the mobile technology allowed you to connect to the main website where the comparison decisions were made. All of the parts existed independent of each other, and your creativity brought it all together as a sellable solution to a real consumer problem.

There is really no limit to the creative ways in which data provided by various sources can be combined in creative ways to offer unique benefits to needy customers in a geographically independent way. Connecting the dots so that it all makes business sense is where you come in.

Differentiating the Technology from the Information

At this point it might be good to spend a few moments talking about the difference between technology, information, and solving a problem that people will pay for.

Buying a powerful smartphone that does not have the ability to do anything functional beyond making a phone call is not solving a problem. It is just an expensive (but very cool) additional weight in your pocket. It does not help you in any way beyond a regular cellular phone. However, if that phone connects to a navigation system that helps you drive to your next location, the vendor has solved a problem for you that you, and many others, would be willing to pay for. The information on the mapping system already existed before you got your phone. Remember also that you got your phone primarily to make calls. Creatively connecting the maps to the phone to give you directions created a huge opportunity. Always be looking beyond the information and the technology toward the customer to find the usefulness that becomes the application upon which to base your new business.

We may be living in one of the most exciting entrepreneurial times I have seen since the introduction of the personal computer in the early 1980s. That powerful technology was looking for applications that solved problems, and I feel the same way about today's technology. Location is becoming irrelevant. Network speed is becoming irrelevant. Voice, data, image, documents, and editing are becoming equally available. The processing power of the portable devices are starting to rival those of desktop computers, and in more ways than ever before our office goes with us.

I will not debate the merits of a 24/7-available office here. But what I will say is that as an entrepreneur, I believe that opportunities for creative solutions to everyday problems are more viable for less money than ever before in my lifetime. Take the time to become familiar with the basic models presented in this chapter, train yourself to see problems as opportunities, and partner with folks who have the technological background needed to make your idea a viable reality.

For Your Plan

When preparing the operations portion of your plan, make sure that you consider the following points:

- Briefly describe the confluence of the various technologies that enable your offering.
- Explain how the information and technology combine to offer something unique and useful for users.
- Elaborate on licensing and other legal issues related to accessing the information and using the technologies.

- Project as possible the technology trends that will impact your offering and how you plan to remain competitive by adapting to these changes.
- Compare your idea to other successful online models while ensuring that your idea's uniqueness is clearly spelled out.

The Least You Need to Know

- Customers buy solutions to problems, not technology. Data, technology, and information can be uniquely combined to create customer solutions.
- Modern technology is useful for connecting your company to a customer's need.
- Mobile technology and networks are becoming more powerful every day.
- There are several standard online business models that can help you focus your idea.
- The online business marketplace is in its infancy, with huge future opportunities available.

Chapter 5

Reducing Risk by Buying an Existing Business or Franchise

In This Chapter

- Understanding the benefits and drawbacks of buying a business or a franchise
- Learning the stages of buying a business or franchise
- Understanding franchise basics
- Knowing when to use the right professionals
- Buying the right business for you

Ben was convinced he wanted to own his own business. However, he was concerned about his ability to start a business from scratch. He knew a lot about repairing cars and had stayed current on the latest trends in car technology. Plus, he had worked for a dealership for 10 years so he knew a lot about dealing with customers. In fact, one of the things that customers continually said about Ben was that they really trusted him to work on their car.

What he did not know much about was how to find customers and how to price what he planned to sell. At the dealership the customers came to him and all of the service prices were set. He just fixed the cars and charged what was on the rate sheet. With his own business he would have to find those customers for himself, and set his own rates.

His concerns were driving him, his wife, and friends nuts because he really wanted to go off on his own but he also had a healthy respect for what would happen if he didn't build a clientele.

Then he saw a notice in the paper that Frank, the owner of the mechanic's shop where he originally had started out just a few miles from his house, had passed away. The shop had been there forever and had a solid reputation. The article mentioned that family members were looking to sell the business. Frank had made enough money off of the shop to raise his family, and Ben figured that he could, too. "Wow," he thought. "I might get my own business by buying Frank's place."

But there on the next page he came across an ad for a company that was selling franchised shops for mechanics who wanted to go off on their own. The income that they claimed the owners could make in two years was double what he made now. Ben remembered that a guy he went to high school with had started a franchise food business and had done pretty well.

Ben went from wondering how he would go off on his own to now having a major decision: should he buy an established business here in town, or buy a franchise and possibly double his salary?

Not everyone is wired to create a business from just an idea. Regardless, it doesn't mean that you have to give up on the dream of owning your own business. You could instead look at buying an established business with pre-existing customers, employees, vendors, processes, and reputation. Or you might be better off buying a franchise, which is a successful business method that you purchase and implement. Either way, a lot of the risk associated with starting a business might be reduced with these options, increasing your odds of being successful.

This chapter is for those of you who know that you want to own your own business but have concerns about starting one from scratch. If you are smart in selecting the right business or franchise, you might find yourself a successful business owner in no time, often faster than if you created it all new.

The Benefits and Drawbacks of Buying an Existing Business

Consider the following key aspects associated with buying an existing business. An established business has a track record that helps you determine if future sales will provide the income you need. It also has an existing customer base that you can tap into for future sales, relieving some of the startup selling pressure. The company is already legally formed, which means that it has a name, a reputation, banking relationship, and other important business foundation aspects that you would have to create for a new business. You can get up and running in your new business in as little as a few weeks, depending on how long it takes you and the seller to come to an agreement. These all sound pretty good, and they are.

Like so much else in business, with all of these benefits there are also some potential risks. If the company has a bad reputation, it could take a long time and a lot of effort to turn it around, even if everyone knows that it is under new ownership. No—your smiling face may not be enough to get customers to buy if they had a bad experience with the prior owner. On the other hand, your great management may be just what is needed to make a poorly operated business succeed.

The company may have some legal or other obligations that would transfer to you as the new owner. You are basically inheriting the prior owner's legal and financial problems once you buy the company, so extreme care and professional guidance is warranted in this area.

It may be possible that the prior owner is the primary reason for the business's success; and if the prior owner leaves, so does what made it successful in the past. This is actually pretty common, so careful attention to this point is warranted. On the other hand, if customers did not like the prior owner, this could present you with an opportunity for improvement.

The employees may be fiercely dedicated to the prior owner and either leave when the company is sold or, even worse, work to undermine your future success simply because you are not the same person they worked with for so many years.

STREET SMARTS

Beware of paying too much for a business when purchasing it; make sure that you factor in purchase payments to the prior owner when doing your financial projections. If the business was marginally profitable when run by the prior owner, it could become a losing venture for you once the purchase payments are included. You might find it cheaper to start your own from scratch.

As you can see, just like any business situation, there are pros and cons, risks and uncertainties. I suggest that you have a heart-to-heart with yourself about whether you are a startup person who likes to create things that are new or someone who is stellar at improving on an existing idea. Once you have an idea about who you are, then you can decide if starting or buying a company is right for you.

Finding the Right Candidate

There are always companies for sale, and many of them may not be advertised. When purchasing a house, it helps to know the number of bedrooms, baths, garage size, and type of neighborhood you are looking for; so, too, does it help to be clear about what you are looking to buy when purchasing a business. Do you want a larger company or one with fewer than 10 employees? Do you want to be in a specific geographic location? Do you want to build things that others sell, or would you rather sell things directly to the buyer? Do you want a newer business or one that is well established? All of these issues and many more will be part of the consideration process when purchasing a company.

So where do you start your purchasing process? Start out by asking yourself the following questions, knowing that other questions will come up as you move forward.

> What type of personal time and energy commitments are you willing to take on?
>
> What type of geographic, financial, and industrial characteristics should the ideal company have?
>
> Do you want a company that is already doing great, or are you up for the challenge of improving one that is struggling?
>
> How much are you willing to spend on the purchase, and how do you plan to find the money?
>
> Are you willing to work with the prior owners after the sale, or do you intend to go it alone?
>
> What assets, experience, expertise, or other capabilities do you bring to the purchase that could improve on what the company already has?

Try to picture what you want your business life to look like in three to five years. You should look at industries that interest you and that are growing because they present a better opportunity for future sales success.

The more questions you ask before starting your purchasing search, the more efficiently the process will proceed and the more likely you are to wind up with a satisfactory purchase.

Remember that this is ultimately a business decision and it must make business sense—if not, it makes little sense at all. No business stays in business for very long if it fails to guard its financial health.

To find potential acquisition candidates, many people work with a business broker. Just as a real estate broker is familiar with the properties currently on the market, a good business broker will be familiar with the businesses currently for sale. If you choose to go without a business broker, then you will have to find the candidates on your own. Try looking at bizbuysell.com or businessesforsale.com to see what comes up in your areas of interest.

Whether on your own or using a broker, you start by determining the general criteria for your candidate companies. Here is a starting list that will help you find three to five candidates:

- Specify a geographic region.
- Pick a company in a growing industry.
- Look for a company with a positive reputation and ideally one that is a leader in its community or industry.
- It should have been in business at least three years.
- Look for one that has something unique about it when compared to the competition.
- If it continued along its current path, would it be on a track to match your particular five-year goals?
- If you are not looking to turn around a struggling company, you should look for candidates with a consistent sales record.

At this stage you are simply trying to make a first-cut determination about which companies are worth more detailed evaluation. Should a company fail this first set of evaluation criteria, then you are best served dropping it from the candidate list unless other attributes are such a strong fit that they warrant further investigation.

Now take a look at what the media has to say about the candidates. A few days of investigation can round out your initial assessment and may even let you know if the company is currently for sale, whether deals have recently fallen through, or if the company has extenuating circumstances that make it an even better *acquisition target.* Local newspaper articles are important for learning about smaller, privately held businesses, as is the local chamber of commerce or rotary club. Perhaps you know a college business student who can help you with this by using the college's library subscription resources. You might have access yourself if you are an alumni.

DEFINITION

The **acquisition target** is the final company selected from a list of potential acquisition candidates that meet your general business purchase guidelines.

The companies you come up with do not even need to be for sale—many great companies are not listed, but the owners would sell for the right price and to the right person. You are simply determining who you should talk to. After the media review, your list of five companies may be down to three or fewer. But notice that your information on these companies is now as current as possible using only publicly available information. You are informed enough to talk intelligently to the company management and represent yourself as a credible buyer.

STREET SMARTS

I have a friend who found the retail service business he bought by keeping his eyes open while shopping for some personal items. He saw a business that interested him, started talking to the owner, and got the impression that he was tired of running the business. My friend asked if he would be interested in selling, and a few weeks later he was a shop owner. It is amazing what can show up if you just start looking for it.

Plan to Buy in Stages

Buying a business takes time. It also takes planning if you expect the purchase to make you money in the future. It may help you to divide the prebuying process into a few stages.

Stage 1: Prepurchase—In this stage, you are doing some soul searching while at the same time cleaning up any credit or other financial problems. You'll want to have as much cash on hand as possible, as little debt as possible, and as clean a credit record as possible. These actions will all pay off later should you need funding for the purchase.

Stage 2: Finding Candidates and Targets—During this stage, you put out feelers with various people to see who might be interested in selling their company. The challenge here is to approach enough companies so that you will find a few interested sellers. During this stage you might contact people by mail or telephone, but preferably through mutual acquaintances. You will probably have a meeting or two with the sellers before moving to Stage 3. A business broker can be helpful at this stage (for a fee), and you might have to sign nondisclosure agreements because the sellers may not want the general public to know that they are for sale. Expect to have the broker check you out as well to ensure that you are a real potential buyer and not just kicking the tires.

Stage 3: Due Diligence—This is a critically important stage for buyers and frightening for sellers because this stage requires sellers to reveal detailed information about their overall company operation. This stage can be a lot of work and potentially expensive if you need consultants, so make sure that the seller is really interested in selling before beginning this process.

Stage 4: Proposal, Negotiations, and Close—This is where final purchase price numbers are discussed along with terms and conditions. At this point, lawyers refine the contractual terms and conditions. This stage ends when the purchase agreements are signed, money has changed hands, and you get the key to the business's front door.

Stage 5: Postsale—Many forget about this stage, which in some ways is the most important to you as the buyer. As the new owner, you get to meet with employees, customers, and vendors while taking over the reins of your company. It is in your best personal and business interest to ensure that this stage goes smoothly, because your future reputation and income will depend on it. This stage is particularly important if the purchase agreement involves stock, loans, or other financial vehicles that are tied to the company's future financial performance.

As you can see, this is not a one-step process, and you should be willing to sign up for the whole trip once you start on Stage 3. This doesn't mean that you can't back out at any time before the actual purchase, but don't expect to do so without suffering some type of professional, financial, personal, or legal repercussions. Understand that the sellers, brokers, and other involved parties are investing time and money in your potential transaction. Clarifying everyone's understanding about what will happen if you choose not to purchase early in the process will help to avoid hard feelings—and unexpected litigation—later on.

Getting the Right Professional Help

As you get deeper into buying a business, you will find that each question generates a few more. And the more complicated the transaction becomes, the more you will appreciate having experienced professionals on your team whom you trust.

Let's start with your accountant. This person is important in that she can evaluate the company's financial information as an objective observer. She should be able to verify the bookkeeping and accounting accuracy of the seller's financial statements.

Make sure that you ask a lot of questions and get the detailed answers you need to understand exactly what type of financial obligations you will have should you complete the purchase. It is not the accountant or lawyer who has to pay off the debts associated with the new company—it's you! Use your accountant for guidance, but know that the decision and estimating future results is up to you alone.

WATCH OUT!

Just because someone such as a CPA understands accounting doesn't make her a good financial or business manager. Just because an attorney understands business law doesn't mean that he understands merger and acquisition law or can make a decent business decision. Get the right professionals with the right expertise for your team; don't rush into a selection. Take the time to understand their strengths and limitations. Referrals from other business owners are helpful. Also remember that their guidance is only as good as the information that they have to work with. Always verify the source of their information. If it came from the seller and was not independently verified, you could find yourself making decisions based on biased data that probably benefits the seller.

The same general advice applies to attorneys. Attorneys are excellent at making sure that contracts and other documents are "legal," but they are not really trained to determine whether something makes business sense.

For example, a "legal" agreement could be one that allows your vendors to instantly change, without prior notification or your consent, the terms on your accounts payable debt so that it is due within 48 hours instead of the initially agreed-to 30 days. If you signed an agreement containing these conditions, you would be legally bound by that agreement even if it made no business sense. Expecting your attorney to make excellent business decisions for you is usually unrealistic, unless you are lucky enough to have an attorney who is also a solid businessperson.

Also consider that company-buying law is a specialized animal that involves specialized areas of the law, and these laws change on a regular basis. For this reason, it's best to work with an attorney experienced with the detailed nuances of business purchase law.

There may be special benefits derived from having a tax attorney on your team in addition to a business attorney. The tax attorney will understand both the accounting and legal aspects of your particular company. The business attorney will understand the legal aspects of the agreements you will sign as part of the transaction. The skill sets involved are unique. Having an attorney who is also a CPA is an ideal combination. If this person also has business purchase experience, you should lock him in a room and not let him out until the transaction is completed. By the way, all of this expertise usually comes with a pretty hefty billing rate that can run in the several hundreds of dollars per hour. Make sure that you pay them for the hours that require their specialized expertise and not for the hours spent on routine legal matters that are far less complicated and do not warrant the higher billing rate.

Franchises: Paying for Their Experience

Buying a *franchise* is a way to start a business using the experience and training provided by an existing company. You are familiar with franchises if you have ever eaten at a McDonald's or been coifed at Fantastic Sams. Franchising is big business. According to the International Franchise Association (franchise.org), franchises employ 18 million people and contribute $2.1 trillion to the economy, and 825,000 businesses are franchises in the United States alone.

The franchise purchasing process works like this:

1. You decide you want to be in business.
2. You look around for business ideas that interest you.
3. You find a *franchisor* that has developed a good business concept with a successful track record helping people start similar operations.
4. You purchase the rights to use their procedures, brand name, and training program in exchange for an up-front fee and a recurring annual percentage of your business's income.
5. After a few years, you start to resent paying the fee to the franchisor and begin looking for ways to sever the link.

(Step 5 might not always happen, but I have heard about it from enough successful *franchisees* that you may as well expect that reaction eventually.)

DEFINITION

A **franchise** is a company that has created a successful business concept and offers to sell the rights to the concept on a limited geographic or market basis. The buyer of the franchise rights is called the **franchisee.** The seller of the franchise rights is the **franchisor.**

You benefit from the franchise relationship because it removes a lot of the risky trial and error associated with starting a new business. A successful franchisor, such as McDonald's, knows precisely how to run your business so that you have the best chance for success. That expertise does not come free, but it might save you from going under while you work your way up the learning curve. They have helped enough people set up a business as one of their franchisees that they have learned what works and what does not. That knowledge is a big part of what you pay for when you become a franchisee.

STREET SMARTS

Just to start up a well-known tax service could require an investment of under $100,000, whereas to start up a well-known fast-food chain could require an investment of over $1 million. The franchisors can usually help franchisees obtain funding.

Four Basic Franchise Formats

The basic franchise flavors are distributor, chain-style, manufacturing, and business format.

The *distributor franchise* is typically used with automobile dealerships where the franchisee (the dealer) is licensed to sell the franchisor's products. The franchisee is given some type of exclusive marketing arrangement for a specific geographic or market segment. The franchisee's main role is to sell the company's products, rather than become involved in manufacturing or other functions. An example of a distributor franchise is the Ford Motor Company.

A *chain-style franchise* is used with fast-food establishments. The franchisee (the local owner) is licensed and required to prepare the food in accordance with the franchisor's standards. The local store is often required to purchase all supplies from the franchisor, maintain quality standards, and (often) hit specific sales volume targets. McDonald's is a famous example of a chain-style franchise.

In a *manufacturing franchise*, the franchisee is licensed to create a product in accordance with the franchisor's specifications. The franchise then resells the product at a wholesale price to the distribution channel. Coca-Cola is an example of a product sold through a manufacturing franchise.

A *business format franchise* is just what it sounds like—a franchisee is provided with the specific steps to follow to implement the franchisor's business model. This model can apply to services such as oil change, carpet cleaning, and educational services, to name a few.

STREET SMARTS

Entrepreneur magazine (entrepreneur.com) offers a listing of the top 500 franchising opportunities at its website. Check it out! Their website typically shows the top franchises for the current year, what it costs to get into one, and general information about the listed franchises. This is pretty interesting reading given the wide variety of businesses that are offered as franchises.

A franchise arrangement allows you to start your own business with proven, experienced knowledge behind you. This improves your likelihood of success and might decrease the amount of up-front cash required because many franchisors assist with the initial funding. On the other hand, it might *increase* the up-front total investment required (cash and loans) because you are buying a share of a proven business franchise concept. Unless you are dead set on "doing it your own way," you should consider the purchase of a franchised operation as a business option.

Franchising in a Nutshell

Franchising took the country by storm in the 1980s, led by the example of immensely successful franchises such as McDonald's, Dunkin' Donuts, and Burger King, among countless others. Today franchising is a great way to start a business for people under the right set of circumstances, which explains their popularity.

STREET SMARTS

The Federal Trade Commission (FTC) regulates franchise operations in the 50 states and requires the disclosure of specific minimum information from any franchisor. In addition, many states require their own level of franchisor disclosure. A disclosure document is usually filed with the FTC and appropriate state regulatory body before the sale of franchises in that state can commence operation. Often these disclosure documents must comply with the Uniform Franchise Offering Circular guidelines. See ftc.gov/bcp/franchise/16cfr436.shtm for more information.

To get a deeper understanding of the franchise relationship, let's cover a few basic franchising concepts:

- A company develops a successful method for performing a specific function, such as changing automobile oil, food preparation, or personal fitness training.
- The company then standardizes its methodology under a legally protected brand name.
- The company prepares a set of franchise agreements and performs the required legal filings with the FTC as well as with every state in which it intends to sell franchise locations. It is officially recognized as a franchisor at this point.
- Interested parties purchase a franchise to offer these specific services or products in a given geographic or market area. Once the purchase is completed, the buyer is then known as a franchisee.
- The franchisor then provides various benefits to the franchisee, such as financing assistance, volume purchase pricing, national advertising, training, and business location research, among others.
- Franchisees pay a franchise fee to the franchisor, usually based on a percentage of their sales revenues. This fee relationship usually continues for as long as the franchise is in operation.

You can see from this quick overview that there are substantial benefits associated with purchasing a franchise, but that you also pay for access to these benefits. A major benefit is that you need not be an expert in a particular field to be successful as a franchisee; the franchisor has that expertise and can train you adequately enough to apply its model to your particular business situation. In theory, you provide the money and the personal motivation and they provide the expertise and training … but, oh, if only it were that simple.

A problem often lies with the franchisor not having adequately prepared the training and support aspects of its franchise network. Or sometimes the franchisor gets lazy and stops delivering anything new to the franchisees. When this happens, the franchisee may be left pretty much on his own but still paying franchise fees to the franchisor. This could become the basis for a class-action lawsuit against the franchisor by a group of franchisees.

In the ideal relationship, the franchisee needs the franchisor to be successful so that the promised purchasing economies of scale, national advertising, research, and new products or services are provided. Otherwise, the financial model upon which the franchisees made their original purchase do not apply. The franchisor needs the franchisees to succeed or the franchisor won't be able to sell additional franchisees on its business and operational concept.

STREET SMARTS

Check with the secretary of state's office as a starting point for specific franchisor information. If they don't have any information, they might point you in the direction of someone who does. A simple Google or Yahoo! internet search might turn up important background information as well.

Getting to Know the Franchisor

The more you know about the franchisor, the more you understand the reality of daily life after purchasing a franchise. The franchisor is like a parent in a relationship; it defines many of the daily working rules. Single moves by the franchisor can have a dramatic impact on the franchisees. It is hard to overemphasize the importance of investigating the franchisor before formalizing any type of legal arrangement.

Start by reviewing the franchisor prospectus for new franchisees to learn about their requested financial arrangements. Do an online search to see if the franchisor has any type of pending litigation against it from customers, vendors, lenders, or franchisees. How long has the franchisor been in business and how many franchisee locations has it sold? Find out how many of the sold locations are still in business and how well how the owners are doing financially compared to the numbers presented in the prospectus. See if you can talk to existing franchisees to see how the relationship is working out. You may have to go outside of your geographic area to get an honest answer because locals may think of you as potential competition. What does the franchisor do to continually merit receiving its franchise percentage fee?

Find out if the fees have changed in the last five years; if so, by how much did they change and for what reasons? Has the franchisor changed management or ownership in the last three to five years? Why? Is the franchisor publicly or privately owned and financed? Are there any pending major financial deadlines or other covenants? How would these affect the franchisees? Try to find out how many new products/services the franchisor has offered to its franchisees in the last three to five years. How many of these are actually making money for the franchisees, and why or why not? Check on the types of national advertising in the last 12 months, and what is planned for the next 24 months?

STREET SMARTS

You can expect to have the franchisor check you out as well. This should be gratifying to you in a way because it means that they likely checked out the other franchisors, too. You want to be part of a franchise network wherein the owners are responsible, motivated, and professional—just like you. If the franchisor simply takes your money and gives you a franchise without asking questions, it could be cause for concern.

Make sure that you check out the franchising resources listed in Appendix D for additional details related to franchising.

The Least You Need to Know

- An existing business has customers, a reputation, and a proven marketing approach that allows you to become a business owner in no time and often with less income uncertainty.
- Get the help of specialized professionals such as accountants and attorneys when evaluating the target company or franchise, but remember that you are the one who ultimately inherits the results of your decision. Be an informed business manager.
- It may be less risky to buy a franchised business than an independently owned one as long as you choose the right franchisor. This is especially true if you are not an expert in the chosen field.
- Franchisees are heavily dependent on the franchisor for new products, services, and technologies. There will be some type of legal obligation and relationship here as well.
- The franchisor should never forget that their future is strongly tied to the success of the franchisee. Make sure that your franchisor is financially stable when you first buy in and stays that way during your longer-term relationship.

Mastering the Business Side of a New Professional Practice

Chapter

6

In This Chapter

- Understanding the unique nature of professional service firms
- Discovering what they didn't teach you in school about running a business
- Keeping a keen eye on ethical and professional standards
- Managing cash in a professional service environment

Briana sat at her desk and took a sip of tea. It had been a rewarding day, as two of her patients had been released from the hospital after nearly dying. Helping people was why she had become a doctor. She took another sip of tea and looked across the desk at her bank statement. The balances in her checking and savings accounts had dropped each month since opening her practice. If it kept up like this she would be out of cash by Christmas, which was not how she wanted to end the year. A knock came from the door. She looked up to see her father, David, a retired doctor.

"I came by to take you to dinner," he said.

"Oh, Dad, I'd love to but I have some thinking to do here. Not sure I can afford dinner," she said with a little self-pity in her voice.

"Okay. What's up? The way you're sipping that tea and looking at the bank statements, it looks like money problems. Close?"

"Yes and no," she said. "No—from the standpoint that we are busier than I thought we would be and we have billed for a lot of appointments and services. Yes—from the standpoint that payment for those services is coming in way slower than I expected and I am on my way to successfully putting myself out of business."

"Yeah. That is a problem with being a doctor with her own practice. We all go through it and I guess this is your turn. Medicare can take forever to pay, Medicaid payments seem to be directly tied into whether the state has money or not, and the insurance companies will hold up payment for months, blaming it on you for not filing a form you have never heard of. Sound familiar?"

Briana laughed. "Hah! Who made you so smart? And okay, Mr. Smarty Pants, what do I do now?"

"First thing you do is go to dinner with your old man, who happens to also be willing to help you turn some of those invoices into quick cash for you—in return for a little profit, of course. Second, I think you and I should meet once a month for a while to discuss the business side of doctoring. Call it School of Hard Knocks 101, and I think you enrolled today. There is an art to being a good doctor, and also an art to making the business side work. What do you say?"

In my years of consulting I have worked with many professionals who run their own businesses. One common theme that has come up over and again is how ill prepared they were for starting their own practice. They were highly skilled in their particular discipline—dentistry, chiropractic, engineering, or medicine—but were clueless about how to make money while running their practice.

I think back on my own engineering education and can relate. I had taken difficult courses in calculus, electromagnetism, nuclear physics, and circuit design, but had never seen an income statement. I could program a computer to analyze the forces acting on support structures holding up a building, but had no idea of how to create an invoice or make a sales call. When I graduated and went to work for an engineering firm, they took care of selling, invoicing, insurance, and other critical aspects of the business. This gave me great engineering experience, but didn't teach me a thing about making it on my own. Attorneys, chiropractors, doctors, dentists, accountants, and engineers have all told me the same thing: "I know my profession really well but don't understand how to run a business." This chapter is meant just for you.

What They Didn't Teach You in School

Professional educational programs are full of courses related to the specific discipline of the profession. I am not really sure what schools have in mind for the students once they complete the programs, other than that they will get a job working for a large firm. The reality of it is that many professionals will want to go off on their own (or with partners) to start and own their business, requiring that they develop a set of business management skills. Oddly enough, statistics show that professionals leave their chosen profession after around 10 years of practice. I wonder if their leaving is in part due to not being able to grow as professionals by starting their own business. I wonder if it is easier for them to leave than to undertake the learning curve and risk associated with starting a business.

This book covers much of what is needed to make a business run in general, but professional practices have their own unique characteristics that differentiate them from other service businesses. They are regulated by a licensing body which dictates a lot of what can and cannot be done within the practice. The way in which a professional finds clients, makes proposals, provides services, organizes his or her practice, and gets paid will differ between disciplines and even by the state in which the practice is established.

STREET SMARTS

Don't assume that all states have the same regulations and requirements for becoming licensed. If you live on the border of two states, you might find that the practicum hour requirements to become a psychologist in one state is very different from the neighboring state. This could mean that in one state you could be licensed today, but 5 miles down the road it would take you another five years of working for the equivalent of minimum wage in order to be licensed. You will make the decision that is right for you should you be in this circumstance, but please make it an informed decision.

A few concepts are common across all disciplines. You will have to be professionally licensed by the state within which you work. This will typically involve a combination of formal education, documented experience in your field working for someone who is already licensed, paying the required fees, and often undergoing additional industry-specific training above and beyond that received at school. Some type of specialized insurance will be required, so familiarize yourself with the insurance standards within your particular industry. I know professionals from various disciplines who have gone back to work for major firms in order to avoid the professional liability insurance fees associated with being a sole practitioner.

I know a couple of engineers who had stopped practicing only to find out that they had to maintain their engineering liability insurance for a minimum number of years after stamping their last set of plans, to cover potential problems with the job. Unfortunately for these particular engineers, the contractors, suppliers, and everyone else involved with their construction projects had gone out of business, making them the last ones in line to sue. This is exactly what happened. Our engineers' insurance skyrocketed to the point that it became cheaper to stop professionally stamping design plans than to work and incur the insurance costs. By the way, not one dime was ever paid out on the liability insurance because the engineering designs were fine. Just the threat of someone making a liability claim was enough to push insurance rates up to the point that their business was financially strangled. I am not trying to talk you out of going into business, just trying to explain how the business aspects of running a professional practice can overshadow the technical aspects that all of us love.

STREET SMARTS

It is important to remember that you are not the first professional to set up his or her own business. Many have done it before, and the problems they encountered are likely the same ones that you will run into. Professional associations exist to help practitioners succeed in their field. They offer seminars, training, advice, guidebooks, and other resources designed specifically for your field. Using the experience of others to address a problem is common to all professions. Doesn't it make sense for your business, too? Make full use of association membership fees. Read books. Talk to others who run a successful business in your field. Don't be afraid to take advice—not so easy for those of us who are usually paid for giving the advice. I know.

In certain fields, the amount you charge for a service might be set by a third party, such as an insurance company. This means that you will have to set up your operation such that your internal costs will allow you to maintain reasonable profit margins when given these market-dictated sales caps. If regulations change, you will have to change with them. In addition, your clients will likely be looking to you for the latest information on regulation changes, which means that regular training to remain current is an important part of doing business. Licensing boards will usually stipulate the minimum number and type of continuing education units (CEU) that you are required to take to keep your license current. The bad news is that you will have to continue in school. The good news is that these courses are often offered in places like The Bahamas or Jamaica or on a cruise. No reason that you have to suffer while keeping current, is there?

If you intend to work in multiple states, you will have to comply with the licensing requirements of all these states. Some states have reciprocal agreements whereby one state's license will permit you to work in another state, but this will vary by state. Don't assume anything and make sure that you have done your homework about each state's individual requirements and take the steps that serve you best.

ED'S LESSONS LEARNED

I think it can be difficult for a professional to separate his or her allegiance to the profession from the realities of making money as an independent practitioner. We have it drilled into our heads from early on that we must adhere to a high standard of ethical conduct and professionalism, with which I fully agree. But we can also become risk averse for fear of what our peers or the regulating bodies might say.

I have seen this get to the point where a professional won't ask for the order from a prospect because he doesn't want to appear like a salesperson. Hey! When you run your own business, you are the salesperson! I have tremendous respect and appreciation for the tough educational road that professionals must complete to become licensed. Always work to keep sales healthy, customers happy, and deposits flowing into your business checkbook. Nothing wrong with being a rich professional, is there?

Selling Within Ethical Constraints

Professional contractors are typically used for specialized situations that require a specialized expertise. That is probably you. Try to put yourself in the customer's shoes when presented with a problem requiring professional assistance. How does someone pick one type of doctor from another when he or she does not have any type of personal relationship with any of them? How does someone find a lawyer who deals with criminal instead of real estate law? How does someone find an engineer who can handle a drainage problem around a multiple flat rental property instead of a shopping mall? How does someone find an accountant familiar with IRS auditing instead of one experienced with preparing publicly traded company SEC filings? The nuanced, complex, and critical nature of professional work makes finding the right person with the right expertise and the right personality a major challenge for most people.

As professionals, we must help potential clients understand the specific circumstances under which we can be of most assistance. Answering the following questions will help you understand where you fit in the overall scope of your profession:

- What type of professional are you?
- Are you someone who offers general services or treatments or are you someone who has developed a specialty?
- What makes you unique to your profession?

- Do you have some type of independent licensing for your specialization?
- What type of person would be looking for your specialization?
- Are you working in a field or specialization about which you are passionate, meaning that you would be interested in it even if you did not do it every day to earn a living?

I believe that alignment between passion and work is critically important for professionals. Running a professional service is complicated. You have to keep up with your profession, work with a wide variety of clients, manage many projects or clients at one time, conduct business within the guidelines of your licensing board, and also make a financial profit. That is tough. If you are not passionate about your work and profession, you might back off on developing the competencies needed to be successful, likely bringing the business down with you. Passion is contagious and it shows in all we do. This is particularly true for professionals.

I may be repeating myself here, but you must understand that potential clients do not yet know you. They do not understand how capable you are in your field or how willing you are to go the extra mile to create a satisfactory outcome. All they know is that they have a need and are looking for some professional to help with its solution. Connecting them to you is the essence of service marketing, and this is usually done by word of mouth: one person asking another if he or she knows anyone who does a certain type of work.

One major marketing challenge with a professional business is that confidentiality is core to its success. This means that you must not talk about what is happening with any of your clients unless the client approves the communication. Should you discuss your work with others, keep it generic and anonymous so that nothing said can be traced back to a specific client. Nobody will appreciate something revealed in confidence being repeated to others in an uncontrolled way.

My rule on this came from my father, who once told me that if you want to succeed with people, "don't talk, and make sure everyone knows that you don't talk." This is good advice but often difficult to do when others seem to live in a world of gossip. You might find yourself the quietest one at the party, but potential clients who are watching will believe that their future secrets will be protected by you with the same level of diligence. This means that successful client testimonials are precarious or even impossible to use.

Try thinking about it from another perspective: you cannot tell one client about another, but that client can tell someone else about your services. You can ask or encourage clients to share their stories, but again you cannot share their stories for them. As with any new businesses you have to create awareness that you exist. Local advertising on billboards, in magazines, in newspapers, on television, or on the radio all work pretty well for this purpose. As part of this advertising, you will want to create an awareness of your uniqueness. In other words, don't just talk about being a lawyer, but explain your personality and specialization so people understand how they will benefit from working with you. When people are satisfied with your work, ask if they would be willing to act as a reference for future prospective clients looking for a personal reassurance from satisfied clients. You cannot offer clients' names without their permission, but you can ask them to offer a reference.

Social networking media offers a wonderful and powerful way for generating word-of-mouth advertising within interested customer and prospect bases. Check out Chapter 11 for more details on how social media can be used for new business advertising.

ED'S LESSONS LEARNED

Once trust is lost in a professional relationship, usually so is the relationship. Guard the client's trust like it is golden—because it is.

Billing Arrangements for Professionals

Different professions will have different norms related to billing for services and when payment can be expected. The medical industry has undergone tremendous change in recent times. Instead of being able to charge what the marketplace is willing to pay, medical service providers might have a cap on what can be charged as determined by an agency or insurance company. The provider could choose to not participate in the network requiring the cap, but then he or she loses the promotion and referral benefits that come from larger company affiliation. To complicate it even more, patients do not understand how billing works, which means that someone on the doctor's staff will likely have to serve as local resource for both the doctor's practice personnel as well as for the patient. This increases the practice's expenses without adding to the revenue stream. Patients will likely pay part of the bill with the insurer paying the balance, but there may be, and likely will be, a delay between the time when the service was provided and when payment is received. This delay may stretch into months, depending on the situation, and the practice owners must have a way of keeping the lights on and the employees paid in the interim. A medical practice might be very busy, generating large accounts receivable, but if there is not enough cash to cover the bills while waiting for payment, a busy practice could go out of business.

A law firm could be in a similar situation, especially if the firm works on a retainer tied to recovery from a lawsuit. Assume that the firm specializes in wrongful death cases and collects its fees when a case is won. The case might take several years to resolve but will involve expenses to prepare, and all along the way the owners must keep employees paid, the rent paid, and the lights on. There might be a very large payout at the end of the case but only if the firm can stay afloat, which means that the financial aspects of the firm are integral to the success of the firm. Oh yeah, and all of this assumes that the case is won. If the case is lost, then all those expenses are incurred with no big payday.

It is not uncommon for engineering firms to spend much time and money preparing proposals for projects that will commence sometime in the future, often the distant future. The time spent preparing a proposal costs the firm twice. The firm pays once for direct expenses involved with the proposal preparation, such as travel, copying, other professionals, clerical, and such. The firm pays again because the professionals involved with the proposal preparation are not generating revenue during this time. Preparing proposals is part of doing business, and the firm must set up an operation and billing rate that allows for things like proposal preparation and contract performance with delays between when the work is done and when payment is received.

Before you start down the path of opening your own professional firm, spend some time researching cash management practices—either on paper, through your associations, or by talking to someone who is already doing it. You can only make it to the long term if you get through the short term. In professions where delays between spending money and receiving customer payments may be substantial and outside of your control, cash management may be the secret to your business success. Or, as they say, good medicine.

For Your Plan

When preparing the operations portion of your plan, make sure that you consider the following points:

- Discuss the business operational norms for your particular profession.
- Clearly document the licenses that company personnel will have earned before working for your business.
- Discuss your approach to maintaining the licenses in good standing.
- Explain how you plan to get the word out about your business while working within the legal guidelines of your profession.
- Describe the unique nature of your professional offerings and how these will be used in the marketplace.

The Least You Need to Know

- For a professional services company, the product is the professional. For other companies, products may be the offerings.
- There may be long delays between when you pay the costs associated with providing client services and when payment is received for those services. Plan your cash management plan accordingly for your industry.
- Not all professionals are the same, and your uniqueness is key to creating customer perception and marketing success.
- Make sure that you preserve your licensing, because without a current license you are out of business.
- Work within the ethical and professional requirements of your industry, but avoid limiting your creativity to historically accepted approaches. You are now the professional who charts his or her own course and pays the bills.

Writing the Right Plan for Your Business Idea

Chapter 7

In This Chapter

- Learning the sound reasons to create a business plan
- Appreciating the questions your plan must answer
- Understanding the sections of your plan
- Building credibility by keeping the plan honest
- Dealing with an idea that does not turn out as expected

Judy looked at her husband Jim with a mix of angst and curiosity. He looked like a cat that had swallowed a bird and just couldn't wait to tell someone how it tasted.

"Okay. What's up?" she asked. He perked up and smiled, clearly glad that she asked.

"You know how I am always coming up with great ideas, and then a year later I find someone else making a fortune off it? Well, not this time. I have an idea that I think is worth taking a chance on."

Judy's stomach flipped as she tried to keep the support and enthusiasm in her eyes. She hoped that he didn't notice her concern, but at the same time she had some questions.

"What is the idea?" she asked supportively. He told her.

"Okay. I have to admit that sounds like a pretty good idea," said Judy, now showing sincere interest. "But how much is it going to cost to try it out, and will it make any money?"

"Come on," cried Jim. "This is a great idea. You got it right away. No doubt others will, too. This will sell like crazy! Don't be a killjoy here."

"Hey, look. My goal is not to rain on your parade, but half of the money we would put into starting this thing belongs to me, not to mention the time it will take—a big chunk of which I sort of have a claim on." She smiled and paused to let that thought sink in. "I am like an investor here and I would like to have a better idea of what this great idea will cost to get started, how long it will take to make some money, and whether we will at least be able to bring home money-wise what we are making now. I don't think that is too much to ask."

Jim hung his head and took a deep breath. She was right, of course. He had wondered exactly the same things once he realized that his interest in this idea was more than casual. The problem was that he didn't really know how to go about answering her questions. But he was not willing to let this idea pass him by just like the others.

Not all ideas are good enough to start a business. Yet many new ideas are the ones that change the way people live their lives while making the entrepreneur rich. Remember that all businesses start out as ideas—it is the responsibility of those with the ideas to put the effort and commitment behind the good ones, creating businesses, careers, and fortunes along the way. The question remains—how do you know which ideas are the good ones? A great place to start that evaluation process is by preparing a *business plan.* A business plan helps you to make sure that you invest in the right areas and consider all of the right steps that will lead you to successfully starting your own business.

DEFINITION

A **business plan** is a document that can be as small as 10 pages or long enough to fill a book, with a reasonably detailed plan usually running 30 to 50 pages. The goal of the plan is to inform its readers about the details of a business idea and to also help the plan writers better understand the idea's financial viability.

This chapter is designed to help you understand the plan-writing process as well as the elements of a respectable business plan. Any project has a higher likelihood of success if you appreciate the magnitude of the undertaking, are clear about what you have starting out, know where you want to end up, and believe that it is worth doing. A plan helps you understand all of this. Even simpler, if you need to get the buy-in from others, a well-thought-out business plan is a must.

Read this chapter and absorb the information to keep yourself motivated and directed as you write your plan. The time you spend here will save you time later on, and might make the difference between getting your business up and running … or not.

Why Prepare a Business Plan?

Although you might have heard that you only need a business plan if you are trying to get financing to start a company, this is not true. Here are a few more reasons to write one:

- Putting your goals and ideas down on paper helps to organize your thinking, which will make you more effective.
- Writing down your plans and goals demonstrates your commitment to your business, which impresses potential investors, suppliers, employees—oh—and spouses.
- Once you have your plan down on paper, you have a game plan for achieving your goals that you can refer to regularly to measure your progress or modify as circumstances change.
- Your plan helps focus your organization on its mission, reducing the chance that the business becomes sidetracked by other less important activities.
- As your own ultimate investor, you deserve to prove to yourself that your business idea is a good one. And if you are funding yourself, it is even *more* important that you write the plan because there is no outside investor reality-checking your idea and approach.

Let's face it: others will not believe in your idea nearly as much as you do. Part of the reason is that they probably don't know as much about your business idea, your marketplace, and your implementation plans as you do. Think of the plan as a sales document; those who read it will be sold on your idea, vision, and approach. There will probably be many different people who want to see your business plan, for their own reasons.

Bankers and other funding sources will use your plan to determine whether you are someone that they want to invest in because you are truly capable of successfully starting and running the business. Strategic partners or joint venture participants may want to look at portions of your plan to determine whether your overall direction is in alignment with their plans. Your future board of directors (if you create one) or management team will want to review your plan to understand the direction of the company. Finally, and perhaps most importantly, family members may want to review the plan when determining how willing they will be to give you up on weekends and evenings so you can pursue your new passion.

As a result of the planning process, you will learn more about your business idea than you ever thought possible. Treat it as a learning experience, and watch where it takes you. The plan will quickly take on a life of its own once you get started researching and writing. The cool thing is that if you still believe in your idea after completing a business plan, your belief will show through in everything you do. That belief is contagious in a very good way—others will be attracted to the idea and will want to help you succeed.

Think of It as a Simulation

A business plan is just a simulation. It is a way of predicting the future success of a business idea before you ever get started. Will the plan be correct? Perhaps, but the only way you will know if you were right with your predictions is after you have already taken the plunge and implemented the plan.

STREET SMARTS

Many people worry so much about getting their forecast estimates correct that they have a hard time finalizing them out of fear of being later found out to be wrong. The only way you will ever know if your forecast was accurate is after it becomes past history. Make your best guess today, and if you believe in your analysis, act on it as appropriate to the situation. History will do its own determination about your accuracy.

Large companies may spend millions of dollars preparing a business plan because the amount of money involved with introducing a product on a national, or even international, scale is huge. Small businesspeople don't have this large planning and funding luxury; as a result, they produce less comprehensive plans and have to be quick enough to adapt to the unexpected. (See Chapter 19 for more about adapting while staying focused on your goals.) But don't forget that the money and time you will invest in a business idea will be important to you and your family, and completing some type of planning process is good protection. (See Chapter 14 for more information on venture capital and other types of funding.)

My point here is that the business-planning process produces more than simply a written document. It produces an objective evaluation of whether the business idea stands a reasonable chance of success. It forces you to think through the numerous details involved with the daily operation of your business. It increases your likelihood of being successful and strengthens your conviction in the idea being a good one. You are much better served spending a few extra days up front adding "meat" to the business simulation (a.k.a., plan) than spending weeks or years and hundreds of thousands of dollars "experimenting" in the real world.

The Questions Your Plan Must Answer

Few people who read your plan will remember everything that it contains. Heck, you probably won't remember everything. Here are a few fundamental questions that your plan must answer to adequately serve your readers as potential stakeholders and you as the future manager/owner:

- What is the business idea and what makes it unique to prospective customers in the current market environment?
- How much money is required to get the business up and running on a solid footing?
- When do you expect the business to not only recover the initial investment, but also begin to show a reasonable profit for investors?
- What are the major opportunities and challenges that this business faces in becoming successful, and how will they be addressed?
- How do you plan to create sales? This must be explained in enough detail to be believable.
- Why does this business, run by you, stand a reasonable chance of succeeding?

The ultimate goal of the plan is to credibly answer the preceding questions for your readers. Remember that you are ultimately trying to decrease as much perceived risk as possible in the minds of prospective investors. If your plan accomplishes that goal with integrity, then it is a success. See Chapter 2 for a detailed discussion about perceived risk and business planning.

STREET SMARTS

Busy people—which includes most investors—won't take the time to read a plan that is too long. They also won't put a lot of effort into figuring out what you're talking about if you haven't been crystal clear. A small plan that clearly and concisely addresses all the major points of interest will be better received than a lengthy one that drones on about irrelevant information for pages and pages. You need to do the work for your readers; spell out your information in a simple, well-written style. Lead them through the plan, step by step, explaining your idea and how you intend to make everyone money doing it.

The Pieces of Your Plan

Effective business planning is a lot like assembling the pieces of a jigsaw puzzle. As you become more familiar with the pieces, the proper fit reveals itself as the most viable way to have the idea work in reality.

I tend to look at a startup business plan as both a sales and an operational document. The flow of the plan presented here is designed to enhance the sales (persuasive) aspect of the plan. Intrinsic to the plan are the operational details and goals that will be used after startup to determine successful operation of the intended plan.

The business plan is broken into sections. Each section deals with an important aspect of your business idea and its investment prospects. The sections combine to present an overall view of your plan's viability. Your business plan should contain the following basic elements:

I. Cover Sheet
II. Table of Contents
III. Executive Summary
IV. Business Description
V. Market and Sales Analysis
VI. The Competition
VII. Marketing and Sales Strategy
VIII. Operations Plan
IX. Management Team
X. Financial Overview and Funding Needs
XI. Summary and Conclusions
XII. Appendixes or Supplementary Materials

The following sections take a closer look at each part of the plan. Refer to the Dog Grooming Services business plan in Appendix B for an example of how these parts were implemented in a basic business plan. A more detailed Kwik Chek auto inspection sample business plan is offered in Appendix C.

STREET SMARTS

One of my early sales managers described an effective sales presentation in this way: first, tell them what you are going to tell them (executive summary); next, tell them what you want to tell them (the detail sections); finally, tell them what you told them (summary and conclusions). A business plan is a sales document that explains your business idea in a similar way. You are ultimately trying to persuade the readers that your idea is one worthy of their time and/or money.

Cover Sheet

This is your plan's first impression, so make it a good one. The layout of the cover sheet should be uncluttered, professional looking, and easy to read. At a minimum, it should contain your company's name, the type of company it is (e.g., corporation, sole proprietorship), home state of operation (e.g., Illinois), address and phone/fax information, email, URL, primary contact person, and date. It is also a good idea to include a statement that this plan is for investment analysis purposes only, is a confidential document, and that it may not be copied or shared without your written permission. It's not a bad idea to add text such as "Copyright © 2011 by <your name>. All rights reserved." It at least lets people know that you feel your idea is unique and that you understand something about protecting your intellectual property.

Some people number their plans and keep track of recipients as a way of maintaining confidentiality control. In these cases, a special "Number" and "Presented to" section is included on the cover sheet. Some people recommend sending a copy of the plan to yourself using registered mail, and then not opening the letter once received. In this way, you have an envelope date-stamped by the post office that verifies when the contents were mailed. Make sure you attach a copy of the plan to the outside of the envelope once you receive it so that you don't forget what is inside. Don't laugh. It happens.

Table of Contents

The table of contents is not a major element of your business plan, but it shows readers what and where information can be found. Because tables of contents are generally found in well-organized documents, you will make a good impression by including one. It can't hurt you as long as you make sure that the section titles and page numbers shown in the table of contents match those actually in the plan. If you use the headings and referencing features provided by your word-processing software when writing your plan, you may be able to generate a table of contents automatically.

Executive Summary

It may seem odd, but you will write this section last. I cannot overemphasize the importance of the executive summary. It is common to write a few sentences to describe each section of the plan. Finish the executive summary by listing the amount of money required, the projected profit to investors, the major advantages your company will have over the competition, and why this is an excellent investment opportunity. In essence, the executive summary should briefly answer the questions posed earlier in the chapter.

STREET SMARTS

Plans are more believable when they include information that is more than just your opinion. Look for third-party research and facts to substantiate what you present and add credibility to your analysis. Readers will ultimately choose to invest in large part because of who you are, but they will appreciate seeing that you know what others have to say as well.

The executive summary should be one or two pages long (at most), and is often the only section a potential investor will read. Based on these few paragraphs, the investor will decide whether to read the rest of the plan, or forget the whole idea. For this reason, your summary needs to catch and hold the reader's attention. The summary is written last because you will learn things as you write the plan, and that wisdom should be included in the final version of the executive summary.

Business Description

The business description part of the plan explains your product or service idea and how it meets the needs of your intended customers. Describe exactly what it is you will be selling and why people, or businesses, will buy it. How is it different from similar items already on the market? If it is a revolutionary concept, explain why the world needs it.

Don't get sidetracked into talking about all of the great things that you believe about your company in this section. This is like hearing proud parents talk about how their child rolled over by himself last night. Instead, make sure you focus on the *benefits* of this opportunity for the intended customers and eventually the investor. You can include all of those other details as an appendix if you still feel the need. You might even consider working with a professional writer when preparing your plan, but definitely have a professional help you with the overall editing and preparing the executive summary.

Start by describing the *features* of your product or service. Explain what the product or service does for the user—what the benefits are and why customers will buy it. If there are similar products or services already on the market, briefly compare them to what you are offering and explain how yours is better. If your new product or service is unlike anything currently available, convince the reader that it is needed.

Remember that there is a plan section dedicated to competitors, so only provide the highlights here.

DEFINITION

Features are the different characteristics of a product or service. For example, the features of a drill bit may include its size, length, and the type of material it is made of.

Benefits are what the customer gains by using your product or service. One sellable benefit of a drill bit could be that it is made from a special material that never needs sharpening. Customers buy something to obtain the benefits associated with using it. The features get them the benefits.

You may also want to include some history about the company; how it is organized; whether and when it was structured as a corporation, partnership, or sole proprietorship; whether any stock has been issued; and who invested any money to start it, and how much. (See Chapter 15 for help on determining the right legal structure for your business.) If your company is already in operation and looking for money to fund expansion, make sure to include some company successes to help decrease the perceived risk on the part of the investor. It might even be a good idea to start with this information so the reader knows that this is an existing business and not one in the idea stage.

Market and Sales Analysis

The market and sales analysis section presents information describing the market need for your product or service. This is where you detail all the information you gathered regarding the size of your market, the number of potential customers for your product or service, and the growth rate for your market or for the industry as a whole (which can mean worldwide). This section not only relies heavily on the results of your research, but also on your ability to present the information in a simple, concise, logical, and easy-to-understand way. (See Chapter 8 for information on market potential estimates.)

WATCH OUT!

Anyone who believes that there is no competition is in for a rude awakening, even if he or she has a totally revolutionary product. There is always someone out there willing and anxious to challenge companies with new and profitable ideas.

The Competition

Who are the established companies already selling products and services similar to yours? How will they react to your company? Depending upon your idea and how long your product or service has been available, your competition might consist of other new and aggressive companies just like yours or established companies from whom you intend to take business. We all think our business idea is unique, but the customer might think it's like dozens of others. Rely more on the market data you've collected rather than your opinion about whether there is a similar idea already in existence. Better yet, ask prospective customers if what you offer is really that unique.

You should be respectful of the competition, but there is no reason to be afraid. Accept that you have competitors and take every opportunity to learn from them. What are they doing right, and what can you do better? It is okay to mimic things your competitors do well and to learn from their mistakes, as long as you don't infringe on any trademarks, copyrights, or other intellectual property rights that they may have in place. Generally, this means that you can copy certain ways of doing business, such as offering free delivery with your service or guaranteeing your work, but not their advertising or designs. I tell you more about dealing with the competition in Chapter 9.

STREET SMARTS

Don't make the mistake of thinking that your product is so wonderful that customers can't help but buy from you. This assumption will almost certainly push away the investor who reads your plan by raising questions in their minds about what other blinding biases you might have, and will probably eventually cost you your company as well.

Provide a list of the other major players in the marketplace to show that you know exactly who your competition is. You should also indicate your impression of their strengths, weaknesses, and overall success in the market. By learning about your competition, the reader of your plan can better understand how you will succeed: either by going after a market opportunity that no existing competitor is addressing, or by doing what everyone else is doing but with a new and improved twist.

Marketing and Sales Strategy

If nobody buys your product or service, you're out of business. Period! Nothing ends a business faster than no customers. In this section of your business plan, you need to explain to the reader how you will attract customers.

As part of your marketing strategy, you should describe how you intend to let the public know that you're in business. You should also explain your sales approach, such as selling by direct sales representatives, by mail-order catalog, online, home meetings, or through a retail storefront, among others. You'll find a detailed discussion of all the different ways you can market and sell your offerings in Chapters 10 and 11.

Notice that the marketing and sales strategy section is included after you have already presented your business idea, detailed the market conditions, and covered competitive information. This section flow makes a lot of sense considering that the whole point of a marketing and sales strategy is to obtain sales. Sales successes are dependent on market conditions, industry purchasing norms, and competitive offerings. Customers will buy either from your company or from one of your competitors, so you have to consider competitive pressures when developing your strategy. The strategy section builds on the information presented in prior sections.

Operations Plan

The operational procedures that will enable your company to meet all of its functional obligations are presented in this section. These include the purchasing of inventory, finding qualified personnel, manufacturing and shipping of products, providing services, arranging licensing, and any other aspects related to providing the product or service defined in the business description. (See Chapter 12 for a detailed discussion of these important topics.)

Make sure that you explain the assumptions related to your analysis. For example, a service business would detail the number of hours per month you, as the owner/manager, expect to spend on billable client-related work, sales activities, and management. It would then break down hours and activities for other employees, too.

ED'S LESSONS LEARNED

We all think that we can work 70- to 80-hour weeks until the business is up and running, at which time we will cut back. I tried this and burned myself out, as have many others I have known over the years. Remember that if your service business starts with just you, then you will not only be doing the work that customers pay for, but you will also be contacting, selling, billing, shipping, etc. Plan at least 20 percent of your weekly hours for these types of activities to keep yourself from fizzling out right when things start to heat up.

The Management Team

One of the most important elements of your business plan is the section telling the reader why you and your partners (if you have them) are the most qualified group to start and run this business. Investors give their money to people, not companies or product ideas. Investors want to feel confident that you have experience in the type of business you're starting and that the other members of your management team complement your skills.

Remember that new company investors cannot look to past company performance as a gauge of future performance. This means that they must guess at what the future will look like based on what is presented to them by you and the other founders. A great idea with the wrong management team will likely crash and burn. A great management team with a solid idea will eventually get funded because it stands the best chance of succeeding.

Briefly describe the background and experience of key personnel. If you have an associate working with you who has 25 years of experience in your intended industry, be sure to mention it; it makes your company much more credible. If you previously managed a company like the one you plan to start, mention it. If you have advisers or consultants who have been working with you, mention them. If you've set up a board of directors, briefly mention the members. You want to show the reader that you recognize you don't know everything and will rely on professionals to round out the skill set. Many business owners think they know everything and don't need advice from other people. These are usually the ones who don't last very long.

Financial Overview and Funding Needs

Now we get down to the bottom line. Everything else up to this point was presented as the foundation for the financial analysis. This section spells out for investors the actual investment required, the details on how that invested money will be spent, and when the business will start making money. Everything else in the plan was background to whet the reader's appetite for the financial feast that follows. You should include a *break-even analysis* that covers the production volume required (in units for manufacturers or hours for service providers) to push the company from red to black.

A simplified plan, such as the dog grooming sample plan in Appendix B, will only need a *cumulative cash flow analysis*. A more complicated plan that involves large amounts of capital or rapid growth also should include an *income statement* and *balance sheet*. Both plan types will detail the first year in months, with the second and third years as annual totals. These reports are called pro forma financial statements. Pro forma just means that the numbers are projections, or estimates, of future sales and expenses. A lot more details related to financials and obtaining funding are presented in Chapters 13 and 14.

DEFINITION

A **break-even analysis** determines the unit sale level at which you are paying your overhead expenses after your product (variable) costs are subtracted. (To put it in terms you can relate to, at break-even, you are living at a subsistence level with just enough money to pay the rent and put food on the table, but nothing extra for movies and popcorn.) The **income statement** reflects all income and expenses for a particular period of time (usually a year). The **balance sheet** shows your total assets and liabilities. The **cash flow analysis** shows exactly how much cash you received and how much you spent on a monthly basis. The **cumulative cash flow analysis** sums (accumulates) the net positive and negative cash flow from prior periods.

Summary and Conclusions

You should include a summary in your plans where you tie up the plan in a neat package. This ensures that readers understand your view of the overall opportunity instead of letting them walk away with interpretation that is not quite accurate. They may not agree with what you present, but they will concisely understand what the plan was about and the conclusions you would like them to draw.

STREET SMARTS

I sometimes include a special section titled "Risks and Opportunities" before the summary and conclusions section. The purpose of the risks and opportunities section is to spell out for the reader what I believe to be the major risks to the success of this venture, as well as the special opportunities associated with it.

Appendixes or Supplementary Materials

The appendixes and supplementary materials may be referred to throughout the plan and are included as references at the end. These may be tables, graphs, résumés, or marketing literature, all of which help to convince the reader that you have done your homework. Including this information at the end instead of within the plan keeps the plan flowing along without getting bogged down with too much detail. You want a plan that moves the big-picture reader along, while still fulfilling the information cravings of the analytical investor. Make sure that you list these materials in your table of contents so interested readers can easily find them.

Dealing with a Bad Business Idea

What a drag! You performed the entire analysis to discover the idea does not hold financial water. Now what? Be thankful! You have just saved yourself from a nasty experience—such as bankruptcy.

If you had pursued the venture based on what you thought true prior to writing the plan, you would be crying over all of the hard-earned savings you lost or apologizing to your angry investors. Take heart! A negative outcome on this round does not negate the entire venture. You know a lot more about the idea than you did going in and can now consider a different, potentially more successful approach to the idea. (See the creativity section of Chapter 3 for more about creativity as a business tool.)

Consider the following questions while reevaluating your idea to see if modifying it can provide a better, more profitable strategy.

- Is the problem with the idea itself or simply how it was presented in your plan?
- Are you the right person to shepherd the idea to success, or should you be looking to involve others to round out critical management positions?
- Do you need more money to allow additional time to achieve the needed market recognition?
- Can you reduce expenses in some ways to make your investment dollars last longer, giving you more time to develop customers and sales revenue?
- Should you initially offer a product or service that is more immediately useful to consumers?
- What could you do to increase sales faster and what would be the additional cost?
- Are you being so conservative in your estimates that you did not give the idea analysis a fighting chance?

These are just a few ideas to get your creative juices flowing. You have learned a lot with the plan writing. Take a little more time to see if there is another more viable solution.

Ethics and Your Plan

Nobody gives money to people they don't trust. If you take liberties with the "facts" in preparing your plan, your exaggeration may be interpreted as lying. If the reader finds out you have done this (which is likely when he or she checks out your plan in detail), you may not be able to recover the required level of trust to make the relationship work. If your idea is a good one, then it will get funded. Trust that to be true and prepare the best possible, most credible business plan you can.

The Least You Need to Know

- The clearer you are about your business idea's benefits to customers and investors, the more clearly you can convey those benefits in your plan.
- The business plan is a simulation of your idea and it can keep you from investing time and money in a bad idea.
- Your business plan is a sales document to investors and an operational plan that you use to keep your business on track.
- It is your responsibility to make the plan easy for the reader to understand. It is not the reader's job to decode your plan in the hope of discovering the investment opportunity.
- Honesty is the best policy. Keep your plan accurate, and don't make factual claims you cannot back up. Instead, state them as your best guess and explain your rationale.

Part 2

Evaluating Your Idea's Sales Potential

Creating sales revenue is critical to the success of any new business because without adequate revenue the business will be out of business. Many plans offer detailed descriptions of the offerings, the personnel, the management, and the financials, but offer little explanation of how the business will create sales. Some are so limited in scope that they essentially say "trust me" to the readers.

Contrary to popular belief, creating sales is not just a matter of working hard, talking slick, or being cheaper than the competition. There is science and art involved with creating a successful sales and marketing process. The basics are overviewed in this part of the book. My goal is for you to understand enough about sales and marketing to develop your plan to a credible level. By "credible," I mean that you will have built a solid case for the number of units you plan to sell, the reasons people will buy from you instead of the competition, and a justifiable estimate of your expected sales revenue.

Investors may quibble about certain aspects of your estimates, about whether people will buy slower or faster than you expect, or if your offering price is too high or too low. But when you are at this level of discussion, you have made a huge transition in their mind in that they are considering the idea credible enough to warrant detailed evaluation. "Trust me, it will sell" is never good enough for any seasoned investor. It shouldn't be enough for you, either. Complete this part to create a marketing and sales plan that will increase the likelihood of getting your plan funded and of turning your plan into a business success.

Calculating Customer, Market, and Sales Opportunities

Chapter

8

In This Chapter

- Determining your available marketplace
- Finding applicable research data
- Extracting and correlating facts to determine market truths
- Estimating your sales revenue based on realistic projections
- Positioning your company in the customer's mind properly to improve success

John stood up from his chair and walked to the window before speaking. "Of course there is a market for my product. It just makes sense that people will want it."

Jason, a potential investor, shook his head and then looked directly at John.

"All right. Let's play it this way. You say in your plan that you will sell 10,000 units next year. And, coincidentally, that gets us just over the break-even point. What percentage of your available market must buy your product before you meet that 10,000?"

"Not that high of a number. I'm not sure, but I know I can sell 10,000."

"I don't doubt that you *believe that you can sell 10,000 units. What I don't believe … scratch that … don't have a sense of is whether that 10,000 represents a small fraction of everyone who can use this product, or is many times the number of those who might really buy it. Do you see my point?"*

John just stood there and looked at Jason.

"John, just because you believe it to be true doesn't make it true. I have faith in you and your ideas, but the market will determine if we make money or not. We have to know more about the market."

Your customers make purchase decisions based on their needs, how your offering fills those needs, and their ability to buy. The more customers you have looking for products or services like yours, the better your chances of selling. The fewer potential customers you have, the worse your chances of selling. That makes sense, doesn't it? Here's the rub: how do you predict their likelihood of buying in general, and then project their likelihood of buying specifically from you? Herein lies the art and frustration of market and industry forecasting.

This chapter looks at some basic marketing concepts and then delves more deeply into a forecasting and research procedure that you can use to gauge your likelihood of sales success.

Understanding and Assessing the Market's Influence

I can't overemphasize the importance of marketplace trends. Just as it is really difficult to find a winning stock when the market is in a tumble, it is difficult to find customers to purchase your offering if the marketplace is in decline and few are buying what you sell. On the other hand, if you are lucky (smart?) enough to be offering a desirable product to a hungry market, you might continually struggle to meet customer demands. Guess which situation is more appealing?

Let's take a closer look at an optimal selling situation before we get into the details of forecasting market trends. Optimal selling conditions would look something like this:

- The overall marketplace demand for your offering continues to grow at more than 20 percent per year when measured by dollar sales, and when inflation is low (under 3 percent).
- The number of units that your existing customers are expected to buy from you next year will increase, and they already have budgeted product purchases from you for the next year.
- The number of vendors providing products like yours within your marketplace is few, which means that customer demand can only be fulfilled by you and a few other companies. Less competition is usually a good thing.
- There is no pending legislation or major social change that will undermine the great market conditions that exist.

- Your customers have enough money to purchase what you offer.
- Your customers are convinced that they need what you offer and are ready to make use of it as soon as possible.

What I just described is a market situation that any vendor would think ideal: lots of customers with lots of money, who all have a recognized need and only a few vendors that they can purchase from. If you can't make money in this type of marketplace, you might as well stay at home and watch TV reruns. And if you are lucky enough to have an ideal marketplace come your way, take maximum advantage of it as quickly as possible because it won't last long. Lucrative market opportunities create interest on the part of other vendors who want a piece of your pie. Somebody, somewhere, will create an offering that at least matches, if not exceeds, the value of yours, putting increased pressure on you to perform. This pressure usually means that your profit margins will start to shrink due to sale price erosion even if your unit sales continue to increase; the opportunity will start to look less attractive than it once did. Take a look at what has happened with the cellphone, iPod, and iPod look-alikes, as examples of what I am talking about.

STREET SMARTS

The forecasting process is one of trial and error. You start with the ideal scenario, and if you find that isn't feasible you try new assumptions to investigate a different scenario. You are always looking for information that helps you better estimate what will happen in reality, always keeping a cautious eye toward things that indicate marketplace troubles. In bad market conditions even the best of ideas can't succeed.

Let's take a look at the negative extreme of the earlier scenario: many vendors competing for the business of a fixed (or declining) number of customers who have decreasing incentive to buy. Now the customers are in the driver's seat regarding when, how many, and how much to pay for your offering. If you don't make it attractive enough, they will go elsewhere. As new products come onto the market that meet the customers' need, you will eventually find that demand for your product starts to diminish. Your business situation is now the opposite to the ideal mentioned earlier:

- The number of new customers is stagnant or even decreasing from year to year.
- Industry-wide sales have flattened or even decreased from year to year.

- Along with decreasing marketplace sales comes a decrease in profit margin, which means that you are struggling to sell product and making less on each sale than ever before.
- There are oodles of vendors selling something that is almost exactly like your offering, for around the same price, making it difficult to differentiate your offering from theirs.

This second scenario is a tough one, and the future prospects for a company in this situation are grim. It would be a mistake to enter a marketplace that looked like the second scenario and wonderful to enter one like the first.

Here is the question that you are trying to answer with your market research and forecasting work: Where does your offering sit on the continuum between "ideal" and "grim"? What are the facts upon which you base your assessment other than your gut feeling? The better you can determine where you stand using objective information and analysis, the more credibility you will add to your business plan. This will help to decrease the uncertainty and risk associated with investing time and money in your idea.

Don't Create a Market Need

I'm going to make this section short and to the point: you can't afford to conjure up a customer need, no matter how much you love your new idea. If you want to survive the startup stages of business, make sure that there are people out there today who are ready and willing to purchase your offering. You don't have the resources to convince potential buyers that they really need this new idea when they aren't sure themselves. Leave the market creation to the IBM, General Motors, and Allstate Insurance companies of the world. Earn your money addressing the secondary and tertiary needs that these big company market creation efforts spawn since they rarely satisfy all of their potential customers. Even a little piece of their existing pie is better than an entire pie that is a figment of your imagination. See? Simple. Done.

Determine Overall Market Characteristics

This section presents a technique for estimating (or *guesstimating*) your current and projected market conditions. There is a lot more art to this process than science, and it is heavily dependent on how lucky you are in finding the information you need.

Not only are you looking for a needle in a haystack, but you also have to mentally correlate the relationships among the various haystacks in the hope of gleaning some type of meaningful trend that helps you predict the future.

You will have to make a number of assumptions when completing your market analysis, and the analysis will evolve in stages. The basic concepts related to market estimation look something like this. In the marketing universe there are a total number of potential buyers for your specific offering. For various reasons such as location, gender, education, income, or other *demographic* characteristics, some people are more likely than others to buy *specifically from you.* Demographic characteristics are traits that can be objectively determined and that allow you to divide people into subgroups.

If I plan to open an upscale Korean restaurant, I might want to assume that anyone who eats is a prospective customer. In a city like Chicago that could include millions of people, and my estimated sales numbers will almost guaranteed be very large if I multiply a $10 meal ticket by 2 million people. Unfortunately, these are just numbers on a piece of paper and mean nothing useful. In reality, only people within a 5-mile radius might make the trek to my restaurant, which means I should exclude those outside of the 5-mile radius. I might also know that only those with an average household income of over $80,000 are my target customers, allowing me to exclude everyone else. Notice that out of the entire Chicagoland area I have now narrowed my total prospective customer base to those who live within 5 miles of my restaurant and have a household income of over $80,000. It is unrealistic to expect that everyone from the more refined list will enter my restaurant; in reality I will likely only get a small percentage of them to become regular customers. The more I know about my potential customers, the more I can narrow the total base until I get a number that represents the core group of potential persons who will make or break my restaurant's success.

Let's present this concept a little more formally. The total number of potential buyers for your particular offering represents your *target market.* This isn't everyone in the Chicagoland area, which is called the *potential market*, but only those within the 5-mile radius because they are most likely to purchase from you. Each of these people will purchase an offering like yours from some company, not necessarily yours, for an average sale amount per transaction called the *average transaction size.* Multiplying the average transaction size times the target market gives you an estimate of the total potential sales that your particular market segment can expect in a year, which is called the *total target market.* In real words, this multiplies everyone who could reasonably buy your offering times the average amount that they will spend with each purchase, which equals the total amount all of them will spend in a year for offerings like yours—with you and also the competition.

Back to reality … only a small number of the prospective customers will actually purchase from you. Dividing the number that you expect to purchase from you by the total target market customer base gives you an estimate of the *market penetration* that you can expect, expressed as a percent. Your market penetration will be a subset of all prospective targeted buyers, and the seasoned marketing person uses this estimate to get a sense of how realistic your forecasts are. Major companies with established brands will typically have less than a 50 percent market penetration. A new company with an unknown product in a wary marketplace should expect much lower numbers, in the maximum range of 2 to 10 percent gained over a several-year period (except in rare circumstances). Why do you think that the stores carry so many different brands of kid's cereal? Remember, contrary to what you may think, not everyone is going to be so enamored with your offering that they will buy it. Your goal with this process is to get a realistic estimate of how many might actually buy from you.

DEFINITION

Market penetration is a measure of the total target market who you expect to buy from you. This is usually projected monthly in the first year and annually after that. If there are 1 million people in your target customer market and you expect 50,000 to actually buy your product, you expect to capture 5 percent of the potential market.

Your **projected sales revenue** is the dollar value of sales you would collect if you multiply your estimated market penetration in customers by your average transaction size in dollars.

Guesstimates are your best guess of something based on factual estimates and a little bit of educated hunch.

Demographic characteristics are objectively determined traits that allow marketing people to divide larger groups into subgroups. Typical demographic characteristics include gender, age, education level, marital status, and interests as measured by group affiliations.

You can come up with some decent projections of potential percentage market penetration through information obtained from other companies who did what you plan to do or from best guesstimates obtained from people experienced in the field. Looking at historic percentage penetration growth over time gives you a starting point for estimating your market penetration growth, which directly impacts your projected sales revenue growth.

No one expects you to know exactly how many sales you will make during the first year, but you can provide fairly accurate estimates by making some educated assumptions. It is important, however, to make it clear when you are working with verifiable industry facts and when you are expressing your personal or professional opinion. In this way, the reader can differentiate between what you "think" is true and what is indeed an objective industry reality.

WATCH OUT!

If you become careless or, even worse, deceptive in how you present the facts in this section, you might create questions about your integrity in the investor's mind. This will almost surely eliminate the possibility of obtaining the funding you require.

Is the Market Growing?

Markets are estimated in two basic flavors: dollar sales and unit sales. Dollar sales deal with the estimated total amount of money spent purchasing offerings like the one you are investigating. Unit sales deal with the estimated number of units (widgets, hours, boxes, and so on) that might actually be sold. Here an imaginary set of market circumstances is useful to demonstrate the procedure you might follow for uncovering overall market potential and characteristics.

Assume that you're interested in selling a special type of cooking dish for use inside a microwave oven. You have looked around and found nothing else like it on the market and are convinced that this product is your ticket to national stardom and big bucks. This is how you could determine if early retirement is on the horizon.

First, what do we know? The product is used in microwave ovens, which means that the only people who will use it are those who currently own, or are planning to purchase, a microwave. Let's start here.

STREET SMARTS

Notice that if you take the total number of industry dollar sales and divide it by the total number of industry unit sales, you get a marketplace average of the sale dollars/units sold, or the average transaction size. In itself, this is a valuable number to know since it indicates whether your intended offering is priced above, even with, or below the industry average. You can also use this for estimating sales revenue if no better estimates are available.

Go to the library or cruise the internet for retail sales information pertaining to the number of households with microwave ovens. You might even find this data in the latest U.S. Census or through the Department of Commerce.

By the way, a quick Google search using "microwave oven marketplace statistics" as the search term showed 4,160 matches and led me right to the International Microwave Power Institute (impi.org), where all kinds of microwave-related reports are available (for a fee, of course). To really show you what is available with a simple internet search, check out appliancedesign.com to view more information about appliances than ever crossed your mind.

Assume that we discover that 12.62 million microwave ovens were sold last year, and that this represents an increase of 6.2 percent over the prior year. That tells us a lot already if you expect your product to be sold primarily at the time of a new microwave purchase. We know that your total available market is 12.62 million units and that the market grew over the past 12-month period, but not everyone will buy one of your units (sorry). Read on.

What if your product is only useful in microwaves above a certain cubic footage? Finding the breakdown of units sold by cubic footage would further help you define your available market, since this 12.62 million number deals with *all* microwaves sold. Search until you find this breakdown by cubic footage, likely on a percentage basis, and then apply that percentage breakdown to the total sales numbers you found at that last site. I went to the Walmart site (walmart.com) to see the various microwave size breakdowns, and they appear to come in the following cubic-foot sizes: 0.5, 0.7, 0.8, 0.9, 1.0, 1.1, 1.2, 1.3, 1.4, 1.5, 1.6, 1.8, and 2.0. We now have a general idea about the sizes involved.

Next assume, for example purposes, that only people in warm climates would be interested in our product. This means that we are primarily interested in the states in the West, Southwest, South, and Southeast as prospects. This will narrow the market even more. From The Weather Channel website (weather.com), I found a map that showed the average temperature by state for the year, which enabled me to pick the states of most interest.

STREET SMARTS

It is tremendously important to know as much as you can about the overall characteristics of your "ideal" potential buyer. Using these characteristics, you can narrow down the overwhelming amount of information available to just that applicable to our specific scope of analysis. Typical criteria include income, location, education, or pertinent social interests such as environmental protection. I call this your "ideal customer" profile.

Perhaps only people above a specific income bracket or under a certain age are expected to buy our product; that would narrow the scope even more. Starting to get the picture? Assume that with this additional refining of the total marketplace, we now determine that of the 12.62 million new microwave units sold last year, only 5 million represented viable prospects for our product. We now know a lot.

We know that 5 million microwave units are sold annually with which our product could be bundled. It is a reasonable "guess" that this figure will increase by 6 percent or so (the national average) next year as well. We could refine this by knowing more about the percentage increases by unit types and geography, and whether that 6 percent is a one-year fluke or an ongoing steady average. Five million times 1.06 (a 6 percent increase over last year) equals 5.3 million.

You're trying to determine the total number of units you could possibly sell if everyone bought your product with their microwave, and then you can scale it back to something that is a reasonable percentage of that total market. Sorry. You are not going to sell 100 percent of the new purchasers on your great product—it just doesn't happen.

The total possible units that the market could purchase next year is 5.3 million, as shown previously. Now, assume that your company can reasonably convince just 10 percent of those new purchasers to buy your product along with their new microwave. By the way, 10 percent would be a high number for the first year, but it is used here to keep the math simple. You will more likely see under 3 percent acceptance rate in the first year.

That means you could expect to sell 10 percent of 5.3 million, or 530,000 units which, if sold for $30 each, would translate into sales of $15.9 million. Not bad for a new company. You can adjust the percentage sold up or down from this starting point, but notice that you now have a benchmark for determining the quantity of units you expect to sell and the amount of sales revenue you expect to earn from those sales. Much of the rest of your plan will be determined by these two numbers, so you want to make them as accurate as possible.

Is the market forecasting process starting to tie together for you a little more? It is a process of curiosity, discovery, learning, and assimilation. The more you learn, the more you know about how to find that specific piece of data that will tie your entire analysis together. Remember that your goal with all of these calculations is to estimate a few values that will eventually end up in the cash flow analysis that you will prepare in Chapter 13. You will explain where these numbers came from in the market analysis, sales process, and strategy portions of your plan. At a minimum, you should include the following points:

- The number of units that can reasonably be sold by month and year.
- The average price per sold unit.
- The length of time it will take to reach a certain sales level, and what percentage of the total prospective purchasing population will have to buy to make those numbers (your market penetration estimates).
- The way you subdivided the total marketplace using the specific demographic traits of your most likely buyer. An explanation of how you came up with these numbers will be included in the market analysis portion of your plan.
- The best way to get to your prospective buyers based on their easily tracked demographic characteristics. You have to be able to find them to sell to them. This will be included in the marketing and sales strategy portion of your plan.

Keep your analytical eye on finding the answers to these questions, and the information will come your way. It always does once you are focused on knowing what you want. Take heart in knowing that if trustworthy numbers don't come your way, this analysis process will teach you enough so you can at least make an educated guess, which will likely be as good as anyone's.

You now have some credible market estimates. It is always hard for me to believe that all of this research, analysis, and investigation come together as just a few numbers on a spreadsheet. But, oh, how important those numbers are. You can never be too careful when estimating your sales numbers because major over- or underestimating can put you right out of business.

Using Market Segmentation to Your Advantage

Within every market and industry are smaller pockets of opportunity called market niches. These are a more specialized segment of a bigger market. For example, attorneys who specialize in construction industry accidents are pursuing a niche within the larger legal profession. Vegetarian restaurants would use marketing to target the segment of the population that doesn't eat meat and eats in restaurants. Each uses a niche strategy.

Larger companies don't waste their time trying to meet the needs of a small portion of the market, but you might want to. Often the larger companies will create niches by not offering add-ons to their main offering. They are more focused on the larger sales opportunities and tend to ignore the niches, but a niche can be very profitable for a smaller business like yours.

These niches are often like a vacuum in that once you make your product available, everything you produce will get bought up by niche customers. Niches are small enough that you can quickly establish a strong reputation that is difficult for new competitors to challenge. Even though niches might have fewer potential customers, they are often easier to sell to. Why would you want to sell to everyone when only a small portion of everyone is actually going to pay for what you offer? Sell directly to those who are the most likely to buy.

By the way, a hot unique product in a hungry niche market means you can likely charge more for your offering, which increases your profit margins. Get a good mental picture of what this means and feel the smile grow on your face.

A friend who grew up in South Africa says that they have a saying: "Many small animals live off of the crumbs from the elephant's mouth." Those elephant crumbs are looking more appetizing all the time, aren't they?

Who Are the Major Players in Your Market?

Your offering and company don't exist in a vacuum. Most likely there is established competition for the type of product you intend to offer. Assume that Competitor A offers your target customer a product similar to yours, has an 80 percent market share, and sells 4 million units per year. This information tells us that your maximum available market—before having to steal sales (and customers) from A—is 1 million units. Why? Because customers are already buying from A, who must already be heavily entrenched in that market to have an 80 percent market share (4 million ÷ 5 million = 80 percent). There are only 1 million units left to sell that are not already being sold by Competitor A. You not only have to overcome the fact that you are the new kid on the block, but also that buying from A is the customer-accepted norm.

If, on the other hand, A offers a similar but inferior product to yours and only sells 500,000 per year with a 20 percent market share, then you might have a great situation on your hands. Competitor A might have created a market need for your type of offering, but it has done a pitiful job of filling that demand with sufficient quality. You might be able to step directly into that market void with your higher-quality offering and sell a ton of product right under A's nose. If this happens, make sure to send A's president a box of chocolates and a thank-you note after you make your second million dollars. See Chapter 9 for additional details related to assessing and dealing with competition.

How Long Will This Opportunity Last?

The saying "nothing lasts forever" is particularly true of a hot marketplace. At some point, it will cool down, and you don't want to be caught off guard when it does. In a few short months you could undo all the success you created over the prior few years. Knowing your industry's maturity level helps you determine the requirements for and time frame of the market activity that will follow. Watching your market allows you to prepare to make money right up until the last minute and adapt to the next evolution.

Some markets, such as the novelty gift market, are highly volatile, meaning that they explode and fizzle in only a few months. Think about the Pet Rock. Others, such as steel manufacturing equipment, last for years or even decades. Your marketing window of opportunity will vary with your industry, and you should have a somewhat intuitive sense about your particular industry's market window and its unique signs of change. International pressures have the ability to quickly change U.S. markets from favorable to challenged. A healthy respect for competition blended with mild paranoia is probably a good recipe for staying competitive.

STREET SMARTS

We all know that much information is available online, but it is often difficult to find very specific information even when it is freely available. Stop by your local library and ask the reference librarian about sources they use for marketplace and demographic information. Determine the specific data you need and ask the librarian to help you find it. That is his or her job, and librarians all seem to like a good investigation challenge.

Finding Your Right Price

Price is interesting in that it often represents more than just the amount of money that is paid for a product. Price is often viewed as a status symbol or a measure of worth over and above the amount that changes hands; the most expensive suit appeals to some people. Pricing a product too low can make it appear inferior and can make people avoid it, even though it's of comparable quality to more expensive models.

Ultimately, the customer pays a price that is consistent with the *perceived value* of the offering. If the customer perceives the name on the product as having high value (such as designer clothing), then he or she might be willing to pay a high price to wear those designer duds.

DEFINITION

Perceived value is the overall value that the customer places on a particular product or service. This includes much more than price; it considers features such as delivery lead time, quality of salesmanship, service, style, and other less tangible items. With a perceived-value (a.k.a., market-based) pricing strategy, you set a price for your product or service by determining what people are willing to pay, yet making sure that you can still cover all your costs. Don't let your ego dictate your product's price. Several companies with a substantial jump on the market have fallen flat because of the faulty belief that people would pay more for their product simply because it was new, different, or had a particular company name on it! People buy benefits that are derived from their perceived value of your offering.

Pricing strategies fall into two basic categories: cost based and market based. You can calculate cost-based prices by determining the costs of producing a product or delivering a service and then adding a profit margin. This means that you'd better know your exact costs or this can really "cost" you the farm. You might think that you're doing great, only to find out that your projected costs were wrong and you are selling for less than your actual costs. You might be super busy because of your low prices but losing money on each transaction.

You determine market-based prices by studying price for competitive products or services and then basing your prices on that competitive information. (See Chapter 9 for more details about competition and weighting of features to determine perceived value.)

You need a lot of information about your product costs, your competitors' pricing, and how customers decide what and when to buy in order to accurately and comfortably determine pricing for your offerings. Here are some basic rules that will help you determine the best price for your services or products.

Never price the product below your cost. You need to make a profit on every sale to stay in business unless you are clearing out inventory for the next year. Some people think that if they sell huge amounts, they'll come out okay in the end. Wrong! You can't lose a nickel on each unit and expect to make up the profit in volume.

If you have a new company or a new product, you generally cannot match price with an established company with a similar offering. This is because the other company is already known and trusted and is a less risky choice for the customer. For the same price, its offering is considered a better purchase value.

You generally have to price lower than the established competition until you get a foothold in the market, unless your offering is perceived by the customer as unique and more valuable because it cannot be found anywhere else. Then you might be able to match, or exceed, competition pricing, but you better have a great sales pitch that explains the added customer benefit. Don't expect the customer to just "get it"; you have to spell it out.

You can generally sell intangibles such as better service, deliverability, and location for up to 20 percent over a competitor's price. Over that price point, the customer will probably treat your offering as too expensive for the perceived value requirements. This is not a hard and fast rule, but one I have found true more often than not.

Don't always price your offering based on your costs. This approach is called *cost-plus-profit* pricing. Although a selling price is pretty easy to compute this way, it often leaves money on the customer's table that you could have otherwise put in your company bank account. *Market-based pricing* (based on competitive options) is generally more complicated but best ensures the most possible profit on each sale. In other words, if you do a better job producing the product and lowering your costs, market-based pricing gives higher dollar profits because you keep your sale price constant. With cost-based pricing you would cut your sale price with each cost improvement, cutting your dollar profit as well. (By the way, if you understood this last sentence, you are getting this accounting jargon and concepts under your belt. If not, read Chapter 13 and then reread this chapter until you do. It is really important.)

DEFINITION

When your price is calculated using the cost to your company plus whatever profit margin is reasonable for your industry, you are using **cost-plus-profit pricing.** A widget that costs $1 to produce with a desired 50 percent mark-up would sell for $1.50 ($1 + [$1 × 0.5]). You're simply adding on your desired profit percentage to your actual costs. By the way, this would give you a 33 percent gross profit margin (0.5 ÷ 1.50 = 0.33).

When you price offerings at a level set by competitive analysis rather than by your costs, you are using **market-based pricing.** With this strategy you can generally make more money, assuming your competition is charging reasonable rates and you can keep your own costs down.

Quantity discounts are an effective way to encourage your customers to purchase more of your product at a given time. However, watch the discount amounts, or you might find yourself selling a lot for a minimal profit.

Obviously, you can set your prices wherever you want, but your ideal price means more sales (and profits) for you. You will have figured out what your customers believe is a fair price for your goods. In return, they will want to buy more.

STREET SMARTS

Profit margins for a company are available, sorted by Standard Industrial Code (SIC), from the Dun & Bradstreet Reports, Robert Morris Associates' Annual Statement Studies, or the annual report of publicly traded companies. Most publicly traded companies will send you a copy of their annual report if you call their investor relations department. If not, buy a single share of stock, and they legally have to provide it. This provides you with a benchmark for what your profits should be. Most of them are available online from the company website under the "Investor Relations" link.

Your Marketing Message and Positioning

I used to regularly play racquetball with two guys who were much older than me, and they whipped me every time. As if getting beaten wasn't bad enough, by the end of the game I was totally exhausted, and they were only slightly winded! One time, I put aside my pride and asked about the secret to their racquetball success. They replied, "It isn't the speed with which you hit the ball or how fast you are as much as your position when you hit it."

Positioning is everything in sports and in business. I don't mean the geographic location of your company, but rather the way your customers perceive your company in their heads. Creating that *market positioning* is an important function of your marketing activities.

Take a moment and think about the hundreds of marketing-related messages that bombard consumers on a daily basis. One important function of these marketing messages is to create awareness in the consumer's mind about your offering so that when they need something that you sell, they think about you. This is called *mind share.* Another important function is to enable consumers to sift through the irrelevant messages and focus on the ones of importance to them. How and what they recall depends on the way the product is presented using a *marketing message.* This message is the key to creating your intended customer perception.

DEFINITION

The **marketing message** is what you want your customers to understand about your company. **Market positioning** is accomplished using the marketing message to create a picture in the customers' mind of how they should think of your company with respect to their needs and the competition. **Mind share** is the portion of a person's thought process that includes perceptions of your company's offerings. One hundred percent mind share means that any time a person needs your type of offering, he or she thinks only of your company.

The message should be simple, easy to remember, and easy to understand. The only way you can effectively position your company or your product in your customer's mind is to understand his or her thinking and lifestyle. By knowing your competition's marketing approach you can make sure that your new company appears unique yet also trustworthy, reducing the customer's perceived risk of trying you for the first time.

Here are some examples of typical positioning statements:

- Lower price with superior quality.
- More convenient, cleaner, and better-stocked store shelves.
- We are never out of stock.
- More fun at a lower price.
- Earn your college tuition in exchange for several years of training.

The range of positioning statements is infinite and limited only by your creativity. Your marketing message clearly and simply conveys the positioning benefit perception you want your customers to understand. Spend a lot of time thinking about this and try several variations on colleagues. The marketing message will appear on almost everything you produce and will create the perception your salespeople work with during the sales process. If your message is off, you are in trouble because your customers won't even think of you when they need exactly the products or services you provide!

WATCH OUT!

Change may be a natural part of life, but it generally causes confusion when dealing with marketing messages and positioning. It takes months (or years) to create a solid market positioning in a customer's mind, and you should not tamper with it in a careless way. Confusion is a dangerous thing when dealing with customers. Decide on the positioning and stick with it unless you are absolutely sure it doesn't work.

Research Data Sources Are Everywhere

One of the best ways to learn about your industry's trends is to turn to the media. Trade newspapers, magazines, reports, websites, and radio and television stations carry so much information that you can become overloaded if you aren't careful. By knowing what you're looking for, you will recognize a research data point gift when it comes across your desk. Where others would read it and move on, you will read it and add it to your analysis.

The best way to undertake market assessment research is to immerse yourself in industry and trade business magazines and newspapers, local newspapers (and local news programs), publications about subjects pertinent to your offering, national news and business publications, related internet materials and websites, and industry association trade journals.

Since you already know what you want to sell but are not sure about pricing or potential sale quantities, you could narrow the focus of your research to businesses like yours. Study them. Read all the recent articles about them in your local library's clipping files, and talk to owners, vendors, or customers about how the businesses are doing.

If local company owners are unwilling to share their secrets, call similar business owners in another town or state. If you are not a competitor, they may be willing to talk with you about what they've done that has worked—and not worked. Check out online sources such as forums and discussion groups with people who can provide advice based on their experiences.

From their experience, you will be able to gauge a reasonable price point and acceptance level for your offering. There is really no better indicator for potential acceptance of an offering than to study how similar products have been purchased. From this baseline, you can assess whether your proposed offering is more or less valuable to the customer and guesstimate this value assessment's impact on what your customers will pay.

Researching Your Plan

The deeper you get into this research process, the more you will start to appreciate your local public library and the reference librarians who work there. Virtually all the information you'll ever need to research your business idea is out there. You just have to know where to look for it. Reference librarians are masters of finding that obscure fact that you simply cannot find. And if they can't find it, it just may not be out there. Get to know these reference gurus well, and use their important talent to its fullest extent.

The whole point of this chapter is to get you started on understanding your marketplace and industry so that you can make some credible predictions about your expected sales levels. Although you might have years of experience in the type of business you want to start (perhaps you've been working in your family's print shop for decades), investors want to feel as confident in your market instincts as well as in your operational abilities.

To show them that your ideas are on target, it is best to give them proof in the form of reliable published articles, reports, and other statistics. Saying that the market for printing is growing exponentially each year is nice, but being able to back up that statement with a report from the Department of Commerce stating essentially the same thing gives you a lot more credibility—and that's what you need at this point. To accomplish this, all you need to do is turn to reliable experts, such as publications, reports, and market gurus. All are available by phone, fax, internet, or at the library.

You can find much of the information you need online. Once you become proficient at internet searches, you might be able to avoid constant trips to the library. However, I still find that trained librarians are often able to point me in just the right direction, particularly for those difficult-to-find yet important, obscure data points. Don't be afraid to contact your local community college or university library as well. Most states have an incredible network of libraries that may provide the information you need, and your tax dollars have already paid for it. The cool thing about working with an established library is that it subscribes to many amazing information services that would cost you a lot of money on your own. Truth is that you have likely already paid for them with tax dollars that support the community college or library.

STREET SMARTS

Subscribe to industry-specific publications and trade groups that make sense for your offering. These targeted groups offer support and research that might not be available to the general public or that would cost you a hefty fee. Find a federal repository, frequently located at a local university, which contains all the latest government document information. You've already paid for the research with your tax dollars, so you might as well use it. A listing of documents is also available from the Government Printing Office (gpo.gov).

For Your Plan

When writing the market and industry analysis of your plan, make sure that you include the following points:

- Show that your new business idea applies to a marketplace that is healthy and growing.
- Provide a detailed description of your ideal target customer, including demographic profile and buying characteristics. Make sure that you explain how you determined this profile.
- Detail your rationale for determining the sales unit volume, average transaction size, market penetration, and revenue numbers used in the financial analysis.

- Offer your intended positioning statement and explain why it was written in just that way. How does it differentiate your company and offering from others—and if it does not, why not?
- Explain how you plan to advertise and promote your company and offering. What are the projected costs of this promotion? What are the projected sales returns for promotion dollars spent? See the social media chapter for more details about using social media during your first year of business.
- Detail your pricing rationale and how it stacks up with the competition. Include discussion and analysis on the profit margins required for each step in your particular marketing/sales approach and how it ties in with the life cycle analysis.
- Outline your plans for expansion beyond your initial market introduction, as applicable.
- Show yourself to be an expert not only on your product and company idea, but also in the industry into which you will sell.

The Least You Need to Know

- Clearly understand the demographic and buying characteristics of your ideal customer as a way of focusing your marketing and sales plan.
- Price is not the only buying criterion; customers look at the total value and benefits of your offering. You must remain focused on creating high perceived customer value.
- Create a simple yet clear marketing message that describes your company's market positioning, and stick with it. This is how people will perceive your company.
- Credible marketplace and industry information are out there, but you may have to piece scraps together to get the overall picture.
- Make sure that you spend your marketing dollars on the target market that is most likely to buy what you offer.

Analyzing and Using the Experience of Your Competition

Chapter

9

In This Chapter

- Determining your direct competition
- Learning about the similar companies or products
- Evaluating your offering against the competition
- Finding your niche in the marketplace

"A few years back I was on a plane going to Minneapolis," my boss said, "and two guys behind me were celebrating a large sale contract they were about to close. When one guy said the name of the company and the contact's name, I realized that it was one of my customers. He then outlined the entire sale situation, including the dollars involved, the basic technical requirements, who was making the final decision, and by when. In short, he told me everything I needed to know to steal the sale."

"Do I have to guess what you did?" I asked. For once this had turned into a pretty good story.

"I called the customer immediately upon landing. I told him that I had heard he was looking for some equipment and that I had what he needed at a price that just happened to be 5 percent cheaper than the bid provided by the guy on the plane," he replied with a big grin. "I closed the deal that afternoon before the other guy even had a chance to claim his luggage."

This is a paraphrasing of a true story (except the luggage part). Believe that there is always some competitor out there who will take your lunch away, and you might not even know how it happened! This chapter shows you how to learn from, meet, and beat the competition.

Is the Competition Real?

It's easy to overreact when dealing with the competition. You might treat your competitors as insignificant (watch your ego on this one) or as a major threat (watch your paranoia on this one). Both of these approaches are inappropriate unless you know something about the competitor. You need an honest understanding of your competition's strengths and weaknesses before deciding how you should respond.

It is very important that you spend time in your plan discussing your competition. Any investor will know that a good idea has competition; either it exists already, or it will appear soon after the new idea is proven viable. A plan that does not include a detailed discussion about competitive risks is a plan that has been created in a vacuum. That is a scary prospect for any investor, since it indicates a naive approach on the part of the entrepreneur.

Direct competitors are companies that your potential customers would call in addition to you when looking for your products or services. These competitors will pose either strategic or tactical threats to your business. A *strategic threat* can affect you negatively down the road but at present might only be a minor nuisance. A *tactical threat* takes money out of your pocket today when your customers buy from your competitor instead of you. A large company that might enter your marketplace a few years down the road would be a strategic threat. A large company that currently offers competition to your offering and your customers is a tactical threat. A tactical threat that persists for a longer period of time will likely become a strategic threat.

DEFINITION

A **direct competitor** is a company that regularly sells a comparable product or service to the same customers that you do. A **tactical threat** is one that has immediate potential impact, whereas a **strategic threat** is one that can hurt you over time.

A strategic threat can easily become a tactical pain in the butt if you don't pay attention to it and take the proper actions to protect yourself. A tactical threat, if large enough, can cause major problems for you today. This is especially true when you have a small customer base that provides most of your sales. If your competition takes one customer, which they will definitely try to do, potential and current customers start to wonder what it was that lured one of your major accounts away.

When you start your business, you are in the enviable position of having no major competitor who takes you seriously. This provides you with a tremendous amount of freedom because nobody will be aiming to eliminate you in sales situations. You know that you are succeeding when competitors start to know your name and change their marketing strategy to go after you. That's both good news and bad news at once.

You should always be collecting as much information as possible about the competitive companies in your particular market segment. When you are starting out, people might not view you as a competitor and thus might be more open with their information. Sit down and imagine the picture that your prospective customers have in their minds about each of your competitors. Your competitors' marketing message and positioning generally creates this image. (See Chapters 8 and 10 for more on this topic and the sales decision process.)

How does your offering compare to your competitors'? If you were a customer looking at the two companies, would you see them as direct competitors or as two companies in separate market segments? Does this perception come from the fact that they offer different products or services, or does their marketing message present it differently?

Remember that you continually want to be training yourself to see things through the eyes of your customer. Those are the most important eyes, after all.

Accumulating Competitive Information

Current and accurate information is the key to making savvy and effective decisions in general, and competitive decisions in particular.

Information is everywhere; keep looking for it, find it, collate it, and, finally, put it into some semblance of organization and order. It is amazing how fragments of information can be combined to give you an excellent overall picture of a competitor.

Where do you start looking for competitive information? Even in today's highly online world, a simple place to start investigating local competitors is in the Yellow Pages. Who is listed in the category you would choose for yourself? Try calling the numbers to see who is still in business. Are they also listed in another category? If so, why? How many companies are listed there? How do they position themselves in the ad? What services or products do they emphasize? Is it a display ad or simply a small-column ad? Grab last year's Yellow Pages and compare it to this year's. Has the number of competitors increased or decreased? Did some of the advertisers advance to a display ad, implying that last year's ad worked? Did their positioning change from last year to this year? Look at how much insight you can obtain about your market by simply looking at the Yellow Pages.

Use a search engine on the internet to look up offerings like yours in your geographic area. Cross-reference the search results with the information you've culled from the Yellow Pages. Check out the websites for those who look like potential competitors and see what information they offer. You can learn a lot right here. Their website may tell you more about the people, sites, plans, products, services, policies, warranties, and pricing than you can get anywhere else. Be aware that your competitors will also check out your website, so don't put information there unless you want it found. Make sure you use search terms like "comparison" or "pricing" or "review" to see if someone has done analysis to help you with your work.

Other useful sources for competitive information include newspapers and magazines, your customers, your competitors' customers, annual reports, social gatherings, networking functions, and sales brochures, to name a few. Check out the Better Business Bureau (bbb.org) or local chamber of commerce (uschamber.com) for more information.

Scour local newspapers, business reports, and trade publications for advertisements, articles, and quotes from any of your potential competitors. Ask your friends to do the same. They might find something that you missed. Start a folder for each of the competitors. (They really each deserve at least a manila folder, don't they?) Your local public library might also keep files on local companies that you can scan for free. Every time you find a piece of information, write it down if you heard it, print it if you found it online, or photocopy it if you found it in print. Date and place the information in that folder.

WATCH OUT!

Beware spending a lot of money for market research reports prepared by professional companies. Having someone else perform general research hurts you on two fronts. First, you have to spend much-needed cash early in the process; second, you give up the opportunity to become familiar with the marketing information yourself. Spend the money on marketing research if you must, but try to find out some of this information on your own first. Having great research but no money to spend taking advantage of that research is poor planning.

Ask your prospective customers what they know about your competitors. How do they like dealing with them? What is their satisfaction level? If they are not satisfied, would they consider using you for the same products and services? Notice that this discussion opens another level of communication with your prospective customers, which is always a good idea.

Some companies specialize in accumulating information about companies for a fee. These *clipping services* review a set number of publications for information regarding certain companies. You tell them which companies you want them to watch for and which newspapers or magazines you want them to read. They generally photocopy any articles that appear and send them to you on a regular (usually weekly) basis. This service is not free, but it might pay for itself in the valuable information about your competitors that you may have overlooked. A clipping service differs from a market research service in that the research service will offer analysis as well as the information. The clipping service will typically only offer copies of the articles and media references.

DEFINITION

Clipping services are companies such as BurellesLuce (burellesluce.com) that read thousands of media outlets such as newspapers, magazines, social media, and other online sources looking for articles about or references to specific companies. Many businesses hire clipping services to watch for articles about their company and the competition. **Industrial espionage** is the practice of collecting secret information about competitors through devious or illegal methods. Using public information sources is intelligence gathering and isn't considered espionage, but rummaging through corporate wastepaper baskets after hours would be.

Finally, you can call your competitors and ask for information. A lot of times, they will send it to you. Don't use a fake personal or company name. If you misrepresent yourself, you are toying with *industrial espionage*, which is really scary. Penalties for fraud and misrepresentation can be severe and can seriously damage your business and your personal credibility. Just give them your name, number, and address—leave out your company's name—and hope that you're talking to someone who doesn't know who you are. Don't volunteer information, and only give what you're asked. This approach is probably a safe bet when you first start out and will become more difficult as your success builds, along with your reputation.

The secret to accumulating competitor information is to have open ears, focused attention, a closed mouth, and organizational skills. It's a job that requires constant diligence but doesn't take much time once you begin. As time goes on and you become more familiar with your competitors, you will get to the point that you know them almost as well as you know your own company, sometimes understanding their next move before it is even announced. If you get this good at predicting your competition, please don't tell them. This is the type of skill that is best kept secret.

STREET SMARTS

If the competitor you are researching is a publicly traded company, you can get a lot of information from its annual report, which you should be able to find at their website. If not, call the company's investor relations department and ask for it. If the company won't send you one upon request, simply buy a share of stock, which entitles you, as a shareholder, to the same information that any other shareholder would receive. Also, try cnbc.com or your personal stock brokerage house to see if either has information you can use.

Comparing Yourself to Them

Okay, so you've played supersleuth and acquired a wealth of information about your competition. Put down your pipe, Sherlock; it's time to get into the trenches and start analyzing the information you've collected. How do you compare to the competition from your customer's perspective? When you find the answer to this question, you are on your way to determining your own position in the marketplace.

Here's an exercise that will help you find some answers.

		Your Company		Competitor #1	
Ⓐ Characteristics	Ⓑ Importance (1-10)	Ⓒ Effect (1-10)	Ⓓ Result (B x C)	Ⓔ Effect (1-10)	Ⓕ Result (B x E)
Years in Business	4	3	12	6	24
Credit Terms	7	8	56	8	56
Hours of Operation	7	8	56	8	56
Depth of Offering	6	6	36	8	48
Prior Experience with Company	8	5	40	6	48
Certification	5	8	40	6	30
		Totals	**240**		**262**
		Sale Price	**$75**		**$95**

Take out a pad of paper or, better yet, create a spreadsheet to automate the following easy calculations:

- Set up six columns: A, B, C, D, E, and F. Add more columns as needed to compare more competitors.

- In Column A, write down the top 10 characteristics that your customers consider when making a purchase decision. Characteristics can include technical competency, service, phone support, convenience, credit terms, years in business, depth of offering, online ordering, and so on. You can add to this listing later if you want, but only use 10 for now.
- In Column B, place a number that corresponds to the amount of importance you believe a customer places on a particular characteristic, based on your experience. Make 1 stand for least important and 10 stand for a must-have. Although these are your opinions, they are still worthwhile to note. You can always adjust these values later on making the spreadsheet approach preferred.
- Create individual two-column sets for your company and each of your competitors (i.e., competitor #1, #2, etc.).
- The left column of the set is where you enter a number between 1 and 10 that is your subjective assessment of how well each company meets your ideal customer's need for that particular characteristic. (See Columns C and E in the example.)
- The right column value of the set (Columns D and F) is calculated by multiplying the importance value (Column B) by the effect value for the respective column set. For example, your company result value is calculated by multiplying Column B by Column C. For competitor #1, multiply Column B by Column E to get its respective result value.
- At the bottom of each results column, total all the numbers in the column for your company and each competitor. This final number provides a relative weighting assessment of how each competitor compares against the others and your company.

How does the relative weighting number for your company compare with those of your competitors? Is your number higher or lower? The same? How does your price compare with the others when compared against the summary numbers, such as in Columns D and F in the example? Notice that you now have a somewhat objective measure of how a customer would assess your offering against that of a competitor. It doesn't just involve features, but also how important those features are to customers. Now we can compare that assessment value to price, which is certainly what your customer will do.

In general, you want your company's total result value to be high because it indicates that you are close to ideal for your customers. Ideal is calculated by totaling the importance column and multiplying by 10—the perfect score for each item. For example, the sum of the importance column in the previous table equals 37, which, multiplied by 10, equals 370 points for the ideal.

Divide your rating (such as 240 in the example) by the ideal (such as 370) to see how close you are from a percentage standpoint (240 ÷ 370 = 65 percent). What is the proper percentage level? It's a relative setting and one that is highly dependent upon your business and customer type. In general, you should strive to have a rating of 75 percent or higher, which would give you a C or better in high school. It should surely be a continuing improvement goal to get closer to the ideal score.

STREET SMARTS

Customers are always looking to buy the best possible value—which means the best fit for their needs—for the lowest price. The closer your results score can come to meeting the ideal for the lowest competitive price for your particular customers puts you in a very strong competitive buying position in the mind of the customer.

Numbers are okay but I think in pictures, so I plot price and the total weighting importance factor against each other for my company and my competitors. Let the horizontal line represent the weighting results, starting at 0 on the left, to the maximum ideal weight on the right. Let the vertical line represent the price of what is being sold. To plot your company data from the example, follow the horizontal line until you get to 240 (your total results). Now move vertically until you match the $75 horizontal line. Put a dot there and label it "My Company." Repeat this process for each competitor. You can now see graphically where you are compared to the competition.

Notice from the example that the competitor charges a higher price and also provides a higher total results weighting factor; now you know why they can get away with charging a higher price. If you match the competitor's features (weighting) and offer a discount price, your plot point will move down along a vertical line because you are decreasing pricing and not changing the weighting. In the customers' eyes, they can buy the same features for less money. Sure, this will keep you initially very busy, but if you have not set up your profit margins to work at the lower price, eventually you will busy yourself right out of business because you ran out of money.

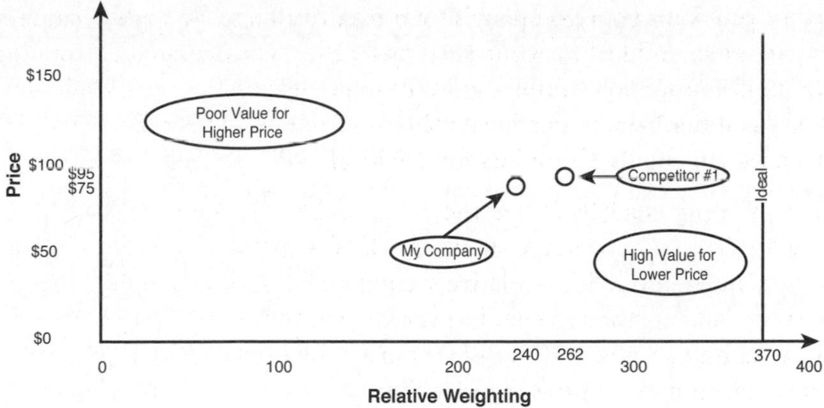

On the other hand, decreasing the weighting results total and keeping the price the same also eventually rings the death knell. In the customers' eyes, they would be getting less value for the same price when compared to a competitor, so they will stop buying from you. Graphically, you would be moving your plotted dot to the left along a horizontal line (keeping the price the same) while decreasing the offering results weighting.

Where do you need to beef up services? Where do you get the best weighting-factor return for the dollars spent? In the preceding example, spending money to offer longer hours of operation or better credit terms increases your weighting factors on two items of high importance (both rated 7 in importance), whereas spending money on certification (rated a 5 in importance) provides a lower weighting return.

Okay, enough of all this graphing and other technical stuff. Will you make decisions strictly by this weighting analysis and chart? Probably not. Will the results from this analysis provide you with a structured way of analyzing your competition so that you can make informed decisions? Absolutely yes. This is a good reality check and one worth performing on a regular basis.

You should now have a pretty good idea of how you stack up against your competition. You might be less expensive than they are, for instance, but you also don't offer the extra services that they do. On the other hand, if your price is lower and you have a higher total value, you might consider raising the price on your offering. Why leave money on the table if you don't have to? But remember that the one who has the ultimate say in the purchase is the customer. Make all of your decisions considering first how your customers will react.

Are You a Specialty Store or a Superstore?

Are the other folks in your industry large companies such as Walmart that have deep pockets and a wide selection of offerings? Or are they smaller companies that provide a specialized, niche offering that a few people use (such as Candles Are Us)? It's important that you understand where you want to fit in the continuum between the two types of businesses. Note that these terms apply equally well to service or product businesses. You could be a full-service health club or a specialty massage practitioner.

If you're trying to be a *superstore* but don't have the money to provide the required variety and volume of products needed, you will probably go out of business. The financial demands of making a business of this size work will affect your ability to maintain appropriate inventory or personnel expertise levels. Once your shelves appear naked or you don't provide a proper service level, customers will quickly take their business elsewhere.

If you're a smaller business that tries to cater to everyone's needs, you will probably fail—not because you lack skills or ability, but because your specialty customers will expect more depth of product offering than you will be able to carry. They will expect many different shapes and sizes of vanilla-scented candles instead of just one. Plus, remember that as a smaller store you purchase in smaller quantity, which means that your product costs and eventual sale prices will be higher. The superstore firms will clobber you on price alone. Think about it: if your customer can purchase the same product for 20 percent less from one of your competitors, you must offer some other very real benefit for them to get them to purchase from you instead. All things being equal, customers tend to buy the lowest price. If you plan to charge a premium price for your offering, then you must make sure that the quality/value perception in the customer's mind is higher when they compare your total offering to your competitors'. This is a tricky balancing act.

Interestingly enough, superstores are wary of the *specialty stores* eroding their business in key areas. A specialty store can provide a much higher level of personalized service and depth of product offerings to customers than a superstore can ever hope to provide. The specialty store can also charge a little more for the service because their customers perceive it as having more value. In this way, the specialty store can keep margins high and expenses low, which is always a good way to run a business. However, you need to know your customers and offer the specialty items they want.

DEFINITION

A **superstore** is a very large discount store, such as a Walmart or Kmart, that offers a wide variety of products at discounted prices. A **specialty store** offers a smaller variety of items that are usually focused on a specific category, such as shoes or candles.

Bookstores present an interesting example of the smaller store holding its own against megastores such as Barnes & Noble. These niche/local bookstores tend to know their local clientele and offer books that are specifically related to their interests. Their bookstore is not only a place to purchase specialized books (e.g., they offer the best selection of local-area gardening books around), but it is also a community meeting place where residents congregate as a social activity. The local bookstore becomes part of the community and is supported as such. They may not provide the wide variety of a larger store, but the shopping experience is ideally tailored for a smaller, more select clientele.

In technical areas, a specialty store may be one that not only sells hardware and software but also customizes computer equipment or software for the customer's particular needs. The company makes money on both the products and the services. The customer wins because she knows that her purchase will be handled in a low-risk, professional manner. Customers will pay for the service, especially if the cheaper or larger department store route has burned them. If the customer is looking to buy a computer and a dishwasher, the smaller store generally cannot compete.

In retail, for example, a specialty store might be one that deals only in candles and related items. The customer might be able to find a cheaper candle in a superstore, but could he find "just the right one" based on color, size, scent, etc.? Probably not, and that is the benefit of a specialty store. People expect to pay more for the added selection and service. Value is what sells; don't shortchange yourself on that count, but don't gouge your customers either. Find that right balance and you can create a dedicated clientele and highly valued referrals.

Trying to be a superstore when you should be a specialty store is surefire trouble, as is the reverse. If you don't have the broad range of products or services to qualify as a superstore in your industry, stick with serving a small niche as a specialty store. You'll probably make more money by establishing a reputation as a specialist in a particular area, rather than a generalist who tries to do everything. And you'll probably have more fun and do a better job of it along the way. Check your ego. Make more money.

For Your Plan

When writing the competition portion of your plan (see Chapter 7), know that your plan readers will be keenly interested in both the competition and your reaction to their potential threat. Make sure that, at a minimum, you include the following information:

- A table that presents important competitor facts such as name, geographic location, public/private, nationally known or local guru, sales revenue, net income, number of employees, competitive products, years in business, and any other significant information.
- A comparison of your offering with that of your competitors. It should outline product features, noting areas where they have an advantage over your product or service and where you are better than them. Pricing, warranty, terms, and other significant purchase-related information should be included.
- A clear outline of your own competitive advantages, so the reader knows you not only understand the scope of the competitive threat, but also are ready to deal with it in a credible way.
- Your strategy for marketing and selling against these competitors, including the specific tactics you plan to use to win business. See Chapter 10 for more details on effective selling.
- If your offering is substantially different from anything else out there, how do you plan to convince customers to go with you instead of staying with the established way they have previously done things? How do you plan to deal with the almost guaranteed reality that your competition will come out with a product that competes once your idea is proven worthy?

The Least You Need to Know

- Competition will always exist, but that's not necessarily bad. Comparing your products and services to those of your competitors helps you stay on top of what customers want.
- Watching your competitors provides insight into what's going on in your market and what they believe customers want. This information can help you better plan for the future.

- Continually collect competitor information and perform a detailed comparison analysis once a year to objectively see how you stack up against your competition when viewed through a customer's eye. You might also perform the relative weighting analysis to ensure that what you think is true is actually true from the customer's viewpoint.
- Customers purchase value, not price. Just because your competitors drop their prices doesn't mean that you have to.
- Understand whether you are a specialty store or a superstore and match your depth or breadth of offering accordingly.

Creating Sales, Sales, and More Sales

Chapter

10

In This Chapter

- Understanding the value of effective selling
- Matching sales procedures to your company's offering
- Evaluating direct and distribution sales
- Selling services

"So, what happened?" asked the board member who provided the most of the initial funding for the company.

"The sales just didn't come in as expected," said the president, a professional engineer and former operations manager. "We've been through three sets of salespeople and can't seem to find a good group. They all seem to just want more money and don't bring in the bacon."

"Have you ever been with them on a sales call?" asked the board member.

"Not really," replied the president. "I have been working with our technical people to make sure the product can do what we promised. Selling is what I have sales managers for. Why pay them if I have to do everything myself?" He felt like he just walked onto shaky ground.

"Let's make sure I understand. We have a product and a production facility that works perfectly due to your involvement, but we have nobody who wants to buy what we build. Is that correct?" Heads nodded around the room. "What is wrong with this picture, and what are your plans to correct it?"

Simply stated, a business does not survive without sales. Period. You won't have to worry about collecting debts from customers because you won't have any customers or accounts receivable. You won't need a perfectly working product because nobody wants to buy it. Much of the rest of the reason that a company exists is out of faith that sales will happen. Sales is the money funnel of your company, and without sales eventually there will be no company.

Understanding the sales process and what it takes to succeed at selling is important to running a successful business. As the founder and owner of your company, the sales "buck" stops with you. You became the top salesperson in your company the instant you started it. The only question is whether you will fully realize that fact, take ownership of it, and then set up your sales operation to support the company needs and your particular sales capabilities and style.

There is arguably no more important skill that a new business owner can cultivate than the ability to create sales. You may create these sales yourself or you may hire people to create them for you, but create them you must. Read on and learn more about how sales fits into your business plan, and also how the sales process can be designed and managed to create your first year of success.

The Importance of Sales to Business Success

It has intrigued me over the years that the sales portion of a business plan is often the shortest and least thought out. The operation plan will be detailed, the product specifications will be precise, the personnel roster will be complete, but sales will be treated along the lines of "we will sell 100 in the first month." No backup details about how that will happen. Just the equivalent of "trust us, sales will happen." Even more intriguing to me is the lack of emphasis that new business owners will put on sales during their first year of operation. They will focus on accounting, manufacturing, design, and just about anything else but sales. Let me just say that those who get themselves into financial trouble, sometimes uncorrectable trouble, are those who don't focus on sales. And I can safely say that I see more companies get into financial trouble from too few sales than from too many. Get my drift?

I refer to sales as the money funnel because no cash comes into the company unless someone has sold your product or service to a customer and you eventually collect the customer's money. Selling is your lifeline to staying in business. To succeed, you must give it the attention and respect it deserves. You can stay in business if your accounting is inaccurate or if you aren't the best of managers, but you will definitely be out of business if you cannot create sales. This doesn't mean that you must do the selling yourself, however. If you lack the interest or the ability to sell successfully, find someone who can.

You need to know enough about sales to manage those actually performing the sales function and to determine when a sales slowdown represents a problem with your sales force or with your company's offering, or if it's due to something happening in the marketplace.

Your potential investors are aware of the importance of sales to your success, too. Any good business plan must include enough details about sales to make the investors believe that the sales targets are feasible. No new business will survive into year two if the company's sales track record doesn't show regular improvement, defined as increased sales revenue. Understanding the sales process for your new company is critical, and this chapter provides you with a framework for understanding how to best present your selling plans.

I developed this approach to sales during my time as a salesperson and sales manager. I use it in my own company and also with my clients. It works and I suggest that you adopt it for your plan and first year in operation, after which you will no doubt find a sales approach that is right for you and your company. At that point, this chapter will have done its job—you'll be funded and through your first year.

Manipulating and Selling: Not the Same Thing

Most of us have had someone convince us to buy something we later realized was not in our best interest. We felt manipulated by the whole process and by the salesperson involved. Manipulation has nothing to do with professional sales! If you manipulate people to buy your offering and they don't want it, they will resent you, your company, and its offerings for a long time. That single sale could cost you a fortune in future revenues, not only from that one customer who will never buy from you again but also from everyone he tells about his negative buying experience with you.

Professional sales is the process of matching your products or services with a customer who truly needs them. You are helping the customer solve a problem by providing a service or a product that will make her life easier. It could be as simple as selling a pair of shoes for a special party or as complicated as setting up an experiment on the International Space Station. If the customer has a need for your offering and you provide a credible product or service that meets that need, within her budget, then the customer will buy! It's that simple. If the customer doesn't buy, there is something wrong with your offering or your presentation, or you are not presenting to a viable (qualified) potential buyer.

Manipulative selling might earn you a fast buck, but it also eliminates the chance for a future sale to that customer. Professional selling is the act of solving a customer's problems through your company's offerings. It is service-based professional selling instead of manipulation based and has a much better chance of creating long-term customers.

Many new salespeople have shifted from average performers who just do their jobs to outstanding performers who like what they do by simply making this conceptual shift. The difference between these two approaches is the difference between not caring whether a customer needs something (manipulation-based selling) versus determining that the customer has a need that your product or service can meet (service-based professional selling).

STREET SMARTS

More satisfied customers result from service-based professional selling than from manipulative types of selling. You don't need to be a business guru to understand that satisfied people buy more and tell their friends to buy from you. This is good.

True business and selling success usually comes from a lot of smaller successful clients instead of a single "killing" with a huge customer. The huge deals make good press and media headlines but really don't reflect the reality of day-to-day business success, which is earned deal by deal.

Getting Closer to Closing the Sale

The sales process takes place in a number of stages. Look at the way you buy anything. You go through your own set of questions and investigation stages before actually forking over your money. You might evaluate the available information, read about the product in magazine or newspaper articles, ask knowledgeable friends for their opinions, flip a coin, and call your mom for her advice before eventually deciding on a purchase.

Professional selling involves a sequence of small events that eventually lead to the sale. At each step along the way, the salesperson makes little requests for customer action, or *minicloses*, which eventually lead to a sale, which is the ultimate *close*. For example, asking to meet with someone face-to-face is a miniclose in that you are asking the customer to take an action that leads in the direction of the sale. If the customer agrees, you are one step nearer to getting him to make a purchase. Once the customer is satisfied that buying your product or service is the right decision, he commits naturally and on his own to a purchase, which is the final closing of the sale.

When talking to a salesperson, people expect to be asked reasonable questions that help them solve their problem, and they also expect you to ask them to buy. If you don't ask for the order, you can't blame them if they don't offer.

Here is the key take-away from this section: customers looking to purchase your company's product or service will follow a natural sequence of predictable steps before making their final purchase. Those steps may happen in a few moments or they may take months depending on your industry, but the steps will be there. Understand those steps, understand how you plan to move the customer from one miniclose stage to the next, and then make sure that you have developed the right automated processes or have the right people who can move that customer through one miniclose to the next. Remember that each step brings your customer one step closer to making a final purchase. More on this important topic later in the chapter.

DEFINITION

A **close** (pronounced *cloze*) is a request by a salesperson for a specific action on the customer's part. Asking for the order is the ultimate close, but smaller **mini-closes** occur at each stage of the selling process to gradually move the customer toward committing to the purchase.

Everyone Has to Sell, but Not Everyone Closes

Everyone in your organization should support the sales process by providing information, support, service, and guidance when requested by the customer. At the very least the employees should make sure that the customer is reliably put into contact with the right salesperson within your company. When it is time for the final order to be placed, the salesperson should be there to take the order.

Aggressive selling is closing when it is inappropriate and unlikely to succeed. Professional selling is closing at each stage as appropriate to move the customer to the next stage in the sales process while still keeping the customer comfortable. The moral of the story: don't rush customers into making a purchase decision, or you might lose them forever.

Taking care of customers is the responsibility of all employees, and when a few drop the customer service ball, especially the owners, the entire company suffers. It is the responsibility of top management and owners to make sure that there is no question in the minds of employees that the customer must be taken care of, and not taking care of the customer will not be tolerated. I can assure you that customers are only a few minutes (or a click) away from going to one of your competitors if you don't provide the service they expect.

ED'S LESSONS LEARNED

I have seen small business owners hire salespeople and then remove themselves from the sales and marketing activities of the company. Wrong move! It must be an organizational mandate that all employees, especially the owners, think of themselves as customer service and sales support personnel when it comes to serving the customer. If the phone rings six or more times before being answered and there are employees there who could have answered it, then that customer is not being served, and a sale might be lost. If a website inquiry is not responded to within 24 hours (4 hours would be better!) then you are telling that customer that you do not monitor your website and that his or her interest in your company is unimportant to you. Always try to see your company through the eyes of the customer to gauge how you are doing.

Is Your Offering a Special or Commodity Item?

Your company's approach to selling is largely determined by your market positioning and message. (See Chapter 8 for more information on marketing and positioning.) Offerings with plenty of competition, where the products and services are pretty much the same, require emphasis on features and benefits such as price, delivery, warranty, and stability to set your company apart. Specialty products and services, such as very sophisticated technology or even tailored clothing, require a higher level of personalized service and credibility as part of the sales process because each product is so different from the others on the market. If the customer software product specifications or the customer's measurements are not right, then neither the software nor the suit will meet with the customer's satisfaction, costing you not only the sale but also the referrals that could come from a happy customer.

Where does your product fit? Commodities rely more on the distribution channel to effectively get products into the hands of customers. There is little or no difference between competing commodity products (milk, white envelopes, and lead pencils), making price and service major factors in the customer decision-making process.

Specialty products require a higher level of technical and sales sophistication because the product's competitive advantage must be explained well. The salesperson has to know about the benefits of the competitors' products and services and how they compare to his own company's offerings in order to sell the customer on why his is better. It is often possible to sustain higher profit margins selling specialty products because the customer is more sophisticated regarding your particular product. This is why fine wine shops, antique dealers, and high-end stereo stores effectively charge so much more for their products than a large discount store. Their products are not widely available and have specialized features for a more sophisticated audience, and the salesperson provides a higher level of knowledge and service as part of the sale process. This is expected in a more complex product or service environment; if it's not provided by you, customers will go elsewhere. The bottom line: match your level of salesperson knowledge to the expectations of your customer and you are on the right track. Don't expect customers to find their own answers if they are paying a premium for expertise, and don't feel obligated to offer a premium service and expertise if they are paying discount store prices.

Is Your Prospect a Likely Buyer?

All the sweet-talking, wining, dining, and fancy brochures in the world will not close a sale from an unqualified prospect (someone who is not able to buy or interested in buying at all). I have seen a lot of new, and even experienced, salespeople invest valuable time on who they believed to be a viable potential customer, only to find out later that they were really never qualified to purchase in the first place. Here is a list of five criteria you can use to determine whether you are dealing with a *qualified customer.*

DEFINITION

A **qualified customer** is someone who is interested in buying from you and has the means, motivation, and capability to do so.

Does Your Customer Need What You Have to Offer?

If your customers don't need what you offer, then you can't blame them for not buying it. Would you buy something you didn't need just to make the salesperson happy? No way, and they won't either! Your challenge is to accurately identify your potential customers' needs and make sure your marketing message addresses them. If you determine that you cannot meet their needs, get out of their way.

Bottom line: work hard to match your offerings to the needs of your targeted marketplace. Don't offer what you "know" they want without checking it out first. In your business plan, present how you determined that your offering fills an existing need in the marketplace and who will be the buyer.

WATCH OUT!

If you are planning an online business, don't make the mistake of thinking that you will not need employees. There is only so much customer-initiated adaptation that you can proactively build into an online tool; when customers hit their frustration level after clicking into deeper and deeper layers, you better have a person easily available to answer their questions when needed, or you will likely lose them and perhaps not even know it. Remember that they are only a click away from leaving your website.

There are powerful online tools (such as web conferencing, video, audio, and cookies) that enable amazing levels of customized user interaction, but remember that they are still machines. The prospect or customer on the other end is human. You should use automation to its full advantage but always remember that people buy online expecting that a person is in the background in case something goes wrong.

Are You Working with the Decision Maker?

Ultimately, a single person will authorize the purchase of your offering. If you are not dealing with the person in charge of the budget—the person who can say yes and sign on the dotted line—then you are only dealing with someone who has the authority to say no to the sale or at best can only influence the outcome. Instead of wasting time and energy convincing someone who is not authorized to make a decision to buy from you, first determine who the decision maker is. This might require that you meet with non–decision makers until you find the right person.

Bottom line: always be looking for and marketing to the person who will make the final decision to purchase your offering. Advertising to the dog makes no sense when the dog's owner buys the food. Get it? Create some type of profile for the decision makers and develop a plan to get to them.

Is There Money Budgeted for This Purchase?

If there is no money available to pay for a purchase, there is no potential for a sale. It is perfectly okay to ask whether money is already in the budget for this purchase or how the customer plans to pay for your product. You might find that the money is coming out of next year's budget and that the sale is on hold until the next fiscal year starts. You might also find that there is no money currently budgeted for this project—currently or in the future—which should set off warning bells in your head. Or you might discover that your customer needs to spend the budgeted money by the end of this fiscal year, which provides an added incentive on his or her part to move the sale forward. Handling budget issues could be as simple as whether the sale is credit card or cash, as in a retail environment.

Bottom line: people can only buy if they have the money, and spending lots of sales time cultivating prospects with no money will not fill your sales funnel. At some point, they will have to pay for their purchases. When planning, discuss the budgeting time frame associated with your sale. If you run a retail business, the time frame will be at the point of sale. If industrial, the time frame may extend months or years, which will have a huge impact on your cash flow and sales cycles.

Is There a Pending Event?

This is an important point that in my experience is most often overlooked by people new to sales, and even forgotten by some sales old-timers. A pending event is something expected to happen in the future that affects when a decision is made. The pending event drives the time frame within which a decision is required. Typical pending events include fiscal year end (when budgeted money needs to be spent or is lost), management orders, moving offices, and mergers. A birthday would be a pending event for a retail purchase, while obsoleting an existing product line or the start of a government-supported equipment purchasing program are examples of a pending event for manufacturing businesses. If there is no pending event, the customer can, and might, take forever to make a decision. Why should they force the decision when a decision is not necessary? If there is no critical deadline, you might spend a lot of time trying to convince an unmotivated customer to buy.

Bottom line: consider pending events that your prospective customers will have, and capitalize on those time frames with special offerings. Explain how your marketing and sales offerings will capitalize on these events.

Is Your Customer Politically Open to Using Your Offering?

Sometimes you can have everything in place, the deal looks like it can't help but close, and then it falls apart. It is almost as though an unknown power stepped in and killed the deal. That is probably just what happened. Many companies have divisions and subsidiaries they are supposed to buy from, and if it is discovered that they are planning to buy from another company, someone might try to kill the deal. Why would a company buy from you if it has a subsidiary that offers the same product at a comparable price? It won't! Not because the product isn't right. Not because you did a poor job of selling. Simply because there's a company policy that says all purchases must first be made from an internal business partner. Period. For a retail sale, the fact that the product is not made in the USA might be enough to kill the deal because the customer only buys American goods. It is becoming more common for compliance with fair-trade or energy-efficient policy to be requirements.

Bottom line: try to find out about these barriers to your sale early and save yourself a lot of frustration and anguish later.

The Nine Stages of Selling

Baking bread can be a frustrating and exhilarating experience at the same time. It is an art form, and anyone who has failed in the bread-baking process can verify this. You must follow specific steps in precisely the right order and at precisely the right time. Reordering the sequence or trying to rush the process invariably leads to a poor-tasting loaf.

The sales process is similar; a sale will go through specific stages before the deal is either lost or won. Performing these steps out of sequence usually leads to poor results, and skipping a step usually leads to disappointment. Plan your sales strategy to include moving the customer from one stage to another, with minicloses along the way, rather than trying to rush the customer directly to the final close. Here are the stages of selling that you should follow.

The Suspect Stage—Stage 1

You hear from a friend of a friend that perhaps Company A needs your products or services. This is the first stage in the process, and it occurs in conjunction with proactive marketing efforts, such as a direct-mail letter, an email campaign, an advertisement, or telemarketing phone calls.

When you don't know much (or anything) about a potential customer but you think it might need your services, it is considered a suspect or a lead. There really is no close at this stage other than to make initial contact with a person on the staff at Company A to verify that he has a need for your services. Once direct contact has happened, you are into the next stage.

The Prospect Stage—Stage 2

If you make contact with a representative of Company A and learn that the company does indeed need the services you provide, you have just received confirmation and can move Company A to the prospect stage.

Confirmation from a prospect can come in the form of a response to your direct-mail campaign, a request for additional information, a website visitor response page, an email response, or a phone call made by your salesperson. The miniclose for this stage is to have Company A agree to an in-depth discussion about its business needs (Stage 3), which will include the involved decision-making personnel from their side.

WATCH OUT!

You do lose control when you use distributors or reps to perform the sales function for your company. Major problems can erupt when distributors make commitments or promises on your behalf that you cannot or will not fulfill. Be sure that you define up front each party's responsibilities to avoid such politically and financially costly situations.

The Entrée Stage—Stage 3

In the entrée stage, you have your first major interaction with the prospect. This discussion can occur in person, over the phone, by email, by online chat, on a web conference, or by other means depending on geography and industry. For complex technical sales in particular, personal contact is often required to understand the customer's needs and to explain your company's complex products and features.

This stage enables you to learn more about the prospect's need for your services and how they plan to make their decision, and to lay the groundwork for the next stage—not your needs, but the company's needs! If you use an online meeting service, make sure that the process is outrageously simple for them to implement, or you could lose them and your credibility at the same time.

Here you qualify Company A regarding money, time frame, and the decision-making process. Your miniclose for this stage is to have the prospect detail for you exactly what it intends to buy: how many, for what purpose, when, at what price, and so on. The more you know about Company A's plans and needs, the better you can convince the company that you are the best choice for this project. It is not uncommon to leave this stage with more questions than answers, which leads to the next stage: discovery.

STREET SMARTS

Start tracking and forecasting a potential sale as soon as you receive an inquiry from the prospect. Monitor the prospect's progression through each of the sales stages so that you can better gauge when the actual sales transaction may occur. This gives you a consistent way of forecasting sales and predicting cash inflow.

The Discovery Stage—Stage 4

In some cases, there is no need for a discovery stage because the prospect has already indicated his or her needs to you and has requested a specific proposal or quote. When this happens, you can proceed to Stage 5, the proposal. There is often a bidders conference date included with the request for proposal so that vendors can get additional information.

When you are dealing with larger companies, you might find that you have to speak and meet with several people before you are prepared to send a proposal. Often this is because many layers of management need to give their okay; this might mean many presentations, meetings, or visits just to be sure you've spoken with everyone involved in deciding which vendor company the prospect should use. When you're meeting with numerous people, you have to repeat the process of learning and addressing each person's needs and concerns.

If you haven't already collected this kind of information in Stage 3, determine the prospect's situation, what might be the best way to improve the situation, the budget, how quickly the work must be done, and the most important factors in picking a supplier. Armed with this information, you can write a proposal that shows you truly understand the company's situation and that you can provide a solution that's also within the budget.

AT THE WEBSITE

A sample Consignment Agreement is included at the website as document 10-01.

The Proposal Stage—Stage 5

Once the prospect's needs are defined and the overall sales criteria are established, it's time for you to present your best solution: your proposal. This can be in the form of a formal written document or bid for a more complex sale, or you can simply tell the prospect that the shoes cost $75 retail. In either case, you now explain to the prospect that you recommend a specific solution to improving his situation, and the cost is such and such.

For a large-dollar sale, this stage might involve a formal presentation to a committee of people. Make sure that you don't have food stains on your shirt or blouse and ensure that you present the benefits that the customer receives from buying from you; don't concentrate as much on your particular offering's features.

Trial Close Stage—Stage 6

In the trial close stage, you ask the prospect for his reaction to your proposal, and whether he plans to buy from you. Don't assume that a no is final at this stage. A no might only suggest that you missed something or that the prospect needs time to consider your proposal. Ask for some feedback on your proposal and just listen to what the prospect tells you. You might be surprised by what you hear. Adjust your proposal accordingly and promptly resubmit it. Feedback at this stage is your friend if the prospect doesn't accept your proposal as you presented it. Notice how thoroughly doing your homework in the discovery stage will keep you from having nasty and unwelcome surprises when you trial close.

Some sellers who are trying to sell to retailers will get over their commitment resistance by offering their product on a *consignment* basis. In this way, the retailer does not pay for the seller's product until it actually sells. If the product does not sell, then the seller simply takes back the product. The only risk to the retailer with this arrangement is the energy the retailer puts behind selling the product and the floor space used up in offering the product. The seller runs the risk of the retailer selling the product and then not paying the seller for the sold products, but this is more of a credit issue than a sales one.

DEFINITION

A **consignment** sale is one where the retailer does not pay the vendor for products displayed until it actually sells.

The Budget Stage—Stage 7

Many large purchases must go through an approval process at the prospect's company, which can take anywhere from a few hours to a few months. This stage is often nerve-wracking for both the vendor and your primary contact who wants your offering. It requires patience. Unfortunately, all you can do is maintain regular contact with the prospect to ensure that nothing stops the positive momentum toward the sale.

For a small purchase, this stage can be as simple as running a credit card through the machine and getting an approval code.

The Close Stage—Stage 8

The close stage is when you ask for the order and either get it, find out what is missing, or simply lose the deal to another company. All prior miniclosing stages lead to this point. If you read the situation properly and had valid information and a qualified customer, you stand an excellent chance of winning the sale. This is an exciting and scary time for both you and your customer, particularly when the sale involves a large amount of money.

If you get a no or a maybe, return to the discovery stage to find out if you missed some crucial bit of information or if the prospect's needs have changed. Then go through the rest of the stages again. If the customer meets the five qualification criteria, you should either get or lose the deal (or at least know what has to happen to obtain the order).

AT THE WEBSITE

The website contains a sample Sales Contact (document 10-02), a sample Purchase Order (document 10-03), a sample Bill of Sale (document 10-04), and a sample Limited Warranty (document 10-05).

The Postsale Stage—Stage 9

You've made the sale and the deal is closed. Everyone should be happy, right? Nope. You are still not finished. You need to check back with the decision maker to make sure things are going okay. Make sure the customer is still happy with her choice and isn't having doubts or misgivings. This is an often overlooked and critically important stage to building long-term customer satisfaction. This is also a great time to ask your new customer for referrals to others who might be able to use your offering. A solid referral from a happy customer is golden and cannot be overvalued. Don't be afraid to ask for the referral, as many new customers want to share their success with others.

It is much less expensive to keep an existing customer than to find a new one. Your most valuable assets are your repeat customers. Guard them jealously. To ensure that they continue to be repeat customers, check back with them after each sale to confirm that they are pleased with their purchase. Show your customers that you have their best interests at heart and weren't just after the sale.

Sales Stage Timing for a Commodity and Complex Sale

The sales stages timing varies, depending on whether you're selling a CD player at a department store, a fancy house on a lake, or a $500,000 computer system to a Fortune 100 company. Although the timing of each stage might differ, the same sequence must be followed or the sales process gets disrupted. What will change is the time frame associated with each stage. Adding all of the individual time frames together will give you the overall sale cycle.

For example, the department store sale cycle looks something like this: the customer walks up and asks for assistance. This incorporates Stages 1 through 3. You ask what the customer is looking for and how much he or she wants to spend. There are Stages 4 and 5. You find a unit that you think matches the customer's needs and ask whether he or she wants to buy; end Stage 6. The credit card is processed, and the customer signs the receipt and walks out the door with the DVD player (Stages 7 and 8). Asking the customer how the DVD player is working out the next time he or she comes into the store covers Stage 9. Notice that this overall sale cycle might take only a few minutes, and many of the sale stages (Stages 1 to 3, for example) combine during different phases of the sale cycle.

The sales process becomes more complex when working with high-dollar items or services, and the cycle will become extended compared to the retail example, but the sequence of the sale stages are the same. For example, trying to charge a consumer's credit card for a DVD player before he or she has agreed on a unit would definitely not work in the retail scenario. In the same way, placing Stages 7 (Budget) and 8 (Close) before the other stages would not work when selling a $500,000 computer system.

Here is how you can use this staged approach for your plan: Map out your total sales cycle from beginning to end, match phases of the cycle against the sales stages, and then set realistic expectations for the miniclose of each stage. Once you have this all clearly in mind, then write down a description of the ideal salesperson for each stage, allowing overlap when applicable, to get an idea of how many salespersons and of what skill levels will be needed to make your sales process work.

ED'S LESSONS LEARNED

Adding up the total time for all stages gives you an idea as to how long it will be from the time you make your first viable prospect contacts to the time when you can expect to cash your first customer payment checks. Make sure that you include normal payment terms in determining the time frame. This is an important time frame to know, since it has a direct bearing on the amount of cash you must have on hand to fund operations until customer payments start coming in to help to defray expenses.

Matching Personnel to the Sales Requirements

Salespeople are important to the success of your organization. Just as important, in many cases, are the people who support the sales team, such as the customer service personnel. In your new business, salespeople will be responsible for finding new customers, but support people who are solely responsible for servicing and selling to existing customers.

These two tasks—finding new customers and supporting existing customers—require different skills and temperaments. The support person has a relatively routine job that revolves around meeting delivery deadlines and keeping account information up-to-date, but the new business salesperson must create new opportunities on a daily basis, which can be chaotic, frustrating, and highly uncertain. Where the service person responds to customer requests, the new customer salesperson must proactively engage unknown prospects with the intent of making them a customer. I have found that these two very different tasks are best handled by people with a temperament matched to each process. Put the service-minded person—someone used to answering the phone instead of calling—into a new sales development role, and she will usually not succeed. Put the new customer salesperson in a support role and he will be bored and likely not respond well to customer requests. We all have our skills, and matching the right skills to the right type of job is one of your important management functions.

Running an efficient and productive sales team requires focused attention, enthusiasm, and commitment. But you don't have to do it all by yourself. Hire the help you need to keep sales coming in, especially for those more routine tasks that take up time and keep you from talking to new customers.

Picking the Right Sales Channels

There are a couple of different ways that you can reach new customers. You can use independent distributors or representatives to give your company rapid exposure, you can build a direct sales force that deals directly with customers, and you can coordinate an online presence that brings business your way. Each approach has pluses and minuses.

Distributors and Independent Representatives as Sales Agents

Distributors and *independent representatives* are organizations with established salespeople or individual salesmen who have established customers that match your ideal customer profile. The distributor will typically purchase large quantities of your product, for a major discount, and then sell it directly to its customers. You get to deal with a single major customer instead of lots of smaller customers, and you can enter a marketplace more quickly through an established distributor because it already has a sales relationship that you would have to develop. As stated earlier, the distributor will want a discount off of the sale price for stocking the inventory, selling the product, and taking on the collection risk. In many cases, this is a discount well spent from your side, as long as the distributor is credible, trustworthy, and financially stable. The independent representative also has customer relationships that can generate sales pretty quickly, for a commission, but he or she does not stock any inventory. Instead, he or she generates orders for your company that your company then must fulfill. As you can see, distributors and independent representatives serve similar customer relationship functions, but in a very different way.

DEFINITION

A **distributor** is a company that purchases products from you at a reduced rate, keeps them in inventory, and then sells those products to its own customers. Distributors are commonly used in commodity industries. Distributors make money on the difference between the sale price to the customer and the cost of the materials as purchased from your company.

An **independent representative** is a person or company who sells your products on your behalf. Reps do not purchase or inventory the products; they only sell them to their existing customer base. They make their money on the agreed-upon commissions earned from successful sales. You are responsible for credit collections. The commissions to an independent representative are lower than those to a distributor.

The advantage of using a distributor or sales representative channel is that you instantly get an in-place sales force of hundreds or thousands selling your product or service. A major disadvantage is that it is more difficult to get customer feedback because you have a barrier between your company and the customer. Plus, remember that the representative will deal with the customer on your behalf, and if the representative does a poor job it will definitely reflect poorly on you. Also remember that the representative or distributor will be representing other offerings in addition to yours, so you should always be looking for ways to keep your offering front and center in their thinking.

STREET SMARTS

It is critical to get customer feedback so you can accurately determine whether you should be developing new products or services. It is also important for you to know how happy your customers are with the distributor, rep, and your company. Can you trust the distributor or rep to make that assessment for you? In most cases the answer is no, so you have to decide whether the additional sales from using this independent organization are worth giving up direct contact with customers. You might have to add personnel to your staff to acquire the information you would otherwise have obtained from your sales force.

Using distributors usually means you need to hire fewer salespeople to cover a comparable geographic area or market, allowing you to keep your personnel costs down. However, you need to interview and qualify distributors as carefully as you would a full-time salesperson because that distributor is going to represent your company. Get references from other companies that they represent and check them out. Remember that you will be giving up a percentage of each sales dollar to pay for the sales rep or distributor fees. That percentage will vary between industries and product lines. In essence, you are trading a fixed cost (your own employees) for a variable cost (the commissions).

STREET SMARTS

Perhaps a blending of in-house personnel, distribution, and representation selling is the right approach for your company. You might sell directly in your local geography, but choose to use distribution or representation in more remote locations such as other states or in foreign countries.

Should You Use Your Own Sales Force?

When is it time to set up your own direct sales force instead of selling through distributors or independent representation? As with many of these questions, the consultant's answer applies: It depends.

Here are a few things to consider when making the choice:

- The overhead associated with an internal sales force is substantially higher than with distributors. The overhead cost eats into your profits every month, whether the sales are there to support it or not.
- You gain more control over your customer relations when you sell direct. This provides you with better management information for decision making, particularly with respect to new product or service development.
- Selling direct does not take advantage of established customer relationships your distributors may already have in place. Your direct sales force must generate its own contacts and relationships, and that can take time to develop, delaying sales in the process.

- An internal sales force that you can fully train is often better able to handle sales of highly complex technical products and services. Your own personnel will be less likely to make promises your company can't keep.
- Some companies start out selling direct on a smaller scale until they determine the proper sales strategy for their offering. They then approach larger distributors about introducing their products or services through the distributor's sales channels. This hands-on approach to selling also gives you critical feedback early on about how your offering does or does not fulfill the intended customer need.

You have more control and flexibility with an internal sales force, but you also have higher expenses. You need to examine your marketing strategy to decide which approach makes more sense for you right now.

Selling Services Instead of Products

Services provide an interesting sales situation. The customer is buying something of value, but when the project is completed, he or she might not have anything tangible to show for it. For example, the result of your service contract with a customer might appear in the form of a new organization structure, better-trained staff, a new logo design, or a piece of software. These items clearly contribute to the company's success, but they are less obvious to the customer.

You have to keep in mind that services solve people's problems through your expertise and experience. Because the customer doesn't receive a tangible product, she must walk away with the belief that she benefited from using your service. Benefit-oriented selling is an important part of any sale, but it is critical when selling services such as consulting or training. I sometimes provide a paper summary of work performed so that the customer has something tangible in her hand to refer to later when looking at how much she paid me for services rendered.

AT THE WEBSITE

A sample Project Management Agreement is included on the website as document 10-06.

Clearly defining the *scope of work* from the beginning is critical to success when selling services instead of products. Because the customer might not have something tangible at the end of a project, it is important to clearly define at what point the project is complete. More than one company has been left holding the bag after submitting an invoice that the customer feels is too high or refuses to pay because he doesn't feel he got his money's worth. The company providing the service may have done everything it was asked to do, but if the customer thought he was getting something else, it becomes difficult to get paid.

DEFINITION

The agreement on exactly what services will be provided to a customer is the **scope of work.** For instance, the scope of a project might be writing a press release. Mailing out all the press releases is beyond the scope of work, meaning that activity was not included as part of the agreement and would have to be contracted and paid for separately.

To avoid such frustrating situations, the best policy is to get adequate detail, in writing, about what is to be done. In your proposal to your potential customer, state clearly what you are offering to do and at what price. Make the desired outcome as specific as possible, preferably including the delivery of a final report, or services provided and benefits received by the customer. If there is nothing tangible you can provide to signify the completion of a contract, such as with service contracts and warranties, set a specific time period during which your services are offered. After that period is up, your services stop.

Always avoid vague, ambiguous statements such as "We will edit the new corporate brochure until the customer is happy with it," which is a time bomb just waiting to explode. What happens after you've done 25 versions of the customer's brochure and she just can't make up her mind? Is your work done, or do you have to continue to edit and reedit until the customer is satisfied? If you state exactly how many rewrites you provide as part of the agreement, the answer is probably no—you don't have to keep working forever. But with vague statements, you will probably never get paid if the customer is not satisfied.

AT THE WEBSITE

The website has a sample Software Licensing Agreement (document 10-07) and a sample Contract Drafting Checklist (document 10-08).

Instead, use carefully chosen and specific wording, such as the wording I used for a sales brochure design proposal: "We will provide an initial concept design followed by a professionally created first draft and then a second final version of the brochure that includes any requested customer changes from the first draft." Establish *milestones*—that is, measurable targets or events that demonstrate that you have provided the service and reached your objective.

DEFINITION

Milestones are important target dates or goals that help you track how well you're performing against your long-term business goals. Milestones can indicate that a specific percentage of a project has been completed, once a certain step has been taken, or they can provide evidence that the project is completed. These smaller percentage completion divisions enable you to bill for portions of the project as they are completed, instead of having to wait until the entire project is finished.

Advance payments (retainers) or down payments are always good, but they are particularly valuable with contracts for service. People have convenient memories, and a little cash on the line always seems to keep the memory of both parties active and on track. It's also an excellent sales qualifier. Any prospect who is unwilling to pay a percentage of the total project cost is not someone you want to do business with. A charge of 25 percent is the suggested minimum, and 35 to 50 percent is not out of the question. Submit invoices regularly (determined in agreement with your customer) if you are billing on an hourly basis so you receive regular payments for your work.

For Your Plan

When writing the section of your plan dealing with sales, make sure that at a minimum you cover the following points:

- Explain whether your offering's sales process will be routine (commoditylike) or more complex (such as a technical sale).
- Define, preferably by sale stage, the required skill set and preferred personality type of your sales force (whether direct or through distribution) and why the direct/distribution decision was made. How will these people be trained, not only in your sales process but also on your offering?

- Describe how customer service issues will be handled once the deal is closed and the next stage of business relationship begins.
- Explain the timeline for a typical sale and the various actions taken, and list a miniclose objective at each stage of the sales cycle.
- Explain the compensation and commission structure that you plan to use for paying your sales force. Include as much information as you can about travel and other sales-related expenses.
- Outline the sales tracking and management procedures you intend to follow and how that procedure will be used for sales reporting to upper management, the board of directors, and investors.
- Explain how leads will be generated, how they will be followed up, and how lead tracking will be coordinated. Will your company use telemarketing, and if so, how? Will a website or social media be used for prospect generation? If so, explain how.
- Lay out a contingency plan to cover the possibility that the initial sales plan does not work and how the determination will be made to move to your Plan B.
- Outline how your sales force will implement the marketing plan's strategy for winning sales from competitors. Deals will have to be won on more than your smile, nice as it may be.

The Least You Need to Know

- Sales are necessary for a company to survive. If you are not highly sales motivated, then you should hire someone who is.
- Selling is a process, not an end in itself, and all company personnel must be sales-service oriented, even if they are not officially in sales.
- Every sale must go through nine specific and sequential stages before the customer is willing to make a commitment. The timing (cycle) will vary with industry and sale type, but the general stage sequence will be followed.
- Closing and selling are not the same thing, and professional selling creates satisfied customers and referrals while manipulation creates resentment.

- Don't waste time on a prospect who doesn't meet the specified qualification criteria.
- Selling direct or through distributors or sales representatives fills different needs and requires different approaches.

Using Social Media as a Powerful Marketing and Sales Tool

Chapter **11**

In This Chapter

- Learning how websites and social media are related
- Understanding how online tools create awareness
- Appreciating the importance of awareness for new businesses
- Creating intersections between your website and online media tools
- Relating traditional marketing tools with social media

"Your phone hasn't stopped buzzing since we sat down. What's going on?" asked Gordon.

"I posted a reply yesterday on my blog and it appears to have gone viral," replied Jim, typing something on his iPhone.

"Viral? Is that good? Sounds serious, even for the internet."

"Yeah. I think it is good," said Jim. "Some guy has been having trouble getting a license here in the city and I told him about a special program designed for businesses just like his. It turns out that there are a lot more like him out there than I expected. All of a sudden, all of these people want me to work with them to help get them into this special program."

"That all sounds like good news. What is the problem?"

"I don't know if this program has a limit on the number of applicants, how long it is being offered, and whether the city is equipped for handling the type of activity that could be coming their way."

"These people are willing to pay you to help them get into this program so they can get their license, right?" Jim nodded. "Well then, I suggest you help as many of them as you can. Try to get them to tell each other online how well you worked out for them, and keep an eye out for similar programs in other cities. What if this same need exists in Milwaukee, Detroit, Minneapolis, and Seattle? This could be your new business." Jim nodded as he typed away. "Hey, rock star! You're buying the coffee."

More than one person has become famous—or, less attractively, infamous—overnight due to the internet. People now have the ability to communicate quickly and easily, from anywhere, thanks to modern technology allowing the natural need to socialize to flourish in cyberspace. Services like Facebook, Twitter, and YouTube have membership numbers that are exploding, and by some reports more people in England have Facebook accounts than have dogs. Many attribute the downfall of Middle East governments during the spring of 2011 to the ubiquitous availability of Twitter and Facebook on mobile devices, which allowed the reporting of on-the-street reality to compare with formal reports coming out from the governments.

This social media trend is something that business owners ignore at their own peril; a new business is missing a great opportunity for creating exposure about its offerings if social networking is not part of its initial and evolving marketing strategy. This chapter is intended to create a framework for understanding how the internet and social media affect your plan development as well as your first year of operation. This is an exciting new area of marketing opportunity that can only be covered superficially in a few pages, but by the time you get to the end of the chapter you will have a solid idea of how to go about getting yourself online and into the social consciousness.

Viewing the Online and Social Media Landscape

Facebook, Twitter, and other social media tools offer powerful sales and marketing opportunities like never before. Any new business plan should consider how these services can help to create brand image as well as attract new customers, perhaps making social media a centerpiece of their new business sales and marketing plan. This section provides an overview of various social media types and provides a framework for understanding how social media fits into the new internet-connected and highly mobile consumer marketing landscape.

Differentiating Websites from Social Media

It can be confusing trying to differentiate the various online technologies from each other and to understand their applications. We covered some online business model approaches in Chapter 4 that helped us find possible business opportunities by integrating technology with information to solve a customer's need.

When you think about online technology from a business perspective, it makes sense to approach it from the usefulness perspective and not simply based on its "coolness." What can technology do to help your business sell something or help the consumer buy? Understanding why a consumer would benefit from using a technology goes a long way toward helping you understand why and how you should use it.

WATCH OUT!

The most frightening complaint from a customer is one that you never hear about. They may tell you that their experience was great or not say anything at all, perhaps to not hurt your feelings, only to later tell everyone else how bad it was. This is a double-trouble situation in that you never learn that you have a problem—which means that you will likely not fix it—and prospective customers are being told negative things about your company that will surely cost you future business. None of us likes to hear negative things said about us or our company, but not hearing the negatives can cost you dearly and you wouldn't even know why.

The essential difference between a conventional website and social media is that social media is conversational and member driven, whereas the standard website is still driven by the website owner. A standard website does a wonderful job of offering pages of information about a company and its personnel, detailed specifications about products, step-by-step instructions about how to repair or order something, and even processes by which bills can be paid or shipments managed. All of this is pretty amazing in its own right, and I think these capabilities are becoming a minimum offering from companies. Instead of online information and ordering being possible, it is becoming expected. Those that have not taken steps to implement this capability will find themselves seriously behind their competition. But this is still not where social media comes into the picture.

Understanding the Uniqueness of Social Media

The social media phenomenon starts to enter into the picture when prospective customers start communicating with each other about something that your company does or does not do, such as not being able to process orders online. User support groups have existed for a very long time, but they were previously limited by the ease with which they could communicate with one another. They historically might have sent a periodic printed newsletter to all members and perhaps had an annual conference, but this is the Stone Age compared to what contemporary social media offers.

In today's world, customers might complain by email to each other about how annoying something is and then forward those emails to hundreds of their colleagues and friends, who then forward it on to hundreds of their contacts. Get the picture? With social media word can spread very quickly, sort of like a disease, which explains why this type of online spread is called *going viral*. A *listserv* is a service that allows people to store a large number of email addresses in a single location. When one email is sent to a central address on the listserv, it will be sent to the whole listserv. Those folks can then respond to the listserv or forward the email to others. You can see how a single email can spread pretty quickly.

DEFINITION

An **online community** is a grouping of online users who share a common interest and communicate with each other about that common interest. A **listserv** is a central listing of email users; sending a single email to the listserv central address will prompt an email to be sent to all members of the listserv. **Going viral** happens when something generated online is shared with a large number of users in a very short time frame (sort of like an online contagion).

People who are members of a given listserv have something in common, which leads us to the concept of an *online community*, a group of people who share some type of common interest. This interest could be about a company, a social cause, a movie star, or people interested in Einstein. The listserv allows members of this community to easily share information with other like-minded persons. Ideally, each member contributes uniquely such that the evolution of the group's purpose is continually being furthered. Google Groups is a commonly used listserv, but it may have a membership limit based on the version you use.

Notice that social media involves a conversation between parties who have some common interest, such as your company. They communicate with each other about aspects of your company that they believe are important; the comments might be positive or negative. The key is that this is not a conversation that you control but, if you think about it, a conversation that you would like to be a part of. Why? Positive aspects are those you want to promote to your current and prospective customers. If the opinions are negative, then you want to know about them before they cost you current or future customers.

STREET SMARTS

Getting customers to talk with each other is an important goal of marketing because this is where customer referrals come from. Positive referrals come from positive customers, so the more you can do to create positive discussion about your company and its offerings, the better off you are. Customers are going to talk. Social media offers the capability for them to do it in such a way that you can listen in and respond. That is pretty powerful in its own right.

It is common wisdom that the more you can involve a prospect with the sale process, the more likely you are to get the person to buy. Think about the automobile dealer's weekend test drive offer, the free food sample, or the free subscription to a magazine. These sale approaches were not adopted by accident—they were adopted because the vendors realized that if someone used the offering and felt like she had a personal investment of some kind with the offering, she would be more likely to buy it. In today's age of personalized, customized offerings, consumer input is even more important. Here is where online technologies simply blow traditional marketing out the window. Modern technology allows a much higher level of timely interaction with customers than ever before.

Let's take a look at how a traditional marketing program was implemented. A group of people from the marketing and sales departments would get together inside a building with a bunch of research data about prospective consumers. This data might have been obtained through surveys, focus groups, prior purchaser demographics, or other conventional research methods. These people then take their best guess as to what their target group of consumers will react to and then implement a *broadcast* media campaign based on those guesses. Broadcast means that the message is sent out on TV, in a magazine ad, or by direct mail, and the sender then waits for a response.

Notice that consumer feedback related to the broadcast communication is very limited in this traditional marketing scenario. If the ad does not get the desired response, the marketing people try something else until they get the desired result or run out of money. This is a simplified explanation of traditional broadcast marketing.

DEFINITION

Broadcast communication is a one-way transmission of information between the sender and the receiver of the broadcast, with no immediate feedback from the receiver to the sender. A conventional newspaper ad is a typical broadcast advertising approach because the advertiser really has no accurate idea about the number of people who read an ad and how they respond after reading it.

Social media sticks the consumer directly into the process and turns the broadcast approach to consumer relations on its ear. Instead of the company being in control of communication, consumers decide what is important. In fact, trying to control the communication will likely backfire on the company. Not responding to serious customer service issues will likely backfire on the company. Treating serious complaints in a cavalier way will likely backfire on the company. Remember, your customers will have these conversations with or without you, so you might as well find out what they are saying.

STREET SMARTS

Facebook and Twitter were primarily intended for personal use, but the services are adapting themselves for more commercial purposes. LinkedIn is intended for professional audiences to talk with other professionals in a more commercially useful way. Link your Facebook, Twitter, and LinkedIn accounts and make sure that all contain information about your website, which is the hub of your company's communication and ordering process.

Let's assume that someone on Facebook has 500 or more *friends* who themselves have hundreds of friends. I might post a comment to my *Wall* about having had a great dinner last night at a local restaurant. My friends read the comment and can respond to the posting or forward the comment to their friends. If all these friends are in the prospective customer group of the restaurant, potentially thousands of qualified prospective customers could know within a short period of time that I had a great experience. If those people in turn eat at the restaurant and then tell their Facebook friends about how great the experience was, the restaurant has obtained wonderful word-of-mouth referrals that we all dream about. Notice that no formal advertising was used in this scenario.

Remember that customer referrals are the most valuable form of marketing you can create, and social media is built to naturally make this happen. Oh, by the way, if a customer has a bad experience at the restaurant, it can all work against the restaurant in the same way. If the restaurant owner can tune into that conversation and respond credibly to the initial complaint, it could make dedication to the restaurant even stronger. Most importantly, the owner will know about the problem and be able to take steps to correct it in a visible way.

DEFINITION

Facebook is an online social media site that allows a central person to connect with selected persons that Facebook calls **friends.** Facebook members post comments to their **Wall.** Friends can read the posting and can then reply—with all friends able to see the reply—or they can forward the posting to their friends. Hot topics can spread pretty quickly this way.

Mobile Technology and Social Media Are Linked

Mobile technology kicks social media possibilities into an entirely new stratosphere. Instead of only being able to communicate with your online community while sitting at your desk, which was already pretty cool, you can now communicate with them while shopping, sipping a hot beverage at a coffee shop, or sitting in your favorite restaurant. So what? A May 2011 Marketwatch.com article reported that Laila Shereen Sakr, a scholar from the University of Southern California, collected 100,000 Twitter *tweets* every five minutes during the spring 2011 Middle East unrest. From reading the tweets, each of which she described as a miniheadline of what was happening in different locations, she developed a feeling for what was happening in each country. Clearly people were following her writing because a Facebook page she wrote titled "Syrian Revolution" received over 175,000 *like* responses. That number represents only those who responded and not necessarily all of those who actually read it.

DEFINITION

Twitter enables users to communicate with each other as a group by sending a single message, called a **tweet.** The messages are short by design, under 140 characters, so they have to be direct.

A **like** response on Facebook means that the viewing person took the time to say that he or she approved of this posting.

A Social Media–Based Approach to Startup Marketing

There are entire books written about the use of social media, and I list a few in the sidebar if you want to get deeply into the subject. I am going to focus our attention here on what you should be doing to get your business started and successfully run during its first year of operation.

STREET SMARTS

There are some wonderful books out there that talk about social networking and media in detail. Two that I have found useful are *Secrets of Social Media Marketing* (Linden Publishing, 2008) by Paul Gillin and *Twitter Power: How to Dominate Your Market One Tweet at a Time* (Wiley, 2010) by Joel Comm. Gillin's books covers the relationship of conventional media to social media, and I would recommend it for a general view of the topic tied in with practical tips for use. Comm's book does a great job analyzing Twitter.

Setting Up Your Website and Domain Name

First, you will need a website. This used to be complicated but it is now pretty simple to reserve a website domain name, create email accounts associated with that name, and have a simple site created. My basic tip for you here is to reserve a domain name that is representative of your company. It looks unprofessional to have a website that is based on some other service such as AOL, and you should avoid creating a website that has a structure something like <yourname>.aol.com. You are going to spend time and money creating awareness of your company and brand and you don't want to repeat the process should you decide to leave AOL for another provider. Own your website domain name. I own edpaulson.com and can transfer it to any hosting company I choose and support it any way I want as long as it is paid for and active. There are many companies that will help you reserve a unique domain name, and it is inexpensive to do. Spend the time to get it right.

Once you have your domain name reserved, set up a few email addresses associated with it. These email accounts will look more professional because they will have a form that looks something like billk@yourdomainname.com instead of billk237@aol.com. It is easy to add email accounts to your domain when you start to add employees. This approach gives you centralized control over correspondences which you lose if workers continue to use their personal email account. My basic and most public email account is author@edpaulson.com because I want to reinforce that when someone sends me an email they are sending it to an author, me. I also have ed@edpaulson.com, sales@edpaulson.com, and info@edpaulson.com, but I don't really promote those because I would have to follow all of them. The more contact mechanisms you promote, the more time you have to invest in maintaining them. My clients know that The Paulson Group is a small consulting firm and that all correspondences come to me. There is no need for multiple email addresses. If I add employees, I add an email at the domain for each of them, as needed. Keep all of this as simple as possible at first and then expand capabilities as you add more people to handle them.

STREET SMARTS

Remember that nobody knows how big your company is from your website. Your new company can look as big as one in business for 20 years if your website presents you as such. Adding different email accounts such as info@, sales@, or service@ offer the appearance of many departments and people when you may actually be the one answering all three. Just remember that all of these email accounts will work against you if you do not stay on top of them.

At first, your website can provide only information: providing details about your company, products, services, employees, location, etc. This gets you out there on the internet. If your business idea is based on your website, then expect to spend some time and money creating the site that will be right for the needs of your customers. Refer to Chapter 4 for more information about online business models. Make sure that you build the site to address not only your needs today but to also address the needs that will show up later on as your business succeeds and evolves. Try not to lock yourself into a technology that has to be scrapped every time you want to add more capability.

Next you want to learn about *metatags* and *keywords* that are used by search engines to categorize your website content. For example, when a person types "korean restaurant chicago" into a search, the engine can easily pick out your restaurant as one that fits this search criteria because of the way you set up your metatags and keywords. Otherwise, you could get categorized under some other area that has nothing to do with your primary emphasis, which would do you little good. Google claims that it does not use metatags and instead reviews the content of the page, but there are some who believe that other engines such as Yahoo! and Ask still use them. You lose nothing by including them. Creating keywords will force you to focus on the primary topics people should associate when thinking about you and your company.

Considering that Google reviews the page content, doesn't it also make sense to ensure that keywords are included in the text so that Google can find the right connections for searches? Think about how many times you personally find a company by doing an online search and you will appreciate how important it is to have the right search terms associated with your company and offering.

DEFINITION

Metatags are places where hidden data is embedded in the pages of your website. **Keywords** are hidden words that tell a search engine where it should classify your web pages for future searches.

Your website becomes the information hub of your online company presence. Your overall marketing goal is to drive traffic to your sales and ordering entry points, which will likely be your website, email, and telephone. If consumers want to learn more about your offerings, they should be easily able to find it on your website. If they want to place an order, the procedure should be easily located on your website. If they need to talk to a manager, that person should be personally represented on the website. If they have a complaint, the process for registering that complaint should be clearly presented. People have come to expect a website when doing business with a company. The more useful you can make your website, the better it will serve your customers—which means the better it will serve you.

I think it is a good idea to also create a YouTube account where you can store video related to you, your company, and your offerings. Video has become an accepted form of communication and it is really effective for creating a personal connection with the viewer. Going back to the Korean restaurant, the owner might want to post a video tour of the restaurant to YouTube with a link at the website connecting visitors. They will watch it on the website, but it is hosted by YouTube. Let's say that the restaurant offers a special of the month. Wouldn't it be cool to have the owner introducing the monthly dinner special, explaining how personal it was to him because it was a family recipe passed down from his Korean grandmother? He might even include a video of him cooking the dish. The owner has the chance to develop a personalized relationship with his customers over the internet without ever meeting them face to face.

If you are a consumer-oriented products company, consider how valuable video can be to you regarding installation of your products. It is really difficult to create clear assembly instructions; coupling written instructions with an online video could save oodles of customer calls, complaints, or even returns. Just Google "product assembly video" to find any number of different samples of how these videos are used, often provided by YouTube.

One final word about reality is probably warranted here. Keep your focus on the goals of your first year in business: to gain customers, to create sales, and to move as quickly as possible to break even. This online world is constantly evolving, in some ways becoming more conceptually complex while also becoming simpler to implement from a technology perspective. Determine the basic steps that will offer the most reward in the short run, and then add to the complexity of your online presence as time and money allow. Your online presence will never be finished; expect it to be constantly evolving. But plan to get into the game from the beginning at some basic levels or you will be missing out on one of the most powerful and valuable awareness development and support tools available.

Creating Awareness of Your Website and Company

Creating awareness is a huge part of marketing, as discussed in Chapter 8, and social media can help you in this regard. Remember that the key to marketing is to have people remember you and your company when they think about a need that you can fill. A massage therapist will want to remind people of his unique treatment approaches such that when someone in his contact network is looking for a massage, that person will think of him. That person must then be able to easily find our therapist to book an appointment, which could all be handled by the website.

Creating awareness is where conventional advertising, public relations, public presentations, and other conventional marketing avenues have served well in the past, and will continue to serve. Social media adds new and efficient avenues for creating awareness.

STREET SMARTS

Owners of any type of business should plan to spend between 15 to 25 percent of their time working directly with customer-related activities. New company owners should spend even more time (50 percent or more) getting new customers in the door. Special emphasis should be placed on having regular, direct, often face-to-face contact with existing and prospective customers when it is productive to the sale process.

For new service companies that start out with a single employee (you), this can be really difficult to do because you only make money when doing billable work, which makes it difficult to focus on marketing and sales work. Social media can allow you to support marketing and sales activities after normal billable hours.

Assume that you belong to a group of 500 people who track a certain topic. Now assume that the most valuable comments you read originate from a specific member. You would typically click on that person's identification and request to become a member (or follower or friend) in his personal network, giving you access to all of his communications instead of just those associated with your special group. From following this person you will learn more about him and become more comfortable with his offerings and unique talents. Now suppose that you have a problem at work and you need someone with similar talents. Wouldn't it make sense to contact this person to see if he can help you out? He has shown a high level of subject matter competence, you have become familiar with him (almost to the point that you feel like you know him), and you have a problem to be solved. You should be working to become this highly thought-of person for your own prospective and regular customers. You want your social media activities to reinforce awareness, credibility, and trust with a large number of followers, expecting that when the time is right they will think of you.

Being online is mandatory for modern businesses and particularly important for new ones. Creating awareness is critical for a new business, and this is best done through word-of-mouth advertising. The goal of a new company marketing campaign is to create discussion between existing and prospective customers, such that those with experience refer new customers to your company. Social media provides the opportunity for creating this word-of-mouth advertising in rapid and uncontrollable ways as never before possible. Your website will be the hub of your online strategy, offering detailed information about your offerings, your personnel, your policies, and how to interact with your company for specific needs and situations. Your social media activities will help to create marketing mind share that will drive people toward your site when they are in need of your offerings.

For Your Plan

When preparing the operations portion of your plan, make sure that you consider the following points:

- Research and reserve the right domain name for your company.
- Register complementary identifications with various online media tools such as Facebook, Twitter, and YouTube.
- Diagram how these various tools will be used for various purposes in the first year and then in following years.

- Understand the personnel implications of implementing a social media networking strategy.
- Include funding for online services, technologies, and professional talent as part of your plan.

The Least You Need to Know

- Social media allows consumers to communicate easily around a common topic.
- Existing and prospective customers have connected supportively for decades, but social media tools make it instantaneous and widespread.
- Your website domain is the hub to your online marketing strategy, and new capabilities will be implemented in stages, continually evolving.
- To be effective in the online and social media space you will have to allocate your own time or that of one of your employees.

Finalizing Your Plan and Making a Decision

Part 3

The most comprehensive paper analysis in the world will not create change if no action is taken. In Part 2 you evaluated the marketplace and potential customers to make sure that if you build it, someone out there will buy it. Now it is time to evaluate the other business functions that must operate well for you to meet customer demands and make a profit.

The sales and marketing process is incredibly important, of that there is no doubt. But other business aspects are critical to your success, too, such as the ability to deliver what the sales process promised, making sure that money is available in the amounts and time frame needed, protecting yourself legally should anything unexpected jeopardize your business, and making a confident decision about whether to start the venture or not.

This part will help you to understand the reality of your startup's daily operation, estimate the amount of money you will need to start the business on a solid financial footing, find the money needed to get started, and decide on a legal structure that will protect you personally when dealing with the taxes or an irate customer. Finally, you will be presented with a process for deciding whether the business as planned is right for you. By the time you are finished with this part of the book, your business plan will be done. After that, as usual, it is up to you.

Chapter 12

Delivering On Your Business's Promises

In This Chapter

- Learning how operations affects your entire business
- Appreciating the difference between product and service companies
- Understanding personnel and efficiency
- Planning to automate
- Properly setting customer expectations

"You have got *to be kidding me," gasped Kendall as he viewed stacks of half-finished inventory on his manufacturing floor. "We can't ship any of this because of a 50-cent part?"*

His manufacturing manager, Brian, just stood there and hung his head.

"Okay," said Kendall, trying to calm himself down. "What happened and how can we make sure that this doesn't happen again?"

"Do you remember how a few weeks back we were celebrating those huge orders that Jill brought in?" Kendall nodded. "Well, what we didn't anticipate is that one of the specialty parts needed to fill the order has a 12-week lead time. We thought that they could accelerate our order and get it to us sooner. Well, they can ship them in 8 weeks instead of 12 as long as we paid a premium for the accelerated delivery."

"So the problem is what?" asked Kendall, still looking at the stacks of stuff and people standing around.

"Eight weeks is still two weeks out. We had all of this inventory waiting to be used, so we started building product just to get as far along as we could and to keep people busy, but now we are held up waiting for the part."

Kendall took a deep breath as he walked in circles a few times. "I promised Jill's customers that we would get these orders out on time and now you are telling me that we are going to be late by at least two weeks. Right?" Brian nodded. "Now I know why I have a stack of call notices on my desk from Jill. To summarize, it looks like I made a promise that we cannot keep, I have a lot of half-built inventory, and now I find out that they might cancel the order over a 50-cent part. Do you have any other good news for me?"

Trust is arguably one of the most valuable business traits any person or business can have. When a customer purchases a product or service from you, they expect that the promises made during the sales process will be fulfilled. After all, it is what you told them to expect, and they know that you will expect to be paid when all is done. That is just how credible businesses work.

Every business has some type of process that must be followed to move a customer from the early sales stage to invoicing after delivery. A little thinking up front can help you better understand the realistic implications involved with implementing the processes that will be needed to fulfill the commitments made during the sales process. This chapter will give you a solid starting point for not only understanding your future business operation, but also for estimating what it will cost you.

Relating Operations to Your Sales Promises

Think of *operations* as the process of fulfilling the commitments that you and your company make to customers. This may entail combining raw materials, labor, and manufacturing equipment into a finished good that is sold to meet a customer need. Or it could mean having nurses, a waiting room, and staging areas for a doctor's office so that patients are seen on time and with professionalism. Or it might mean having the right people with the right programming skills available to meet an immediate customer service requirement. How you fulfill your customer obligations will be as varied as the entrepreneurs who create the companies. What they all have in common is that to become and remain a successful business you will have to deliver on what you promised your customers.

DEFINITION

Operations is the overall process by which your company fulfills its promises to customers, vendors, employees, and other stakeholders.

I find that it really helps to create a high-level diagram that shows the various stages of the operations process. I start with the first customer contact and mentally walk through receiving the order, providing the offering, and eventually following up after the invoice is received. Each section of the diagram will eventually warrant its own more detailed picture, but a lot can be learned from this general chart.

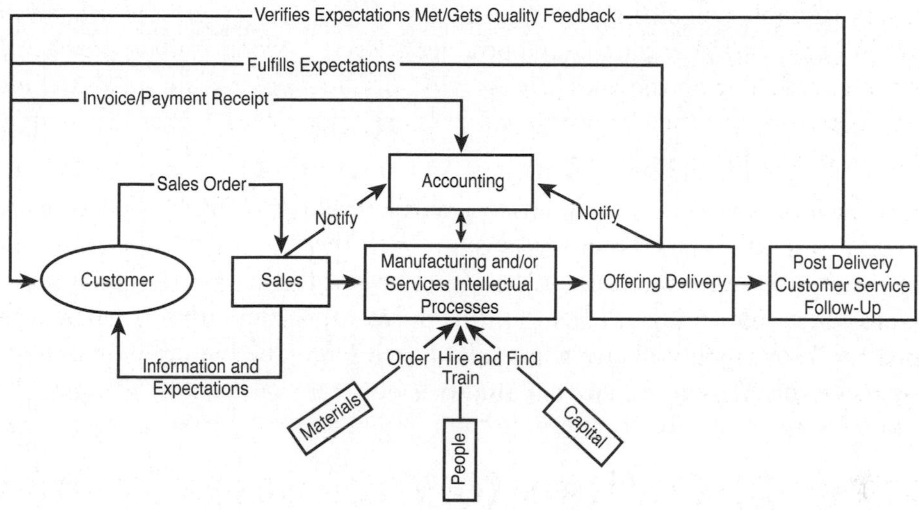

Operations diagram at a higher level.

Operations is really an interconnection of all other departments of your company. Starting from the left side of the diagram, we see that salespeople set expectations with customers, either by what they say or by the printed materials they provide. Customers then place the order, which is forwarded to accounting for administrative purposes and production so that they know what they have to deliver and when. Notice that production will have already put in place people, materials, and capital (money) so that the unique expertise associated with forming your offering can be applied. Accounting is also involved with recording what is happening in production and elsewhere in the company. The offering is eventually delivered, after which accounting invoices the customer in accordance with the sales agreement and then follows up with collections so that you get paid. Finally, somebody in your customer service group should follow up with the customer to determine the level of satisfaction with your product. This group might also ask for a referral to potential other customers and/or a follow-up order from what is hopefully a happy customer. Any break in this operational chain can create an unhappy customer, negatively impact cash flow, hamper future sales efforts, or all of the above. When a company has serious uncorrected problems in any of these areas for any length of time, its livelihood becomes jeopardized.

STREET SMARTS

You, as the overall manager of the company, have the responsibility to ensure that all these pieces are working together.

Certain aspects of your operation will be complex and always changing. Other aspects will be consistent and routine in nature. As an example of the more complex aspect is that each prospective sales situation is a little different from the next because no two customers are exactly the same, even though there may be similarities. A routine situation would be one such as entering sales order information into a computerized accounting system, which will be pretty standard from one order to the next. The more you know about the characteristics of each stage, the better you will be able to manage the reliability, efficiency, and cost of the overall process. The rest of this chapter looks at these important topics in more detail.

Matching People to Tasks for Efficiency and Savings

Your operation will involve a series of tasks that vary in complexity, and how you match people to tasks will impact the likelihood of their successful completion. I won't go into all of the theory here. Just accept that you will want to give the more complex tasks to your more experienced people and put your newest people on the simpler, more *routine* tasks. If you properly match the experience of the person to the complexity of the task, you will make the best use of your money and better ensure the reliability of your operational processes.

DEFINITION

Routine tasks or situations are those that are simple to understand and accomplish. Nonroutine tasks or situations are complicated to understand and complete.

Oh, and it will also save you money. Why? Think of it this way. Your most experienced people are often your most expensive and those most qualified to handle complicated tasks with the highest likelihood of completing them successfully. To have an experienced writer like Stephen King transcribing minutes from a meeting is a pretty inefficient use of his main talents. On the other hand, expecting a clerical assistant, fresh out of a community college office assistant program, to write a nationally acclaimed best-selling thriller is unrealistic. In this extreme case you would match the right person to the right job. Yes, that means that you should put King on the novel.

ED'S LESSONS LEARNED

There is always some aspect of an operation that is more critical than others. Critical in this context means that if it fails it can stop the entire process with catastrophic consequences. The 50-cent part in the story that started this chapter is a good example of a critical item. Collecting accounts receivable is a critical item. Creating sales is a critical item. But there are others in your process, too. For example, should your product not pass Underwriters Laboratories (UL) compliance testing with the Federal Communication Commission (FCC) regulations, it may never be eligible for purchase by a major customer or the government. When planning and running your business, always look for and pay special attention to those critical items that can put you out of business and create backup plans to protect yourself.

A service company's operation has places where the task routineness analysis can apply. If you look at a doctor's office, you see a blending of routine and nonroutine tasks and how they are delegated to the proper personnel. For example, taking temperature, blood pressure, and weight and performing other routine tasks are handled by a nurse, whereas the nonroutine tasks—the examination and diagnosis of each patient's unique symptoms—are performed by the doctor. The patient might be in the office for an hour, but the doctor might only be with the patient for 15 minutes. In this way, the doctor can see four patients in an hour instead of only one, which wouldn't be the case if she performed all the routine tasks and the patient illness diagnosis on her own.

Fairly routine tasks are those like order entry, bookkeeping, shipping, vendor delivery confirmation, making appointments, etc. Typical nonroutine tasks involve situations that are outside of the norm, such as major customer contract cancellation, major product reliability issues, legal problems, forming alliances between companies, presenting to investors, and the like.

It turns out the routineness is tied into not only the task to be accomplished but also the experience of the person assigned to the task. Everyone is new at some point, which means that they have little to no experience, which makes most of what they do new or nonroutine. But once they have done it a few times, they learn more about it and what before was confusing moves into being more familiar, or routine. Experience can move situations and tasks from nonroutine to routine, even though the complexity of the task or situation has not changed that much. Okay, enough theory.

Take the time to evaluate your operational diagram in light of the complexity of the included operational tasks. Now evaluate those tasks in light of the personnel skills required to complete those tasks—how many you will need to keep up with sales demands and the cost of each person—and you are on your way to an objective estimate of your personnel costs.

STREET SMARTS

The more times you do something, the more efficient you become at doing it. Increased efficiency usually translates into reduced costs and increased profits.

Comparing Operations for Product and Service Companies

Product and service companies have different operational characteristics. As a result, each type will require that you place emphasis in different ways, not only when planning but also when running the company. A product company can sell 100 units today and 900 units tomorrow, averaging 500 units over the two days. As a service company you cannot work 2 hours today and 28 hours tomorrow and average 15 billable hours over the two days (no matter how much coffee you drink). It is just not a physical possibility, which means that service businesses have to look for ways of managing hours as a limited resource, building that scarcity into the pricing and personnel decisions. Once a day of billable hours is over, as a service company, you can never get it back.

The two company types also differ in customer postsale perception reality. When customers buy a product, they walk away from the transaction with something tangible in their hands. They will receive a bill for the products and they will be able to look at the new car in the driveway and know what they are paying for. Services, on the other hand, disappear once they are completed. You may feel great while getting a massage, but 30 days later the memory will fade and there will be no physical reminder of having received it other than the invoice. For this reason, billing for services promptly after received and looking for ways to provide customers with some type of tangible evidence of having received the service is highly recommended.

It is common for service environments such as consulting to involve nonroutine situations. Customers don't usually call a consultant to help them solve a problem to which they already know the answer. They call a consultant because they have a problem that is strange to them and they want someone with experience to help them navigate the way forward.

On the other hand, providing a pedicure or a manicure is fairly routine, meaning that a lower employee experience level may be totally okay. The same may be true of someone who changes the oil in a car, given that this process is pretty standard and should not involve a lot of unknowns. Repairing a transmission would be a different story. Both are automobile related but involve very different skills from those doing the work.

ED'S LESSONS LEARNED

I have some friends who run a small business that specializes in custom injection plastic molding of very large parts. Once the process is set up, they might produce fewer than five parts for a customer. To handle these types of low volumes, they use a unique process methodology that streamlines the design and prototyping process in a reliable and efficient fashion. If they based their pricing model on large production costs, they would be out of business. They realize that their offering is unique and charge the premiums needed to cover the higher costs associated with a small production run environment, yet they also ensure that the customer does not get gouged.

Product businesses are based on a process that is relatively independent of the people performing the tasks; service businesses often get their work because the client wants a specific person performing the task. Product businesses rely on efficiency and reliability. Service businesses rely heavily on the expertise of the personnel. The jobs typically performed by service personnel are nonroutine in nature, meaning that each time the job is done it is potentially different from the next.

Here are a few general guidelines for understanding product and service companies:

> Product-based operations tend to be more routine in nature with mass volume efficiencies and consistency as the goal. Service-based businesses tend to be more time dependent because the overall project variations can fluctuate from one time a task is performed to the next. It is difficult to estimate the amount of time something will take if you have never done it before.
>
> Service-based businesses should look for a methodology that makes the nonroutine tasks more routine, allowing less skilled personnel to perform the tasks without compromising quality. More skilled people can then focus on the nonroutine aspects that more fully utilize their higher skill level.

Personal customer contact and relationships are critical to a service business (would you go to a doctor you didn't like?), whereas product performance and quality are critical in a product business (have you ever met the designer of your MP3 player?).

The similarity in developing product and service processes is that you always want to find the common tasks involved in each process. This commonality presents an opportunity for applying automated, money-saving strategies to this stage of the process. Of one thing you can be sure: you will never reach high production volumes if everything you produce is a custom act of creation. You must take this into account when establishing your offering prices.

Linking Purchasing, Production, and Marketing Forecasts

If you have ever worked in a product manufacturing environment that did everything by hand, you understand the importance of automating the purchasing and inventory processes. Manual processes work well when an operation is small, but once it starts to grow quickly, or involves many different products or locations, some type of systematic production management approach becomes mandatory. Without it, production errors will happen, costing money, time, and credibility.

The intricacies of managing a manufacturing floor are pretty complicated but the general concepts are really important, so bear with me as I give you a glimpse. Consider the following: you need to order parts from your vendors before you can build your product. This means that you must have quantity projections about the products to be built. In addition, each of the components that you include in your product has some delivery lead time requirement from the vendors. This lead time can be as short as overnight or as long as several months for a custom casting part. This means that before the components can be purchased, you must know how many you plan to build and by when, which means that you must know how many your sales and marketing people plan to sell. And more specialized parts are generally more difficult to find and more expensive to purchase. Remember poor Brian in the story at the beginning of the chapter?

The service equivalent of a specialized part is finding a person with the unique skill set needed to address your customer needs. You must hire a person with the required skills, hire a less capable person and train him to have the required skills, or train one of your internal personnel to have the proper skills. In any case, the lead time involved with getting the right person with the right skills must be considered. You even have a lead time involved if you already employ someone who has the proper skills. Why? Because if you are operating profitably, that person is already busy on another project and might have to finish it before he or she can start on the new one.

Oh, by the way, you also need to ensure that you have the financial means to purchase the components (or hire the personnel). Remember that there will be some lead time on your side between the time when you start building product to when it is in the customer's hands and you receive the payment. Before you flip out, take a look at Chapter 17 for techniques for correctly managing your cash flow.

How can you manage the critical gap between your sales forecast and your production and purchasing requirements? You can handle this gap in a rigorous, yet manual, manner at first, but as you succeed and your production volume grows, you will eventually wind up paying someone to develop custom software, or scour the industry for a software package that addresses your specific company needs. These packages are out there, but you might pay thousands of dollars finding the package that is right for you. They are generally referred to as *manufacturing requirements packages* (*MRPs*).

DEFINITION

A **manufacturing requirements package (MRP)** is a software system that integrates the various aspects of operations that relate to manufacturing of products. It may be custom designed for a specific application or a modified version of a standard package.

Is an MRP software package worth the initial investment? It depends on how large you plan to grow and how substantial your initial funding is. Paying a lot for the perfect production control software package when your company is first starting out could deplete your cash reserves to the point that you jeopardize critically important sales and marketing activities. Clearly not a good idea. But those with aspirations of growing a large manufacturing company want to take a hard look at automating with an MRP system early on in your company's life. At the least, start today setting up a paper tracking system that is easily adapted to an automated MRP system. If you don't and you do turn out to be successful, you will likely lose sales, customers, profits, and sleep as you deal with the intense demands that arise from rapid manufacturing growth. Make sure that you hitch your MRP wagon to a solid software product provider who will be around in the future to keep your software purchase reliable and contemporary.

In keeping with my "automate from the beginning" philosophy, I suggest that you train yourself to think of your company as a process. It starts with the sales lead to the order and continues through purchasing, production, shipping, receipt of the product by the customer, receipt of the payment check from the customer, to the final cashing of the check. Ultimately, it also includes generating the operational and financial reports on a periodic basis. The more clear you are on your needed processes, the easier it will be for you later on to automate it with an MRP system.

Maintaining Quality

Nothing will put you out of business faster than being a new company that gets a reputation for bad quality. Happy customer referrals are critical to the success of your business, and if you let the quality suffer, your referrals will become negative instead of positive. Ouch—then bye-bye!

I recently gave a speech to a group of quality professionals on the importance of instilling quality in small business environments. Here are a few of the high points from my talk for your consideration and application to your specific company and plan writing.

Know what you sell and what your customers buy. Make sure that you or someone you trust inspects the critical qualities that your customers expect from your product or service before your customers see your offering. This applies to both product and service companies. If your company offers massage services, get a massage by each of your massage personnel every now and then to ensure that they meet your standards. If you offer tax preparation services, have one of your senior people randomly spot-check the returns to ensure that they are accurate.

Never let your customers become your final product inspection team. Make sure your product or service meets your expectations before you let them see it. Customers never forget that you sold them deficient goods.

Don't overpromise and underdeliver. You can deliver exactly what all of your brochures promote and still have an unhappy customer if the customer was promised additional items that were not delivered. Overpromising happens when you make commitments to customers that you cannot fulfill; you get caught trying to impress a customer with all the stuff you can do, just like the big guys. You know that you have overpromised when you start cursing yourself on evenings and weekends as you do extra stuff for a customer that are not part of your normal offering. Even worse, you work like crazy to fulfill the unique promise, only to eventually disappoint the customer by not fulfilling the promise or by completing it late. If you had just promised what you could deliver, everyone would have been happier—assuming that you got the deal.

Try to underpromise and overdeliver. People rarely get upset when you deliver more to them than they expected for the same money. This is overdelivering, which is usually possible when you underpromise. It is a completely natural tendency in a sales situation to promise the customer anything just to get the order. The problem is that you are going to have to deliver on those promises. Try to promise what you can definitely deliver and keep a little extra as a secret, so that you can deliver something to the customer that is over and above what was ordered—and for the same money. Underpromise and overdeliver is a surefire way to keep customers happy. Work to promote open communication between sales and operations personnel so they tend more toward cooperation than antagonism. When these relationships become toxic, the entire organization can suffer along with your sales and quality.

Personally spot-check the products or services before they leave your business, and let everyone know that you do it. This tends to keep employees on their toes and keeps you informed about your offering's ongoing quality level. Perhaps you should set up some type of financial incentive system that is tied to acceptable quality levels.

ED'S LESSONS LEARNED

Cisco Systems, the communications products manufacturer, has set up annual surveys of both customers and employees as a way of gauging satisfaction. Employees are paid a bonus or raise based on the results of their respective quality surveys. In typical Cisco fashion, they automated the survey process to make it simple and fast. Perhaps there are a few lessons here for your company as well.

Work with customers up front to establish their expectations. This is particularly true for service agreements, or you can find yourself working for a client forever, with the best of intentions, not getting paid for it, and still having an unsatisfied customer even though you delivered what you thought the customer wanted. For example: "My company agrees to supply your company with a draft of the document, circulate the draft to the client for comments, and then incorporate those comments into the final draft." Notice how only one level of revision is included in this agreement; this means you do not waste time and resources endlessly revising your work.

Define specific, concrete expectations, and do not leave them general. General (not recommended): "To deliver a product or service to the customer's satisfaction." Concrete (recommended): "To deliver a product that meets the specifications as outlined on product specification sheet 01-A, dated 09/27/2007."

For Your Plan

When preparing the operations portion of your plan, make sure that you consider the following points:

- Make sure that you understand the routine and nonroutine aspects of your offering and adjust your operation and personnel accordingly. This approach helps to ensure higher quality and avoids wasteful personnel spending.
- Spell out how and where you intend to perform your manufacturing and operation activities.
- Estimate the product and labor costs associated with your offerings, taking into account the cost decreases that typically come from higher volume and more experience. This information is critically important to setting your prices and maintaining healthy profit margins.
- Present any labor- or skill-related issues that directly affect operations process.
- Explain how you intend to define and maintain an appropriate level of quality for your intended customer audience.
- Present a flow chart of the operational process from order receipt until after the offering is received by the customer. Specify the critical components, skills, or operational steps associated with your operation environment and how you plan to address these important concerns.

- It is common for the operations plan to present the details associated with lead generation, order receipt, processing, invoicing, and collections. They are all part of the operation process associated with a healthy business. You might also include the sales and marketing related items in those sections.
- Include an explanation of how you intend to finance and create new offerings, whether service or product oriented. At some point, a new offering must come along to take the place of the ones you initially offer, and it is good to present some thought in this regard.

The Least You Need to Know

- You must understand how your company creates and delivers its offerings, and then ensure that the quality that makes you successful is an integral part of the process.
- Understand the routine and nonroutine aspects of your business, and assign appropriately skilled personnel accordingly.
- Play your operational processes from the beginning with an eye toward eventually automating them as much and as soon as possible.
- Map out your production process and specify the personnel skills, raw materials, space, time, and equipment needed at each step of the process.
- Underpromise and overdeliver.
- Know the relationship between the time needed to produce your offering and when and how your customers buy.
- Spot-check quality yourself, and never let your customers do your final quality inspection.

Estimating Your Startup Financial Requirements

Chapter 13

In This Chapter

- Appreciating the basic accounting principles
- Comparing cash and accrual accounting methods
- Reviewing balance sheets and income statements
- Understanding cumulative cash flow analysis and the importance of break-even

Jake, who lived in Tulsa, was in Chicago for a business seminar and was excited about seeing his friend, Dan. They had worked on cars together in high school and now each owned their own auto-repair businesses. It was great to talk about business; they shared the same problems and could be honest with each other because they were not competitors. Dan's business was in its fifth year of operation. Jake started his about two years ago and was clearly not making it. Things were tough, and this seminar was his last shot at turning things around before he had to bag it and get a real job.

"I don't understand," said Dan. "You're a great mechanic and you love working with people. What's wrong with your business that you aren't making ends meet?"

Jake looked out the window and back at Dan. "Good question. I'm busy as all get-out and often have to turn business away, but at the end of the year, my accountant tells me I don't have enough money to pay myself what I need. Something's wrong, and if it doesn't get fixed soon, I go back to work for the dealership."

"What is your percentage profit margin?" was Dan's initial question. "And how does your pricing compare with the competition in town?"

"I have the lowest prices around," said Jake proudly. "I dropped our prices 20 percent last year, and that was when things really cut loose. We're doing more work than ever, and my sales are twice what they were last year. I even had to add space to my garage to handle the new business."

Dan smiled and then looked Jake squarely in the eye. "High sales and profits do not always go hand in hand. If you can't keep your profit margins where they need to be, you're in trouble. What's your percentage profit margin?"

"I don't know," replied Jake. "I let my accountant take care of all that financial stuff for me. I do cars; he does numbers. I just tell him what I want our prices to be and he takes it from there. That's what I pay him for."

"So he makes your financial decisions?" Dan asked. "What does he know about the car business? Does he care if you don't make money? You really don't review your financial statements more than once a year? I have a bad feeling that you're a great mechanic who never made the transition to being a business manager. Let's get a copy of your financial statements and compare them to mine. I bet we can get an idea of where things are going wrong. Your business means too much to you to let it go under due to bad pricing and financial decisions."

Jake nodded somberly, silently hoping that Dan would buy lunch. He started to realize that just looking at sales instead of the whole business might have hurt his dream of independence. This time, he would stay awake during the seminar's financial analysis segment.

Like Jake, most business owners treat accounting as a necessary evil. I understand that attitude completely because I did the same thing. And because I did not treat the accounting aspects of managing my company seriously, I made a few major financial decisions based on bad information, much to my regret. I now strongly believe in the value of accurate accounting, and I encourage you to learn from my mistakes.

This chapter won't make an accountant or bookkeeper out of you. Relax. It will, however, introduce you to important accounting terms and methods so that you will learn enough to manage an accountant in a way that is valuable to your own business situation. Remember that your accountant works for you, not the other way around. Get him involved early so that he understands your needs, but remember that *you* inherit the financial impact of your decisions, not your accountant.

It is important to remember that your books have to be right for tax accounting purposes, but they also have to provide you with the information you need to make solid business management decisions.

Accounting 101

The purpose of the highly structured world of accounting is to provide business managers and others with the information they need to manage a business or evaluate their investments. Accounting is how business keeps score, and, just like keeping score in baseball, there are rules and procedures that have to be followed to accurately reflect the results of the field action. The structured formats allow others to understand your financial situation in the same way which is really important when talking to bankers and investors.

STREET SMARTS

If you're publishing financial information for use outside of your company, you need to consider an additional set of special accounting rules (called GAAP, or Generally Accepted Accounting Principles) when you prepare your financial statements. For managing a business, however, you only need to make sure your accounting system makes sense to you and to your financial advisers. Most software packages will handle the bookkeeping part of things. Your accountant can help you set up the procedures that keep you GAAP compliant without a lot of complexity.

You need to accumulate information that is timely, reliable, and useful, and you don't want to take valuable time away from making money. Fortunately, there are several software packages on the market that make accounting a much simpler task than ever before. Talk to other business owners about the accounting software that they use to give you an idea of which one will be right for you. I have had very good luck with QuickBooks over the years and have found that the package evolves from one version to the next, making it more valuable to me with each revision.

The following sections provide some basic accounting concepts so that you can understand the considerations involved in not only creating your plan financials, but also for setting up and maintaining your accounting systems. Time spent up front planning and developing good accounting procedures can save you countless hours of frustration down the road. Plus, it will show your potential investors that you intend to handle their investment money with care.

Accounting Periods

Accounting periods are periods of time, such as months, quarters, or years. Keeping records by accounting periods allows a company's financial reports to be compared from one time frame to another. It's a good idea to review your company's performance on a regular basis so you can become aware of potential problems, such as running out of cash, higher product or fixed costs, or lower sales figures, before it's too late. Watching how your financial condition changes from one period to the next provides important trend information that tells you early on if you are doing better or worse than before.

To file your tax returns, you have to determine in what month you want your year to end, called the fiscal year, so you can report your profit or loss for that year. Most small companies use a calendar fiscal year (January to December).

I suggest that you review your financial performance on a monthly basis and report to your investors based on an agreed-upon interval, usually quarterly or annually. If things are happening quickly within the company—such as rapid growth or decline, or operational change—then you should review the statements more often. When you look at the quarterly statements, try to measure your progress toward long-term goals. It's always good to know where your sales are coming from and how your money is being spent, and if you are moving in the direction you planned.

Recording Sales Revenue and Expenses

Assume that your client pays you today for work you intend to perform in 60 days. Let's take a look at whether you should declare that customer payment as *sales revenue*. (In other words, can you spend the money today knowing you won't have to give it back, or should you wait?)

DEFINITION

Sales revenue is the first item on your income statement and represents the total amount of sales that your company earned during the accounting period. This means that you substantially completed the work *and* expect to be paid for it.

You should not record a transaction as sales revenue unless you have a formal or informal agreement between you and the customer, *and* you have a reasonable expectation that the customer will pay you as agreed. When you receive payment from a customer for work that hasn't been completed yet, you need to record that payment as unearned income until the work is done. When the earning process is complete, you can record the transaction as sales revenue. If the customer can cancel his order, then the money really hasn't been earned yet, has it? You are essentially holding the money for him until you complete the work. In short, if you haven't finished earning the money by meeting all the terms of your contract with the customer, you shouldn't consider the revenue from those sales as truly yours. Many businesses hedge on this requirement and eventually get themselves into cash trouble when the orders get cancelled and the customer wants the money back. Treat unearned income as a refundable deposit until you do the work to earn it. Then it is yours!

If you use the *cash basis* of accounting, everything you receive from sales is considered revenue when it is received, and all expenses are recorded when paid. If you use the *accrual basis* of accounting to track your business, transactions are recorded when commitments are made, even though no cash may have changed hands. More than likely you will report your taxes using the cash method and monitor your daily operation using accrual accounting methods, especially if your business involves credit or inventory.

WATCH OUT!

Beware simultaneously tracking part of your business on cash basis and part on accrual. This can get very confusing when reading financial statements. And it is guaranteed to make your banker question the validity of the rest of the numbers. But if you use the cash basis of accounting and you use or offer credit, you must make a nearly obsessive commitment to tracking what your customers owe you along with when and how they pay. Or, simply use the accrual basis of accounting. All this accounting stuff is important and interesting, but your business success starts and ends with creating sales, collecting customer debts, and enabling your company to pay its bills. Never lose your emphasis on creating sales and collecting customer payments, no matter what accounting procedures you use.

Any business will have to spend money to stay in business; these payments are called *expenses.* Typical expenses include rent, utilities, salaries, and the purchase of materials that are needed to manufacture what the business will eventually sell to generate revenue. Taxes are also an expense, as you already know. *Net income* is what is left over when all expenses are subtracted from all revenues. Accounting procedures try to match the timing of when revenue is earned with the timing of the expenses needed to earn that revenue. This is done by recording them in the same accounting period if possible, which is much easier to do with accrual accounting. Matching is desirable because it allows you to better determine how successful you were at earning revenue for the money spent. You want to always be working on making sure that your revenues are greater than your expenses, or you will be spending more money than you are earning—a recipe for going out of business if it continues for very long.

DEFINITION

Expenses are payments that you make to keep the business running, such as utilities, salaries, parts for products you will sell, and rent.

Net income is the amount of money left over after *all* expenses have been deducted from the sales revenue figure.

Comparing the Cash and Accrual Accounting Methods

Business transactions are pretty simple to track if you receive payment from customers at the time of sale, do not manufacture anything, and pay cash for all of your expenses. This type of business is basically a cash-in, cash-out type of operation, and accounting records can be maintained accurately using the cash basis of accounting. What happens when you offer credit to your customers or use credit to purchase things that you sell to customers? Things start to get complicated because the process of earning a sale was completed when the product was sold (or service provided) and the revenue should be recorded as earned income. The timing for receiving payment is something else completely and tied into whether you offered credit, not into whether you completed the work. The accrual basis of accounting allows you to track your revenue and expenses based on the commitments that were made instead of when cash was received or spent. As soon as you offer credit, use credit, or involve manufacturing in your business, you will most likely have to start using the accrual basis of accounting. Beware that accrual accounting might report handsome profits while you have no cash in the bank to pay suppliers, because all sales show up as revenue and accounts receivable (money owed you by customers), even though your customers haven't actually paid you any cash yet if they purchased from you on credit.

This is a great topic to discuss with your accountant in detail once you are up and running so you understand the implications associated with this important transaction recording difference. For purposes of preparing a business plan, your level of understanding does not have to be that detailed.

ED'S LESSONS LEARNED

My primarily service-oriented company runs on the accrual basis for management and tracking purposes, but files taxes using the cash basis. I usually recognize the sales revenue at the time of invoice generation, track my accounts receivable, and monitor my balance sheet cash account like a hawk. I found that tracking only cash transactions while also providing credit payment terms to customers became too confusing. It impaired my credit collections and did not give an accurate assessment of my company when I ran my financial reports.

The following table summarizes the advantages and disadvantages of cash basis and accrual basis accounting.

Cash vs. Accrual Accounting

Cash Basis Advantages	Accrual Basis Advantages
Relatively simple to use	Provides a conceptually more correct picture of the results of your business operations if not compared to cash
Understandable to anyone who has balanced a checkbook	Consistent with the way bigger companies report their financial results
Reports income when you have cash to pay the taxes	Required by the IRS if your business has inventory
	Simplifies accounting during change in ownership
	Makes reporting to outsiders (bankers, potential investors, and so on) more comprehensible because they are used to accrual basis statements
Cash Basis Disadvantages	**Accrual Basis Disadvantages**
Can distort the results of operations, possibly leading to bad business decisions	Can be costly and time-consuming
Not acceptable to the IRS if your business has inventory	Might not match reported income and cash availability
Not comparable to the way bigger companies report their financial concepts and their reported results	Requires some thought and expertise to understand
Complicates accounting during changes in ownership	
Can make your company's financial condition appear worse than it is if you offer credit terms to your customers	

Understanding Financial Statements

Financial statements aren't that hard to understand. Yes, even you can pick it up. Again, for business plan development purposes, you do not need to fully understand all aspects of the statements. But you will definitely improve your chances of selling your plan's financial projections and managing your business to success if you better understand financial statements. Why? Using financial statements effectively, along with a valid sales forecast, gives you a preview of good and bad times before they hit, so you can take proactive measures if necessary. Investors appreciate working with people who will take steps to protect their investment.

There are three basic financial statements: the income statement, balance sheet, and statement of cash flow. The income statement shows you the sales revenue, expense, and net income level of your company during a specific accounting period. The balance sheet shows you how much you own and how much you owe at a particular point in time, which is usually calculated at the end of a fiscal quarter and on the last day of the year. The statement of cash flow shows exactly how much cash you actually received and how much cash you spent on a periodic basis. You really need to watch your cash flow statement carefully, especially if you use accrual accounting. Your cash flow statement keeps you informed about how much money you actually have in your bank account to pay all your bills. Accounting transactions are stored in accounts, and each type of statement will have its own specific types of accounts. All of the accounts together are referred to as a *chart of accounts*. Many of these accounts are standard between companies, making the statements easier for others to understand.

The Income Statement

Your income statement (a.k.a., profit and loss statement, or P and L) tells you whether your business made or lost money during a specific accounting period such as a month, quarter, or year. All revenue is totaled and listed at the top, and then the expenses associated with making that revenue, not including federal and state taxes, is subtracted. The result is the *pretax profit* and, after taxes are paid, net income.

Expenses fall into two categories: cost of sales and operating (fixed) expenses. Cost of sales (also called the *cost of goods sold*, or *COGS*) are those directly related to producing your product or providing your service. These generally include the cost of raw materials, the cost of labor to run the machine that produced the widget you sold, and other expenses required to obtain or create the product or service. COGS will vary with sales volume and are often called *variable expenses* (sell nothing and COGS = $0). Fixed expenses do not change with sales volume (sell nothing and rent stays the same).

For example, assume that you sold a coffee mug for $5 and it cost you $3 to purchase it. The cost of sales is $3, which is what you paid for the mug. The *gross profit* calculation associated with this single mug's sale is revenue – cost of sales = gross profit, or $5 – $3 = $2 gross profit. The cost to your company of providing products for sale varies with the quantity sold, or is said to "vary with sales," so it is called a *variable expense.* The relationship of revenue, cost of sales, and gross profit explained in this paragraph is important enough for you to keep going over it until it makes sense.

Operating (fixed) expenses are those expenses associated with the daily stuff that keeps your business running. You still have some amount of these expenses regardless of how much you sell in a month. These include your salary, your rent payment, the cost of the electricity in your office, insurance, administrative salaries, commissions, and other similar costs of operating the company. Operating expenses are paid out of the gross profit.

DEFINITION

Pretax profit is the amount of money left over after all expenses, except for tax payments, have been deducted. **Cost of sales,** also called **cost of goods sold (COGS)** are **variable expenses** that change with sales volume level and include costs such as raw materials and labor. **Operating expenses,** or **fixed expenses,** are those expenses associated with running your company (salaries, rent, utilities, and so on).

Your **gross profit** is the amount of money left after you cover the cost of sales: gross profit = revenue – COGS. Out of gross profit, you pay your operating (also called fixed) expenses. Sorry for the jargon confusion, but I wanted you to see the various terms here first.

Now that I've given you an overview of what the income statement provides for you, take a look at one.

A Simplified Income Statement
Jackson Surveying—Income Statement
For Fiscal Year Ending December 31, 20XX
Income Statement

Item	**Dollar Amount**	**Description of Its Income Statement Function**
Sales	$250,000	All revenues
Cost of Sales (variable costs)	$95,000	Variable costs associated with the revenues
Gross Profit (Gross Margin)	$155,000	Sales - Cost of Sales
Operating (Fixed) Expenses:		All nonvariable expenses:
Salaries	$65,000	Usually administrative and executive salaries
Rent	$18,000	What you pay to keep your doors open
Marketing and Sales	$55,000	What it costs you to sell your offering
Total Other Expenses	$138,000	Total of All Other Expenses
Pre-Tax Profit	$17,000	Gross Profit - Total Other Expenses
Federal/State Taxes	$5,950	Taxes due on the Pre-Tax Profit
Net Income	$11,050	Pre-Tax Profit - Federal and State Taxes

A simple income statement.

Remember the earlier coverage of accrual and cash basis accounting? Look at the income statement that follows in the next section and notice how the relationship between expenses and revenues is linked directly to profit calculations. Unless the two are synchronized, there is no way to accurately determine if you made money during the time period that you're examining.

The Balance Sheet

Whereas an income statement reflects the flow of money in and out of a company during a specific time frame (as videotape records events over a period of time), the balance sheet shows how much a company owns (its assets) and how much it owes (its liabilities) at a specific point in time (a snapshot of how things are at a particular moment). When what is owed is subtracted from what is owned, the remainder is called *owner's equity*. Stated another way, the balance sheet is based on a fundamental equation of accounting: assets = liabilities + owner's equity.

Assets are those items of value that the company owns, such as cash in the bank account, accounts receivable, inventory, equipment, and property. Current assets are those that can be converted into cash within 12 months such as accounts receivable and inventory. Long-term assets are those that would typically take longer than 12 months to convert into cash, such as equipment, buildings, and land.

Liabilities are amounts that you owe. Typical liabilities include accounts payable, which reflects amounts you owe to suppliers, loans, credit cards, taxes, and other people or organizations. Short-term liabilities, which are paid back within 12 months, are also called *current liabilities*. Long-term liabilities include the portions of mortgages and equipment loans that are not due in the next 12 months.

Owner's equity is the portion of the balance sheet that displays what is left over when all liabilities are subtracted from all assets. Take what you own, subtract what you owe, and you are left with owner's equity. This is the number that you want to maximize over time because it indicates you are building value. The initial investment of your company stock and accumulated retained earnings are added together to calculate owner's equity.

The amount of net income (see the sample income statement earlier in this chapter) determined at the end of the year is added to an equity account named *retained earnings*. You add the current period's net income to the prior period's retained earnings to calculate the company's retained earnings at the end of the period in question. A negative retained earnings is often a flag for a company in financial trouble. If you think about it for a second, it will make sense to you. The only way that the retained earnings can become negative is if there are negative net income values added to it from the income statement, which means that the company lost money during the period that created the negative net income. Again, this concept is pretty important and worth spending some time thinking about. I also understand that I threw a lot at you in a few paragraphs, so find someone who knows this topic in more detail to teach you over time. It will eventually become second nature, but it can be confusing at first.

The following table is an example of how to organize your accounts in preparation for making your balance sheet.

Typical Balance Sheet Accounts

Assets	**Description**
Cash	Bank accounts, petty cash, investments.
Accounts Receivable	What other companies (customers) owe you on a credit basis, to be paid usually within 30 days.
Inventory	Raw materials, finished goods, products being built, retail merchandise, product manuals, and so on.
Fixed Assets	Land, buildings, machinery, office equipment, depreciation expense.
Liabilities	**Description**
Short-Term (Current)	Must be paid in less than 12 months. Includes accounts payable to suppliers, unpaid wages, taxes, credit card debt, short-term loans, and long-term notes with less than 12 months left on their term.
Long-Term	Due over a period that is longer than 12 months. Includes mortgages, equipment loans, bank loans, and other long-term financial obligations.
Owner's Equity	**Description**
Equity Equation	Owner's equity = assets – liabilities.
Capital Stock	Owned by shareholders. Includes common stock and preferred stock.
Retained Earnings	Current and cumulative prior years' net profits or losses as accumulated from prior- and current-year income statements.

STREET SMARTS

It is common for small business owners to manage their business so that they show a negative net income and, as a result, pay no taxes. Since privately owned companies do not have to face the scrutiny of the public investor marketplace, there is minimal pressure to show a positive net income. You can also take this approach with your business, but be prepared to answer some pretty tough questions if you ever need to present your negative income financial statements to outside investors, bankers, venture capitalists, or the IRS.

So here you are with accounts and numbers. Now look at the following figure to see how to put them together to create a balance sheet.

A Simplified Balance Statement Jackson Surveying—Balance Sheet Period Ending December 31, 20XX	
Current Assets	
Cash in Bank	$15,000
Accounts Receivable	$25,000
Inventory	$18,000
Other Current Assets	$7,000
Total Current Assets	$65,000
Fixed Assets	
Land and Building	$250,000
Machinery	$75,000
Office Equipment	$35,000
Accumulated Depreciation	($25,000
Total Fixed Assets	$335,000
Total Assets	**$400,000**
Current Liabilities	
Credit Cards	$3,000
Wages Payable	$9,500
Taxes Payable	$3,000
Line of Credit	$5,500
Accounts Payable	$4,500
Total Current Liabilities	$25,500
Long-Term Liabilities	
Mortgage Loan	$185,000
Machinery Loan	$55,000
Equipment Loan	$30,000
Total Long-Term Liabilities	$270,000
Total Liabilities	**$295,500**
Owner's Equity	
Common Stock	$45,000
Retained Earnings	$59,500
Total Owner's Equity	$104,500
Total Liabilities and Equity	**$400,000**

This simple balance sheet shows the format for organizing all your balance sheet accounts.

As your company grows, the numbers on your assets and liabilities and equity lines will grow larger because you'll be purchasing new equipment, increasing your accounts receivable because of higher sales, and (hopefully) improving your cash situation. Companies just starting out will typically have a small number on their assets and liabilities and equity lines. Focus on having a positive net income, which will create a positive and growing retained earnings, thereby increasing your owner's equity.

STREET SMARTS

The balance sheet is not as critical as the income statement and statement of cash flow when preparing the financials for a new business plan. Savvy investors know that your focus for the first year must be on creating sales, managing expenses, and collecting cash. Two of these three important focus areas are tracked on the income statement—sales and expenses. The cumulative cash flow statement presented later in this chapter is a modified income statement which tells you how much money you will need to get started. Focus your attention on the income/cash flow statement, because that is where investors will pay most of their attention.

With all of that said, please also understand that your focus will eventually have to shift to managing the balance sheet, or you could find yourself running out of cash just as your business starts to take off. This is usually after you make it successfully through your first year.

Once you are up and running, your balance sheet might not change drastically from week to week, but it is still a good idea to regularly review whether you are taking on more debt or increasing the equity of the company. Most financial software packages can easily provide you with a balance sheet and income statement whenever you want to look at it. Always make sure you know if you are looking at an accrual or cash basis report, and watch your cash and accounts receivable like a hawk.

Cash Flow Analysis

There is a statement of cash flow which can be your most important financial statement once you are up and running, because it tells you how you are managing your cash. Never forget that cash is as important as air for your business. Period. Although tracking your assets and liabilities is important over the long term, when you're just starting out, a key challenge is keeping more cash coming in than is going out. But, because we are now preparing your plan to get your business started, the statement of cash flow is less important.

The cumulative cash flow statement is a very important statement at this stage. It represents your best guess at a series of monthly income statements assuming a cash basis of accounting, but it will include another line underneath the net income (loss) line. This additional line is named "cumulative cash" and represents the cash totals either received by the company over the period in question (when the company is making money) or the amount of money required by the company to keep running during the months when it is operating at a loss. It is specifically designed for analyzing the early months of a company's operation, which will usually involve 12 to 24 months. The figure on the next page gives you an example of a cumulative cash flow analysis for a new company, starting from three months before its grand opening up through its first year of postlaunch operation. Remember that this represents nothing more than a best guess at this stage.

Referring to the cumulative cash flow analysis, you can see that the company will need to spend $19,000 before it even opens its doors. It will then lose money in its early months through July of the year listed. Assume that the company opened its doors in January. If you add up all of the negative net incomes (losses) from January through July, you get a grand total loss of $49,092. This figure means that you must have at least $49,092 on hand before you start your business to cover what you predict to be the total amount of loss before you begin to make some money in August. August is called your "break-even" month because it is when you sell enough of your offering to create enough gross profit to cover your fixed expenses.

The break-even dollar sales value can (and should) be translated into a unit sales level by dividing the break-even sales revenue number by the average sales revenue per unit sold. This number tells you the number of units you have to sell at an average price to generate enough gross profit to pay your fixed expenses. Selling more than the break-even level means that you are making money. Below that sales volume level means that you are writing a check every month to cover your fixed expenses. To me, this sounds like a pretty important number (and initial target) to know.

	October	November	December	Grand Opening January	February	March	April	May	June	July	August	September	October	November	December	20xx Total
Startup Expenses																
Licensing		$ 2,000														
Plan Preparation	$ 3,000															
Legal Expenses		$ 2,000														
Build Out			$ 10,000													
Deposits		$ 2,000														
Revenues																
Product Sales				$ 1,200	$ 1,560	$ 2,028	$ 2,636	$ 3,427	$ 4,456	$ 5,792	$ 7,530	$ 9,789	$ 12,725	$ 16,543	$ 21,506	$ 89,192
Services				$ 300	$ 390	$ 507	$ 659	$ 857	$ 1,114	$ 1,448	$ 1,882	$ 2,447	$ 3,181	$ 4,136	$ 5,376	$ 22,298
Net Revenues				$ 1,500	$ 1,950	$ 2,535	$ 3,296	$ 4,284	$ 5,569	$ 7,240	$ 9,412	$ 12,236	$ 15,907	$ 20,679	$ 26,882	$ 111,490
Cost of Sales																
Product Cost				$ 300	$ 390	$ 507	$ 659	$ 857	$ 1,114	$ 1,448	$ 1,882	$ 2,447	$ 3,181	$ 4,136	$ 5,376	$ 22,298
Services Cost				$ 45	$ 59	$ 76	$ 99	$ 129	$ 167	$ 217	$ 282	$ 367	$ 477	$ 620	$ 806	$ 3,345
Total Cost of Sales				$ 345	$ 449	$ 583	$ 758	$ 985	$ 1,281	$ 1,665	$ 2,165	$ 2,814	$ 3,659	$ 4,756	$ 6,183	$ 25,643
Gross Profit				$ 1,155	$ 1,502	$ 1,952	$ 2,538	$ 3,299	$ 4,288	$ 5,575	$ 7,247	$ 9,422	$ 12,248	$ 15,923	$ 20,699	$ 85,848
Fixed Expenses																
Salaries				$ 3,500	$ 3,500	$ 3,500	$ 3,500	$ 3,500	$ 3,500	$ 3,500	$ 3,500	$ 3,500	$ 3,500	$ 3,500	$ 3,500	$ 42,000
Payroll Taxes and Benefits				$ 700	$ 700	$ 700	$ 700	$ 700	$ 700	$ 700	$ 700	$ 700	$ 700	$ 700	$ 700	$ 8,400
Advertising and Promotion				$ 300	$ 300	$ 300	$ 300	$ 300	$ 300	$ 300	$ 300	$ 300	$ 300	$ 300	$ 300	$ 3,600
Depreciation				$ 150	$ 150	$ 150	$ 150	$ 150	$ 150	$ 150	$ 150	$ 150	$ 150	$ 150	$ 150	$ 1,800
Supplies and Postage				$ 100	$ 100	$ 100	$ 100	$ 100	$ 100	$ 100	$ 100	$ 100	$ 100	$ 100	$ 100	$ 1,200
Professional Fees				$ 175	$ 175	$ 175	$ 175	$ 175	$ 175	$ 175	$ 175	$ 175	$ 175	$ 175	$ 175	$ 2,100
Printing				$ 200	$ 200	$ 200	$ 200	$ 200	$ 200	$ 200	$ 200	$ 200	$ 200	$ 200	$ 200	$ 2,400
Telephone				$ 250	$ 250	$ 250	$ 250	$ 250	$ 250	$ 250	$ 250	$ 250	$ 250	$ 250	$ 250	$ 3,000
Equipment Rental and Repair				$ 50	$ 50	$ 50	$ 50	$ 50	$ 50	$ 50	$ 50	$ 50	$ 50	$ 50	$ 50	$ 600
Travel				$ 650	$ 650	$ 650	$ 650	$ 650	$ 650	$ 650	$ 650	$ 650	$ 650	$ 650	$ 650	$ 7,800
Miscellaneous				$ 225	$ 225	$ 225	$ 225	$ 225	$ 225	$ 225	$ 225	$ 225	$ 225	$ 225	$ 225	$ 2,700
Office Rent				$ 900	$ 900	$ 900	$ 900	$ 900	$ 900	$ 900	$ 900	$ 900	$ 900	$ 900	$ 900	$ 10,800
Total Fixed Expenses				$ 7,200	$ 7,200	$ 7,200	$ 7,200	$ 7,200	$ 7,200	$ 7,200	$ 7,200	$ 7,200	$ 7,200	$ 7,200	$ 7,200	$ 86,400
Net Income (Loss) Before Tax				$ (6,045)	$ (5,699)	$ (5,248)	$ (4,662)	$ (3,901)	$ (2,912)	$ (1,625)	$ 47	$ 2,222	$ 5,048	$ 8,723	$ 13,499	$ (552)
Income Tax																
Federal Income Tax				$ -	$ -	$ -	$ -	$ -	$ -	$ -	$ -	$ -	$ -	$ -	$ -	$ -
State Income Tax				$ -	$ -	$ -	$ -	$ -	$ -	$ -	$ -	$ -	$ -	$ -	$ -	$ -
Net Income (Loss)	$ (3,000)	$ (6,000)	$ (10,000)	$ (6,045)	$ (5,699)	$ (5,248)	$ (4,662)	$ (3,901)	$ (2,912)	$ (1,625)	$ 47	$ 2,222	$ 5,048	$ 8,723	$ 13,499	$ (552)
Cumulative Cash	$ (3,000)	$ (9,000)	$ (19,000)	$ (25,045)	$ (30,744)	$ (35,992)	$ (40,654)	$ (44,555)	$ (47,467)	$ (49,092)	$ (49,044)	$ (46,823)	$ (41,774)	$ (33,052)	$ (19,552)	

Note: Tax deductions not included to simplify analysis.

A simple monthly cumulative cash flow analysis.

ED'S LESSONS LEARNED

Use the cumulative cash flow analysis as a starting point for your needed investment. It is not uncommon for sales to come in smaller and slower than you expected and expenses to be larger and quicker than you planned. For this reason you want to obtain more than the maximum cumulative cash flow number to protect yourself from running out of cash just as things start to take off. For the example, I would ideally shoot for between $70,000 and $90,000 in investment money and be thrilled if you only needed $49,092 of it before becoming profitable. It is like a cash cushion insurance policy.

Notice also that the company starts to make money pretty quickly after August such that between August and the end of November, enough positive net income is predicted ($29,539) that it pays a large portion of the initial $49,092 required to get you past July. After December, this company is really expected to generate substantial positive net income of around $13,500 per month which means that the whole initial investment will be repaid by February!

Notice that a few important goals present themselves with this cumulative cash flow analysis:

- You know the absolute minimum amount of money you have to have in savings or from investors to cover your company during those lean early months ($49,092). Notice that this does not cover your personal expenses, although you have a salary built in. That salary might be for others working with you for free. Sorry. It is common when first starting out.
- You know when you expect the company to start generating a positive net income (August).
- You know the sales level you have to reach to have the company generate a positive net income ($9,412).
- You know the approximate amount of product and services you have to sell to generate the needed break-even revenue ($7,530 and $1,882, respectively).
- You know that your fixed expenses are $7,200 per month and if there is a way you can reduce them, at first, you will more quickly get to a positive net income.

Are you starting to see how important this simple statement is to your overall business planning and analysis procedures? I hope so, because much of the work you do preparing the rest of your plan will wind up as numbers inserted into the cash flow analysis cells. Get to know the numbers you put in here, believe in their reality, and see how the numbers fall. If you can show that your plan makes you money within the required time frame and you have access to adequate cash to cover the initial losses, then you have come a long way toward determining if this business idea is right for you.

STREET SMARTS

You can and will spend cash in ways that will not show up as an expense on your income statement. For example, the interest that you pay on a loan is deductible as an expense, but the principle portion (the part that decreases the amount of outstanding loan balance) is not an expense. You pay cash to reduce the loan payment, but it does not become an expense. For this reason, the statement of cash flow will not match your income statement.

For Your Plan

The mathematics involved with creating a cumulative cash flow analysis are actually pretty simple, requiring only a basic understanding of Excel to put together. Much of your work in preparing a solid financial projection for your business idea will involve researching the figures that you will include in the spreadsheet analysis cells. As you get better at preparing business plans you may want to modify my recommended approach, but for now take the following steps:

- Start collecting the data you will need to create an income statement and balance sheet for your new business.
- Follow the standard format shown in this chapter for all statements that you include in your plan.
- Use a spreadsheet package like Microsoft Excel to prepare these statements so that you can tweak the numbers once the initial analysis is completed. This is usually a pretty interesting time and perhaps my favorite in the whole plan-writing process.
- Calculate the cumulative cash flow requirements at least until the break-even month to determine the total amount of cash you will need to cover the initial startup negative net income.

- Plan a cash safety net as part of your analysis and investor discussion. For example, if you think you need $27,000, based on cumulative cash flow analysis, then you might try to find $35,000 to $40,000 just in case you don't ramp up sales as quickly as expected. Life almost never turns out like we predict.
- Make sure that you spell out all of your assumptions and sources related to where the numbers contained in the cash flow analysis came from. Why? First, you will forget where you got them from if you don't write them down. Second, investors will want to know how you estimated future sales growth and associated expenses.

The Least You Need to Know

- Accounting is integral to business, and you should pay close attention to it from the start.
- Financial statements include an income statement, statement of cash flow, and balance sheet.
- The cumulative cash flow analysis is a specialized approach to determining the startup cash requirements of a new company.
- Accrual and cash basis accounting provide different profit and loss information for the same accounting period. Make sure that you always track your cash once up and running.
- Bookkeeping is basically clerical in nature once the procedures are set up; financial accounting involves analyzing financial performance and comparing current results with prior accounting periods.

Chapter

14

Finding the Money You Will Need

In This Chapter

- Understanding the relationship between risk and reward
- Match funding risk with company stage
- Understanding different funding methods
- Differentiating between debt and equity funding

Frank tossed his presentation materials on the front seat of his car, got in, and slammed the door. Taking a deep breath, he let back the seat and closed his eyes. A moment later his phone rang. Caller ID showed that it was his friend, Milton, a personal finance adviser.

"So how did the presentation go?" asked Milton.

"Not well. They were polite, but I could tell they really didn't get the idea and I'll be stunned if they buy in."

"Sorry. Did they give you any feedback on what they did or didn't like about the plan? I, for one, like the product's second-generation build-on idea a lot. What did they say about that?"

"Nothing," replied Frank with a slight pause. "I didn't tell them about it." He waited.

"Hmm. That was a good idea," sighed Milton with sarcasm in his voice. "Isn't that where you really expect your sales to increase and ramp you up enough to be a viable acquisition target?"

"Sure. It is. But it's also the most unique part of the plan, and I'm afraid someone will steal it if I'm not careful. Until I know they're interested, I'm not going to tell them about it."

Frank could imagine Milton shaking his head on the other end of the phone. "Look, Frank. Your plan just isn't very attractive without revealing that second development stage. No credible investor will give you money if they don't see that part. Sorry to be the one to break the bad news."

"So what you're telling me is I won't get the money if I don't reveal the second stage details. And my fear of revealing it may keep us from getting funded at all. Is that right?"

"Exactamundo," replied Milton enthusiastically. "If they can't see a way to make money off of their investment, why would they invest?"

Hard to believe that people aren't lining up to give this great idea of yours money, isn't it? Be honest. Why are they all being so negative about your company's prospects? You know your idea will work. You can feel it in your bones, and all you need is a few hundred thousand dollars of their money to turn it into reality. Sound familiar? Or am I the only person who has ever had the experience of asking people for business funding, only to walk away confused and a little disheartened by their response?

It might not be them. Sorry. Perhaps you have unrealistic expectations about how they should react given your specific situation. Perhaps they are reacting more objectively to the risk inherent in your venture than you are. Perhaps they're telling you something that is worth knowing about where your idea or plan falls short. Or, perhaps, they didn't understand the real financial, and possibly personal, benefit to them of getting involved because it wasn't explained to them very well.

This chapter helps you to sort through these points before you make those important investor presentations. It helps you anticipate the concerns that your investors may have so that you are better prepared to address them. The more credibly you can address their concerns, while infusing them with a strong dose of your own belief in the idea, the more likely you are to get the funding you are looking for.

Investors Give Money to Get Something Back

There is an unbreakable link between the level of risk that an investor sees in an investment and the amount of reward that he or she expects. Understanding the investor mindset is critical to making the right pitch. More about risk, uncertainty, opportunity cost, and risk tolerance can be found in Chapter 2.

If you want a gift, go to your wealthy Aunt Sally. Oh, don't have a wealthy aunt or uncle? Hmm. That is a little bit of a problem. Now we have to deal with people who have no personal interest in us at all and who will get involved as an investor only if the investment makes financial sense. Let's take a look at what "financial sense" means to a realistic investor.

People with money are always looking for ways for it to make more money while best ensuring that they don't lose the money along the way. Anyone who has lost money in a stock market decline (which is probably all of us) knows that there is no such thing as "a sure bet."

So why put your money in the stock market? Simple. Assume that your bank savings account is now offering an annual interest rate of just under 1 percent. Assume also that you can tie up your money in a certificate of deposit (CD) for several years and perhaps get around 4 percent. (This rate fluctuates all the time, so just use this for example purposes.) Finally, assume that the stock market, on average over the past few decades, has shown annual returns of around 10 percent. Let's look at what this means: no risk (savings) provides 1 percent. The CD is essentially risk free, but it ties up your money for a few years (which involves the risk that you might unexpectedly need it and have to pay a penalty when you cash in the CD); the CD pays 4 percent, which is 3 percent more than the savings account. The stock market, which we all know is highly volatile and may require tying up your money for years to get a decent return that might or might not happen, is estimated to pay 10 percent on a prospective average basis.

Are you starting to see a pattern here? Why would you put money into something that is riskier than a savings account if you get the same percentage rate of return (1 percent for the example here)? You can get 1 percent from the bank without taking any risk at all, so if you are taking the stock market risk of losing part or all of your money, then you are going to want to be compensated for taking that risk. How much more compensation? Therein lies the art of financial negotiations.

The Greater the Perceived Risk, the Greater the Required Return

The basic friction that exists in the investor/borrower conversation comes about as follows:

- Investors are ideally looking for huge returns on their investment, within a short period of time and with no risk.

- Borrowers ideally want to borrow as much money as possible for as long as they need it, to pay nothing to the lender for the use of that money, and have no obligation to repay it if the money is lost.

Disconnect! Notice that investors and borrowers come at the transaction from completely different points of view. The more seasoned you get at lending or borrowing, the better you get at resolving the friction points. There are also industry norms that help provide some ballpark within which typical financial transaction terms should fall. But realize that there is a huge gap between how investors and borrowers look at the lending/borrowing transaction.

Every investor has some level of risk tolerance. This means there is an investment risk and uncertainty level beyond which the investor will not provide money. Some have a higher level of risk tolerance (venture capitalists) and others a lower risk tolerance (bankers). To go to a banker with a high-risk investment, like your new startup company, is asking a low-risk tolerance investor to invest outside of her comfort zone. It is likely not going to happen, and if it does, she will be uncomfortable with having taken the risk and, likely, make you uncomfortable along with her. Plus, banks have legal constraints within which they must work to maintain their insurance and other protections that define the circumstances under which they can lend money.

You should now see that there is a fuzzy balancing act you must perform between assessing an investment's level of *perceived risk*, the risk tolerance of the lender or investor, and the rate of investment return that this investor will require. Keep reading, and you will learn methods for assessing and presenting the risk level while also making sure that you are talking to the right type of investor for your situation.

DEFINITION

Perceived risk is the risk assessment as seen through the eyes of the investor. You always want to be working to realistically assess and minimize the level of perceived risk.

Expect That Investors Will Check You Out

Remember that investors are always looking for all those hidden or obvious risks to their investment—where they could lose all or part of their money or simply not make on the investment what they could have made if they had put the money elsewhere.

Remember also that your new company has no track record of its own on which to stand. Its only track record is your track record and that of the other founder/owners.

For these two reasons, expect that investors are going to check you out personally along with your business idea. Actually, they may be checking you out more than your business idea. The idea won't be using their money—you will be.

STREET SMARTS

Always keep investor discussions professional and try not to make them personal. Once you make an investment decision personal for either you or the investor, you run the very high risk of turning a business relationship into a battle of personalities and egos. Keep it business all the way when talking money with investors, and it will work out better for both you and them. You may sometimes need to play the "personal card," but know that it has risks.

Keep your personal finances as clean as possible and try not to commit them if you don't have to. Just be aware that the early round of investors may want a piece of your personal wealth as protection for their investment. Notice that the more you guarantee, the lower the risk becomes to the investor, which should also lower their return on investment requirements. If someone wants high returns and a 100 percent guarantee of his funds within the agreed-upon time frame, then he has unrealistic expectations. Explain this in a businesslike manner, without making it personal, and you might be able to educate him along the way. You can't blame him for asking for the sky, can you? It doesn't mean that you have to give it to him.

Comparing Loan to Stock Sale Funding

Investors come in two basic flavors: those who provide *debt funding* and those who provide *equity funding*. Debt funding must be repaid and is a loan of some type. Equity funding means that an investor gave you money in exchange for stock (equity) in your company. Equity funding is usually paid back when the investor sells his stock either to the company, on the public market, or to another investor.

Notice that debt funding has risk associated with it in that the loan may not be paid back. But debt funding usually has required payments along the way that reduce the level of risk to the debt investor every month. Plus, don't be surprised if the lender asks you to *personally guarantee* the debt, which means that she can go after you personally if the debt is not repaid by the business. Personal guarantees are a last resort, for sure, but when you first start out it might be required, so be prepared.

DEFINITION

Debt funding must be repaid and is usually a loan of some type. **Equity funding** means that an investor gave you money in exchange for stock (equity) in your company. A **personal guarantee** is often required by lenders of all types as a way for them to go after you personally for debt repayment should the business cease to exist and default on a debt payment.

Equity, on the other hand, is a completely different story. An investor gives you his money today in exchange for a percentage of the outstanding shares of stock in your company. More than likely, the investor will not see a dime on that money until the stock is sold, unless your company pays a dividend, which is unusual for a small startup company since cash is always at a premium. If your company is an S-corporation, it is even possible that the investor may have to pay tax on income passed to him through the Schedule K-1 but not actually receive any cash. By the way, if the company goes under, the equity investment is lost, and the investor gets nothing in return for the initial risk. Now that is a sweet deal for an investor, isn't it? See Chapter 15 for a detailed discussion about the various business legal forms and their benefits.

For these reasons, equity investors will likely only give you money if they can see (and believe) that a relatively large return on their investment will come their way within a few years. This "relatively large" return is usually anywhere from between 5 and 30 times their investment per share. For example, if she pays you $1 per share of stock today, she will likely want to have a reasonable (not risk free) chance of receiving $5 or more in a few years or so. Venture capitalists will generally want to see a chance of 30 times or more from their investment within three to five years before they will take the plunge.

Equity investors will generally only invest in a startup with money that they can afford to lose, since they know the risk level is that much higher. It is not quite like gambling, but it is close. If you have someone close to you who intends to invest his total savings as an equity investment, make sure that person *completely* understands the risk associated with the investment and that he may never get it back. More than one friendship has been strained or lost when friends equity invest, thinking that it is a loan to be repaid, and then lose all their money when the company goes under.

Company Maturity Stages and Funding

The perceived risk level associated with you and your company will change over time with the success history of your company. In the early stages, the risk level is high since there is no historical track record from which to estimate future performance, which adds to perceived uncertainty. As that track record gets established, the perceived level of risk decreases—assuming that you create a good track record. This is why companies like IBM are perceived by customers and many investors as less risky than your startup. This section tracks the various stages that your company will go through and that stage's relationship to funding requirements and risk.

Seed Stage

As the name of this stage implies, your company is a kernel of an idea waiting to sprout. You have an idea and might have scratched a few notes on the back of a cocktail napkin, but that is really it. You may now need some money to free you up from your day job so that you can write a great business plan using the recommended steps outlined in this book. Those looking to develop a product-based business will likely create some type of prototype of the product at this stage. This could mean a mock-up of a website or a plastic model, or bread board, of a more complicated electronic product.

The uncertainty level here is high because you will be learning a lot about your idea, but the funding needs are likely pretty low. Many people fund this stage out of their own pockets or treat it as a part-time job, without pay, while they keep their regular job. This approach is particularly applicable to those looking to eventually break out of the "big house" of corporate America, as presented in Chapter 1. If your idea is complicated with national or international implications, then some people look for outside funding at this stage to just investigate the viability of the idea. These types of investors are out there, but they are pretty rare and will want a hefty return for taking the early highly uncertain risk.

Startup Stage

Plan and prototype in hand, you are now ready to start making your company a reality. You start to hire key people, set up an office, and create preproduction prototypes as opposed to the mockups from the seed stage. You have likely also beta tested your idea to see if actual customers are interested in what you have to offer. All of this information helps to convince investors that your idea and company are worth some more money. This is a typical time for venture capital firms to become interested in getting involved. Know that funding at this stage is critical, and it may take quite some time to find, so planning ahead is a good idea. Also know that you may need to ask for additional funding from the same people who funded you initially should you not achieve your initial projections, so you want to keep on good terms with these folks.

The uncertainty is still high, although not as high as with the seed stage, and the financing requirements are still relatively modest, although much greater than the seed stage. Many unknowns exist that can squash the entire deal, but you now have some management success that works in your favor. Keep the faith and keep asking for that money. If the idea and your team are as solid as you think, someone will buy in to your idea. Make sure that you conserve money as much as possible at this stage, since it is a waiting game in that you have to last, financially, until you get your first stage startup funding.

First Stage (Early Stage)

By this stage, you have a real company, with a real product and some real customers. You have bumped your head a few times, had some wins, and learned a lot along the way. Your plan has been adjusted from what you initially thought in the seed stage, and you are rapidly moving forward.

Uncertainty is substantially reduced when compared to the previous stages, but the funding amount needed has increased a lot because you must now add manufacturing personnel, inventory, advertising, sales force, and any number of other expensive capabilities. This is when you can viably make the case to the venture capital folks, assuming you have an idea that shows that type of large-industry merit. This is also a time when people around you will be seeing that you have something going that is working and want to get involved. Selling shares is now easier, and less expensive, than at any other time. See how reducing perceived risk works in your favor?

ED'S LESSONS LEARNED

The personal dynamics of first and second stage success can be pretty intoxicating. You may be the darling company that everyone wants a piece of and the talk of the town. People all over are asking you for a job, and they actually know your name. Keep your ego and aspirations in check. All this attention can get you believing that things are better than they are or that customers will now start sending you money in buckets just because you are you. It may all be true, and if so, great. If it is not true, and you believe it to be true, you and your company could be in for a rude, and possibly catastrophic, wakeup call. It is the adrenaline rush of the first and second stage that keeps Silicon Valley startup people coming back for more.

Second Stage

Now you really need big money, and the requirement for effective cash flow management has never been more important. Revenues are growing at double-digit or higher percentage rates, and cash management has become almost an obsession. Sales activity is soaring, and production demand is growing like a weed. If your company has adequate operating margins and effective cash management (prompt accounts receivable collection and attractive vendor payment terms), then you might be able to internally fund this stage. More than likely, you will be short on cash and need to have some cash in reserve to cover the deficiencies that arise from having to pay vendors and employees before, sometimes months before, you have received customer payments. See Chapter 17 for details related to effectively managing cash on an operational basis.

There are firms that specialize in providing this second round of financing. These firms not only provide investment capital, but also offer expertise on managing this perilous stage. Uncertainty is again reduced from the first stage because you have not only a history but also a future with respect to forecastable orders and expenses. Accounts receivable can be used to fund this cash shortage, as can other methods covered in Chapter 17.

It is not uncommon for a company at this stage to sell additional shares as a way of obtaining equity funding, which does not increase the cash drain on the company yet provides an important infusion of cash. This cash is really a safety net that protects the company from serious cash shortfalls, decreasing stress on management and improving the likelihood of making it to the third stage. Equity funding is not as expensive for the company to obtain, since the level of overall perceived risk to the investor is much lower than at prior stages.

Third Stage (Mezzanine)

Your company is now a well-oiled machine. Your employees know their jobs, your operational systems are in place, you have an established name in the marketplace, and you are developing the next generation of products and services that will take you into the future. You are hiring managers specifically oriented toward management of a larger company, standardizing offerings, and maybe even broadening to international markets.

This level is often called mezzanine financing in that it is a growth and financing stage between (or bridging) two other levels: second and harvest. Management is now actively working on ways to foster the right environment within which they can harvest their prior work. This stage involves refining the company operation so that it appears as financially viable and profitable as possible, and laying the groundwork for having the share selling price seen at harvest be as high as possible. Financing obtained at this stage is usually for a relatively short period of time, and everyone involved knows that the next step is the harvest.

Harvest Stage (Exit Strategy)

This is the stage when employees, founders, and early shareholders reap the benefits of their earlier investment. This stage can be the sale of the company to another group of investors or to another company, or the offering of stock in an initial public offering (IPO). The prior shareholders offer their shares for sale and take the money, often making very large sums of money in the process. If a company does a public offering, it will likely sell founders' shares as well as shares over and above those already outstanding as a way of filling the company's cash coffers while providing a way for the prior shareholders to cash in on their investment. Now your startup is a real, live, mature company that must carve a life for itself as an adult. It is a player in the marketplace. The shareholders who sell their shares "exit" the company in that they will sell some or all of their founder shares, even though they may still remain on as employees.

This is a time of management, employee, and focus changes, when leadership skills are incredibly important. Keeping now-wealthy shareholders focused on creating the next level of company success is not always an easy task. There is a big party on the day that the harvest transaction becomes final, but everyone still must come to work the next day to get on with it.

Typical Funding Action Sequence

Here are a few steps that will likely happen independent of your selected method of funding:

- Determine what you want to do and how much it will cost to do it by writing a solid business plan.
- Prepare a presentation that provides a prospective investor (even if it is you) with a justification for making the investment.
- Put the word out to the appropriate people that you are looking for funding.

- Meet with prospective investors and professionally present your case and funding need request.
- Give them some time, along with a desired decision deadline, to verify what you have told them.
- Get your money or find out why this investment is not right for them at this time. Say thank you either way because it is a learning experience for you when dealing with the next potential investor.
- Report to investors on a periodic basis (quarterly and annually are usually minimum) about the performance of the company and the state of their investment.
- Always be on the lookout for people who can provide your next required level of funding as your business becomes more successful.

As the top manager of your company, one primary responsibility is to ensure that the company has the money it needs to not only survive but also to capitalize on its next level of opportunity. This is a never-ending process, so just accept the fact that it is now part of your management landscape.

Basic Types of Funding

Without funding, your business idea will go nowhere. You must find a way to support the business (and you) while it grows into a profitable, self-sustaining entity. Here is an overview of the various funding methods and how they may apply to your particular situation. Think of this as an à la carte menu from which you can select as needed to create the funding meal that is right for your situation.

Funding Out of Your Own Pocket

Depending on the size of your new venture and your own financial situation, you may be able to fund your new venture out of your own savings. If you are not so financially fortunate, you should at least have enough savings to cover your own living expenses for a minimum of six months while you get the business up and running. I prefer 12 to 18 months of living expenses on hand to handle unforeseen delays, but 6 months should be the minimum. There is no cookie-cutter right way to fund your new venture because so much of it depends on how much you can afford to put into the venture along with your living expenses before hitting your pain threshold. With that said, here are a few words of advice I hope you take to heart before using your own money.

Don't cut your estimated need too close, or a cost overrun of some type or a slower sales ramp-up could put you in a painful cash crunch. Make sure that your significant other(s) all buy in to investing money for this purpose, or you could really feel pressure later when it will be the least appreciated. If you are younger, you might be able to use a larger percentage of your nest egg, but those closer to retirement (50+) should be a little more conservative. After all, you don't have 35 years to make it back before retiring, do you? Ideally try to only use money that you can afford to lose. If the amount required will use all of your nest egg, then you might consider bringing in investors even if on the surface it doesn't look like you will need them. Sleepless nights over losing everything because a major client defaults on a receivable is a terrible way to live. Trust me on this one, or check it out with someone who has already been through it.

Some people use the equity in their home to fund their business. This might also be a solid approach, as equity lines of credit are offered at lower interest rates than unsecured loans and you can (hopefully) sell your house to pay off the debt if the worst happens to your business. You don't get back the equity or money put into the business, but you at least aren't in debt if you end up closing your doors.

ED'S LESSONS LEARNED

If you're starting a corporation, you might consider taking out an equity line of credit on your house at the prevailing percentage interest rate and then lending that money to your corporation at some reasonable market rate that will typically be a few percentage points higher than the equity interest rate, amortizing the loan over a five-year period. Check with a bank on these rates. The company gets the cash, and you get to make several percentage points of interest income on your home equity. Make sure that you execute a loan agreement, just as you would if you were lending the money to a third-party company, to keep the IRS happy.

Finally, there are people who start their companies using credit card financing. This is pretty expensive. Plus, once you run up your credit cards, where do you go to charge those daily items that will definitely be required? I have done this before and got myself in trouble in that I was making minimum payments instead of paying off the whole thing. I strongly recommend that you not take the credit card route unless the amount you need to start with is low enough that you could pay it off in a few months if things don't go well. Otherwise, I fear that you might dig yourself into a credit charge hole that is difficult for some, and impossible for others, to dig out of.

STREET SMARTS

Angel investors are people, or groups of people, who invest in ventures that are thought too uncertain or risky for typical investors. They are willing to take the risk for any number of personal and professional reasons, such as helping the local community, working with women to get started, or helping recent high school graduates become financially independent. Don't let your pride get in the way of starting a solid business that you believe in. Talk with local community organizations to see if there is some angel investor who might be interested in your type of company. This is particularly true for those of you starting philanthropic type of ventures.

Brother, Can You Spare a Dime? Family Funding

Family and friend funding is a double-edged sword: (1) family may feel more inclined to help with your business idea because of a personal need to help you out—such as making sure that you don't come live with them; (2) they may have faith in you because they know you; but (3) they may hold it against you for years to come if the business fails, taking their investment with it. Can business be done with family members? Absolutely. It happens all the time. Should you be overly cautious when dealing with friends and family as potential investors? Absolutely, again. It is one thing to lose an investor. It is something altogether different to create a rift with a good friend or family member.

I have a tendency to go overboard on disclosure when dealing with friends and family. My belief is that I can always find another investor, but it will be difficult to replace this personal relationship. If they still want to be involved after all the disclosure, then so be it. At least everyone's eyes were open. Also, make sure that you execute the same documents (such as loan agreements) with friends as you would with a third party. This is still a business arrangement and should be treated as such. Even (especially?) with family and friends.

Venture Capital—Not for Everybody

Venture capital (VC) is a term that gets bantered around a lot as one Silicon Valley startup after another got funded, grew, almost became profitable (sometimes), and then went public. A common question I get is, "Who are these venture capital people, and how do you get some of their money?" The venture capital market today is much different from what it was in prior years. So beware assumptions about what venture capitalists are or are not investing in. Consider that your venture will have to meet certain requirements before typically a VC firm will even look at it.

Your initial investment amount should be at least $500,000 or it is not worth their time and money to investigate. You and your management team must be top-notch since the VC invests in you first and the idea second. These people know that large amounts of money behind a great team with a hot product in a growing market will strain the seams of the company and its management personnel. They want seasoned people at the helm who know how to responsibly manage this type of growth. The idea must support large sales growth over a short period of time. The business plan must show that the VC can make at least 10 times their initial investment within a five-year period or less, or they will not likely fund the company.

Run the numbers and see what has to happen to a company's value to meet the VC valuation increase requirement. Assume the $500k in VC funding buys 25 percent of the company. This puts the initial company value at $2 million (4 × $500k). Ten times that value is $20 million in market valuation within five years. Possible? Sure. Easy to do? Not usually.

Venture capital funds like to work with companies that have an existing marketplace, workable (or proven) product, and are credible so that the provided money enables rapid expansion. VC-funded companies are always racing the clock, so time is scarce and rapid sales growth essential.

Just on these points alone, particularly the required company valuation growth, most smaller businesses will not qualify for venture capital funding. If you feel that your idea could qualify for venture funding, you should get solid professionals involved as a reality check and for refining your plan before going out for VC funding.

Agency-Guaranteed Bank Funding

You might find that your local state or perhaps federal agencies have put together special guaranteed loan programs that you can tap into. The general theme is that the public agency guarantees the loan to the lender, who evaluates and processes the loan for you, the entrepreneur and borrower. If you default, the agency pays the lender for the lost loan. The intent of these programs is some type of greater economic good to the community, such as promoting small business growth as a way of stimulating the economy and increasing employment. Don't be afraid to talk to your banker about possible programs that would apply to your situation, not only today but also as you grow and become more stable. Perhaps you can personally fund the company until it is large enough to qualify for one of these types of loans.

SBA and Governmental Program Realities

Without question, you should get to know the programs provided by the Small Business Administration (SBA). This is particularly true if you plan to purchase property as part of your business operation. SBA programs change, so I will not go into detail on any particular program here. The website is your best bet for initial information (sba.gov), but also look around your area for financial institutions that are SBA-approved to see if they can help you find and qualify for a loan that is right for your particular business. Be forewarned, however, that the SBA typically will want substantial collateral to back up loans for buildings or general business loans. Even the government understands risk and reward. The programs offered by the government change on a regular basis, so make a point of checking to see what is available. It might surprise you.

Finally, don't overlook any leverage that you may have in qualifying for a special governmental program. This leverage may come from you being a woman, a member of a minority race, your geographic location, industry, age, education, income bracket, military background, or any number of other criteria. It never ceases to amaze me at the number of programs that the various governmental agencies offer. Someplace, somewhere, with patience and tons of paperwork, you might be able to find some funding for yourself.

STREET SMARTS

Needing advice on how to take your successful company public with an IPO is what my brother would term a "high-class problem." If you eventually get to that stage, make sure that you carefully pick your partners on that important journey and be thankful you have that opportunity.

Stock Sales (Not an IPO ... Sorry)

One reason to incorporate is to be able to sell stock for funding purposes. Notice that a stock sale makes the shareholders owners of the corporation, and you do not need to repay their stock investment. They are taking a risk with their investment and often get a say in the company operation in exchange. This is called equity financing or equity funding.

Equity funding is obtained through three basic means: selling shares of stock to private investors, selling shares of stock to professional investors such as venture capitalists, and going public, which involves selling shares to the general public on one of the stock exchanges. You will initially deal with the first two financing options and, if you are successful and lucky, eventually have the opportunity to go public, which is beyond the scope of this book.

Selling shares of stock looks pretty good on the surface: you sell a portion of the company in exchange for some cash. All you give up is a little ownership in the company to get the cash you need. What is the downside? As usual, it comes down to whom you choose as your investors. The more sophisticated the investor, the better an ally he or she will make down the road. A professional investor knows the pitfalls associated with running a business and can guide you through potential minefields. However, professional investors also tend to be demanding and relatively heartless when you do not perform as expected. From their perspective, not living up to your plan indicates a lack of business control. A professional investor will take you to task if needed because he or she has a vested interest in your success.

Your Uncle Billy, on the other hand, might not need monthly reports from you on your progress and might purchase your company's stock on his faith in your ability alone. This makes getting your initial funding easier, but might hurt you down the road. Suppose that the company has a rough quarter, for reasons that are out of your control, such as a flood or economic calamity. Billy might not understand why that dividend check you promised didn't arrive. He might not understand why you need more money due to unforeseen circumstances. Billy might not even have deep enough pockets to fund the next round of investing.

Seller Financing When Buying a Business

If you plan to purchase an existing company, you may find that the seller is willing to finance a portion of the purchase price. This is sort of like a house seller taking a second note on the purchase with the bank being in first position. In this case, the seller might be the primary lender and you make monthly payments to him instead of to the bank. There is something to be said for this approach since it keeps the seller interested in the business's success and gives him an incentive to work with you to make it successful. A successful business after purchase is a win for everyone. Plus, the seller may get some tax benefits with this approach, which you could factor in to the purchase price. Check with your accountant.

Ethics and Funding

It is hard to overemphasize the importance of keeping your ethics intact when looking for investors. People might take a chance on an idea that they feel is risky but has merit. Few people will give money to someone they don't trust. If you find yourself wanting to shade the truth, take a deep breath and ponder the ramifications of what you are about to do. If you are found out, the impact on your business could be devastating, not to mention the impact on your relationship with this investor. Plus, it really is a small world out there. The word will get out that you cannot be trusted, and it will take you forever to regain your good name. Do your work up front and watch the investors convince themselves that your idea is one worth funding.

Never knowingly involve someone in your business that you do not trust. You will be busy enough worrying about expanding your business; you do not need someone questioning your every move and undermining what you do. Stall, work harder, cut expenses, and play with cash flow before getting involved with an investor who might be a potential integrity headache.

For Your Plan

Here are a few points that must be included in your business plan related to your need and request for funding:

- Prepare the cumulative cash flow analysis presented in Chapter 13. Proper preparation will involve financial analysis along with an explanation about the underlying assumptions associated with the analysis.
- Explain why you are structuring your funding requirements as you are with respect to the use of debt and equity funding.
- If you already have investors, provide that information in your plan to include their relative percentage ownership.
- Outline the projected harvested returns for an investor who gets in now. Explain how and when they can plan to harvest their investment. Make sure that everyone knows that these numbers are *not guaranteed* but are simply estimates.
- Tell how the funds will be used and how the investors will be kept informed about fund usage and progress toward the achievement of outlined business goals.

The Least You Need to Know

- Debt funding must be paid back but allows you to retain total company ownership.
- Equity funding requires that you give up company ownership but also does not require that you make payments on a loan.
- Venture capital funding is usually only right for a select group of new companies that have huge growth potential.
- Banks don't typically lend to risky ventures.
- Funding requirements, and perceived investor risk, vary with the stage of company growth.

Selecting the Right Legal Structure for Your New Business

Chapter

15

In This Chapter

- Understanding the difference between sole proprietorships, partnerships, and corporations
- Learning your business structure's legal implications
- Determining how taxes affect your business
- Selecting the legal structure that is right for your business

Bill shouted, "What do you mean I could lose everything I own? I didn't even know Ted bought that equipment for the company."

"The problem is that you never incorporated as you planned, and the law treats the two of you as a partnership," replied the attorney. "Under the law, you are responsible for the company obligations whether you agreed to them or not."

"No way," shouted Bill. "I'm not going to pay. Let them go after Ted first."

"The equipment company will first go after the business and then you and Ted at the same time. As far as the law is concerned, you and Ted are both equally liable for paying off the debt. Sorry, but you have no choice. Next time, pick your partners more carefully and consider incorporating to avoid this situation again."

Bill didn't like it, but he accepted what he heard as the truth. How could his life savings and a thriving company take a dive so quickly based on the irresponsible actions of one person? What could he have done differently? How could he have known?

The legal structure of a business is usually invisible once set up, but it becomes very important should anything go wrong. Just as one house style doesn't meet the living requirements of all families, no single business structure meets everyone's business needs. Depending on your current situation and future business aspirations, one business structure might meet those needs better than another. Take the time to determine where you want the company to go not only in the next few months but over the next few years, at least. A long-term perspective helps you decide on the best structure for your specific situation. In this chapter, I review the different legal business structures and discuss the pros and cons of each.

You should use this chapter as a general starting point. Understand the information presented and then apply it to your situation. This is your homework portion of the process. You should then run your assessment by the proper legal and accounting professionals to ensure that you are on the right track and to help set you up properly for your particular situation. Try to avoid the temptation to "go it alone" at this stage, because an error regarding your company's structure can have serious business, personal, and tax consequences later on.

An Overview of the Various Business Structures

The three basic business organizational structures are *sole proprietorships*, *partnerships*, and *corporations.* Under each category are subclasses that apply to specific situations.

A sole proprietorship is the most common and easiest type of business to create. Anyone who performs services of any kind, such as a gardener, caterer, or even babysitter, is by default a sole proprietor unless he or she takes specific action to set it up otherwise. A small company with only one employee is often kept as a sole proprietorship, but there are no restrictions on how big a sole proprietorship can become. It depends exclusively on the desires of the owner, or proprietor. The majority of small businesses in the United States are sole proprietorships.

A general partnership is formed whenever two or more people decide to enter a for-profit business venture. Typically, each partner owns a portion of the company's profits and debts, which can be set up in a written agreement among the partners. You do not need to file any special paperwork to form a partnership, but you should make sure you and your partners sign an agreement to minimize misunderstandings regarding each person's rights and liabilities. If you do not have an agreement signed by all parties, then any partnership-related disputes are handled under statutes based on the Uniform Partnership Act (UPA) used in most states.

Most larger online and on-ground bookstores carry books that cover creating partnerships for your particular state. There are also websites that will help you create a partnership that is right for your particular state. These sources are inexpensive and helpful in making sure that you and your partners dot the right i's and cross the right t's. Once you have done the grunt work using both the book and the forms provided at the website (idiotsguides.com/startingyourownbusiness), I suggest that you present it to an attorney to make sure all of the proper legal lingo is included and that everyone's interests are protected.

Corporations are often treated as an indicator of how serious you are about being in business. This may be because a corporation is more involved to set up and manage than a sole proprietorship or partnership.

When you form a corporation, you actually establish an organization separate and distinct from you personally. You may ask why that's such a big deal; what's the advantage? A primary advantage is that if the corporation is sued, you are not personally responsible for any damages that might be awarded (unless, of course, you are also named in the suit, which can always happen—corporation or not). This aspect of corporations provides you with limited liability. Paperwork and record keeping are fairly involved with a corporation, which is why some people decide it's not worth the hassles. You may find it more advantageous from a tax perspective to be incorporated, which can and should completely separate your personal and business income.

Sole Proprietorship: Going It Alone

Assume that Judy makes wooden dolls and gives them as presents every Christmas. Her historical doll-giving activities would be considered a hobby. But today she sold her first one to a neighbor, which means that today Judy became the head of a sole proprietorship business.

Once you begin providing and receiving money for products or services, you become a sole proprietor. Your business expenses are deductible, all income is taxable, and you assume the liabilities of the business. (More on the tax implications later in the chapter.)

Notice that Judy did not have to create a separate name to start her business. She simply started her business and began selling her product, using her own name. This is why the sole proprietorship is such a popular business structure. You are the person doing the work and also making the money (if there is any) making you the sole proprietor of the business.

WATCH OUT!

Be very aware of the dangers of the sole proprietorship and partnership business types. They can leave the owners personally open to any type of litigation filed against or debt incurred by the company. Years of work and personal wealth acquisition can be lost in a short period of time using these forms of business structures.

Judy could change the name of her business to Dolls and Such, by filing a Doing Business As (d/b/a) form with the local authorities, usually the county clerk's office in the area where she plans to do business. The d/b/a filing is sometimes called a trade name, a fictitious name statement, or an also known as (a.k.a.). If no one else is using the name she chooses, after filing her d/b/a form, Judy can transact business as Dolls and Such. Filing the d/b/a gives her legal rights to the name within the jurisdiction of the governing body, which is typically the county. If someone else later uses the name within the county, Judy can ask the courts to order that person to cease operations under the name she legally owns. The other business is then forced to rename itself. Notice that this name registration is only for the county and not for the state, which could hurt Judy if she branches out to do business in other parts of the state. A corporation's name applies statewide.

AT THE WEBSITE

A sample Certificate of Assumed Business Name is provided on the website as document 15-01.

A sole proprietorship is easy and inexpensive to create, and all profits go directly to the owner. The major disadvantage is that all legal and financial obligations incurred by the company are also passed directly to the owner. That means that if the company is sued for any reason, such as if a child eats one of Judy's dolls and is hospitalized, Judy is personally responsible for answering that lawsuit. Judy could lose everything she personally owns if the business-related lawsuit is lost and the damages are high. For this liability reason alone, many people choose to change their structure from a sole proprietorship to a corporation.

Liability insurance is strongly recommended for those transacting business in general, but particularly for those running sole proprietorships. Make sure that your insurance agent knows the type of business you are in and how you expect to be protected.

Being a sole proprietorship does not limit whether you have employees, although many sole proprietorships are one-person businesses. You can hire employees as a sole proprietorship, but you, as the owner, become the target for any claims made against the business as a result of any of the actions of your employees. You must apply for an employer identification number (EIN) just as a corporation does since this is the IRS's tracking mechanism for employers. (See Chapter 18 for details on obtaining an EIN.) Oddly enough, you as the owner are not an employee of the company even though you draw a salary. (Who said that IRS regulations had to make sense?) You file your sole proprietorship business taxes on Schedule C of your personal Form 1040 tax return and then will be required to pay self-employment tax. Sorry.

The flexibility associated with being the only owner is often attractive enough to keep people in business as a sole proprietorship, even after the company grows large in revenues.

AT THE WEBSITE

A sample General Partnership Agreement (document 15-02) and sample Partnership Minutes (document 15-03) are included at the website.

A sample Limited Partnership Checklist (document 15-04), Limited Partnership Agreement (document 15-05), Certificate of Limited Partnership (document 15-06), Limited Partnership Consent Resolution in Lieu of First Meeting of Partners (document 15-07), and Limited Partnership Minutes (document 15-08) are also included at the website.

Partnership: A Business Marriage

Partnership is a wonderful term that evokes warm, comforting feelings. Who wouldn't want a partner to share the good and bad times in a business? Well, if you have ever been in a bad relationship, you know the damage it can do to your psychological and financial well-being. You should treat business partnerships with the same amount of respect. Your personal partner may move the ketchup from the pantry to the refrigerator, but your business partner can bankrupt you, which is a way bigger problem than cold ketchup.

When two or more people form a partnership, they are essentially married, from a business standpoint. Either party can obligate the other via the business, and everything the business and the partners own individually is on the line. In essence, a partnership is like a sole proprietorship owned by several people. All liability is passed to the partners.

A special partnership type, called a *limited partnership*, provides certain partners with a maximum financial liability equal to their investment. To maintain this limited financial liability status, these partners, called *limited partners*, cannot participate in the daily operation of the business. The *general partner* is responsible for the day-to-day management of the business. Limited partners invest in the company and rely on the general partner to run the business. When the general partner is a corporation, personal liability is avoided for all partners.

DEFINITION

In a **limited partnership,** some partners (called **limited partners**) invest money but do not participate in the daily operation of the business. They are liable only for the amount of money that they each have invested. A **general partner** is responsible for the daily operations of the business.

A **limited liability partnership (LLP)** is a special type of partnership that is created by a special filing with the state where the partners operate. Partners who are part of an LLP protect their personal assets from being taken if the partnership gets into financial trouble. There is really no reason not to become an LLP.

Special laws govern the operation of a limited partnership, and if they are not precisely followed, the courts might hold that the partnership was general, not limited. The formerly limited partner might find himself as liable as a general partner for business-related debts. Be aware that you must complete and file special paperwork with the state to form a limited partnership.

AT THE WEBSITE

A sample Limited Liability Partnership Checklist (document 15-09), Limited Liability General Partnership Agreement (document 15-10), Application for Registration of Limited Liability Partnership (document 15-11), and Limited Liability Partnership Consent Resolution in Lieu of First Meeting of Partners (document 15-12) are included at the website.

Corporations: Share the Wealth

As mentioned earlier in this chapter, a corporation is a special legal entity that has most of the same legal abilities of a person except that there is no living person who is a corporation. A corporation is created in accordance with the laws of the state within which the corporation will have its main office. It is financed through the selling of shares to people who then become owners in the corporation. The owners and the founders of the new corporation are almost always the same people, and there are generally only a couple of them. The percentage company ownership of each shareholder is based on the number of shares owned by that shareholder compared to the total number of shares issued or outstanding.

WATCH OUT!

If you are not careful with how you handle the administrative aspects of your corporation, you can lose your limited liability protection. So do it right to avoid unwelcome surprises later.

Many corporations are formed in the state of Delaware because of its less restrictive incorporation laws. Delaware was one of the early states to allow you to incorporate while conducting business and keeping headquarters in another state. Most other states now allow the same procedure. Realize, however, that if you incorporate in Delaware and then operate in Illinois, for example, you will have to register your corporation with the state of Illinois and pay taxes in that state. Now you have two states to deal with instead of one, which takes away from the Delaware incorporation benefits. Naturally, if you live in Delaware, that is where you would most likely incorporate.

WATCH OUT!

Don't make your business organization decision based solely on tax implications. The tax laws change on a regular basis, and the impact of the laws vary depending upon your personal income and your company's income levels. But you are right to investigate the tax benefits or drawbacks associated with each business type so that you make this important decision with the right information. Select the business structure that is right for you based on where you are today and where you want to wind up down the road. Consider the advantages and disadvantages of each business structure before making a decision.

It is important to understand that the various business structures have their own sets of tax-related problems and benefits. Just remember that the best business structure is the one that provides the required level of legal and tax protection along with enough flexibility to address future business and financial needs. This is a tricky balancing act that requires attention on your part perhaps along with a strong dose of professional guidance.

Creating a corporation is like creating a new business life. A corporation is a separate and distinct business entity that is responsible for itself. Upon formation, the corporation issues shares of stock in exchange for something of value to *shareholders*, who then become the business owners. Shareholders exchange money, goods, or services to receive their shares of stock. If you plan to start a corporation, it is absolutely imperative that you keep the difference between you and the corporation straight. Beware, however, that stock obtained in exchange for an item of value or cash is tax free, but the IRS considers stock obtained from providing a service to the corporation as income and is subject to income taxes. You see, the IRS never sleeps.

For some smaller and all larger corporations, a *board of directors*, elected by the shareholders, manages the corporation. This board then appoints *officers* of the corporation to handle the day-to-day affairs of the company. In essence, the board members represent the interests of the shareholders in the company operations. Depending on the state in which the business is incorporated, the business owner in many small corporations may be the primary, or only, shareholder and only board member. This same person is listed as the president, secretary, and treasurer of the corporation. A small company rarely has a board of directors except in an informal advisory capacity that does not usually involve any legal obligation on the owner and shareholder. Some states, such as Indiana, do not require a board of directors at all.

The corporation pays taxes on its annual profits and passes the profits to the shareholders in the form of *dividends*. The board of directors, who represent the shareholders, determine the amount of the dividends. A Sub S-corporation is taxed differently from a standard corporation; this topic is covered in another section of this chapter.

DEFINITION

In a corporation, **shareholders,** or stockholders, own a percentage of the business, expressed in terms of the number of shares of stock they own in relation to the total number of shares issued. The corporation is managed by employees who take their overall direction from a corporation's **board of directors.** A small company with few shareholders will likely not have a board of directors. Annual profits are passed on to shareholders in the form of **dividends,** although annual dividend payments are not mandatory. The amount of the dividends is determined by the board of directors. Corporation **officers** have the ability to legally commit the corporation, whereas standard employees have limited commitment ability, if any.

The major benefit associated with a corporate business form is that the corporation is liable for its own financial and civil liabilities. The shareholders risk only the amount of money they have invested in their respective shares of stock. This is referred to as limited liability. Liability issues can also be addressed through insurance, so while limited liability is one reason to choose a corporate form of organization, check with knowledgeable advisers before making a final decision.

Using the earlier Dolls and Such example, assume that the business is now a corporation with $500,000 in its bank account. If someone were to win a judgment against Dolls and Such for $1 million, the company would probably go out of business, and only $500,000 would change hands. The person who won the legal judgment against the corporation would have no immediate legal basis for getting the rest of the money from the shareholders personally.

However, this is not the case with a partnership or sole proprietorship. As a partner or sole proprietor, your personal finances are put squarely at risk in this scenario, and you could lose a lifetime of work. You might end up owing an additional $500,000 to the judgment holder if that situation ever came to pass.

Another major corporate benefit involves raising money for the business by selling shares in the corporation. Once the buyer and seller agree to a price per share of stock, the buyer simply purchases the number of shares needed to equal the amount of money to be exchanged. For instance, assume you need to raise $100,000. If you find a buyer who is willing to pay you $4 per share, then you sell that person 25,000 shares of stock to receive the $100,000.

To further illustrate the point, again assume you need $100,000 but don't know anyone with that kind of money on hand. Instead of selling 25,000 shares at $4 each to one person, you could sell 2,500 shares to 10 different investors for $4 each and still get the money you need. You now have 10 shareholders instead of 1, but you got the money you needed. This approach is often more attractive to investors in that they can share in your success but do not have to risk more money than they can afford to lose. Forming a corporation is the route to take if you eventually plan to raise a large sum of money by selling stock to a number of different people. Make sure that you check the stock sale registration regulations for your particular state and the Security and Exchange Commission (SEC) when doing any type of stock sale offering.

AT THE WEBSITE

A sample Corporation Checklist for Offering Memorandum Checklist (document 15-13), Corporation Subscriber Questionnaire (document 15-14), Corporation Investor Letter (document 15-15), and Installment Promissory Note (document 15-16) are included at the website.

Standard corporations are separate entities from their shareholders and, as such, the corporation files its own tax return. It shows revenue, expenses, and net profit before tax on which state and federal taxes are paid. Net income is what is left over after all taxes are paid. (See Chapter 13 for the details associated with financial statements and terminology.) Notice that the corporation may have money left over in the form of net income, but none of it has been paid to the shareholders. If the corporation wants to reward the shareholders for owning its stock, then the board of directors (or shareholders) can issue a dividend to the shareholders, who then must pay tax on the dividends they receive, just as if they had received a dividend from owning General Electric or Microsoft stock.

So the corporation pays tax on its net profit before tax and the individual shareholder pays tax on the dividends received from the corporation. This is called double taxation. It is considered a major drawback to corporation ownership and was the motivation for creating the S-corporation.

Subchapter S-Corporations: Protection with a Smaller Tax Bite

Suppose you want the legal protection provided by a corporation but want the income to pass directly to you so that you can declare it on your personal income tax statement and avoid double taxation. For once, you can thank the IRS and Congress because they created the *subchapter S-corporation* for just this purpose.

AT THE WEBSITE

A sample Cover Letter to the IRS for S-Corporation Election (form 2553) is included at the website as document 15-17.

In a subchapter S-corporation, instead of the corporation paying taxes on its income, the business net income is passed to the shareholders, who then declare the income and pay taxes at their personal rate, on their personal income tax statements. Subchapter S-corporations retain all the legal protection provided by a standard

C-corporation (any corporation that is not converted into an S-corporation). It might be worth noting that there is no such thing as a C-corporation, but instead it is a common way of referring to a standard corporation as not being an S-corporation.

Why opt for the S instead of C-corporation? If you are personally in a lower tax bracket than the corporation, then passing the business income to you decreases the overall taxes paid. In addition, if the corporation loses money, you can use part of that loss to offset personal income earned from other investments you may have, up to certain limits. You can also avoid *double taxation* if you use an S-corporation, which can have a welcome tax-reduction effect around April 15 of each year. However, if you don't plan properly or if the company does better than you expected, you can find yourself with a huge personal tax bill at the end of the year.

DEFINITION

A **subchapter S-corporation** is a type of corporation with no more than 100 shareholders and a single class of stock. All profits are passed directly to the owners and taxed as income, which avoids double taxation. For this reason, the S-corporation is often called a pass-through entity.

Double taxation happens when you are taxed on income at both the corporate and personal levels.

There are some creative cash flow issues that must be addressed every year for an S-corporation because all of the corporation's net income is passed to shareholders who pay tax on it. In essence, most of the cash available to the S-corporation is used to pay shareholders what they have coming from the fiscal year. To keep the company from running out of cash, shareholders (who are often founders and large shareholders) take only as much cash as they need to pay their personal taxes resulting from S-corporation ownership distribution and leave the rest in the corporation as an operating cash loan. As the new fiscal year starts and the corporation starts to make money, it pays back the shareholders for the loan, and usually by March or April the shareholders are paid back and the corporation is again running business as usual.

If you think the S-corporation is right for you, check with an accountant and an attorney before taking the plunge. A little prevention goes a long way to avoid unforeseen problems down the road. Notice that the decision is heavily based on how much revenue and net income you anticipate the company will generate and your personal tax bracket. This is why the planning and forecasting aspects of business are so critically important.

Limited Liability Company (LLC)

How would you like the advantages of a corporation or partnership without some of the stock and shareholder restrictions regarding the number of shareholders? That's what a *limited liability company* (*LLC*) can provide.

DEFINITION

A **limited liability company (LLC)** is a type of business structure available in almost every state that has many of the pass-through tax advantages of a partnership or subchapter S-corporation, but fewer of the disadvantages related to stock ownership. LLC shareholders are called **members** of the LLC.

Limited liability companies are now authorized in all 50 states. The reason for their new popularity is that LLCs provide business owners, called *members*, with personal liability protection, just as corporations do, and still provide tax benefits at the individual level only, as subchapter S-corporations do. This all gets pretty complicated; suffice to say for now that you can set up the LLC to look to the IRS for tax purposes as a corporation, partnership, or sole proprietorship, depending on the specifics of your business situation.

For most small business owners, setting up an LLC may be overkill. Think of it conceptually as an S-corporation with much more flexibility with respect to shareholder types and numbers.

AT THE WEBSITE

A sample Limited Liability Company Checklist (document 15-18), Limited Liability Company Articles of Organization (without manager) (document 15-19), Limited Liability Company Articles of Organization (with manager) (document 15-20), Limited Liability Company Operating Agreement (without manager) (document 15-21), Limited Liability Company Operating Agreement (with manager) (document 15-22), Limited Liability Company Member Certificate (document 15-23), Limited Liability Company Consent Resolution in Lieu of First Meeting of Members (document 15-24), and Limited Liability Company Minutes (document 15-25) are included at the website.

Professional Corporations

The *professional corporation* is a special business structure that addresses the needs of professionals who share a practice, such as lawyers, doctors, engineers, architects, and accountants. The professional corporation provides tax benefits to the participants, but with the special added benefit that one owner of a professional corporation is not liable for the malpractice actions of another owner. This is different from a standard corporation where the malpractice actions of one employee would affect the entire corporation. In a professional corporation, all owners must be of the same profession. If you are a licensed professional who falls into this special category, check with your accountant to determine whether a professional corporation provides you any special benefits. Professional corporations use the letters P.C. or PC after the company name.

DEFINITION

A **professional corporation** is a special corporation sometimes used by lawyers, doctors, architects, engineers, and accountants. It is often subject to restrictions related to malpractice matters.

Dealing with the Tax Man

Taxes never go away, but the good news is that you only pay taxes when you are making money. At least that means you are making money! All you can do is try to minimize their negative impact on your profits. The impact of taxes on your choice of organizational structure is worth a brief discussion. I present only general concepts here about income taxes; talk to your accountant about your specific situation. Remember, there are many other taxes your business will have to pay. You need to learn about all of them in your area—city, county, state, sales, franchise, and so on.

Start to think of you and your business as separate entities and understanding taxes will become easier. The business will have income and expenses, just as you will personally have income and expenses. How the business income and expenses are related to you personally is what all of this tax discussion is about. For simplification purposes, I will divide taxes into a couple of categories: business income tax, personal income tax, and employment/payroll taxes that include Social Security and Medicare. Remember, too, that as an employee of a corporation you will receive a salary, even though you will also be an owner, which means that you will receive a standard W-2 at the end of the year.

With most business structures, except for the C-corporation, the company's net income will pass directly to you as an owner or stockholder. You then declare that income on your personal tax return and pay tax at your personal tax rate. In

C-corporations, all salary expenses (including the owner's salary) are deducted from the company's revenues prior to determining how much company tax must be paid, but the corporation pays its portion of the payroll taxes on it as well. You then pay personal income tax only on your salary and give up your portion of the payroll taxes throughout the year, just as you have probably done up to this point working for another company.

Self-employed individuals such as those running a sole proprietorship really feel the bite of FICA (Social Security) and Medicare taxes a little more strongly because they pay both the employee's share and the employer's share of these taxes in the form of self-employment taxes. This is a little misleading, though, in that the overall payroll tax rate is the same whether as a sole proprietorship or corporation. It is simply paid in a different way and out of different funds when talking about a corporation or sole proprietorship.

Keeping the various income, expense, and tax relationships straight is difficult for the owner of any small business. Sometimes you emotionally feel that your fate and that of the company are intertwined to the point that they cannot be separated. But they should be separate from a personal perspective, and they *have* to be from a tax perspective.

Take a look at this table to see a summary of the various ways that company income and loss transfer to you as the owner, shareholder, and/or employee.

A Summary of Various Business Tax Situations

Business Type	Income/Loss Transfer	Tax Impact	Comment
Sole Proprietorship, Partnership	Company profit/loss passes directly to the owners with no restrictions on loss transfer.	Taxed at the owner's personal income tax bracket. Self-employment tax (15.3%) must be paid, which is basically FICA for both company and personal portions.	A successful business could quickly put the owner in a high tax bracket. Owners must make separate tax deposits to cover their own tax liability. Owners are not employees and do not receive a W-2, but other employees are and do receive W-2s.

Business Type	Income/Loss Transfer	Tax Impact	Comment
C-Corporation	Corporation itself shows a profit or a loss that is carried forward.	Corporation pays tax at the corporate rate. Dividend payments to owners are taxed at the owner's personal tax rate.	Owner is likely also an employee and receives a W-2 and pays payroll taxes just like all other employees. Nearly all employee benefits are deductible by the corporation.
Corporation, LLC	Corporate profit or loss passes to the shareholders with some restrictions on loss transfer.	Corporate income or loss is transferred to the owners, who are then taxed at the owner's personal tax rate that may or may not be lower than the C-corporation tax rate.	Owner/employees pay personal income and payroll taxes on their salary as shown on the W-2, just like any other employee. They must also pay personal tax on their portion of the corporation profits but also absorb corporate loss from Schedule K-1. Many benefits are deductible by the S-corp, but the owners must show these payments as income upon which they pay tax at their respective rate.

By the way, the tax laws change all the time and often make no sense at all. So don't feel bad if you are not up-to-date on all of the various tax implications. You would have to dedicate most of your efforts to tracking taxes and not to making money in your business. Make the money first and then worry about the tax implications, but be as smart and prepared as possible along the way.

STREET SMARTS

Your company must pay FICA (Social Security), unemployment, and Medicare taxes for each employee over and above the standard salary. This currently amounts to around 7.65 percent. The employee also pays these taxes. See Chapter 18 for more information on payroll taxes.

Picking the Right Structure

Here is how I suggest that you determine the right legal structure for your business. Determine how many people you expect to have on payroll. If it is a small number or just you, then a sole proprietorship should be okay, but if you expect to have a lot of employees then look at another structure. Evaluate how vulnerable you would be to a liability lawsuit that could take away all that you have personally. If low, then a sole proprietorship might be alright. If high, then definitely go with some type of liability protecting structure such as a corporation.

Estimate how much money you will need to get started. If the amount is small, then a sole proprietorship should be okay. If you have to raise a larger amount of money and many investors will be involved, then definitely go with a corporation. Estimate your expected salary including the payroll taxes either as self-employment tax or payroll tax. Would you pay more total tax combining the company and business taxes as an individual sole proprietorship, C-corporation, or as an S-corporation?

If you expect your company to show a loss for the first few years, which is not uncommon, then you might consider being a sole proprietorship or S-corporation so that the loss can be used to decrease your personal tax liability. Note that the S-corporation has some relatively restrictive loss limits, whereas the sole proprietorship loss limits are limited only by your total income.

For Your Plan

As part of your business plan, you want to address your reasons for choosing your business's legal structure. Make sure you address the following:

- Explain the type of business legal structure you plan to use and your primary reason for selecting that structure. Make sure to discuss liability or other specific legal protections related to this decision.
- Where do you plan to incorporate? If a corporation, add the names of key officers and board members (if applicable).
- How did you legally protect the company name (including whether it is available)? Even better, reserve the website name and trademark as well. This is particularly important for those starting an internet business.
- State your intentions related to opening offices in other states or countries and within specific time frames, if applicable.
- Explain how the legal documents were created, signed, and recorded to provide confidence that the company creation documents are legally binding.
- Analyze the tax implications of the business type choice and thresholds at which various other changes, such as from an S- to a C-corporation, will be performed.
- Where are the legal formation documents stored and how will they be maintained and updated?

Your goal with this section of your plan is to provide the reader with a solid understanding of the company's legal structure, why that structure was selected, and how that selection benefits the company and its shareholders in the future.

The Least You Need to Know

- Editable legal forms that you can adapt to your business are included at the website (idiotsguides.com/startingyourownbusiness). Take your best shot at completing them and then run them by an attorney for final okay.
- Select the business structure based on your expected business goals. Each form has its own benefits; you want to choose the one best suited to your needs.

- Sole proprietorships, partnerships, and corporations are not the same. Choose your business structure based on operational, legal, and tax considerations.
- Corporations provide the highest level of legal liability protection, but remember that dividend income can be subject to double taxation if it's a standard C-corporation.
- Taxes are a part of life for any business. Recognize that you have to learn about them or find competent help to pick the right business type that fits your business and tax needs.

Chapter 16

Putting All of the Pieces Together

In This Chapter

- Evaluating the answers to your plan's fundamental questions
- Understanding your own reaction to the completed plan
- Learning the importance of action once you start your business
- Making the final go or no-go decision
- Dealing with a plan that isn't viable

Bernice and Shawn sat next to each other across the table from Lance, Bernice's teacher from business school. They were at a coffee shop to discuss Bernice's new business plan that she had sent to Lance for his review. Lance placed the plan in front of him on the table. Bernice could see that he had written all over it, just like back in school.

"I can't stand this anymore. What do you think?"

"Okay. The good news first—I like the idea," he said. Bernice smiled and looked at Shawn, who looked relieved but was still a little concerned. "You have definitely put a lot of time and effort into this plan and it shows. For the most part, I think you are right on track."

"And what is the bad news?" asked Shawn.

"The bad news comes in two forms. First, I think the sales portion needs a little more work detailing about how you are going to find prospects and handle the specifics of the sales stages to sign them up to your service. That is very doable, I think." He took a drink of his coffee and let it sink in.

It was Bernice's turn to look concerned. "And second?"

"It is almost time to decide. After you tweak the sales portion a little, you have a pretty good plan here that looks like it could make you some real money. You've wanted to own your own business for years, and now you have a plan for an idea that is really viable. In other words, I think you are close to having to decide if you are going to start this thing." They all took a drink of coffee and a deep breath, then Bernice smiled at Shawn.

Congratulations on all of the hard research and writing work you have done so far on your plan. At this stage you are far more knowledgeable about your idea, and also about yourself in the context of starting your new business. So it is very possible that the working and analyzing is about done and it is time to decide. Feel some anxiety combined with excitement? That is good because it means that you have really done the work. Now let's put all of that good work through a final analysis that will help you determine if it is time to start it up.

Revisiting the Six Questions Your Plan Must Answer

Remember back in Chapter 7 where we talked about the questions that your plan must answer? In this section, we will review them to see how well you answered them. After all, you are the primary investor of time, and most likely money, for your new business, so looking at your more refined idea as a potential investor makes a lot of sense. We talked about the ultimate goal of the plan being to credibly answer these questions with the intent of decreasing perceived risk to the point where the investment of time and money looks rewarding instead of just plain scary. Let's see how you did. (See Chapter 2 for a detailed discussion about perceived risk and business planning.)

What is the business idea and what makes it unique to prospective customers in the current market environment?

When you were first captivated with your idea, it was probably a general concept like, "Hey—let's build a house!" People around the table might have looked at you like you were crazy or perhaps agreed that it was a great idea, but at that point in time it was just a general concept. With all of the work you have done at this point, the idea should be far more developed.

Continuing the house-building analogy, you should now know the number of bedrooms, baths, location, square footage, style, and type of flooring. Oh, yeah—and the number of cars for the garage. You probably have a rendering of the house, floor plans, possible towns where you would build it, and perhaps even a few specific lots that you are interested in buying. In short, what was previously a general idea is now a detailed vision.

But that just covers the idea itself. What have you discovered about the likelihood of selling that house? Who would be the prospective buyers? What neighborhoods are they attracted to? What types of houses are they looking for? How will they likely purchase the house? What types of houses are already out there, and why would they buy your house over the others? In other words, you should have a pretty realistic guess about who will buy your house, for how much, their motivations for buying, and how long it will take you to close the deal. Sure, it is all still a best guess at this point, but it is a far more developed view of the initial idea.

Here is the question: do you still like your idea and believe that customers will buy it? It is okay to say no, by the way. You have a much deeper appreciation of the reality of this idea than you did when you batted it around sitting at the dining room table with friends. It is sort of like the difference between dating and living with someone. Dating, we only see small portions of a person's life and can be captivated by those small time segments. Living with someone, you get to know them on a much more intimate level; it is not uncommon for people to move in together with the intent of getting married, only to break up in a few months. That is too bad on one level, but maybe for the best in the long run. The same is true with your idea—just because you were captivated with it early on does not mean that you have to pursue it once you have learned the realities of making it a success. If you can see both the positive and negative aspects of the business, appreciate the challenges offered by the competition, and understand how to attract customers, you know a lot. If the business still looks attractive, that is a pretty positive sign. Remember, if you don't believe in the idea, nobody else will either.

How much money is required to get the business up and running on a solid footing?

You should have a much clearer idea at this point about the amount of money you will need to get the business up and running. This estimate was developed throughout the chapters of this book and came together in the cumulative cash flow analysis you performed in Chapter 13. Recall that all of the sales revenue, variable expense, and fixed expense estimates you made came together to show a loss for a while after opening your new business doors. After a period of time, you hit break-even, after which you start to make money. At break-even you calculated a total cumulative cash value that represented the minimum cash you needed available to start the business. I just threw a lot of concepts at you in one paragraph, and if you understood what I said, congratulations! You have learned a lot about how to start a successful business.

Ask yourself a fundamental question about the financial analysis: Are you comfortable with the numbers? If so, at what percentage level would you feel comfortable saying that the analysis represents a reasonable estimate of the future? Fifty percent? This means that the estimates are about as accurate as a toss of a coin. Thirty percent? This means that you feel that the numbers are mostly estimates that you are not comfortable with. Eighty percent? This means that you not only believe the numbers, but also believe how they came together in the analysis. Notice that I am not asking you to assess the likelihood of the business succeeding—only how much confidence you have in the numbers used to make the analysis. These two points are different. Make sure that you do not try to make the numbers fulfill your own expectations; instead, they should present what you estimate will be the marketplace and business reality. Very different.

If you are comfortable with the estimates, picture yourself in front of a room of potential investors who are throwing questions at you about how you came up with the numbers. Can you objectively justify the sales estimates from both a units and revenue perspective? How did you come up with your fixed expenses? What is your basis for the variable expenses? Do you really have faith in the sales revenue ramp-up estimates beyond just that you "believe" they can happen? What about the sales sequence, timing, and prospects makes you believe that your estimates are accurate?

Remember that you will not get it 100 percent right. You are trying to perform a detailed-enough analysis to give you a solid estimate of what will happen. You prepared the numbers—if you don't believe them, nobody else will or should! Be brutally honest with yourself at this point because reality will certainly not feel constrained to perform in accordance with your estimates.

WATCH OUT!

Remember that you do not dictate reality—all you can do is make your best guess about what reality will look like once you enter the marketplace with your new business. Be diligent but also a little humble with your estimates.

When will the business show a reasonable profit for investors?

Now we get into the area that will be of most interest to investors. After all, they invest their money to get something back for taking the risk. First, they want to know how long it will be before the business has succeeded to the point that it could repay the investment. Second, they want to know how much they can expect to make from taking the investment risk, and when. This is the harvest strategy we talked about in Chapter 14.

Can you clearly see how and when these investor points are met? Are you comfortable with making the commitment to people about how and when it will happen? Would you invest your money, if you had it, based on what you know about how the plan's financial numbers were prepared? If the answers to these questions are yes and you really believe them, then you have a solid plan that is defensible when challenged. If not, then look to see where you are uncomfortable and then see what can be done to reduce your level of discomfort. Quite often more information or a different analysis and presentation of your current information is all that is needed to get things back on track.

What are the major opportunities and challenges that this business faces in becoming successful, and how will they be addressed?

In this section we get back into brutal personal honesty. Remember that nobody knows your plan as well as you do. Only you know about all of the assumptions that went into the projections, any shortcuts you took in coming up with the spreadsheet numbers, and the things that you wish that you could have included in the analysis. As you wrote the plan you might have had times when you thought, "Wow—that could be a great opportunity," intending to follow up on it at a later time. You may also have had times when you thought "Ouch, that could be a problem," and kept on writing. You might or might not have included these two different topics in the plan, but they were in your mind at some point.

ED'S LESSONS LEARNED

Early in my career I worked for a boss who was heavily analytical and pretty risk averse. I did not understand these aspects of his personality and my young entrepreneurial mind couldn't understand why no level of analysis was ever enough for him. "Why can't we just move on this now?" I would ask. Instead of trying to understand him we butted heads, which was completely unproductive. We eventually found an accord but the learning period was pretty tough, and I place much of that struggle on my shoulders. He could not control his risk-tolerance level—it was just a part of who he was. He also had one of the most brilliant analytic minds I had ever seen coupled with decades of experience—a very powerful combination.

Here is where you review open items to see if they deserve further attention. Is that opportunity you did not pursue, because you were focused on something else, actually one that could bring great rewards to the business? Or is an earlier evaluated challenge (threat) to the business bigger than you initially thought, and should now be addressed? Next, think about the things that must be done right to make the business succeed. It might seem like everything is important, but in reality a few issues are so important that if they become problems the business could be jeopardized. Have those been addressed in adequate detail and to your satisfaction?

Finally, be honest with yourself about where this business plan is excellent and where it is troubling. What about the idea and the plan make you particularly excited, and what will keep you up at night worrying? These worrisome aspects are the ones that you will have to monitor diligently after startup. In essence, where is the plan strong or weak? Be honest. Better to find out now so that the strong areas can be capitalized upon and the weak areas can be shored up to present less of a threat.

How do you plan to create sales? This must be explained in enough detail to be believable.

If you have any doubt that sales are critical to the viability of your plan and the success of your business, then you should go back and reread Chapter 10. This is the portion of many plans that is given short attention to the detriment of the entrepreneur looking to start the business. Your investors will want to know how you plan to make money, which means "make sales." But as you will remember, the most effective sales come about through a combination of marketing activities, web activities, social media, telemarketing, and other activities that are specifically tailored to your idea and your customers.

Here is the fundamental question to ask about sales: will the approach as presented in the plan win customers in the numbers and time frame needed to meet plan projections? Step back from the details and think about the whole process and see how comfortable you are with the overall sales plan. Where is it really good? Where is it questionable, either in its approach or in its likelihood of being implemented? Do you have access to the people, contacts, resources, and skills needed to implement the plan? Is your marketing plan adequately funded to be implemented as stated? Have you been too aggressive (or pessimistic) with the projections? Would you believe the plan as it is presented, or should something else be added to make it more believable?

If you can look at your sales projections and believe them, then congratulations! You have done a great job of working through a complicated and often troublesome process. That is no trivial feat and you should pat yourself on the back. And perhaps treat yourself to a hot fudge sundae—my particular weakness. If you don't believe the projections, then take the time to review where you are the most uncomfortable with the sales approach, and determine what can be changed to make it all more believable.

The sales portion of your plan is in many ways the toughest because it involves issues over which you have no control—the prospect's final buying decision and the actions of your competition. When all is said and done, the sales projections are nothing more than an educated guess. Just make sure that your guess goes way beyond "trust me—they will come," and you will make a more credible showing than most new business plans.

Why does this business, run by you, stand a reasonable chance of succeeding?

When we started out on our journey I told you that the success and character of your venture came from you. The investors know this and they will be relying on you to use their money in a way that aligns with their expectations, as set forth in the plan. But they will not be there for the daily, detailed decisions that you will have to make. They are going to have to trust you to do that on their behalf.

Here is a fundamental question at this point: If you were an investor, would you trust you to run this company? Are you the right person to be leading this venture into the success that you have outlined in the plan? If you can't do it alone, have you already gotten the right people on board, or at least defined the skill set of those you need to find? In other words, do you have the drive, energy, health, personal resources, and management skills needed to pull this plan off? Remember that I am not talking about any single area of the plan. I am talking about the totality of running the entire company. Try to look at the overall idea and its execution when making this determination.

ED'S LESSONS LEARNED

Years ago I was canoeing on a river in Northern California when we saw a group of local guys jumping from a bridge into the river. It didn't look that high so I decided to give it a try. Let me just say that the jump looked a lot higher from the bridge than it did from the water. As I climbed over the railing onto the edge, getting ready to jump, one of the guys on the bridge came up behind me and spoke these words of wisdom: "Once you step off, don't think about whether you should have jumped or not. Just control the flight and the landing. Otherwise you can get really hurt." He was right. Once you say yes, don't second-guess the decision. Just make it work. Control the flight and prepare for your landing into the successful entrepreneur's chair.

If the answer is yes, then go get 'em! Perhaps one of the coolest feelings in the world is realizing that a specific and unique job has come your way and you are the right person at the right time to fill that job. In this case it is even cooler in that this could be your last job if it all works out as planned. If the answer is no, then take a deep breath and see if you are being too hard on yourself. You had the motivation and skills to get your idea to this point in the planning process. You had the vision, did the research, performed the analysis, and wrote up the details. You might have investors in the room ready for a presentation and might even have gotten the buy-in from a skeptical spouse or partner. In other words, you have accomplished amazing things in getting the plan to this stage. Do those amazing things help you better see yourself successfully running this business? If the answer is still no, then take a few minutes to glean what you feel is missing. Perhaps you are the right person to lead the operation but know in your heart that you will not be able to do the prospecting needed to create the sales. That is okay. Have you figured out a way to include the person who can create those sales? It might even be a third-party company that you contract for a while to get you up and running. Of critical importance is that this reality is thought through and the financing for this extra person is embedded in your plan.

Of one thing you can be sure—investors, employees, and customers will be looking to you to lead them and this business to success. Picture yourself sitting behind a desk with the title of president of your corporation. Picture the decision making, hiring, firing, pricing, selling, and other daily activities that come with the job, and see how you feel. If you get excited and feel ready for the challenge, then good for you. If not, then perhaps you should let your plan set for a little while and come back to revisit it. With renewed vision it might look different. Remember that investors will be trusting you, but you will also be taking on a job that is difficult to get out of. The last thing you want to do is take on a job that obligates your money and time in a way that you won't feel comfortable with.

Comparing Your Needs and Tolerance to the Plan Risks

There is a very real possibility that you might get through the planning process, evaluate the plan, revise your plan, and still not be comfortable with it. Don't get discouraged or depressed about it. It happens. Let's take a look at why that may be happening and then look at some options.

Remember our discussion in Chapter 2 about risk, risk tolerance, and your natural tendencies? You might be smack dab in the middle of their confluence. To review a little, we all have a natural tendency to avoid uncertainty, and if you think about a business plan it is really a lot of uncertainty rolled up onto a single document. Unless you have already taken action on your plan, it is still only a future projection of what can happen. Every aspect of the plan that you researched, analyzed, and refined helped to reduce uncertainty. Our goal with all of the analysis was to reduce the uncertainty to a level where the plan as presented will be acceptable to investors and other stakeholders, including you. But in reality, the future is uncertain. No matter how confident you feel about your projections, there is always some uncertainty. What might be happening is that as the plan writer you intuitively know more about the level of plan uncertainty than is reflected in the document. In essence, your intuition might be telling you something about the overall plan that your rational mind doesn't comprehend. I am a firm believer in intuition as a guide; if it is raising concern, listen. Mentally survey the plan in your mind, see which areas draw your concern, and then take a quick scan of that section to see which areas pop out. Perhaps your intuition is telling you that this area is a potential trouble maker. If you go through all of this and the section details look right but you are still stuck, then it might be something else. Read on.

Remember that we all have an intrinsic level of risk and uncertainty tolerance that in some ways is out of our control. You might be one of those people who just don't like uncertainty, and the plan will never be certain enough for you to risk. That is okay; that is just who you are. Maybe you should consider taking more of a back seat advisory role in your business instead of being the person in charge. Decision makers never have all of the answers when making decisions, but they still have to make decisions. They are able to make better decisions if they have the best possible information and analysis at their disposal. Perhaps you are better suited as an analyst supporting the company coupled with someone who has a stronger tendency to act. Action tempered with wisdom is very powerful. Wisdom without action does not make a successful new company. Get my drift?

Running It by the Other Stakeholders

You are probably pretty excited. You have performed the reviews outlined in the prior sections of this chapter and so far all systems are go. Very cool. Now it is time to let your plan see the light of day. This means opening it up to the scrutiny of others. Why? Because you cannot see your idea objectively no matter how hard you try. Trust me on this one. When you believe an idea and your analysis behind the idea, it is very difficult to see it with an unbiased eye.

Before you run it by critical people like investors, run your plan by someone who can offer you a supportive yet critical analysis. Ideally this would be a mentor, teacher, relative, friend, or consultant. Make it someone who has an investment in your success but not a stake in the investment itself. What you are looking for is that independent review of the idea that may confirm what you believe to be true or find areas where additional work is needed. Again, all you are trying to do is create the best possible projection of the future, and if this person can help you do that, great!

Try not to be defensive (this is hard to do) and let them know that you value their honest, critical, yet supportive feedback. Avoid people who will pick the plan apart just to be contentious. What you want is constructive feedback on the viability of the plan—not a debate about matters of little consequence. The color of the brochure is not a reason to shelve your business—having existing competition that you did not know about is a reason for concern. Get it?

This is probably a good time to run the plan by any significant partners, spouses, family members, or others who will be impacted by your pursuing the plan. Remember that these folks will also have to live with the business and their buy-in is important. You might find that what was previously reticence on their part has become appreciation for your commitment as demonstrated by creating the plan. They now know that you are serious, and if the plan makes the viability case intended you might be surprised how well it is received. Think about how much better it would be to have their support! If they believe it is in their best interest as well as yours, future decisions should be easier.

Making a Choice and Beyond

At this point you have analyzed, intuited, and disclosed about your plan as much as you can. It is time to decide. Yep. It is that time. Are you going to do it or not?

Yes. It should be just that simple at this stage. Yes means yes. If you are in the yes category, then understand that once you start signing lease, funding, employment, and other agreements, it will be hard to get yourself out. On the other hand, if the answer is yes, then you should execute with as much resolve, belief, and confidence as you can. You have done the preparatory work needed to prove the idea viable and the only thing left to do is execute. Make it so.

What if your answer is no? No does not mean no forever—it might just mean no for now. Try to determine if your no is coming from the plan being a bad idea or from your own natural reticence to take the risk needed to make the plan work. If it is the plan, then make sure to check out the later section on dealing with a bad plan. If it is your reticence, then accept that about yourself and take it as a learning opportunity for your future business decisions.

ED'S LESSONS LEARNED

Once you move forward with your business, you will have to make commitments in the form of legal agreements to create the business, trademark, and copyright filings to protect your intellectual property; website name reservations and hosting; lease agreements; printing of letterhead and business cards; and dozens of other areas. Don't question whether these things need to be done—you determined that already when preparing your plan. Execute your plan with resolve and commitment. It is okay to have your moments of doubt and concern (and they might be intense, by the way), but don't let those stop you from executing your plan. That would be like trying to take back stepping off of the bridge and would only cause you harm. Keep moving, take action, and control the flight. Check out Part 4 for tips on handling your first year in business.

Dealing With a Plan That Does Not Work

It sometimes happens that the planning process shows that the idea is not one around which a viable business can be created. First, be thankful that you found out now instead of six months into the process, when you might have already quit your job, borrowed a bunch of money, made vendor agreements, and made commitments to customers that you cannot fulfill. Anyone who has ever had to close down their business because of financial reasons will tell you that it is not a pleasant experience. I am a firm believer in the planning process as an extra measure of insurance that the idea is viable before taking the plunge.

Now, just because the idea as originally conceived does not work out on paper does not mean that the kernel of a good idea isn't in there somewhere. Why? Consider the following points.

When you started down the planning road you probably expected to prove your idea was viable. That it turned out the opposite, to your surprise and disappointment, says that you learned some things along the way that you did not know when you started. That is good. You know more about your idea, the industry, potential customers, the competition, and other areas that materially affected the initial idea's value. But that does not mean that a variation on the idea cannot work. This is pretty important and I need to revisit creativity again to make my point.

Remember from Chapter 3 how creativity comes from a convergence of experience, knowledge, and openness that form the creative moment when opportunities can show up? You cannot control when this will happen, but if you have not done your homework in the other areas there is a good chance the creative moment will not show up. Here is my point—you have spent a lot of time and effort becoming more knowledgeable in the industry associated with your initial idea. You also are much more knowledgeable about what will be required to make an idea work in that industry. Ask yourself: What is missing in the industry that you now know about that you did not know before? What would need to be done to make that idea work? Can you modify your existing plan in such a way that the resources you were going to put into the first failed idea could be put to better use with this new idea? If so, the first plan was not a waste by any stretch. In fact, without the first plan you would likely have never uncovered the second opportunity that could become your business. The first idea got you into the game—once in the game you realized that the touchdown pass was the second idea.

Open yourself up to an idea by asking yourself the above question and then keep your mind open as ideas show up. It might take minutes, hours, or weeks before they start to flow, but trust that they will. Carry a pen and paper around with you so you can write the ideas down when they come. Don't expect to remember them later. I appreciate that this is a difficult exercise because most of us are always looking for answers. In this case, the first answer did not work out. Why not take the time to see if the right one will show up for your next planning round? That seems like time well spent to me.

The whole intent of doing a business plan is to create a best-guess simulation of how the future will look. The structure of the plan is there to help you cover all of the important things that will affect your success. But the plan is full of uncertainty because by its very nature it is a future activity that is subject to change. All of your research, analysis, writing, and evaluating help to decrease future uncertainty by providing a reasonable range of possibilities over which things can occur. Eventually, you will have to decide if the level of risk and uncertainty is within your tolerance range and whether the idea is ready for scrutiny by other potential stakeholders.

At that point you will need to decide if the idea is worth pursuing on your own, worth pursuing in conjunction with others, or simply not a very good idea at all. No matter the answer, planning offered a detailed look into a complex process and you are now much better informed. Remember that if the plan shows itself not to be viable, let it sit for a while and come back to it with a renewed perspective. Time and distance have a way of making things look different and it could happen with your idea, too.

The Least You Need to Know

- Your plan has to answer the fundamental stakeholder questions presented in Chapter 7 before you show the plan to others.
- Trust your intuition and don't give into unfounded enthusiasm or fear.
- Expect that you will have concerns and perhaps doubts as you make commitments without a revenue stream. Don't let that keep you from executing your plan.
- Look for ways to involve others who can help you improve the likelihood of the plan and business being successful.
- A business plan that shows an idea to not be viable can be used as a spring-board for the next idea that could be great.

Part 4

Surviving the First Year

Creating a viable business from an idea is an amazing feat, but once your business is running, other influences come into play that can hurt or help your success. It may sound strange, but success can create challenges that, if not handled properly, will put you out of business right when success starts to knock.

Right up there with creating sales in business importance is effective cash flow management. I dedicated a complete chapter to cash flow management because cash is like air for your business—without cash, your business won't last much longer than you would without air. We also spend time discussing the impact of growth on your personnel needs and your need to hire the right people at the right time to help your business grow on a solid personnel footing. Success presents new opportunities that you cannot anticipate. Some of these opportunities will be amazing and perfect, while others will take you off of your chosen path, potentially jeopardizing your hard-earned success. Chapter 19 is full of lessons and tips for remaining flexible but focused as you manage your successful first year.

I added Chapter 20 at the suggestion of prior readers who wondered how they could tell if their business was in trouble. I truly hope that you will never have to close down a business, but also know that you will be in good company if you do. It is a painful but common experience, and this chapter will help you recognize trouble before it becomes crippling. It will also help you determine if an alternate approach to your business might actually be more successful than the one you were previously following.

As with all parts of this book, my goal is to help you create the success that you want and deserve. Surviving the first year is a mandatory step toward creating a successful future. Perhaps the best approach is to treat each year like it is the first?

Chapter 17

Treating Cash Like Air for Your Business

In This Chapter

- Knowing the value of cash in your organization
- Turning receivables into cash
- Learning how rapid sales growth can jeopardize your business
- Using credit and credit cards to your advantage

Lori stared in disbelief at her staff sitting around the conference room table. She had heard of this happening to other companies; she couldn't believe it happened to hers.

"We're out of money," she said with a sigh. "I can make payroll, but I don't have enough left over to pay our suppliers."

"That's impossible," said Philip, the VP of Sales and Marketing. "We just had three of our best months this quarter. In fact, our current revenues are triple that of last year at this time, and our income statement clearly shows a profit for this quarter. What gives?"

Jerry from accounting shifted uncomfortably and then spoke up. "The net income shown on our statements is right—we have recently closed some great deals, but our cash is way low. As you know, we haven't collected payments on those large sales. And we've had to pay our workers and suppliers even though our customers haven't yet paid us. It'll be great when all those sales are collected, but if we keep growing as we have been, we're likely to need even more cash."

"So are you trying to tell me that our sales success has put the company in jeopardy?" cried Philip.

"Not at all," said Lori. "We simply did not plan for the rapid increase and came up short with our lines of credit and other ways of getting cash into our bank account. It was my and Jerry's responsibility to plan for this, and we blew it. We need to tell our vendors our dilemma. I think honesty is the best policy. Let's just hope they will let us stall our payments. We can't let it happen again!"

Everyone nodded his or her head at the seriousness of the situation. They had been so happy about being successful that they had forgotten that without cash the business would be out of business.

Keeping the cash flowing into your business is key to growth and expansion, not to mention paying your bills in a timely manner and sleeping at night. This chapter will help you develop strategies for keeping cash flowing into your business so that you don't run into the same trouble Lori's company did. It also shows you how to determine the amount of cash you will need to keep afloat.

When You're Out of Cash, You're Out of Business (Usually)

Love may make the world go 'round, but it's cash that keeps the lights on while you're spinning. Try to retain an employee when you can't pay him, and you will understand that cash is the business equivalent of air. Lose your employees, especially the good ones, and you have substantially hurt your business. Once they're gone, they're usually gone for good.

Take a look at your vendors. How long will they keep providing you with the materials you need if you can't pay your bills? About as long as a snowball would last in a west Texas desert. Once again, you can't blame them for putting a stop to your credit line. Guess who is paying employees out of his own pocket because he gave you credit that you can't pay? Your vendor! Your vendor has to cover his own behind just like you do.

And what about you? What happens if you can't pay yourself? How long will you keep the business alive and pay your employees when you are not being paid? A few months, maybe, but when it becomes a way of life, you will be seriously tempted to pull the plug and "get a real job." Not because you don't love what you do, but simply because that's what an organism does when its air supply is taken away. It looks for a more favorable environment.

Lack of cash might cause your usually professional employees to become disgruntled, might cause the quality of your product to decline, and might lead to your own loss of enthusiasm. The result is that your customers will be affected, and they probably won't like it. Their opinion of your company might drop as employees become snippier over the phone or in person. Unfortunately, customers don't really care why the quality has declined; they just recognize that it has, and they might decide to take their business elsewhere if it continues.

All this because you forgot that cash is king! Income is great. Equipment is wonderful. Receivables are heartwarming. Inventory gives you something to count on boring weekends and at the end of the year. But cash is the oil that makes it all work smoothly on a daily basis.

How Success Can Kill Your Business

How good can it get? Here you are with a 300 percent increase in sales over the past six months. Your people are flying high, and you just can't seem to do anything wrong. As a matter of fact, the projects coming your way are larger than you ever thought feasible, and it looks like you'll get them all! Your initial dreams have come true, and you're on the verge of becoming unbearable to everyone around you. Don't worry. Life is about to humble you, unless you have taken the proper steps to deal with the growth.

Timing is the secret to success, and that is particularly true when working with money. The time that money is in your hands, or in someone else's, either makes you money or costs you money. You must make every possible effort to turn your sales into cash as quickly as possible, paying as little as possible to get your money faster, such as by factoring, lines of credit, or offering fast-payment discounts.

There is a fairly well-defined relationship between when you order the parts needed to build your products, when you pay your vendors for those parts, how long it takes you to convert parts into sellable goods, how long it takes you to sell the finished product, and how long after the sale you actually collect the customer's money. This relationship is graphically demonstrated in the following figure. Notice how much time passes between when parts are ordered and paid for on the left side of the diagram and when you receive payment from customers on the right side. Quite often several months may transpire between the date you pay your vendors and the date the customer pays for purchased product. If you do not manage this float period properly, it can severely hamper your ability to keep your head above the cash-need waterline. And don't forget that you will have to pay all of the normal fixed expenses that keep the lights on and water running.

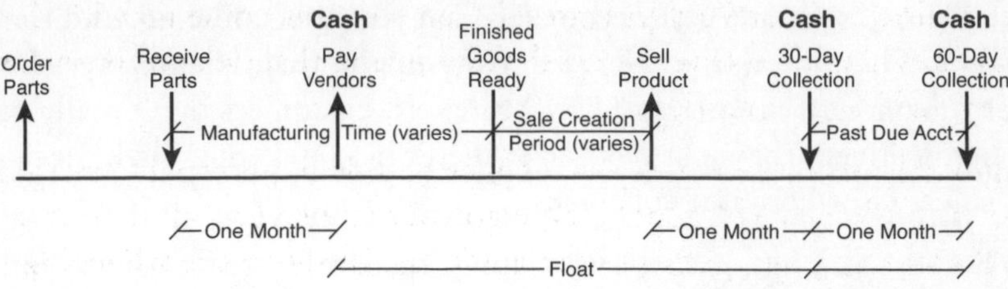

Typical cash inflows and outflows for a manufacturing company.

Picture this scenario: you used to provide $10,000 per month in services, and all your customers paid cash on delivery or by credit card. When you completed the sale, you got the cash and it went straight into your business checking account and was used to pay your bills. Everyone was happy. Then customers began asking for credit terms. After all, your competitor offered them credit, and they have consistently used your company instead. It wasn't such a big deal, and they were stable. Why not offer them credit? So you did.

Take a look at what happened when you agreed to offer credit payment terms instead of cash. Your customers can now pay you a month later than they would have before. In essence, you voluntarily delayed receiving cash payments for at least a month. You, however, still need to pay your employees and vendors at the end of *this* month. Where is that cash going to come from? Unless your company has a lot of cash on hand (and wouldn't we all like that situation?), it will have to come from you, the owner. When the customer pays, you will simply pay yourself back the amount you loaned the company and all will be fine. So far, so good. Sort of ....

WATCH OUT!

Don't put all your eggs in one basket. As dangerous as it is to grow your company quickly, it's even more risky for that growth to be the result of a relationship with just a few big customers. Keep trying to expand and diversify your customer base while managing your growth, or a lack of payment by a single large customer can seriously cripple your business and will cost you some sleepless nights.

Now let's be really successful and bump your monthly sales to $30,000. Wonderful! Who is going to provide the cash needed to cover the month-end bills? You? Do you have the $30,000 (or perhaps more) on hand to lend the company? Even if you do have the cash at $30,000, you might not when monthly sales hit $50,000 or $100,000. What about if customers start to take liberties with the net 30 day payment policy and start paying in 60 or 90 days instead? Can you now come up with the $60,000 to $90,000 it will take to cover the cash flow during that delayed payment period? I should now have your attention.

My point is this: someday you will no longer be able to personally provide cash advances to the company. Uh oh! There go your employees, all those wonderful vendor relationships, and perhaps your company. In short, the whopping success that you enjoyed has just put you precariously close to being out of business. Isn't it amazing how a few short weeks can turn your business on its ear? That is exactly what will happen if you don't take steps to avoid a cash crunch.

I'm not trying to talk you out of making your business as wildly successful as you can imagine. I'm just trying to open your eyes to the fact that success can destroy all that you have built if you don't also deal with its potential risks. Use the information in this chapter to help ensure that your credit and collection policies are rock solid, which will minimize the cash pressure on you and your business.

Factoring, Credit Terms, and Loans

Here you are, all dressed up to go to the dance with a hot date and no cash to pay for the cab. Now what do you do? You go to someone and borrow money against your next paycheck or income tax refund. Well, the same thing can be done with a business, and it's called *factoring*. With factoring, a third-party company gives you a large percentage of what customers owe you, sort of like a short-term loan using what is owed you by customers as collateral. This is pretty expensive short-term money to get, but it is common practice and viable if you are in a cash crunch.

You can also improve your cash situation by providing your customers with a discount incentive for paying their bills early (or even on time) and delaying payments to your own vendors with whom you have credit. This improves your cash position (for the short term) by decreasing the time, often called *float*, between when you must pay your bills and when you receive money.

Finally, you can get a short-term loan that is secured by your customer receivables from a bank or other funding source. This technique is less expensive than factoring and provides greater stability, along with other benefits such as improving your lending relationship with your banker.

DEFINITION

Factoring is the process of receiving money now from a third-party company for payments your customers are expected to make to you in the next few weeks. There is a cost for having that money now, however, which is paid in the form of a percentage fee to the factoring company. It is expensive to do on a regular basis but can be effective when needed. But you must plan ahead with the factoring company to factor your receivables. **Float** in this cash management context refers to the time frame between when you earned the money due you and when it is actually received. It can also mean the time frame between when you actually receive money and when portions of the money are due payable to others.

Factoring Receivables

If you need cash now to cover business expenses, there are companies out there who will provide you with cash for your receivables in exchange for a fee. Here's a general outline of how factoring, or discounting, of receivable notes works. (Use this as a way of understanding the process and verify the percentages with prospective factoring companies that you can find with a simple internet or Yellow Pages search, or preferably from a peer referral.)

1. You close the deal and the customer agrees to pay you for your product or service.
2. The company that plans to factor your receivables issues an invoice to the customer (on your or perhaps their letterhead), which the customer is to pay.
3. The factoring company immediately gives you cash worth between 80 and 95 percent of the receivable value, even though the customer has not yet paid.
4. The factoring company may also give back an additional portion of the fee (up to half of the initial 5 to 20 percent discount) if the customer repays within the specified time frame.

For example, assume that a client contracts to buy $10,000 worth of your product or service. Assume also that you realistically expect to receive that money within 45 to 60 days, which can put you in a bind, depending on your company's cash situation.

AT THE WEBSITE

A sample Receivables Purchase Agreement is included at the website as document 17-01.

Finally, assume that you sell the receivable to a factoring company and receive an 85 percent factoring rate with a 10 percent additional payment if the customer pays within 30 days. This means that you immediately get $8,500 and then will receive an additional $1,000 if the customer surprises you and pays within 30 days. You gave up 5 percent, or $500, to get your money up front instead of later, while also pushing the collection issue over to the factoring company. Collection becomes their problem, not yours. If the customer never pays, you still keep the $8,500, which all of a sudden sounds like a pretty good deal!

If you are in a cash crunch, factoring can save your hide. However, the downside is the expense, which is not trivial. That 45-day cash advance cost you $1,500. If, rather than factoring, you used a typical bank line of credit, with interest-only payments, at a 5 percent per year interest rate, then borrowing that same $10,000 for one month would cost you $10,000 × 0.05/12 = $41.67 instead of the $500 (or $1,500) that factoring would have cost you. When you receive the $10,000, you pay off the line of credit. Simple. Wow! You have saved a lot of money using the line of credit instead of factoring. Oh yeah—but if the customer does not pay you the $10,000, you will still have to pay back the bank for the loan if you spent it all. As you get to know your customers, you will be better able to determine when factoring or line of credit financing is the right approach. Factoring notes from good-paying customers makes little financial sense if you have a bank line of credit, but factoring new customer receivables might make sense. Let the factoring company absorb the risk of nonpayment. The best solution is a solid credit policy that decreases the chances of nonpayment altogether.

Factoring is a pretty expensive way to have your cash earlier instead of later. On the other hand, if you need it, you need it. Don't stand on principle and put your company in cash jeopardy.

STREET SMARTS

You can minimize the sour taste that factoring percentages can create by becoming your company's own factoring services. If you have the personal resources and you own a corporation, you can use your personal money to replace the need for a third-party factoring company. You buy the receivables from your corporation with your personal funds and provide the same terms as a factoring company, just like a third-party factoring company. At least the interest is going into your favorite account (yours!) instead of some other company's and you get to generate a substantial return on your personal savings. You will, however, need to declare the interest income on your personal tax return. After all, it is income that you earned as a private individual even if the money did come from your own corporation. Prepare a factoring agreement using the form provided at the website and perform the transaction just like you would with a third party.

Offering Early Customer Payment Discount Terms

You have an excellent opportunity to improve your cash flow by simply changing the way you pay your bills to vendors, how you set the criteria for offering credit to customers, and how efficiently you collect receivables from your customers. If you must pay your vendors in 30 days and your clients must pay in 60 days, you have a problem in that you are collecting money 30 days after you have already paid the expenses associated with that collection. On the other hand, if your customers pay you in 10 days and you pay your vendors in 45 days, you are in excellent shape in that you are receiving payment from customers 25 days earlier than when you have to pay your vendors for the parts needed to produce that sale. You can give customers an incentive to pay earlier by offering them a discount (such as 2 percent of what they owe you) for payment within 10 days. Many companies will jump at the chance to save the 2 percent, and it's certainly cheaper for you to offer this discount than to pay a factoring service 5 to 15 percent for the same result! From your customer's perspective, they are saving 2 percent off of their product costs (which improves their gross margins) by simply paying early, which may not be a problem for many of them. You will hear this credit policy referred to as "2 percent in 10 days/net 30 days" credit terms.

It is important to mention here that the simplest way to help ensure that customers pay for their credit purchases on time is to only offer credit to customers with a solid payment track record. If a customer wants to purchase $10,000 worth of product from you on credit, you are essentially loaning him or her at least your cost for manufacturing the product or providing the service, and arguably the whole sale price if you could have resold it to a more reliable customer. Whenever approving a sale with credit terms, ask yourself if you would trust the customer with cash in the amount of the sale. If the answer is yes, then make the deal. If no, then you might be better off walking away. Definitely ask the customer to complete a credit application and then run a quick credit report check with any of a number of online services. It could save you major costs and headaches later on. Customers with solid credit expect you to run a credit check, so don't be afraid to ask. If someone gets irate when you ask for a credit check, it might indicate that he or she has something to hide—you are better off finding out now instead of 90 days after the bill became due.

AT THE WEBSITE

Sample Credit Application (document 17-02) and Authorization to Release Credit Information (document 17-03) documents are included on the website.

Think about it all as you look at the earlier diagram of cash inflows and outflows. Notice that the arrows pointing up to indicate money going out and the arrows pointing down to indicate money coming in have a delay between them that usually doesn't work in your favor. You must pay the suppliers months before you receive customer payment. Now take a look at how much easier it is to receive the money just 10 days after the sale instead of possibly months. Plus, when you have the money, you don't have to worry about it becoming uncollectable, a horrible circumstance in which I hope you never find yourself.

Buying on Credit

Your grandmother may have always told you to stay debt free because a person in debt is a person in trouble. Well, that might be true for certain people, but credit is the lifeblood of a growing company. Credit in itself is not bad. It is how you use this credit that can either save your hide or hang it out to dry.

Try this technique for increasing your cash situation. Instead of paying $25,000 in cash for that bunch of computer equipment you intend to buy, why not go to your bank and have them give you a loan secured by the equipment? The bank will probably want 20 percent ($5,000) down and the rest financed over 24 to 36 months at the going interest rate. Notice that your monthly expenses go up, but you have $20,000 cash in your bank account, that you avoided spending today because of the loan, to handle unexpected cash shortfalls.

You can also negotiate to purchase raw materials from your vendors on credit. Instead of paying cash for the materials when received, arrange to pay for them 30 days after receipt. This gives you 30 days more time with the cash in your bank account, while also using the materials to create sellable finished goods. Heck, some vendors may offer "buy now, no interest or payments for up to two years" payment terms. This could become really pretty scary from a customer perspective because you could take full advantage of this offer, run up a huge debt to this vendor, spend the customer payments on growing your business, and find yourself unable to pay the debt when due in two years. It takes a lot of self-discipline to manage this type of debt/credit opportunity properly and not put your company in jeopardy. Remember that credit is never free, and at some point charged items must be paid for with real cash.

Even your grandmother would agree that paying your bills while keeping some cash on hand is a healthy state of financial being.

AT THE WEBSITE

Sample Security Agreement (document 17-04) and Personal Guaranty (document 17-05) documents are included at the website.

Taking Out a Loan Secured by Receivables

You can imagine that every business has the same problems in turning its receivables into cash. It should not surprise you that people, even banks, provide loans designed to cover exactly this short-term timing situation. It is essentially a line of credit secured by the receivables, and you are expected to pay it down as quickly as possible. The interest rate is some variation of prime plus a few percentage points annually, instead of the large percent that you pay with a factoring company, and you establish a credit history with your bank. That always pays off in the long run because the bank can become an integral partner as your success requires higher and higher borrowing levels. Just make sure that you set up the line of credit before you will actually need it because bankers are well known for only being willing to give you money when you don't need it. Look too needy and you might not get the loan.

Properly Handling Credit Card Sales

Credit cards may well be the new form of legal tender. I know people who carry credit cards and an ATM card but little or no cash. You simply cannot ignore the implications of credit and ATM cards on your business no matter what type of business you run. It is important to consider whether offering your clients the opportunity to pay using a credit or ATM card, instead of cash or a check, is a good thing.

More than likely you will find that taking credit cards is a convenience that most of your clients will want, especially if you deal with consumers instead of established businesses. However, if you'll be selling consulting services to companies and billing tens of thousands of dollars, a credit card is probably not the best way to get paid on a regular basis. Instead, request a completed credit application and a company check to verify that they will pay, and save the credit card processing fees.

The Way Credit Cards Work

A person (consumer) obtains a credit card from a bank that provides a line of credit to the person whose name is on the card. The credit card is issued as a Visa, MasterCard, American Express, Discover, or some other brand name. The line of credit will have a limit, depending on the way that the bank evaluates the person's credit worthiness. This person can now charge purchases using the credit card virtually like cash.

The customer's credit card is generally *unsecured*, meaning the bank has nothing that it can take and sell to repay the person's debt if the person defaults on payments. The only recourse is to cancel the card, destroy the person's credit record, and bother her until she pays. Fortunately for you, the business owner, you get paid for the purchase whether your customer pays the credit card company or not. That's what you pay the credit card companies for. They, not you, absorb the risk of their credit card holder not paying her balance. You can really look at the credit card processing fee as inexpensive payment insurance.

STREET SMARTS

There are all kinds of new services popping up to make it easier to accept electronic payments in almost any physical location. There are iPad and iPhone applications that will allow you to accept credit cards for payments at craft fairs, swap meets, or even at a customer's location. With the increased importance of working from a virtual office, it makes a lot of sense to make the way you accept payment mobile as well.

You, as a business owner, set up your own merchant account so that you can process credit card sales. You are issued a *merchant number* by your credit card processing company that helps it identify exactly who you are, the applicable processing fees to charge, and where your money should be deposited, which will be your business checking account.

Think of credit card users as people with a line of credit from a bank whose name appears on the card, such as Citibank or Chase. The company that processes and clears your company's credit card transactions is called a *card processing company*. It executes the transaction by subtracting available credit in the amount of the sale from the customer's credit card line of credit account and depositing the sale amount, less a processing fee, into your checking account. Instant cash—well, almost. The deposit will usually take one to two days to complete. When you contact your credit card processing company for authorization to charge a customer's credit card, you will need to provide your merchant number, the customer's card number and expiration date, the security code shown on the back of the card, and the amount of the purchase before approval is given along with an authorization code.

The processing company may be independent or it might be affiliated with a bank, perhaps even your bank. You can find a comparison of credit card processing companies online by doing a simple search using terms like "e-commerce credit card processing comparison."

DEFINITION

A **merchant number** is a number given to your company that is used to identify which account should be credited when a customer makes a purchase. It also verifies that you're allowed to accept credit cards in payment. An **unsecured** line of credit is a line of credit that is not backed by some form of collateral. The interest rate on this type of credit line is usually much higher than a loan secured by something of value other than your good name and promise to pay. The **card processing company** handles the details associated with processing the purchase in your store, deducting the sale amount from the customer's account and getting the cash into your checking account (less a fee, naturally).

Covering Your Legal Bases

We are always happy to sell our products or services and receive payment, but what happens if the client later contests the charge and refuses to pay? What if the person using the card isn't supposed to be using it? You could be stuck with a huge bad debt that takes a large number of healthy sales to correct. The following table lists a few things you can do to minimize the chance of those situations occurring. Without question, ask your credit card processing company about its recommended (or required) procedures for verifying credit card purchaser identities. The following list gives you a general idea of what is involved, but work with your processor for the most current specifics.

Credit Card Sales Protection Procedures

When Someone Charges Something in Person	Actions and Reasons
Check the expiration date to make sure that the card is still valid.	Look at the "valid from" and "good through" dates on the card to make sure that the card is still valid. Check that the information is embossed and not just printed.

When Someone Charges Something in Person	Actions and Reasons
Look for a hologram or other security mark.	These emblems are difficult to duplicate. If you can't find one, you might be holding a fake card.
Disclose the terms of the sale and get a signature, if possible.	The more that's in writing and signed by the customer, the harder it is for him or her to contest the charge. Make sure the terms, conditions, and return policy are easily spelled out on the receipt.
Run the card through an imprint machine or electronic terminal, fill out the sales draft completely, and get a signature.	Take the customer's card and run it through an imprint machine or electronic terminal using the proper sales receipt. Make sure that you get a signature and that it is legible and completed with all pertinent information included. Verify that the signature on the card matches that provided by the customer on the sales form. Don't accept an unsigned card.
Get an authorization number for each transaction.	Run the card, amount, and expiration date through the electronic terminal to receive a sales authorization from the service company. Write the authorization number on the sales draft if not automatically printed.

The preceding information is taken from the December 1992 issue of the Agency Inc. Newsletter, Volume 3, Number 12, *and is applicable today.*

If you plan to take orders over the telephone without seeing the customer and getting his or her signature, you can still take a few steps to better protect yourself. Because the chances of getting burned over the phone or by mail are much higher than in person, the credit card companies will probably charge you a higher discount rate for this type of transaction. These types of transactions are often called mail order, telephone order, or internet (MO/TO) orders. You want to do everything you can to avoid getting burned by a chargeback, which happens when a customer contests a charge and you as the merchant have to prove that this person did indeed make the purchase indicated. If you do not have the right paperwork, this customer could get your product or service and you won't get paid.

Hopefully you now believe me when I say that "cash is like air for your business." You can persuade employees, vendors, and customers to go along with a lot of things, but not being paid is not one of them. Understand that you have to manage your cash position while you also work to increase sales. Otherwise, you can sell yourself right out of business, like Lori in the opening example.

The Least You Need to Know

- Cash is the lifeblood, or air supply, of an organization. Without cash to pay employees or vendors, you are out of business.
- Cash will become scarce at some point in your business growth; of that you can be certain. Set up credit lines today that will help you when it happens.
- Factoring is a convenient, yet expensive, way of turning receivables into cash.
- Banks will give you short-term lines of credit secured by receivables, but you generally need to have set up this line of credit before you actually need it.
- Businesses must accept the various electronic payment types or risk losing customers, especially if you run a restaurant, retail store, or other end-user, consumer-related business.

Chapter 18

Hiring Good Employees and Staying Legal

In This Chapter

- Adding people to your organization can be a good thing
- Knowing the value and risk of a personnel manual
- Realizing when a contractor is really an employee
- Test-driving employees before hiring
- Understand payroll tax complexities

"Tell me this again," said Julie. "Didn't you smell it when you went by her desk?"

"Sure I did," said Bill, the company lawyer. "But so what? There's nothing in your company procedures manual that covers drinking on the job."

"Because of that, I can't fire her?" asked Julie. "She carries a bottle in her purse. She takes a nip in the bathroom on a regular basis. I have even accidentally picked up one of her coffee cups to find that she was drinking Irish coffee. She's drunk on the job, and I want her gone!"

"That is understandable, but not legal. Has her drinking affected her job performance in any way? Can you definitely point to business lost because of her drinking? Has it disrupted the normal flow of business in such a way that it has cost the company money?"

"I know that it must have happened, but I can't point to a specific instance," said Julie. "So you're telling me that I'm stuck with her because firing her would open us up to a wrongful termination suit based on our not having a no-drinking policy in our manual."

"Pretty much. You need to watch her closely and look for signs of poor performance that can then be documented. Then you can let her go for poor performance. In the interim, you should never mention the drinking problem to her and act as though nothing is wrong. Otherwise, you play right into her attorney's hands when you finally let her go. Sorry."

A corporation is a legal entity that draws its life from the employees and owners who move it forward. When a company has the right people, the energy of the corporation is great and customers buy because they like doing business with positive people. But when the company has a toxic personnel combination customers can feel that, too, definitely costing you sales. At some point customer demand for your product or service will be so high that you will not be able to complete the required work on your own. At that point you will start to look at hiring employees to help out. Yet managing other people brings with it a number of legal and management issues that you don't have to deal with when you work alone. In this chapter, I'll show you how to add the right people to further your success, while making sure that you do not get into legal trouble.

When You're Successful, You'll Need Help

If you follow all the great guidance throughout this book and add your own special flair, you will probably become so successful that you just won't be able to do it alone. At that point, you need to add employees to your organization. It might be a clerical person who handles billing and answers the telephone, or a complete staff of people who handle all those new projects you just brought in as a result of your incredible sales skills.

We talked about operational personnel planning in Chapter 12 using the process flow diagram as a way of understanding the skill sets needed to accomplish process tasks. We also included a management section in the business plan outline presented in Chapter 7. Hopefully you are getting the impression that people are critical to the success of your business—not only when selling the idea to investors, but more importantly once you are doing the daily work to make your idea a success.

There is a reasonable chance that you will start the business on your own and eventually add employees as your activity level increases. Adding your first employee creates new challenges that are unique for you as the founder and owner. There are lots of ways to find employees, but before I jump into how to find the right employees, how to manage them, and all that detailed stuff, let me present a few bigger issues for you to consider.

You have been on your own, and possibly working alone, since you started your company. Make sure that you actually need an employee for functional reasons, not simply because you want someone around the office for business companionship.

Have you gotten to the point that you are losing business because you don't have enough help? Lost business is a financial justification and not just a personal justification for hiring a new employee. Are you losing enough business to pay for this new person, and then some?

Know that a small business is different from a large corporation in that one employee out of a total of two makes up 50 percent of the personnel. If that person becomes a poor performer, 50 percent of the company personnel has performance trouble. Be aware of the large effect one person can have on your business, your customers, and your earnings. Your first hire could be one of your most important, because he or she can have a dramatic tactical and strategic impact on your continued growth.

I have had both excellent employees and poor employees work with me over the years, and have found that poor performers have a much bigger and longer-lasting impact in smaller companies than they do in larger corporations. Larger companies can afford the luxury of one or two poor performers; smaller companies cannot. If you find employees with performance problems, such as employees who can't seem to do the work right or at a reasonable pace, let them go quickly before they do serious damage to your business.

Unfortunately, the tendency in small businesses is to take care of employees as if they were members of your family. I say "unfortunately" because small business owners tend to keep trouble employees on for a much longer time than do larger corporations. One of the biggest mistakes I have seen in small business is when owners are "fast to hire and slow to fire." You should do just the opposite; be "slow to hire and fast to fire." You simply cannot afford to have the wrong people working for your small business for any substantial length of time.

Never forget that you started this business. It is yours, not your employees'. Try to let go of the daily decisions so that they can carve a place for themselves in the operation of the business, or you will wind up with morale problems down the road. Remember, however: you sign the checks, co-sign all company debts, and ultimately make the big decisions. They might also need to be reminded of this as you give them increasing responsibilities and they naturally take more initiative. How you do this is a matter of style; don't be too heavy-handed—an overbearing boss can easily drive away a good employee. (Besides, they obviously know that you own the company.) It is an interesting balancing act to promote employee initiative while also making sure that the employee doesn't get you into financial trouble.

STREET SMARTS

One thing that you will learn about vacations when you own your business is that vacations cost you twice—first, the money that you pay for the vacation and second, the money that you did not earn while you were on vacation. This is particularly true for those who run service businesses. Look to define your operation so that the business makes money even when you are not there. The solution could involve outsourcing of routine operational components, hiring employees, or possibly more effective use of technology by going virtual.

After all of these cautions, let me say that once employees successfully take on more responsibility for the company's activities, you might wonder how you ever did everything yourself. There isn't a more satisfying business experience than to find a series of orders, invoices, projects, and bank deposits that your employees created without your involvement. To call in from a well-deserved vacation and find thousands of dollars worth of revenues and profits coming into the company while you are gone is the essence of small business success. It makes me smile today just thinking about the times that happened to me. Thank you to my employees who made this happen. You know who you are.

Your business needs to be able to create revenue without your involvement, or it will never grow beyond your own abilities. That can only happen when employees get involved and have the freedom to act on their own, within certain guidelines you set.

If you want to keep your company small, then you might never need another employee, other than an occasional relative or temporary helper to handle clerical stuff. If you want to grow so the company works on a relatively independent basis, then you need employees. Accept that as a reality and plan for it in advance. That way, you can be on the lookout for the right person and get him or her onboard when the timing is right.

Employee Practicalities

Employees cost money and must pay for themselves, either today or in the near future. Once you hire an employee, you assume the responsibility for paying him or her regularly, no matter what the business's financial condition is. Even if you have a really poor month, you still have to sign those paychecks to your employees. Are you ready to absorb that expense, or would it be smarter to push yourself a little more for a short while and build up a nest egg? Is the lack of that employee costing you sales and net income yet? In other words, is hiring this person a convenience for you, or is it a business necessity?

When you add people to your organization, you inherit a responsibility for their financial support. If you aren't making enough money to support yourself, you probably can't afford to support someone else. Also, the reality of the situation is that you become the last employee to be paid if the company has cash flow problems. Are you ready to accept not getting a paycheck for a week or two (or three or four or ten) without resenting the other employees who have gotten paychecks?

Employees take up space, use telephones, have opinions, and make decisions; you must expand your business operations to include them. They need to take responsibilities from you to help the company grow. Are you ready to let go enough to use them effectively?

ED'S LESSONS LEARNED

Even if you have managed large numbers of people for a large corporation, expect that managing people in your own business will be a completely different experience. In a large company, a manager is implementing the policies handed down from corporate. In your company, you *are* corporate. Employees know that you make the rules and that all they need is for you to okay something to make it a reality. They also know that you can basically hire and fire at will, depending on the size of your company and some other legal details. Suffice to say that managing people in your own company is a far more personal experience than managing in a large corporation, so be prepared for the difference when making personnel-related decisions. The buck really does start and stop with you.

Have you ever managed people before? Are you familiar with the challenges of encouraging and leading employees? Do you need to take some classes in effective supervision before taking the plunge? Even if you have managed workers before, a refresher is probably a good idea, especially in the context of a small business.

If you are in a service business, make sure that your employees reflect the proper attitude and image you have worked hard to establish. A few weeks of poor telephone attitude toward your customers can unravel years of consistent service on your part. If you are really lucky, one of your established clients will tell you about the problem first, but few customers ever complain; they just leave! Teach your employees early about the level of service they are expected to provide, and reinforce it with your own actions.

Your customers will need to adapt to working with someone on your staff. Make sure that the new employee maintains the same level of concern and dedication to customer satisfaction. The best thing that could happen to your business is for your customers to like working with your employee as much or more than they liked working with you. Now you can focus on other business issues besides customer satisfaction. It is a good sign when customers want to work with your employees instead of you, assuming that you and the customer are still on good terms. This means that you are successfully transferring your unique style throughout the organization.

Don't forget that employees can always (and probably eventually will) find another job. This is your business, and you will be around long after they are gone, unless you are very lucky and find the right long-term fit with an employee. If an employee leaves, you inherit his or her decisions. This means that commitments made by an employee can obligate you long after that employee is gone. You, on the other hand, can't just leave and find another job because this *is* your job. Period. Find that balance between delegation and monitoring that provides the employee with effective freedom to make decisions while ensuring that the decisions made will work for you as well.

I like to set dollar thresholds under which employees can make decisions within their business area before they have to contact me. For example, I might let an office manager make any decision under $250 on her own, up to a total of $1,000 in a month. I then review the purchases with her at the end of the month. In this way, I let the employee know what I expect and teach her how to make decisions that I would have made on my own.

This is beneficial to the employees in that they get to work with some autonomy, and it is better for me because I don't get bothered about each expense. If money is tight, I drop the thresholds, or I start the employees at $100 per purchase and $400 per month and increase the limits as I become more comfortable with their decision-making ability.

There are legal issues related to having employees that you could ignore when it was only you working at the company. Some form of a personnel policies manual would help you avoid situations such as the one Julie had in the introductory scenario. On the other hand, personnel policies that are too elaborate can get you into unnecessary trouble. Here might be a good place to involve someone with employment law experience—a lawyer or someone with a human resource management background.

WATCH OUT!

You might be tempted to hire a friend or relative so you'll have someone on your staff whom you can trust. Be sure he is qualified for the job. Don't let trust be the primary reason you make this hire, or your company will suffer. Go over the details of what you really know about him, compared to what you have simply assumed or heard since you first met. The last thing you want is a surprise that causes you to fire a friend or relative, which disrupts the business, ends a friendship, and makes holidays even more stressful than they already are.

Good Help Isn't Hard to Find

Depending on your personnel needs, there are a few avenues you can take when you begin seriously looking for employees. First, you can try out potential employees through a part-time employment arrangement before making a full-time hiring commitment. You can also hire candidates for a specific project, as independent contractors, and see how they work out. Finally, temporary help agencies can serve as excellent sources of candidates who have already been screened for your particular job opening.

Fellow business owners are a tremendous referral source for temporary people who do their jobs well. Start asking for referrals even before you have a need so that when the need does arise, you have a list of qualified people from which to choose. You will probably need these people when some type of emergency occurs, so it helps to have the relationships already established before the crisis.

You might consider hiring people as independent contractors before taking them on as employees. An independent contractor is a worker typically hired on a per-project basis. They usually have a specialized set of skills that you do not have, which enables you to add capability without having to invest in a full-time employee. Contractors expect to be let go at some point, so the parting is rarely accompanied by hard feelings. I think it's a good idea to have the contractor sign an agreement specifying the length of the project, the work that needs to be done, and the payment for that work. He may cost more in the short term, but he is not on payroll when his temporary project ends, which saves you money in the long run. This arrangement also shifts the payroll tax burden onto him because he will receive a 1099 from you, making him responsible for the payroll taxes, instead of an employee's W-2, where you pay the payroll taxes. This can make a big difference at tax time. If you keep hiring him back, then it might be time to consider him for a full-time position.

When hiring an independent contractor, remember that the IRS has specific criteria that determine whether a person is a contractor or an employee. If you hire someone as an independent contractor but the IRS decides later that she was really an employee of your company, you might be liable for past payroll taxes, Social Security payments, and penalties. Be clear up front about how the IRS would characterize your relationship before taking chances with an independent contractor. Get your hands on IRS Publication 15-A (Employer's Supplemental Tax Guide), 1779 (Independent Contractor of Employee), and Form SS8 (Determination of Worker Status for Purposes of Federal Employment Taxes and Income Tax Withholding) to determine whether you have employees or contractors (irs.gov).

Other temporary personnel sources include college and university co-op programs where students learn on the job through structured programs that help them apply what they've learned in their course work, as well as high school programs that match interested students with part-time employers. Many colleges and high schools also encourage students to apply for internships during summer and winter vacations, where they work for an employer full-time during those breaks from school. Although internships are generally shorter term than co-op programs, you can have a student help on some important projects during a summer vacation. All these options are excellent ways to give students a chance to gain real-world experience, while benefiting from their efforts at your company. You will typically use them for more routine tasks.

Don't forget about all of those folks who are now retired that have decades of work experience. They often do not want to work full time, have time flexibility, and appreciate the chance to be productive without the stress of full-time employment. Money may be less of an issue for retired folks because they might already have a pension that pays their daily bills and medical benefits from other sources. Bringing on a retired person with the right experience could be a great way to add experience to your organization without the full-time price tag. This is particularly applicable to you younger entrepreneurs who have drive but not a lot of business knowledge. What a great deal it would be if you could hire a part-time employee and also a business management mentor at the same time!

As your operation becomes more stable, you will want full-time employees on your staff so that you are not constantly having to train new hires who may only be around for a few months. Take your time finding the right people.

Start out the hiring process by getting a clear picture of what you want this person to do. Write out a detailed job description. Then picture the personality type you want in that job. Ask other business owners about personnel that they have worked with who might be right for your job opening. Place ads in the paper or online, and prepare yourself for hours, or days, of reading résumés and interviewing applicants.

AT THE WEBSITE

A sample Independent Contractor Agreement is included at the website as document 18-01. A sample At-Will Employment Application is also included at the website as document 18-02.

More Employees, More Restrictions

All companies are not created equal when it comes to employment law. Depending on the state where you are doing business and how many employees you have, you will be affected by different rules and regulations. One way to deal with these various state and federal government regulations is to develop a *company policy manual*, or employee manual, for everyone's reference.

DEFINITION

A **company policy manual** spells out what the company expects of its employees and what they can expect in terms of benefits and other topics related to employment. New employees are given a copy of the policy manual and are made aware that they will be held responsible for adhering to these policies.

A company policy manual spells out what the company expects of its employees, and what they can expect in terms of benefits and other topics related to employment. New employees receive a copy of the policy manual and are responsible for adhering to these policies. A well-defined policy manual clears up employee confusion because everyone is given the same information. It also specifies who should be contacted with follow-up questions. Know the laws of your individual state, and create the proper policy manual to address those state laws.

A few personnel issues apply to all companies, regardless of the number of employees. You should clearly spell out the number of company holidays provided to employees each year and the amount of vacation and sick time a person is eligible to take during the year. If you have other company policies that employees need to know, state them in the policy manual.

Drafting your own handbook is cheaper than having an attorney write it, but a legal review is essential to make sure you haven't made significant errors.

State and federal laws kick in at different company size levels:

- If you have fewer than four employees (depending upon the state), you are the master of your domain and can hire, fire, and reward pretty much as you see fit.
- As an employer, you have to worry about a wide array of federal laws that address discrimination and other important personnel-related issues. See the Equal Employment Opportunity Commission website (eeoc.gov) for more information.
- If you have 15 or more employees, you need the same level of policy manual as IBM or General Motors. It must include policies on family and medical leave, harassment, drug-related issues, discrimination, and virtually any other workplace-related issue, such as smoking.

AT THE WEBSITE

See the Employee Handbook Checklist (document 18-03) and Acknowledgment of Receipt of Employee Handbook (document 18-04) documents at the website. A sample Sexual Harassment Policy is included at the website as document 18-05. A sample Employee Noncompete Agreement is included at the website as document 18-06 as is the Employee Confidential and Proprietary Information Non-Disclosure Agreement as document 18-07.

My recommendation regarding your personnel policy is this: until you need a comprehensive manual as outlined in the previous paragraphs, simply include only those items that you specifically want and intend to enforce, such as no drinking on the job, no smoking in the workplace, excessive tardiness or absenteeism as grounds for dismissal, no sexual harassment, no discrimination in the workplace, no stealing, and other rules that you feel strongly about and will not tolerate.

WATCH OUT!

If you write a policy manual, make sure that you and your employees comply with the written policies. It is a good idea to leave out statements regarding policies that don't apply to your company yet because of its size. Whatever you state as a policy, you must be prepared to follow so don't limit yourself unnecessarily.

Make sure that new employees get a copy of the personnel policies manual as part of the hiring process and that they know you expect strict adherence to these policies. In this way, if someone is caught drinking on the job, you can let him or her go for being in violation of the company policy, even if job performance has not suffered. (Thus you can avoid Julie's position as outlined in the chapter opening.) Some firms make new employees sign a statement that they have received the policy manual so that there is no possibility of later confusion on either side of the desk.

Beware the "policies in a can" approach, which uses a standard software package or standard forms to define your personnel manual without getting the advice of a human professional. The created manuals are probably overkill for your small organization and could open you up to unnecessary exposure to legal action. I would strongly recommend creating a draft of your policies using sources such as the forms with this book or a software package, and then running the draft by someone who can ensure that the policies are right for your company. This is one area where you don't want to be your own lawyer, because employment laws are complicated and often change.

No Solicitation and Noncompete Clause Realities

How could these former employees do this to you? You spent three years building up that account, and your two best people just stole it away within a few days of voluntarily leaving your company. Their overhead isn't as high as yours, so they undercut your price by 30 percent. Are you hurt and a little mad? You bet! What could you have done to prevent this? A *noncompete clause* might have been one way to go. A noncompete clause is an agreement that your employees sign, saying that they won't steal your business ideas or methods, or go to work for a competitor, or become competitors by starting their own firm.

STREET SMARTS

The noncompete and no solicitation section is included in detail because it is likely that one of the first people you will want to hire is a salesperson. This is natural because one of your biggest jobs is to create sales; if you are not a salesperson, you better hire one. More than one new owner has been disappointed about how the relationship with their first salesperson ended, perhaps losing customers to a competitor in the process. The situation might have been avoided with the signing of a noncompete agreement.

Although noncompete clauses are treated differently from state to state, you should definitely look into them as one way to protect yourself and your company from ex-employees stealing your ideas and opening a competing business across town. When an employee signs a noncompete agreement, he or she essentially agrees not to compete with you in a specific geographic area (such as in a particular city or region of the country) for a specified period of time (such as one to two years) by performing the same function for another company that he or she did for you.

The theory says that your director of sales couldn't quit and go work for your competitor right away in a sales-related position. The reality of an employee noncompete is that it cannot keep a person from making a living in his chosen field. In other words, you really cannot keep a person from taking a job as a sales manager or design engineer with a competing firm. You can, on the other hand, keep that person from using any privileged, confidential, or proprietary system information in his new job because this information belongs to your company. A salesman can still sell; she just can't use your customer list. An engineer can design; he just can't use design procedures that are proprietary to your company. Making employees complete a confidential nondisclosure and noncompete agreement lets everyone know your expectations if the employee separates from the company. After that, it is up to them to determine what they will do and up to you to decide if you want to legally go after them for enforcement of the signed agreements.

Enforcing an employee noncompete that keeps a person from being able to earn a living in their selected field is a difficult, and usually fruitless, endeavor. You are better served making sure that people know that contact lists obtained at your company stay at your company and are not to be removed when employees leave. Company confidential documents, which you should make sure are marked as such, cannot be removed from the company premises. Diligence on your part during hiring and while protecting sensitive information on a daily basis is the best defense you have against an employee using your information against you.

Think of an employee noncompete as a mechanism for keeping honest people honest. Some states treat signed employee noncompete agreements very seriously and prevent a former employee from taking a job at a competing company if you file suit to that effect. Other states take the view that noncompete agreements limit where a person can work, and don't uphold them. Check with an attorney who specializes in employment law to find out whether your state supports noncompete agreements. If it does, work with an attorney to write an agreement that protects you rather than do it on your own. You might just create more headaches for yourself down the road if you handle this stuff yourself.

There is a way to uphold a company's rights to retain its customers without worrying about a former employee stealing those customers away. This is called a *nonsolicitation clause*, which says that the employee agrees not to pursue your existing customers for business that is related to your company. This agreement lasts for a specific period of time after leaving your company, usually one to two years. Former employees are restricted from using the customer contacts acquired while working with your company to aid another company, including their own.

DEFINITION

A **nonsolicitation clause** is an agreement that your employees sign, saying that if they leave your company, they will not pursue your existing customers for business that is related to your company.

The best way for you to cover yourself in this situation is to have the employee sign a noncompete agreement as well as a nonsolicitation agreement as part of his or her employment. This is particularly true for an employee who has regular customer contact. It makes you seem a little paranoid, but it might also save thousands of dollars of business from walking out your front door. When a customer or competitor starts to wave cash in front of a former employee, his or her loyalty to you will be severely tested. Without these signed agreements you might end up with a personal disappointment and a financial loss without legal recourse.

By the way, if a newly hired employee starts sharing confidential information with you about his last employer, even though he signed a confidentiality agreement with that employer, then you should reasonably assume that he will do the same with your information when he goes to the next job.

Payroll Taxes: You Can't Avoid Them, So Learn How to Deal with Them

With employees come payroll taxes. No one I know thinks payroll taxes are fun or interesting, but as a business owner, you need to have a basic grasp of the legal requirements … otherwise, you can get tangled up in bureaucratic red tape and headaches that make asking for a loan sound pleasant by comparison. You don't have to be a rocket scientist to calculate payroll taxes, but you do have to pay attention to the details. By the way, as a sole proprietor, you still need to pay self-employment tax on your salary, so you really don't get around it even then.

Here's one of my favorite business secrets: just because you have employees doesn't mean that you have to do the accounting for your payroll. That's what staff (and service bureaus and accounting software) is for! I have clients with as few as five employees who use an outside service for managing their payroll. Read on for an introduction to the regimented, deadline-filled world of payroll tax accounting—so that at least you can find out what you'll be delegating to someone else.

The three basic categories of payroll taxes are state and federal income taxes (which you withhold from wages), Social Security and Medicare (you pay half, the employee pays half), and unemployment (you pay it all).

States and some cities have income taxes, as does the federal government, so you need to consult both the federal guidelines and relevant state and local guidelines to determine how much to withhold and when to pay it over to the taxing authority. Social Security (6.2 percent for the employer and 6.2 percent for the employee) and Medicare (1.45 percent for the employer and 1.45 percent for the employee) are easier to figure out because they are only federal taxes and subject only to the federal rules. Combined, the employer plus employee portion of Social Security and Medicare (referred to as FICA) is 15.3 percent, which happens to equal the federal self-employment tax for those who go that route (more is offered on the self-employment tax later in this section). Unemployment is subject to both state and federal rules, with potentially complex interactions between the rules, requiring even more detailed record keeping.

To find the federal rules, contact the IRS, which has a package of tax rules and guidelines for businesses, including "Publication 15, Circular E, Employer's Tax Guide." It's not the most fascinating reading in the world, I'll admit, but it's something you need to know about if you have employees and handle your own payroll tax accounting. The website has a wealth of information, including the forms and instructions, and is located at irs.gov.

For the state rules that apply to you, contact your state department of revenue (for income tax withholding information), department of labor (for unemployment tax information), or secretary of state (in case you can't find the right bureau to answer your question). Look in the blue pages (governmental section) of your phonebook under "Federal Government" or "State Government" to find out where to get the information.

Your employees will give you information about their tax status, number of dependents, and withholding allowances on a federal Form W-4. You can use this employee-provided information to determine the right withholding dollar amount in the tax tables or apply the right percentages for your state's formula. Some states have their own version of the Form W-4, which might contain different information from the federal form. In fact, some states don't have personal state income tax at all. You must check the rules for your particular state and proceed accordingly.

However, just because you figure it out once, don't think you're done for the year. If your employee's pay rate, marital status, dependent status, or address changes, the withholding amounts may also change, and you also have to be aware of the relevant ceilings ("wage base," in IRS lingo) for Social Security taxes and unemployment taxes. Providing detailed, repetitive calculations is what payroll tax reporting is all about, along with weekly, monthly, quarterly, and annual reporting requirements. If you like this sort of stuff, you will be in heaven. I, on the other hand, use a software package to keep me out of trouble.

You've filled out the forms and followed the instructions; now you just drop them in the mail and relax, right? Wrong! Federal taxes and some state taxes are subject to depository requirements, and you can't just mail a check with your return. In essence, you deposit the taxes at your local bank either using a payroll tax coupon with your *employer identification number* (*EIN*) on it, or by paying electronically. The depository schedule might not be the same as the reporting schedule or payroll schedule, so read the regulations carefully.

DEFINITION

Your **employer identification number (EIN)** is a number given to any company that has employees, whether it is a corporation or a sole proprietorship. You need to complete IRS Form SS-4 and submit it to the IRS to get an EIN. You can do it over the phone by calling 1-800-829-4933 with the information required to complete SS-4. Additional EIN information is available in IRS Publication 1635, "Understanding Your EIN." You can even get an EIN from the IRS website, irs.gov. If you have employees, even if it is just you, you must have an EIN to ensure that all your tax payments are credited to the correct account, which is indicated by your unique EIN.

I mentioned earlier that adding the employee and employer portions of Medicare (2.9 percent) and Social Security (12.4 percent) gives a total of 15.3 percent, which is the amount paid as self-employment tax. Self-employment tax is the same amount paid by those who work for themselves as a sole proprietorship, completing a Schedule C for their business and Schedule SE (self-employment) on their personal return. Some people complain about this tax being higher than if they were an employee, but you can see that the amount the government receives is the same (15.3 percent); it just seems higher because the self-employed pay both the employee and employer portion of the tax, which makes sense in that you are your own employer. The IRS says that you are self-employed if you "carry on a trade or business as a sole proprietor or an independent contractor," "are a member of a partnership that carries on a trade of business," or "are otherwise in business for yourself." You can figure it out from there—just know that you are not being penalized by being self-employed.

Fudge on payroll taxes, and you will pay big time and without mercy. It is one thing to be late on a payment to a creditor. It is another to be late on payroll deposit payments to the IRS because you are essentially playing with the employee income deductions. The employer is a trustee of these trust fund taxes, and as such has fiduciary responsibility to make proper payment to the IRS. The IRS will eat you alive in late-payment fees and interest if you delay, so make sure that you read the next section and file on time. Think of it this way: you are holding the employee payment portion for the IRS, so if you do not make the payment, you are essentially stealing from the employee. That puts a little different spin on it all, doesn't it?

For Your Plan

Your company might have a fresh new offering, but the people who work for the company will determine its success. It is important that you take the time to present details about key management personnel as well as your intended approach to hiring and keeping key future personnel. As part of your plan, make sure that you discuss the following points:

- Present the backgrounds of the founding management team, showing why they are the right people to start this particular business at this time.
- Discuss the startup personnel requirements from the perspective of not only finding customers but building a solid customer base.

- Provide job descriptions of the major positions that will perform important functions for the near term.
- Provide estimates of the annual salaries of these personnel, as well as your own and the other founders' salaries.
- Present a plan for expansion and how tasks will be divided as the company gets larger.
- Discuss benefits and how you plan to handle them, not only for the founders but also for the staff.
- Include a copy of the personnel manual (if available) so that investors can see that you have taken the right steps to protect the company and you from employee suits.
- Discuss the intended management style, culture, and general operational policies that you intend to implement on a daily basis.
- Show that you and the other founding members recognize that employees will eventually need to be added if the company meets with the success that all hope to happen.

The Least You Need to Know

- No man or woman is an island when it comes to succeeding in business. You must have the assistance of others if you want the company to grow beyond your capabilities.
- An ineffective employee in a large organization can be disruptive, but in a small company, that person can be disastrous because of the effect he or she has on others and on customers.
- Define processes, procedures, and policies that can be easily understood by new hires. Set up your minimum personnel policies to cover you on the "must adhere to" issues, and add others later as needed.
- Try to use temporary personnel at first before making a permanent hiring commitment.

- State and federal employment laws kick in at different company size levels, based on the number of employees.
- Employee-paid payroll taxes include Social Security, Medicare, and federal and state withholding. The company and the employee pay equal amounts of Social Security and Medicare. The company pays all the federal and state unemployment tax. Payroll tax deposits are your responsibility, and mishandling them can have very serious consequences.

Seizing Unexpected Opportunities While Remaining Focused

Chapter 19

In This Chapter

- Learning a new reason for planning
- Understanding that the first year will happen in stages
- Believing that once you start to succeed the competition will start to take you seriously
- Treating your customers and stakeholders as special partners
- Keeping an open mind while remaining focused on getting to break-even as soon as possible

"You look about as glum as I have ever seen you," remarked Peter as he looked across the table at his friend Bill.

"No doubt," said Bill shaking his head. "I've gotten myself and my company into a huge mess, and I'm not sure what to do to get out of it."

"What happened?"

"Remember when I decided to take on the large distribution contract for South America earlier this year? Well, I just found out that our major customer in Argentina is going under and taking a chunk of my receivables with them. They fell behind on their payments and we kept shipping, believing—perhaps more accurately, hoping—that they were good for it. Now, I'm not sure that I can make payroll since those receivables were used to secure my line of credit with the bank."

"Ouch! That really hurts."

"Not as bad as knowing that I could have avoided the whole thing by staying with my original plan instead of being seduced by the prospect of making 'big money' in a short period of time. We never planned to go to South America in the first place and had no initial interest in carrying those products. I just got greedy and now have put the entire company and a year's worth of work in serious jeopardy. When will I learn to listen to my own advice?"

Who among us hasn't felt that pang of jealousy when talking to a friend who took what you thought was a really silly chance only to have it work out, making them a lot of money. "If I had only …" went through your mind as you thought about the lost opportunity. I've had it happen to me. My clients have had it happen to them. You have, or will have, it happen to you. That is just the nature of business life.

What if it had turned out the other way and the opportunity had cost them a lot of money? What if you had taken the chance and it had cost *you* a lot of money? How would you feel then? Not so hot, for sure. The worst that happened to you by not taking the chance was that you lost opportunity cost, but you did not lose your hard-earned money.

As your business becomes more active, more opportunities will come your way, and you will not have the financial or personnel resources to follow them all. Selecting the ones that are the best fit for you and your business is very important and is the focus of this chapter. We will review the reasons that you wrote a plan in the first place, look at the typical stages your business will go through in its first year, and then offer some guidelines for how to handle the various new opportunities that will come your way as you succeed.

Revisiting the Reason for Planning

Do you remember way back in Chapter 2 when we talked about risk, uncertainty, opportunity cost, and personal risk tolerance? Do you also remember how the business plan was intended as a structured way for you to evaluate your new business idea with the intention of reducing uncertainty to the point that the uncertainty was within your risk tolerance level? If you don't remember this, you might want to take some time and review that chapter because these concepts apply across a wide variety of business situations outside of planning, but they are integral to understanding how to use your plan in moving forward.

WATCH OUT!

I have known people who treat their plan like an unchangeable set of edicts with which they, their stakeholders, and (naively, in my opinion) reality must comply. Reality doesn't much care what you thought would happen, and you are silly to ignore the reality of the situation around you after you open your doors. Compliment yourself for having created a plan that got you up and running, but then adapt to what reality sends your way.

The plan was created initially to help you decide if the idea was worth pursuing, and then to enroll the financial or personal commitment of others who could help you and your business idea succeed. Once you are up and running, the plan takes on a different purpose. Your initial planning was nothing more than a detailed and (hopefully) sophisticated guess at how reality would look once you got started. Now that you have started, reality is what it is. Your guess was credible and effective as far as it could go—but reality is unavoidable. Go with reality every time.

Short- and Long-Term Planning

Nothing happens in the long term without *short-term* actions that move you toward your desired outcome. Short-term actions cannot help achieve any particular goal if no goals have been set and no plan has been developed. You have to know where you're going before you can figure out a route to get there, right?

Taking the time to determine your own goals and your company's *long-term* mission and objectives will guide your daily actions. Without this framework, you and your employees may be busy, but the business will not move forward because everyone is pulling in separate directions. Making sure everyone knows and understands the goals and objectives of the company will make life a lot easier—for you as well as for your employees. Defining the company's goals will minimize employee frustration because they will know what they're working toward. You can minimize confusion by identifying and eliminating activities that don't directly support the goals of the company. (Remember the story at the beginning of this chapter.)

As the business owner, it all starts and ends with you. The time you took early in the book to learn more about yourself, your personal motivations, and your long-term goals helps to ensure that you move the company in the proper direction for you and your investors. If your business starts to grow in a direction or at a speed that makes you uncomfortable, you may start to resent the business and eventually unravel what was otherwise a good thing. We tried to avoid this by deciding up front what kind of business you wanted to have, both short term and long term. Now you are making that happen.

You should review and revise your plan every year to make sure that you are headed where you initially intended, and also that any new information acquired along the way is incorporated into the plan. In this way you keep on track while also ensuring that you and your company don't head in a direction that looked good when planning, but one that is not supported by business reality.

DEFINITION

Short-term goals are those you expect to complete within one year. **Long-term** goals are those you intend to meet within one to five years.

Adapting to What Life, Competition, and Customers Throw Your Way

Your company will move through stages as you progress through your first year of operation. Remember how your idea evolved from the back of a napkin, to a plan, to buy-in from stakeholders, to making commitments, to finally opening your doors? Remember also how each stage of this early startup process had its own characteristics and you had to be willing to adapt to each to succeed? Well, the same is true for the first year of operation.

When you opened your doors, nobody knew who you were. You had no customers, you might not have had employees, and the competition was not taking steps to protect themselves from you because you were not a threat. Now they know who you are. Customers are starting to learn about you and are using your offerings; competitors who might have lost deals to you are now paying attention, and investors are wondering how things are going compared to the plan they bought into. Employees are adding their expertise to the mix, perhaps offering new and viable perspectives on how to best move forward. In other words, it is no longer just you, even if you are a one-person company.

In the very early days you are doing what I call "missionary" work in that you are talking up your company and its benefits at every chance you get. You should be attending meetings, making cold sales calls, promoting your internet presence, offering special deals, and doing just about anything else you can to get the word out that you, your company, and your offerings exist. If people don't know that you exist, they can't do business with you. Creating awareness is the first heavy lifting you will have to do once your doors open. In fact, you would be well served to have started this process before opening your doors. Check out Chapter 11 for details on how to use social media to promote your business. Your typical sales call during this period will involve introducing you and your company, and explaining why they should give you a try. They will most likely not have heard about you; if they have, what they have heard will likely not be accurate. It is critical during these early days that you continue to promote your company no matter how discouraging it might become. And, believe me, there will be days when you will question your sanity at ever having started the business. Trust in the planning process and in the faith that your various stakeholders have in the idea (and you). Keep trudging along, making that cold phone call, completing that email blast, posting that blog entry, or updating Facebook or Twitter. You never know how all of this will piece together later on, but I can promise you that if you do not do this early promotion, you will not reach the next stage except by pure luck.

An interesting thing starts to happen as you get known. You might receive the dubious acknowledgment of your credibility from your competition by finding them pricing their offering or changing their terms to be more competitive. Nothing gets a competitor's attention faster and more deeply than losing a few major deals to a new player. I say it is dubious in that prior to getting their attention, you could play under their radar and not have to worry about them retaliating. Now that you have taken business away from them, they will start to watch out for you. This means that you have become a viable threat, which is a compliment and a heads-up call all at the same time. Now is when you will have to become sensitive to the power of your competition and their prior relationships to your new customers. Always remember that you are the new kid on the block and your customer performance track record is pretty short. Your competition could have been a vendor to that customer for years. You are going to have to be good, and remain good, to keep these new customers from going back to their prior vendors.

The moral of the story here is that you should not get complacent with your success, but must become more attentive. Kick your game up another notch because the competition will start gunning for you and customers will have higher expectations of you based on the great experience they had in the first round.

Another interesting stage is when you start to get calls from clients that are unsolicited by you or some activity of your company. This could be a contract from someone with whom nobody in your company ever had contact—they are not on a mailing list and have not received any direct solicitation of any kind from your company. This is a glorious day, actually, because it indicates that the word-of-mouth advertising that we all try to cultivate is working. This person is calling because he or she heard from a friend of a friend, or read something somewhere, or found your name on a Google search and decided to call. The snowball effect of your marketing efforts is now showing up and it is an exciting time. This means that the marketplace can start pulling you along in your sales activities instead of you having to constantly be pushing for the next deal. Congratulate yourself and your marketing and sales people, and have a little celebration. You have crossed a major milestone.

All of this said, once the congratulations party is over, get back on the phone or the internet and start drumming up new business. Don't take your minisuccess for granted because it can disappear in a heartbeat. This can be a precarious stage for a young company in that you have been pushing for so long and you feel like you finally have some breathing room. I am not saying that you should not appreciate your accomplishment, but I am saying that you cannot take this success for granted. If you keep up the sales push effort along with this positive snowballing pull from the marketplace, you should get a multiplier effect—your efforts now will be amplified through the marketplace, offering the chance for even more and easier sales success.

It is quite common for companies to go through explosive sales and operational growth during this period. If the cash flow is not monitored carefully, you could grow yourself out of business by running out of cash. This is particularly true for manufacturing companies which will have a longer float time between when raw materials are purchased and when the customer payment is received.

Eventually you will hit a point where your sales forecasts are more than just wishful thinking, you have regular customers, crazy hours and new opportunities are the norm, your employees have become really good at what they do, and you are taking home a decent income. This may happen in the first year or it might take a few years, depending on your particular business model and industry. When it does happen, I suggest that you take a little time to reflect on what has developed from the moment that you had the idea to today. You have created a viable, successful business with employees, vendors, customers, and investors—and all from an idea. That is the essence of entrepreneurial success and I hope you get to experience it one day. It is what keeps many serial entrepreneurs coming back for more.

Don't Forget Your Existing Customers and Stakeholders

As you bask in your entrepreneurial success, I think a word of caution is due here. I have seen many entrepreneurs start to take for granted the very customers who made them successful, believing that they will always be there. Instead of treating these valued customers as special clients with a special relationship, owners often focus their attention on newer opportunities, letting the quality of service suffer for these long-time supporters. This is a huge mistake and one that you should diligently avoid.

Your early customers believed in you when nobody else did and probably stuck with you through the "learning opportunities" that invariably occur with a new company. These same customers will stay with you through the long term, too, if you take care of them. But if you don't take care of them and treat them with the appreciation they deserve, then you cannot blame them for taking their business elsewhere. Your new customers are valuable but they are untested and you do not know how they will react when something comes up to strain the relationship. Your established customers have proven their dedication, and you need to prove yours by making sure they understand their special place with you and your business.

A similar type of thinking should be applied to your stakeholders, particularly your investors and early employees. Remember, they took a chance on you and your idea before much about it was proven. Investors parted with money to help you out and your key employees might have left great jobs to sign on to your dream. This is pretty valuable stuff that should not be taken for granted as you start to succeed. There is a social and ethical aspect to this suggestion that is the topic of many movies and television shows, so I won't go into it beyond saying that it is proper to show respect for those who showed you early faith and trust. There is also a practical side to keeping these folks in your corner.

Your early investors saw your vision and believed in it when it was nothing but a few pieces of paper and you telling them about this great opportunity. Now that you are up and running the successful business that they imagined, they are the ones most likely to contribute more money to help fund the next stage of growth. And it makes sense for them, too. There is much less risk investing now than there was earlier. You have demonstrated a marketplace need, your ability to provide your offerings, the ability to lead others in support of the business goals, and the ability to manage financial investment to a level of success. These are not trivial accomplishments and all contribute to reducing the level of uncertainty with a new round of investment. A new investor does not have that insight and will be evaluating a potential investment with a clean and more skeptical slate. As your business succeeds, it may need more money to fully capitalize on its success. Your early investors may be that source of cash or the needed referral to others who can.

ED'S LESSONS LEARNED

An interesting balancing act may appear with the company's success as it relates to your early employees. They may feel like they deserve a bigger portion of the later success pie. I had this situation come up with a couple of my service business employees after landing a major contract. They saw the large sale dollar figure and asked for more money. I called everyone into a room, told them that I would make this presentation only once, and then showed them, in detail, what happened to each sales dollar received from a customer. They were candidly shocked to learn how little actually became profit and that the largest percentage of each sales dollar was spent on their salaries. I was glad that I did. They worked harder, didn't resent me for making the "big bucks," and better appreciated that more went into creating business success than just good sales technique.

As for employees, who has more experience with your company than you and your first employees? These people committed early on to your dream and have been part of the early successes, failures, blunders, and ah-ha moments that got you to today. This experience is incredibly valuable and can show up as seasoned recommendations for future changes to products or services, smoothing over rough customer relationships, training junior members of your staff, or even as your successor should you choose to move onto other endeavors. Don't interpret my comments to imply that these people should not pull their fair share of the workload or that they should be given highly preferential treatment. But these people do have an experience base with you, your customers, your investors, and the company that you cannot buy. Keep that in mind as you determine how these seasoned contributors can help promote the next round of success for your company.

Going Back to Your Plan's Initial Assumptions

Every three months during your first year in business you should check your initial planning assumptions against what is happening in reality. Much of your planning and projections were based on a set of assumptions, and if those assumptions are inaccurate, your plan will be, too. By checking your assumptions against reality, you can get some advance warning of where things might not turn out as planned, which could be either good or bad. You might have been too conservative in your average price per sale, which implies that your total sales could be higher than planned. Or you might find that fewer people in your target prospect group buy your product than was expected, which would have a negative impact on sales. Either way, changing the assumptions changes the way you can expect things to work out in reality.

Once you double-check your assumptions, plug your updated assumptions into your financial projection spreadsheet and see what happens. If revenues are higher and expenses lower than expected, then you might not need that second round of funding you planned. If, on the other hand, revenues are lower and expenses higher than expected, then start planning now for additional funding so that your investors don't feel like you are desperate when you come with your hand out. Funding someone who is desperate is very different from funding someone who understands his situation, how to correct it, and needs additional resources to get him there.

You might find that your assumptions about your ideal customer were off, which would affect your marketing campaigns. No reason to sell to people you *thought* would buy when you now know who *is* buying. Get it? Or you might find that your variable product costs are different from what was projected, changing your gross profit and possibly impacting how you set up your fixed expenses. A higher gross profit with higher sales revenue might allow you to continue your growth by adding that extra person earlier than planned. Lower sales revenue and higher costs might force you to hold off on hiring that person you have been talking to for six months.

Should You Go in a Completely New Direction?

Every now and then reality will throw you a curve ball, potentially taking you and the company in a completely different direction from what you initially planned. Assume, for example, that you started a software services company with the intention of being a premier outsource talent provider. Now imagine that a client comes to you with an idea for a software product that she not only needs for her own company but believes is also badly needed for a specific industry segment. She is willing to work with you to create the product specification and test the product if you do the development. In exchange, she is willing to split the revenues from the sale of the product, but she wants you to be involved in the sales process. Where before you were selling software services, you now are being tempted with becoming a software product provider. Is this the right move? Should you diffuse your focus and resources by taking on what arguably is a different business model? Good question, and one you should think about *before* getting too far into this new arrangement.

In the end it all comes down to opportunity cost, risk, and uncertainty. How much money do you project you can make in your current direction? How much in the new? How much certainty is there with your current path and how much with the new? Would pursuing this new path interfere with your success to date on your current path? Would you be willing to sacrifice your current success and path for the chance of this software product path working out? Oh—and very importantly—are you even interested in becoming a software product developer and provider? There is really no "canned" answer to this type of situation. If it looks like quick money, it can be very tempting to run down that path. But if running down that path would seriously jeopardize your success to date, you should strongly consider the impact of losing out on both. Ideally you would maintain and grow your current path, assuming that it is working, and have enough money and manpower left over to pursue the software development project on a "kick the tires" basis. But if it is an either/or, think twice before you sacrifice hard-earned success on your current path for greener grass that might turn out to be not as green as expected.

Your first year in business will be like no other year to come. Everything is new and you are unknown. The marketplace will go through stages of awareness about you and your company and your energies should adjust to these changes. Understand the role that your plan played in getting you this far, and understand that it is now a guide against which you can monitor your progress. It is not a straitjacket into which you must make everything else fit. Periodically check your plan's assumptions and projections against reality. Adjust your plan moving forward accordingly, including your financial projections.

Keep your investors and other key stakeholders informed about how things are progressing. Be open to new opportunities, but be selective where you put your focus, money, and energy so as to best ensure that you get to profitability just as quickly and inexpensively as possible. Once you get past your first year and to the point where you are making a decent living from your new business, much of the uncertainty about survival shifts from "Will you survive?" to "What should we do next year?" This is a pretty cool transition that may happen so gradually that you barely notice it, but cool nonetheless.

The Least You Need to Know

- There are some typical stages your business will go through in its first year. Be aware of the various opportunities that will come your way as you succeed.
- The assumptions in your plan may not match reality. Learn from reality and adjust your assumptions and projections accordingly based on real feedback.
- Be open to new ideas but remain focused on getting past break-even to profitability as quickly as possible.
- Avoid the tendency to rest once you start to succeed, because that is exactly when the competition will be working hard to cut your success short.

When Commitment and Perseverance Are Not Enough

Chapter

20

In This Chapter

- Recognizing when your business is in trouble
- Understanding marketplace feedback that does not support your perceptions
- Appreciating the importance of secrecy
- Evaluating the personal impact of closing your business
- Relying on accurate financial tracking of your business's performance

Corey's desk was completely clear except for the most recent set of financial statements just delivered from John, her business consultant. Attached to the report was a short analysis that essentially stated that if the business kept on at its current pace she would run out of cash in 90 days. Corey was stunned. She had no idea where she would get more money and she also knew that closing her business was the last thing she wanted to do. She had personally guaranteed the $200,000 loan used to start up the business and it seemed like activity was picking up with new customers coming in all the time.

What really bothered her was the customer analysis that indicated that the company did a good job of selling new customers but a poor job of keeping them. John tied this into the rate of product returns, which were higher than he thought normal for a business of her type, indicating possible product problems. He suggested that these product problems could be causing dissatisfaction with customers, hurting repeat sales and probably Corey's reputation in the marketplace. Not to mention that higher returns would increase her product costs. Her first impulse was to call in her manufacturing and sales managers to discuss the report, but then thought twice about it. Maybe she should keep this to herself for now? What if John was wrong and she created a panic in her company for no good reason? The real question on her mind was, "Now what?" She picked up the phone and called John. "I read your analysis and think we should meet someplace off-site. Don't you?"

The best-thought-out ideas may not work for reasons which are beyond the owner's control. No amount of prior planning can with certainty keep customers from making alternate choices, control the state of the economy, control competitive actions, or predict a personal health crisis. Recognizing a business that is heading toward failure is difficult, especially when it is your business. The passion that led you to believe in the idea is the same passion which may keep you in denial about serious underperformance. The hope of this chapter is for you to recognize when your business is in trouble early enough to either correct it or to responsibly handle getting out.

Know Your Business's Success Metrics

We have discussed in prior chapters various actions you should take to ensure your success, and we have defined success in various ways depending on the topic under discussion. When all is discussed and evaluated, there is one ultimate measure of success: is the business generating enough gross profit and eventual net income to support you and the business with a little left over to reward you for taking the startup risk in the first place? This analysis should be done using the cash basis of accounting, not the accrual basis. As we discussed in Chapter 13, accrual accounting statements may show you making a sizeable net income when actually little of that net income is turning into cash—and cash is like air for your business.

Start by taking a look back on the company's performance since opening. How have sales revenues grown? You probably had a slow start, but once sales started to pick up you should ideally show consistent growth month after month. It might not be a straight line, but when you look back it should show a level of consistently improving activity. If not, then something is wrong.

STREET SMARTS

I don't know if it is a natural law of the universe but I have found that the 80/20 rule applies in a large number of circumstances. In this context, you might find that 80 percent of your business comes from 20 percent of your customers. If so, that is normal and nothing to be concerned about as long as you have a somewhat large number of customers. If you have only ten customers and the two who account for the 80 percent of revenue go under, they could well take you with them.

How has the number of customers grown? More than likely you had a couple of customers that started buying from you early on, and hopefully continued to buy from you. Those few customers should have expanded into many customers who are now buying from you on a consistent basis. If you still only have a few customers, and that was not your initial plan, then you could be in real trouble if those customers stop buying from you. And they might stop buying for reasons that are beyond their and your control. Government regulations might change and put them out of business. An owner at that company could get ill and no longer be able to keep the business running. A fire might bankrupt them. These are things that you cannot control and if they happen, you do not want a few major customers to be such a large part of your revenue that their extinction takes you with them.

Have you been getting repeat business from customers, or are they only buying from you once? I think this is one of the most important tests of how your company will do in the long run. I say this because great sales skills can get you initial orders and an expanding customer base, but if your company cannot keep customers once they use your offering then your business model must be based on continually adding new customers—not impossible, but tough to do. In addition, it prompts asking why they did not use you again. You might think that your company is filling their needs in a credible way, but if they use you and then turn around and buy from someone else, you would be wise to find out why they left. What if small changes could turn a dissatisfied customer into a happy one who refers others? This is a multiple win in that it takes some pressure off your sales force. It is always cheaper to keep a customer than to find a new one, and happy customers referring others is the best form of sales and marketing you can have.

ED'S LESSONS LEARNED

At one point when my business was struggling from a downturn in the economy, my father made an interesting observation. "I am not so much worried about a major event putting you out of business. That will probably be obvious," he said. "I am more concerned that every month you lose money but not enough to close you down. After several months you could be so far in debt you cannot get out." I have seen this happen and the only way I know to keep on top of this potentially slow destruction is by monitoring your financial performance. By the way, we came out of the downturn by finding a major company that knew about us and needed some custom training work done in a rush. A little luck was definitely involved, but we also created our luck by having developed a quality reputation and by not giving up.

How are your variable costs trending? How close are your percentage costs to your planned projections? If you expected your gross profit to be 65 percent of sales and it is 35 percent of sales, then you are spending 30 cents more of every sales dollar buying the parts needed to sell your offering. That is a huge difference and one that will put you out of business if you do not get it under control or find a way to control other fixed costs.

STREET SMARTS

A powerful financial management technique called ratio analysis is used by business managers to get insight into what is or is not working within their company. Talk to your accountant or a business consultant to help you determine the ratios that are right for your business. Developing the right ratios and then tracking them monthly will help you uncover problems before they become threats.

How are your fixed costs trending and how do they compare to your plan projections? Fixed expense management is a common problem area for newer businesses, especially those that get funded with a lot of investment capital. They tend to think that they can spend now in anticipation of the big money that will later come their way. They often later find out that being frugal today would better ensure that they have the money later on to address slower sales or higher costs. Fixed expenses are just that—fixed—which means that the same amount of money flows from your company month after month. Until you reach break-even you will have to pay those fixed expenses out of savings, further depleting your cash reserves, and each month you do that reduces your ability to remain open until you reach break-even. Tracking and controlling your fixed costs is critical during your first year of operation, and if you have let those costs get ahead of your sales success, then you should take a hard look at what can be cut out if it isn't already too late. Check out the cash flow analysis portion of the Dog Grooming Services business plan included in Appendix B for an example of monthly revenue and expense projections and break-even.

Monthly Status Check of How You Are Doing ... Again

I cannot overemphasize the importance of doing a periodic financial check on your business. Periodic for the first year means monthly. As you get into your second or third years and business becomes more predictable, you might be able to back off to every two months, but in today's world of instant report generation, I don't see any reason to check your financials less frequently than monthly. Don't react to small changes in dramatic ways, but if you see a small change in the same direction month after month, then you might be looking at a trend which would warrant attention.

Not checking your finances because you believe everything is going along okay is simply a mistake.

I have had clients working 60 hours or more per week who call me because they are on the verge of bankruptcy. They cannot understand why they are so busy and yet have no money. When we drill down into their operation, we often find that they are busy doing things that do not directly contribute to increasing sales, decreasing costs, or ensuring account receivable collections. They often have a few people too many on their payroll and do not realize that they have been losing money for the last few months. Once we get a set of accurate financial statements, including a proper ratio analysis, they get pretty quiet. It mentally sets in that the lack of attention to the financial side of their business might have cost them their business, and perhaps their house as well if personal guarantees were made to get financing.

The Danger of Believing Your Own Advertising

It is almost impossible to consistently sell a product or service that you do not believe in, and as the owner of a company you have to believe more than anyone. That said, be cautious about believing your own advertising about how good you really are while simultaneously ignoring the objective reality happening around you.

ED'S LESSONS LEARNED

I worked for a Silicon Valley startup company that sold a great product, but for a much higher price than the established competition. The company founders and management believed that "by selling harder and better" we should be able to close deals and repeatedly blamed slower sales on the sales force. I made a detailed presentation, based on market information and customer feedback, to one of the executives that we needed to drop our prices 20 to 35 percent or we would be out of business. He listened patiently, sincerely processing what I presented to him. When I finished he remarked, "If you are right, then we are in serious trouble. I don't think the others will buy in to that type of price decrease, not to mention our margins won't support the price drop." My response was, "We don't really have any choice if we want to close sales." That company does not exist anymore.

In your sales pitch you might talk about having the "most satisfied customers in the industry," but if you can honestly make that statement about only 2 customers out of 20 then you have a problem. If you have a number of unhappy customers that you hope prospective customers don't call, then you have a problem. If you believe that your products are the best in the industry yet you find few repeat buyers, few happy customer referrals, or, even worse, buyers that have returned to their original vendor (your competitor), then something is happening that you do not understand. Or if you find yourself dealing with a large percentage of product returns, you have a problem. It is important to believe in your offerings, your people, and your intentions, but don't be so fixed on believing that you miss constructive feedback that can better ensure your survival.

Living in the Question—Again for Your Survival

There is nothing pleasant about coming to the realization that the business you thought would change the world is not succeeding. Or even worse, is on life support. I sometimes get called in by clients who are looking for an objective assessment of how things stand, and I dread performing the analysis only to find out that they are on their way to bankruptcy. The conversation that follows is often a mix of "We knew it" to "Are you sure?" to "Is there something we can do?" I want to focus on the "something we can do" in this section.

It is almost guaranteed that your company has had successes since its opening. If not, then closing down the company is a pretty easy decision. If so, it can be confusing trying to reconcile the successes with the dire financial condition of the company. My suggestion to you at this point is to take a deep breath and revisit the creativity section of Chapter 3. I suggest that you again live in the question for a while.

The question to ask yourself is, "What else could we do with the company to make it more successful in the future?" Think about it this way: you have customers. You have some type of offering. You have a reputation. You have employees. You have some type of financial/banking relationships and perhaps some cash left in the bank. You might have accounts receivable that you reasonably expect to collect. In short, you have a lot of value embedded in the current company. Perhaps it just needs to be shuffled into a different mix, or oriented toward a different marketplace to fulfill its true value.

STREET SMARTS

I sometimes watch the television show *Shark Tank* and find the interactions between the entrepreneurs and the expert panel fascinating. On one show in particular, the entrepreneur had an idea for bottling wines from his own vineyard that he was looking to get funded. One of the panelists offered to give him money for the intellectual property of the bottling process and had no interest in the wine. The entrepreneur declined. He was committed to the vineyard idea but would not let it go. There was a heated exchange that ended in no money changing hands. By the way, the panelist offered $600,000 for 51 percent ownership of the idea and the entrepreneur could still sell his wine! I don't know how the entrepreneur did after the presentation, but I have to admit that my gut is telling me that he missed a pretty good opportunity to see his idea become a reality.

Remember the earlier discussion in Chapter 19 about using your plan as a guideline instead of a straitjacket? Perhaps you have adhered too tightly to your initial plan and missed opportunities along the way that would have been more beneficial. Perhaps a company you have intensely competed with could actually be a better ally if you combined forces against the other competition. Perhaps one of your customers asked you to pursue a novel project that you passed on but that now makes more sense. Perhaps one of your investors made a passing comment in a meeting about trying a different approach to the marketplace that was more viable than you initially thought.

We all have to believe that we are right on some level or we would never be able to make the wide variety of decisions needed to run a business. But we also need to step back at times and see if we are getting in our own way. This is particularly true if you are considering closing your doors. Imagine the relief you would feel if you found out that the product you were manufacturing was not as valuable as the patent upon which it was based. You could stop selling the product and just sell licenses to the patent. It might be that the patent was more valuable in the first place, but you were too tightly committed to the product to see that.

I don't mean to suggest that performing this creativity process will bring a magic bullet solution to your business woes. You might take your best shot at "living in the question" only to still close down. All I am suggesting is that you lose nothing by taking a little while to consider alternatives. A little more time won't probably make much difference. After all, you are looking at closing down the business anyway. What else can they do to you as the business owner, and what difference will another week or two really make?

Keep It Secret

One thing that you must do if you are considering closing down your business is to keep it a secret. You might find yourself wanting to talk through the decision, and that is probably a good idea. Just be very selective about who you tell and let them know in advance that your conversations are confidential. Nothing will be more of a self-fulfilling prophecy than telling customers, employees, investors, and other stakeholders that you are considering closing your business. Who would continue to lend money to someone looking to go out of business? Would you continue working for someone who may not be able to pay you for your work? As a vendor, would you offer credit to a company looking to close down? Would you buy a product or service from a company that may not be in business in 60 days? My guess is that you answered no to all of these questions and for good reason. Collecting money from a business that has closed is a lot like collecting money from someone who has passed away. Enough said.

This is where trusted colleagues, other business owners, accountants, lawyers, and consultants can play an important role. Part of their job is to keep what you discuss confidential. They would be hurting themselves by sharing private information. Because trust is critical to their business relationships, others will not trust them if they believe their secrets would be shared. They also have an interest in your success but are likely not dependent on you for that success. This combination of familiarity, support, and independence is just what you need when making this type of decision.

Avoid the tendency to talk with key employees during this phase. It is the rare employee who would tell her boss to close down knowing that she did not have another job lined up, and I think it is asking too much of the employee to expect that level of selfless honesty. Plus, if you stay in business or decide to sell the business you want to keep your key and best employees with you and if they think you are closing down, you could not blame them for looking for and accepting another job. This is one of those times when you are the boss and owner, and you may find it isolating. Find other ways to deal with your own personal feelings and get solid professional feedback on how to assess your current situation to determine your best future direction.

Evaluating Your Personal and Business Commitments

Another aspect of business ownership reality kicks in when you start to look at closing your business. There is a very real likelihood that you had to personally guarantee certain debts, which means that these debts will follow you after closing down. This means that you could close the business down only to find that you have to continue making payments on loans but do not have the revenue stream needed to make the payments. Your employees can leave clean and find another job. As the owner, you will drag the business around for a while in reputation, in obligation, or both.

Remember that your business probably made commitments to your customers and they will want to deal with resolving those commitments. If you took money from them in anticipation of receiving certain products or services that you can no longer deliver, you can expect some interesting and heated conversations to come your way ... maybe even a lawsuit or two. Lawyers and other professionals who help you with the closing will want to be paid in advance because they know that once you close down they will not be paid. Don't take it personally. It shows that they have been through this before—exactly the type of experience you want in your corner.

STREET SMARTS

If you are seriously considering closing down, then you should evaluate your situation from two viewpoints: what will your financials look like in two years if you keep operating, and what will they look like if you close up shop and get another job? Closing down a business is messy, disruptive, emotionally draining, and often expensive. I have seen owners near closing down who gamble by staying open with the hope of finding that right mix that made things work. Often the gamble pays off and they (amazingly sometimes) come out of the desperate situation stronger personally, financially, and as a business manager! If closing down the business also makes declaring personal bankruptcy a real possibility, there is a solid rationale for keeping it open. You might have little to lose that is already not committed, and much to gain by giving it another shot.

You might be thinking, "I can always go get a job to pay off my debts." That might not be as easy as you think. Word has likely gotten out that you had started and run your own business for a while. This might raise concerns in the mind of prospective employers about whether you would do it again. Even worse, would you learn about their business and then become their competitor? But you might find that your experience running a business, even one that has failed, will be valuable to an investor or owner looking for a new leader. As the owner of your own company you demonstrated the ability to make an idea into a functional reality. The possibility of failure is a part of business. Most seasoned businesspeople can understand taking a chance and having it not work out. But expect that there will likely be caution from prospective employers as they evaluate your sincerity about again becoming an employee.

Taking Action—Either Way

Back in Chapter 16 I told the story about jumping off a bridge into a California river and the importance of not second-guessing yourself after jumping. The same rationale applies here. If you look at your business's performance since opening and see that everything is trending in a negative direction, then you would be doing yourself a disservice to not perform an honest evaluation as outlined in this chapter. Should you decide to keep the business open, then keep it open on full throttle. Commit fully just as you would jumping off a bridge. There is no halfway to jumping off of a bridge. There is no halfway to pulling a business back from the brink of extinction. Don't confuse desperation with energized resolve and commitment. They are very different. Desperation can create a negativity that shows in every step, and people avoid working with desperate people. Energized resolve shows up, too, but it is contagious in a positive way. People want to be part of success, and if you show up ready to succeed there is a reasonable chance that you just might. Faking it until you make it might be the right attitude if you decide to keep your struggling business open. Ask successful entrepreneurs and more than one will tell you that this approach has saved their hides at one time or another.

If you decide to close it down, then take the steps needed to close it down in the most advantageous way to you possible. Keep it secret but start to cut back on making new commitments that will follow you after closing down. Keep closing deals but try not to get into longer-term deals that could turn into lawsuits if you close. Have a strategy for how you want your finances to look after you close your doors, and work toward that strategy. Talk to an attorney about the legal implications of closing down the business and take the legal steps needed to minimize the personal impact on you and your family. Avoid the tendency to maintain the status quo hoping that it will all change. If you continue doing what did not work before, you can expect to get more of the same in the future.

Facing the reality that your business is not succeeding is difficult and the repercussions to you personally, your employees, customers, and other stakeholders can be pretty serious. Tracking your cash-basis financials on a monthly basis should help you spot financial trouble before it can compromise your success. The sooner you see potential problems, the sooner you can take steps to correct them or minimize their negative impact. Sometimes external forces come into play that you cannot control and that put the success of your business in serious jeopardy. Whether the struggles of your business are something externally caused or something of your own making, those struggles must be dealt with in a candid way. Try not to be so locked into your own beliefs that you are not willing to see what the marketplace is telling you. Perform an honest evaluation of whether you are better served by keeping the business open or closing it down. Look for ways in which your successes can be recombined to create opportunities that you had previously not noticed. No matter which path you choose, take action to correct your situation. Avoidance will not make the problem go away and there can always be another business.

The Least You Need to Know

- Life rarely goes as planned—the same applies to new businesses.
- Monthly monitoring of your financial performance is mandatory in your first year of operation.
- Negative trending on revenues, net income, or expenses should be seriously evaluated because it indicates problems.
- Lack of sales success or customer retention should be evaluated to ensure that the assumptions made while planning were accurate.
- Closing down a business is messy and best done in secret for as long as possible.
- Careful analysis might indicate that you lose nothing by keeping the business open if your personal assets are tied to the business's success.

Glossary

accounting period A period of time used to correlate revenues and expenses, usually defined as a day, week, month, quarter, or year.

accrual basis of accounting A method of accounting that relates revenues and expenses based on when the commitments are made as opposed to when the cash is spent or received.

action plans The steps needed to achieve specific goals.

advisory board A group of business associates who act as advisers to your company on an informal basis. You can set regular meeting dates and times for the group to come together to discuss business issues, but you do not compensate advisers for their advice. You may want to pay for dinner, however, so they know you appreciate their time.

also known as (a.k.a.) *See* doing business as or d/b/a.

analysis statement A statement provided by your bank that details the various deposits and charges associated with your business account. It is used to detail the bank account service fee amounts.

angel investors People, or groups of people, who invest in ventures that nobody else wants to touch.

articles of incorporation A set of documents that are filed with the secretary of state's office that formally establish your corporation in that state.

assets Those items of value the company owns, such as cash in the checking account, accounts receivable, equipment, and property.

authorized shares The total number of shares of stock the corporation is permitted to issue. For instance, if 1,000 shares of stock are authorized at the start of the corporation, only a total of 1,000 shares can ever be sold to shareholders—no more than that unless the articles are amended to allow more authorized shares.

bad debt ratio The amount of money you believe customers will never pay (also called uncollectible funds), divided by total sales and expressed as a percent.

balance sheet One type of financial statement that you (or your accountant) create for a specific date to show all the company's assets and all the liabilities and equity owned by investors. The value of your assets must equal the value of your liabilities and equity for the statement to balance, which is where the term came from.

banking day The days of the week that banks are open for business. You must make deposits at the bank before a certain time of day, which is usually around 2 P.M., for the deposit to be credited on that same day. If you make the deposit after the 2 P.M. cutoff, the deposit is not credited to your account until the next banking day, which may be the next day. If you make a deposit at the end of the week, the next banking day may not be until Monday of the next week.

benefit What the customer gains by using your product or service. For example, the benefit of a drill bit is that it makes holes.

board of accountancy The group of accountants who make decisions regarding generally accepted accounting principles.

board of directors A group of experienced business leaders who are asked or elected to serve as formal advisers to a company. The board votes on major corporation changes, plans, and procedures. In return for assuming responsibility for the long-term growth of the company, directors generally receive either cash compensation or shares of stock. In other cases, the largest shareholders may ask for or require a seat on the board of directors as a means of protecting their large stake in the company.

bookkeeping A system for accurately tracking where your money is coming from and where it is going. You can hire a bookkeeper to manage your record keeping or invest in a computer program to do much the same thing. Bookkeepers are not necessarily accountants, although they do help organize all your information for use by your accountant.

break-even analysis An analysis technique used to determine the quantity of an item that must be produced or sold to cover the fixed expenses associated with the time period in question.

break-even point The quantity point where the gross profit equals the fixed expenses for the period in question. Above the break-even point, the company makes money, and below the break-even point, the company loses money.

browser A software program that runs on a computer and allows internet HTML (website) pages to be properly viewed.

business inertia The inability of a company to change its thinking or ways of doing business. Generally, larger, more bureaucratic companies have more inertia than smaller, leaner businesses that can respond quickly to changes in the marketplace, giving small businesses a competitive advantage in many cases.

business judgment rule A concept that protects members of corporate boards of directors from lawsuits filed by shareholders, customers, or others if the decision that caused the lawsuit was made in the best interests of the corporation.

business plan A document that outlines your overall business objectives, their viability, and the steps you intend to take to achieve those objectives. Can be for internal use, external use, or both.

bylaws The overall rules for operation of a corporation. Bylaws are an integral part of the corporation filing procedure.

C-corporation The default corporation structure used primarily to protect owners from liability exposure. Most major corporations are C-corporations so that they can sell shares of stock to the public. Other forms of a corporation, such as a Sub S, have restrictions on the number of shareholders that can exist, but a C-corporation does not.

calendar fiscal year A financial year that starts on January 1 and ends on December 31.

card processing company A company that processes the credit card transactions for the retailers by verifying the account validity, the credit amounts available, and the transfer of funds into your company checking account.

cash basis of accounting A method of accounting where expenses and revenues are tracked based on when cash is received or actual checks are written.

cash flow analysis A financial statement that shows how much money the company had at the beginning of the month, how much money came in through sales and payments, how much went out in the form of payments, and what was left at the end of the month. Successful entrepreneurs carefully watch the amount of money coming in and going out of a company (cash flow) so the business doesn't run out of cash.

chain-style franchise A franchise arrangement where the franchisee pays a fee for an established chain store outlet like Midas or McDonald's.

chargeback When a credit card processing company charges a sale back against your account, usually because the customer denies having actually made that particular purchase. It is the merchant's responsibility to show that this purchase actually happened, or the merchant could have to take the loss on the transaction.

chart of accounts A list of all the categories a business uses to organize its financial expenditures and sales.

class of stock Corporations can issue different types of stock that each have different legal rights with regard to dividends, voting, and other rights. Each of these different stock categories is called a class of stock.

clipping services Companies such as Bacon's and Luce Clipping Services that read thousands of newspapers and magazines on the lookout for articles about or references to specific companies. Many businesses hire clipping services to watch for articles about their company and the competition. Unless you have the time to read virtually every major business magazine and newspaper, you might want to hire some professionals to do it for you.

close A request by the salesperson for a specific action on the customer's part. Asking for the order is the ultimate close, but there are smaller closes that occur at each stage of the selling process to gradually move the customer closer to the sale.

close corporation A company where owners or shareholders are active in the daily management of the corporation, which has no public investors.

commodities Products that have no distinguishing features or benefits, such as flour, salt, and pork bellies, so that there is little or no difference in pricing between competitive products.

company policy manual A manual that outlines the overall company policies that apply to all employees.

consideration Something of value, such as money or a right to do something, that is usually given at the signing of a contract.

content (website) The information included in a website that is viewed by internet visitors.

contractor Someone who is paid for doing work for a company but who is not an employee.

corporation A legal entity that is created as an umbrella under which business operation can occur. Corporations are chartered with the state and come in various forms, such as the S-corporation and the limited liability company (LLC).

cost of sales The costs directly linked to the production or sale of a product or service; also called the cost of goods sold (COGS). These generally include the cost of raw materials, the cost of labor to run the machine that produced the widget you sold, and other expenses that were required to sell the product or service.

cost-plus-profit pricing Calculating your price using the cost to the company plus your desired profit markup. A widget that costs $1 to produce or purchase with a desired 50 percent markup would sell for $1.50 ($1 + [$1 × 0.5]).

credit card transaction processing company An organization that processes the typical credit card transaction and handles the transfer of funds from a credit card account into yours.

cumulative cash flow The total amount of cash needed to handle the sum of all month-to-month negative cash flow (loss) experienced, at least until the company starts to make a monthly profit when it hits break-even but often until the initial investment is recouped.

current assets Company assets that are liquid or can be converted to cash in less than one year.

cyberspace A term used to designate the networked computer world that continues to permeate business.

debt financing A means of securing funding to start or expand your business by way of a loan of some sort. The business takes on debt, instead of investors, as a way of getting the money it needs immediately while not giving up ownership.

demographic profile Usually refers to a specific set of demographic characteristics used by sales and marketing to target likely sales prospects. Sometimes called an ideal customer profile.

demographics A set of objective characteristics that describes a group of people. Includes characteristics such as age, homeownership, number of children, marital status, residence location, job function, and other criteria.

depreciation A tax-related accounting procedure that deducts a certain amount of an asset's worth for each year of its operation.

DGS The Dog Grooming Services business plan included in Appendix B of the book.

direct competitor Anyone who can, and will, eat your lunch today if you let them. Companies that sell the same product or service your company does, going after the same customers.

direct shareholder vote A voting procedure where the shareholders personally cast their votes instead of voting by proxy.

discount rate Refers to the amount (percent) that a credit card processing company charges a merchant for processing each transaction.

distribution channel However your product or service gets from your facilities into the hands of customers. Different ways of distributing your product include direct sales, employees selling your offerings, retail stores, mail order, the internet, and independent sales representatives or manufacturers' representatives.

distributor franchise A franchise arrangement where the franchisee actually acts as a distributor for a major manufacturer's products, such as with a large auto dealership.

dividends Money paid to shareholders out of the C-corporation's net income (after taxes are taken out). This is a form of compensation to the shareholders for having made the investment in the corporation by purchasing shares. Shareholders declare and pay tax on received dividends when filing their personal income tax return.

doing business as or **d/b/a** When you start a sole proprietorship that is named something other than your given name, you must complete some forms to officially use that name. The form you complete is a doing business as, or d/b/a, form. For instance, Jane Smith & Associates would need to file a d/b/a at the county clerk's office because the name is something other than just Jane Smith. Sometimes called a trade name or a.k.a. (also known as).

domain name A unique name used to define an internet location.

double taxation A business pays tax on its annual profits and then passes part of that income as a dividend to you, the majority shareholder, who again gets taxed at the personal level; thus, the same sales revenue dollar is taxed twice.

earned income Income attributed to completed business operations during a specific period of time.

email A method of sending mail from one location to another using an electronic delivery medium such as the internet.

employee manual A document prepared by the company and issued to all employees, indicating the company's policies and procedures.

employer identification number (EIN) A number issued by the IRS to any company with employees. May also be called FEIN or TIN.

entrepreneur Someone who is willing to take personal and financial risks to create a business out of a perceived opportunity. A cool person who bought this book and wants to make more money than the rest by running the show.

equity financing Someone gives you money in return for ownership of a portion of your company. You are giving up equity in the business in return for capital, which is equity financing. The other kind of financing is debt financing, which is when you get a loan that is paid back later. Equity financing does not get paid back. Investors get their money back by selling their shares to someone else, receiving dividends or Sub S-corporation distributions.

exchange rate The rate at which one form of international currency is converted into another.

exchange rate liability The uncertainty that comes from holding a purchase/sale agreement that is not in your home country's currency in an environment where exchange rates change.

Facebook An online service that easily allows users to create their own website on which they can share information for others to see and comment on.

factoring The process of receiving money now for payments your customers are expected to make to you in the next few weeks. There is a cost to having that money now, which is paid in the form of a percentage fee to the factoring company or factor.

feature The different objective characteristics of a product or service. For example, the features of a drill bit might include its size, length, and the type of material it is made of.

federal tax deposit coupon Coupon issued by the IRS for collection of employee withholding taxes on a regular basis. Your employee identification number (EIN) and the amount due for the tax period are printed on the coupon. The coupon then accompanies your check made payable for the amount due.

fictitious name statement *See* doing business as or d/b/a.

firewall A hardware or software device that is designed to keep those already on the internet from entering your particular systems or network unless specifically authorized by you to do so.

fiscal year The period of time over which you track and report your annual business accounting operations for tax and regulatory purposes.

fixed expenses Business expenses that do not vary each month based on the amount of sales, such as rent, equipment leases, and salaries. Payments for these expenses are essentially the same each month, whether you achieve $1 million or $1 in sales.

float The time period during which you have to cover expenses that should have been paid out of money received from customers. During this time, you are essentially lending money to your customers.

forum A site on a computer service in which people with similar interests can post and read messages.

franchiser A company that has created a successful business operation and concept that offers to sell the rights to the operation and idea on a limited geographic or market basis. The buyer of the franchise rights is called the franchisee.

freelancer An individual who works for several different companies at once, helping out on specific projects. Freelancers are like consultants; they are paid a set rate for their services and receive no benefits, no sick pay, and no vacation allowance. The advantage is that freelancers can usually set their own hours, earn a higher hourly rate than they would get from full-time employment, and work with more than one company at a time.

freight forwarder A company that specializes in shipping, duties, customs, and other administrative complexities related to international commerce.

friend A Facebook term used to designate someone as being within your selected online community group.

Gantt chart A simple yet effective method of tracking project items so that their order of completion, time frame, dependencies, and status are easily monitored.

gating item The section of a process that limits the overall process speed. Increase the gating items throughout, and you increase the overall process throughout.

gross profit The amount of money left after you cover the cost of sales. Out of gross profit, you pay your operational expenses. Gross profit = revenue – cost of sales.

harvest A term used to describe how investors can expect to recover their investment.

hypertext markup language (HTML) The programming code embedded in a website's pages that is interpreted by a browser for display on the user's computer.

imprint When a credit card transaction is recorded by running the customer's credit card and carbon paper through a special roller machine.

income The amount of money left over after all expenses and taxes are deducted from the sales revenue amount.

income statement A type of financial statement that reflects all the income and expenses for a particular period of time, which is generally a year.

independent contractor Another word that the IRS frequently uses for a freelancer. It means that the company you're doing work for is not your employer. You have the freedom to decide when, where, and how you will get the work done that your client has given you. You pay your own taxes and benefits, but you can also deduct expenses associated with getting your work done, such as a business phone line, travel, and supplies.

industrial espionage The practice of collecting information about competitors through devious methods. Using public information sources that everyone has access to isn't considered espionage, but rummaging through corporate wastepaper baskets after hours would be.

inertia Indisposition to motion, exertion, or change; resistance to change. "This is the way we have always done things, so we will keep doing them this way even if they don't work" is an example of ineffective inertia.

initial public offering (IPO) A stock trading event where the stock for a corporation is offered to the general public for the first time.

interests Things that you enjoy doing, including the parts of your current job that you like the most, as well as what you do for fun in your spare time. Combining your personal interests with your business interests is a great goal.

internet An electronically connected network of computers that spans the globe. Once you are connected to it, unlimited usage is typically provided at a flat fee.

internet service provider (ISP) A company that provides access to the internet for users who provide their own computer, modem, and the proper software.

job description A detailed listing of the duties to be performed by the person filling the job in question; a listing of the required skills, education, certification levels, and other criteria directly related to the job.

job shop operation A company that has a process flow that creates unique items at lower production volumes for each of its customers, as opposed to producing a standardized product in high volumes.

Kwik Chek A complete business plan for an auto inspection service that is included in Appendix C.

letter of credit (L/C) A financial note that is set up through international banks by buyers and sellers who reside in different countries. Establishes a third-party, bank-to-bank handshake to ensure that both sides of the financial transaction are executed properly.

liabilities Amounts that you owe. Typical liabilities include loans, credit cards, taxes owed, and other people to whom you owe money. Short-term liabilities, which are paid back within 12 months, are also called accounts payable. Long-term liabilities include mortgages and equipment loans.

life cycle The four general phases that a product or service goes through between being introduced to the market and being discontinued or taken off the market.

like A Facebook term used by friends to indicate that they approve of something posted to your Facebook page.

limited liability company (LLC) A new type of business structure available in almost every state that has many of the advantages of a partnership or subchapter S-corporation, but fewer of its disadvantages.

limited liability partnership (LLP) A special type of partnership wherein the partners protect their personal assets from being taken if the partnership gets into financial trouble. It blends the benefits of a general partnership with the liability protection of a limited partnership.

limited partnership A special form of partnership in which one partner acts as the general partner and is fully liable for the business, and the other partners are limited partners and as such can limit their liability to what they invest in the partnership.

link A technological tool used to connect one internet site's pages with website pages either on the home site or on another. A simple click on a link takes the viewer to the next page location attached to the link.

liquid assets Anything the company owns that can be quickly sold and turned into cash, such as accounts receivable, computer equipment, or stocks and bonds. Assets such as buildings or huge machinery would not be considered liquid because selling them would take a considerable amount of time.

local area network (LAN) A network setup inside of a company that connects computers and peripheral devices such as printers so that all network components can be shared.

logistics The set of activities that deal with making the daily routine effective. The daily grind of answering the phone, mailing letters, and dealing with customers takes time. You will probably need clerical help once you become successful to offload the daily routine paperwork so you can have time for other activities.

long-term goals Goals that typically extend beyond the next 12 months. However, for dynamic industries, only a few months can be considered long term.

maintenance temperament Preference for keeping established systems running like a well-oiled machine and not creating new stuff.

managerial accountants People who help you use your financial information to make business decisions. Generally, these accountants are on staff at a company and are responsible for record keeping and specialized reporting.

manipulation When customers feel that they are not in control of the sales process—that they will be encouraged and persuaded to purchase something they don't really need. Underlying this activity is the sense that the salesperson really doesn't have the customer's needs and interests at heart. Can be useful when repeat sales are not desired or needed, but generally counterproductive if repeat sales are desired.

manufacturing franchise A franchise arrangement where the franchisees are licensed to manufacture a specific product, such as Coca-Cola.

manufacturing requirement package (MRP) A software package that integrates production forecasts with purchasing volumes to ensure that component parts needed to assemble a final product are available to meet production schedules.

market maker A company with the clout to create an entire market opportunity simply by its involvement. IBM and Microsoft are examples of market makers in the high-technology area.

market niche A segment of the market that has an existing need for a product or service that nobody currently offers.

market penetration The percent of prospective users of your products or services who are already existing customers.

market positioning Creating a positive image in the minds of potential and existing customers. The purpose of market positioning is to have potential customers perceive your product or service in a particular way that makes them more likely to want to buy from you.

market segmentation Dividing the total available market (everyone who may ever buy) into smaller groups, or segments, by specific attributes such as age, sex, location, interests, education, number of children, industry, or other pertinent criteria.

market value The value of a product or service as determined by what the market will pay for it. Market values change with market activity and represent a type of collective marketplace survey of perceived value.

market-based pricing Where offerings are priced at a level set by what everyone else is charging, rather than by what it costs you to make it (see cost-plus-profit pricing). With this strategy, you can generally make more money, assuming your competition is charging reasonable rates and you can keep your costs down.

marketing Selecting the right product, pricing strategy, promotional program, and distribution outlets for your particular audience or market. Effective marketing makes it easier for salespeople to sell.

marketing theme The overall thought that pops into people's minds when they think of your company and its offerings. For example, Pepsi's theme is "youth." Its soda is the drink for people who feel, or really are, young—the "new" generation.

markup The amount of money over and above the cost of producing a product or service that is added to pay for overhead expenses and profit.

mass producers Companies that produce the same product(s) in very high volume, as opposed to a large number of products with very small production runs.

merchant number A number given to your company that is used to identify which account should be credited when a customer makes a credit card purchase. It also verifies that you're allowed to accept credit cards in payment.

mind share The portion of a person's thinking processes that includes perceptions of your company's offerings. One hundred percent mind share means that any time a person needs your type of offering, he or she always thinks of your company.

mission statement A simple statement that clearly defines the overall goals, or mission, of the company.

MO/TO A credit card processing company acronym that refers to mail orders and telephone orders. Has also been extended to include internet orders.

momentum Describes the direction in which things are naturally moving and implies the amount of work or energy that would be needed to change the natural course of the business as it is currently operating.

net income Money left over after all company expenses and taxes have been paid out of revenues. Net income can be either positive or negative, depending on how good a year you had, but it can't stay negative for long or you'll be bankrupt.

noncompete clause An agreement that employees or suppliers sign indicating they won't steal your ideas or business methods and go to work for a competitor or become competitors by starting their own firm. Generally, noncompete clauses are one section in a larger employment agreement.

nonsolicitation clause A statement included in most noncompete agreements that restricts former employees from contacting prior customers with the intention of soliciting business from that customer for the employee's current employer.

objectives Goals that define the overall direction of an organization, which can be divided into a number of shorter-range action items.

officers Senior members of a management team or board of directors elected to serve as secretary, treasurer, president, and vice president of the corporation or board. Officers can usually legally commit a corporation in contract negotiations.

operational expenses Those expenses associated with just running your business. No matter how much you sell this month, you will still have these expenses. These include your salary, your rent payment, the cost of the electricity in your office, and other similar costs of operating the company.

opportunity cost The profit that would have been gained by pursuing another investment instead of the one currently in process. For example, if you go out on a date with one person, you lose the potentially good time you could have had with someone else. Sound familiar? That is opportunity cost.

outsourcing Corporate-speak for hiring outside consultants, freelancers, or companies to provide services that in the past have been provided by employees.

overdeliver Delivering more to the customer than was agreed to, or more than the customer expected. It is usually a good idea if you can afford it.

overpromise When you promise more to a customer than you actually deliver. It is never a good idea if you want to keep happy customers.

owner's equity What is left over when the liabilities are subtracted from the assets. Take what you have, subtract what you owe, and you are left with owner's equity. This is the number that you want to see increase from year to year because it reflects the value of your company. The initial value of your company stock and retained earnings are added together to calculate owner's equity.

partnership When you and one or more people form a business marriage; your debts and assets are legally linked from the start. Any partner can make a commitment for the business, which also commits the other partners.

pending event A future event with a specific date that forces businesspeople to make decisions that they would otherwise put off until later.

perceived risk The risk assessment as seen through the eyes of the investor or customer. You always want to be working to minimize the level of perceived risk on the part of the investor.

perceived value The overall value the customer places on a particular product or service. This includes much more than price and considers other features such as delivery lead time, quality of salesmanship, service, style, and other less tangible items than the price. Essentially, a perceived value pricing strategy means determining what people are willing to pay and charging that amount, assuming you can still cover all your costs.

percentage markup The amount of money a business adds into a product's price, over and above the cost of the product, expressed as a percent. A piece of candy costing $.05 to produce that has a markup of $.10 (meaning that the price to the consumer is $.15) has a percentage markup of 200 percent. This is calculated by taking the original cost, dividing it into the amount of markup, and then multiplying the result times 100.

performance to plan A measurement tool used by investors to determine how close an organization is to performing according to the initial business plan goals.

personal attributes Things such as being patient, working with other people, taking initiative, and other intrinsic personality-related traits.

point-of-sale system (POS) This is a system set up to automatically record a customer sale transaction. Often, these systems are tied into the accounting system so that the sale transaction is automatically added to the accounting system, keeping sales automatically current.

potential sale revenue A measurement of the total amount of money that can be made from a specific customer or event.

pretax profit The amount of money left over after all the business expenses and costs of goods sold are subtracted from total sales, but before taxes have been subtracted and paid.

price erosion When competitive sales present enough alternative product selections to your customers that you must drop your price to keep their business. This erodes both price and profit margins and usually occurs when market maturity is reached.

price war When all competitors compete based on price and keep undercutting their competitors to get sales. As each company lowers its own price, others drop their prices to compete, resulting in profit margins in the industry as a whole falling to critically low levels.

pro forma balance sheet A balance sheet comprised of numbers that are calculated based on historical performance and known future events. Typically used to project future financial expectations.

probationary period A time frame within which an employee is evaluated by the company, and vice versa. At the end of the probationary period, the employee and company can part ways with no negative implications or connotations.

processing company A credit card–related company that acts as an intermediary between your customer's credit card sale transaction and your bank account where the sale amount, less a processing fee, is deposited.

product positioning A conscious attempt on the part of your company to differentiate between your offering and those of your competitors. You position your product in people's minds by creating a perception of your product or service so that potential customers think of your products or services when they have a need.

professional corporation A type of corporation, such as the subchapter S and subchapter C, used by professionals such as attorneys and accountants. Such corporations have P.C. after the company name to indicate the company is a professional corporation.

profit The amount of money received from the ongoing sales activity of a business after all expenses are deducted.

prospectus A formal legal document a company prepares before being able to sell shares of stock to the public. The prospectus details all the pros and cons of investing in that company, so the potential purchaser of the company's stock is fully informed of the potential risks up front.

proxy statement A form distributed to shareholders who will not be attending the company's annual meeting so their votes regarding the election of the board of directors, or other issues, can be counted. If a shareholder cannot attend the company's annual meeting but wants to vote, he or she can submit a signed proxy statement turning over the right to vote a certain way to the board.

publicity Working with the media to have your company covered by the professional media such as magazines, newspapers, TV, and radio.

pull and push marketing strategy A pull strategy convinces your potential customers to request your offering through their suppliers. In essence, the end user pulls your offering through the distribution channel by putting pressure on suppliers to carry it in their inventory. A push strategy sells your product to distributors, who then promote it to their customers. A pull strategy is driven by customers. A push strategy is driven by distributors.

registered agent The official contact point for all legal matters. The registered agent is located at the registered office, which is the official address for corporate business.

retained earnings A balance sheet item shown in owner's equity that indicates the amount of net income that is accumulated year after year. A positive net income increases retained earnings and a negative net income reduces retained earnings. When stock ownership does not change, the retained earnings provide a quick measure of year-to-year income performance.

return on investment (ROI) A measure of the amount of money to be gained from making an initial investment, usually expressed as a percentage of the initial investment and reported over a period of time.

revenue Money you receive from customers as payment for your services or the sale of your product. Some people also call it sales, and it is the first item listed on an income statement.

reward What an investor expects to receive for having made the investment in the first place. This is usually some form of payment to the investor within a specified time frame.

risk The possibility that something, like an investment, will not turn out as well as expected. The higher the risk associated with an investment, the higher the expected return on investment.

risk tolerance The natural inclination a person has for dealing with uncertainty and risk in their life.

routine tasks Things you do that are pretty much the same as the last time you did them, except for minor variations. Printing out monthly invoices or counting inventory are two routine tasks that don't take much brain power but that have to be done.

S-corporation A type of corporation, formed by making a special filing with the IRS, that has a limited number of shareholders. The profits are passed directly through to the owner, avoiding double taxation.

sales Begins where marketing leaves off and involves all the steps you take to get the customer to buy your product or service.

sales revenue targets The sales goals you set that affect all the other financial and production figures.

scattergun marketing A scattergun sends buckshot in a wide pattern in the hopes of hitting something. Scattergun marketing sends marketing information everywhere in the hopes that someone will hear it and buy—the opposite of target marketing. Target marketing is usually more cost and time effective.

scope of work An important section of a proposal that defines the overall intent of the work to be performed. This can be detailed or simple, depending on the work to be performed.

search engine Internet technology that allows a program to categorize website information in such a way that a search can be performed on the site based on specific keywords.

secured line of credit A line of credit that has some form of asset such as accounts receivable or equipment as collateral for the loan.

Securities and Exchange Commission (SEC) A regulatory body that monitors and defines policy for the exchange of stock on the public markets.

shareholders Any individual or organization that owns shares of stock in a company.

short-term goals Goals that occur within a short period of time, typically less than 12 months, and ideally lead to the completion of a long-term goal.

short-term loan A loan that is to be paid off within one year.

shrinkage The loss of product due to any number of means including loss in shipment or theft.

skills Acquired skills include typing, speaking a foreign language, playing golf, and so on. Natural skills are inherent and less quantifiable, such as speaking voice quality, physical appearance, running speed, and so on.

social media Technology that enables a community of users to easily communicate directly with each other, easily facilitating the creation of a social network.

social network A collection of people joined by some common interest such as a company, a person, or a topic.

sole proprietorship You transact business without the legal "safety net" associated with a corporation. You are personally responsible for all the business's obligations, such as debt, and report your business activities to the IRS on your personal tax return's Schedule C.

startup temperament Someone who thrives on (or even craves) new and exciting projects and challenges.

strategy A careful plan or method; the art of devising or employing plans toward a goal.

suite A term used in relation to software where a number of different application programs are sold under the same name, so that purchasing a single product actually provides a variety, or suite, of other software packages.

sunk cost Money already spent that you cannot recover. Does not take into account opportunity cost or how else you could have spent the money.

superstore An organization that provides a little, or a lot, of everything as opposed to specializing in a specific area.

swipe card The action of running a credit card through a machine so that the magnetic strip on the back side is automatically read for transmission to the processing company.

SWOT A way of analyzing the strengths, weaknesses, opportunities, and threats associated with a business situation.

tactics Relating to small-scale actions serving a larger purpose, such as a strategy.

target marketing A marketing approach involving focusing your marketing efforts on those groups—those potential customers—most likely to buy your products or services.

tasks Things that need to be completed as part of working toward goals.

tax accounting A type of accounting concerned solely with how much money you will have to pay in taxes. Tax accountants can help you take steps to minimize your tax bill.

tweet A simple message sent on Twitter.

Twitter A social media that uses text messages for simple social network communication.

uncertainty What is not known about a situation that can be corrected by learning more about the topic.

underdeliver Delivering less to the customer than you promised. Guaranteed to create a disappointed customer.

underpromise Promising less to a customer than you actually plan to deliver.

underwriter A company responsible for marketing and selling shares of stock in a company to outside investors.

unearned revenue An accrual accounting term for payments made by a customer for work that has not yet been performed but still shows up as revenue on the financial statements. There will usually be a special account with this name.

unqualified prospect An individual who says he or she needs your product or service, but who has not yet confirmed the ability to make the purchase decision or met the other five qualification criteria.

unsecured line of credit A line of credit, such as a credit card, that a company can turn to for cash and that is not backed by some form of collateral. Secured lines of credit are usually backed by some form of deposit, accounts receivable statement, or other company asset that the bank can use to pay off the debt if the company can't pay off the line of credit.

variable expenses Those costs that vary according to how much of a product or service is produced. Just as things usually cost less when you buy them in bulk, producing a product in large quantities works the same way. The more you produce, generally the lower the cost per product. The cost of sales varies according to how much is produced.

Wall A Facebook member's page where information is available for viewing by friends.

wealth Consistently having money left over after all your bills are paid. Real wealth is usually built by continually saving money over a longer period of time and is rarely acquired in a single "huge deal."

website A location on the internet where people and companies can provide information or services related to themselves or their company.

World Wide Web (www) The interconnection of many internet locations, or sites. These sites consist of HTML-coded pages that are read by a user's browser. These sites also refer to each other through links so that users can easily move from one internet site to another.

Dog Grooming Services (DGS) Business Plan

Appendix

B

The Dog Grooming Services (DGS) plan is intended to give you a basic idea of where you should be going with the plan you write for your own business idea. Read the DGS plan to learn how you should be looking at and analyzing your idea. The DGS plan is primarily a learning tool and is not presented as a viable, fully fundable business plan. And in my experience, if you complete a plan as detailed as the one included here, you have gone a lot further in the planning process than most budding entrepreneurs who do not pay for professional plan-writing assistance. As a bonus, however, you will find another layer of analysis built into this appendix—the sidebars offer a critique of the presented plan to help those of you looking to add the next level of sophistication to your plans. Think of the DGS plan as two learning opportunities in one—a basic plan to get you started plus a more sophisticated analysis to move you your thinking to the next level, when you are ready.

There are some nuggets of fact in the plan based on conversations with folks who run retail dog grooming services, but please understand that this business as it is presented does not exist. Adjust and adapt all expense-, demographic-, and revenue-related numbers to your particular geographic location. Dog grooming may not change much with geography, but the financials involved will vary widely based on how you go about offering the services.

Here are my suggestions for using the plan to create your own:

1. Read through the DGS plan, skipping the sidebars to get an overall idea of what is involved with a basic analysis.
2. Read through the various "For Your Plan" sections included at the end of many of the chapters to see how the topics align with the information presented in the DGS plan.
3. Start writing the sections of your own plan that you feel the most comfortable writing. Don't worry about sequence at this point. Write what you know using the "For Your Plan" nudges as a roadmap.

4. Once you have a draft of your overall plan, reread the DGS plan, but this time read the "Street Smarts" sidebar comments. Consider where you might have left something out of your own plan.
5. Modify your plan as needed to get it to a quality level that you feel is right for your needs.
6. Sit back, take a deep breath, and congratulate yourself. Writing a business plan is a lot of work and a process that can be tedious but amazingly rewarding when completed.

I look forward to comments about DGS and this instructional approach. Please drop me a line about how it worked for you so that we can continue to improve the book as a learning tool for our readers.

Cover Sheet

Plan Number: __________ Presented to: ___________ Date: _________

Dog Grooming Services, Inc.

(An Illinois Corporation)

(Corporate Office)
123 Giant Schnauzer Lane
Great Dane, IL 78751

Phone: (888) 555-5555
Fax: (888) 555-5556
Web URL: doggroomingservices.com

Primary Contact: Big Dog, President and Founder

The management of Dog Grooming Services has prepared this business plan for the expressed purpose of securing funding from the parties to whom the plan is presented. This business plan and all of its contents, methods, data, procedures, and other proprietary information are company confidential information. No part of this plan may be revealed, copied, or duplicated in any way without the expressed written permission of Dog Grooming Services management. Copyright 20xx by Big Dog. All Rights Reserved.

Table of Contents

Executive Summary

The proposed Dog Grooming Services (DGS) is a retail operation that offers a wide range of pet-related nonveterinarian services with major emphasis placed on full-service and self-service pet bathing and grooming. DGS's founders have extensive retail management experience and intend to actively manage the business. A geographic locale of sufficient population and limited existing competition has been found that presents a unique opportunity. Dogs require periodic grooming services, creating a recurring pet owner business relationship opportunity for the entire time that they own a pet. DGS intends to keep a customer for life by becoming their one-stop resource for all aspects of nonveterinarian pet care. Offered services include pet grooming and bathing by professionals, training to enable owners to bathe and groom their own pet, and the opportunity to connect with other pet owners, creating an on-ground and online community. Ongoing educational and obedience classes will be offered, potentially creating a social outlet for pet owners. None of the existing competition offers the extensive full- and self-service opportunities. This unique offering is strengthened by the strong pet owner community development emphasis proposed by DGS. DGS has a lease pending for a 3,000-square-foot retail space located on the corner of a busy strip mall that already contains several major retail anchor stores, offering a unique and inexpensive way to gain marketing exposure within the target community.

STREET SMARTS

Notice how the readers learn quickly about the idea, its uniqueness, the investment amount, the time frame for recouping the investment, and something about the management, all within a few paragraphs. Hopefully this will entice them to read the rest of the plan.

A total of $110,000 in outside investment is sought. Nominal target market penetration is needed to meet the financial projections, and investors are projected to start recouping a portion of their initial investment in the first year of operation and full repayment by year 5. In addition, investors will receive approximately 30 percent return on investment (ROI) annually as a Sub S distribution after year 5.

DGS management believes that the proposed business is an excellent investment opportunity and we welcome inquiries from interested investors.

Business Description

The proposed dog grooming service will be a Sub S-corporation that offers a comprehensive array of retail dog grooming services. The full-service grooming will be performed by trained dog groomers who will groom dogs appropriate to the specific breed. Both general purpose and show grooming services will be provided. Facilities will be provided for owners to self-bathe and groom their pets. See Appendix 3 for the intended floor plan.

STREET SMARTS

The plan does not include any specific geographic location because it was written to be general in nature. Any retail plan must include specifics about the intended location so that automobile and foot traffic potential can be assessed, demographic information can be confirmed, and so the readers can verify for themselves what is presented in the plan. Location is critical to retail but less critical for industrial or online ventures.

The shop will be located in a busy retail mall that includes a Super Target, Walmart, and Sam's Club. This convenient location will enable owners to optimize their time by combining the grooming trip with other shopping needs. Six grooming stations will be available for the professional groomers and four equipped grooming stations will be provided on a rental basis for consumers who wish to groom their own dogs. Two bathing areas will be provided as well—one area with three bath stations for professional use and another with two bath stations for consumers who want to bathe their own dogs. Three drying areas will be provided for use only by the professionals.

Supplemental services will be provided such as nail trimming, obedience training classes, general pet health education, and private grooming/training sessions for owners interested in learning how to groom their own pet. DGS will provide high-end grooming tools for sale, such as clippers, scissors, detanglers, and shampoos. There will be qualified staff groomers to help with recommendations. DGS will offer a range of shampoos, conditioners, and other products that are formulated for pets.

DGS believes that by offering a higher-end shop focused on the grooming and training needs of dog owners, we will create a dedicated clientele who will use the service on a regular basis.

The DGS is unique in that it will offer a full range of dog grooming services that support owners and dogs independent of breed type or owner level of involvement. Some owners will want to use the turnkey grooming and bathing services. Some will want to learn how to groom their dogs as a bonding experience with their pets. Others will use a mixture of both. DGS's goal is to become the one-stop dog grooming resource for dog owners in the area. As will be shown in the competition section, shops fall into two major categories: those offering turnkey grooming services and those offering bathing facilities. None offer the owner training and grooming facility resources that DGS will offer.

Market and Sales Analysis

The American Pet Products Association (APPA) estimated that pet ownership had increased from 56 percent of households in 1988 to 62 percent of households in 2008. They estimated that 46.3 million households had at least one dog and that 78.2 million dogs were owned in the United States, an average of 1.7 dogs per household. Pet industry total expenditures for all types of pets are estimated at $50.84 billion with the spending category details included in Table 1.

The *Chicago Tribune* (2011) reported on research studies that show dog ownership providing measureable health benefits that include lower blood pressure, lower cholesterol, and lower triglyceride levels. Studies also indicate that dog owners tend to be more extroverted, have higher self-esteem, and are less fearful. Dog ownership can improve human convalescence, too. It has been shown that dog owners who suffered a heart attack typically recovered more quickly than those victims who did not own a dog. Word is spreading to an increasingly health-conscious population that owning a dog has many personal rewards above and beyond the pleasure of owning a dog. Dog people tend to be dog people for life, which means that support services for dogs is a stable and arguably growing business opportunity.

Table 1: Annual Total Pet Expenditures by Category

Category	Amount (Billions)	Percent of Total
Food	$19.53	38.4%
Supplies/OTC Medicine	$11.40	22.4%
Live Animal Purchases	$2.15	4.2%
Pet Services:		
Grooming and Boarding	$3.65	7.2%
Vet Care	$14.11	27.8%
Total	$50.84	100%

The American Veterinary Medical Association (AVMA, 2007a) estimates that 49.7 percent of pet owners consider their pets to be members of their family. Their formula (AVMA, 2007b) for estimating the number of households in a given area with at least one dog is to multiply the number of households by 0.372. To calculate the number of dogs owned in a given area based on the number of households is 0.632 times the total number of households.

The Humane Society of America (2011) reports that 60 percent of dog owners own one dog, 28 percent of owners own two dogs, and 12 percent of owners own three or more dogs. Male and female dogs are owned equally on a percentage basis.

STREET SMARTS

The reader quickly gains key insights into the nature of the pet services marketplace by reading research offered by reputable companies. This is not just your opinion, but the viewpoint of others with whom you are not related. You can adapt these national figures to your local target market to determine some basis for market projection. Readers may disagree with you about certain aspects of the percentages, but if they accept the overall analysis framework, you have accomplished a lot in the way of establishing the credibility of your overall plan and analysis.

Dogs require grooming every 4 to 12 weeks depending on the breed (Grooming Angel Pet Salon, 2011). Dogs should be bathed every one to four weeks depending on lifestyle and activity level (Ruff Ideas, 2008). The ASPCA (2011) recommends bathing at least once every three months depending on dog activity level and lifestyle. Anecdotal discussions with fellow dog owners often indicate that they are less vigilant with their pet grooming than they would prefer because of time, convenience, or their lack of grooming skills and equipment. Dog grooming offers a great bonding opportunity between an owner and pet (patz-dogs.com, 2011), and infrequent bathing can increase the likelihood of allergens in the homeowner's living environment (achooallergy.com, 2011).

The American Society for the Prevention of Cruelty to Animals (ASPCA, 2011) reported that people will use a grooming service when they do not have the time, tools, or experience to groom their dog themselves. The ASPCA also recommended that people check with their veterinarian, family, friends, animal shelters, boarding kennels, pet supply stores, or dog trainers to find a trustworthy groomer. They recommend the following attributes for a dog grooming organization:

- The location should look clean and smell clean.
- The staff should be friendly and knowledgeable.
- Dogs and their owners should be handled gently and respectfully.
- Ensure that dogs are held in safe, secure areas before and after the grooming session.
- They should allow you to watch a grooming session.
- They should ask for your pet's vaccine records and emergency contact information.
- They should not use any kind of medication to sedate dogs for the grooming session.

The Competition

DGS has four major competitors within its target market, assumed to be within a 5-mile radius of the DGS retail location. None offer the breadth of service proposed by DGS or the opportunity for like-minded dog owners to come together as a community with grooming and dog-care professionals. DGS's excellent location in a high-traffic shopping area, competitive pricing, distance from other competition, and higher-end context present an excellent competitive value proposition. This section offers details related to each of the four principle competitors within DGS's target market. Local geography is defined as within a 5-mile radius of DGS's location. A competitive fee schedule is included in Appendix 1 at the end of the plan.

STREET SMARTS

This section of the DGS plan discusses competitors as general names, such as Competitor 1. Your plan should include the actual name and detailed information about each competitor. If your offering is at all complex in its value proposition to customers, you would also include a relative weighting analysis to indicate how your offering compares to the competition, in detail. The analysis presented here is greatly simplified. The goal is for the reader to understand that the competitors are geographically far away, that they offer only pieces of the comprehensive care services that DGS plans to offer, and that DGS is competitive from a pricing perspective. A real plan would show how your offering would stack up against each in a one-on-one competitive sales situation, which is what is happening in reality in the customers' mind. Any similarities to existing companies are coincidental.

Competitor 1

This is a local shop that has been in business for over 10 years and primarily services a local, relatively affluent suburban community. It is a small shop of less than 1,000 square feet that does not offer any self-service bathing or grooming options. Their location is near an active commuter station. They offer early opening and late closing hours to facilitate pet drop-off in the morning for owners who are heading to the train to go to work and pickup at the end of the day while heading back from the train. Their overall approach is to provide a variety of grooming and convenience services to their clientele who commute taking the train. They offer a pet pickup and drop-off service, for a fee. They offer day boarding, for a fee, as well as limited overnight boarding, again for a fee. They charge a day boarding fee for pets left over a certain number of hours. For their clientele, the extra boarding fee is worth paying because of their higher income level and busy schedules. Added to the convenience of dropping off on the way to the train and this becomes a compelling value proposition for the residents of this local community, which is 4 miles from DGS targeted retail location. It is not expected that the residents who live outside of the specific community of Competitor 1 would view this shop as competition to DGS unless they commuted using this specific train station.

Competitor 2

Competitor 2 is a major national pet supply warehouse that offers a wide variety of pet supplies and grooming services along with obedience training. The location is in a large mall and is around 4 miles from the DGS location. Their focus is primarily the selling of food and other pet supplies and less on the grooming and other services, although these services do appear to be evolving into more of a primary business focus area.

The grooming aspect of its operation is small, with all groomers working in an area of approximately 450 square feet. Self-service and self-grooming are not available, but a variety of a la carte grooming services are offered. Groomer employment turnover is reportedly high for this organization, meaning that owners could bring their pets in for grooming multiple times and get a different groomer with each visit. Employees are paid on an hourly basis (around $7/hour) instead of on a commission basis, as would be applicable for DGS. For many pet owners, this would be the equivalent of bringing their child to a barber and never knowing who will cut his or her hair. The personal relationship with your barber is important when dealing with children and is assumed applicable here as well.

STREET SMARTS

For a real plan, you would offer very specific information about any major national company that could be seen as a competitor to your company. A national chain has the ability to set market conditions in an area, so the more you know about their operation the better. What you are reading here is a cobbling together of information from various sources about several companies, including a large dose of my imagination to make the point that their turnover benefits DGS. For the following bookstore example, you would include a little history about the specific company mentioned, something about their business model, how they have succeeded, and how that successful model can be adapted to your business.

DGS will employ well-paid, school-trained groomers who will have no financial incentive to change jobs. Plus, the dog owners might have been trained in grooming from a particular groomer, allowing them access to the DGS person who trained them should they use the self-grooming services. We believe that the community atmosphere of DGS in conjunction with the variety of pet service options will create adequate differentiation for customers to choose DGS over this major chain store. This assumption has precedent with the independent book store industry, where many local bookstores have survived against the national brands such as Barnes and Noble by offering a community atmosphere in conjunction with specialized services that cater to the needs of the localized clientele.

Competitor 3

Competitor 3 is a local organization that we believe may have aspirations for becoming a national franchise organization, distracting their focus from dominating the local market. They offer a wide variety of pet services around their core offering—boarding. Other services such as grooming, bathing, and obedience classes as well as self-service bathing are offered as supplements to boarding. The self-service option is expensive compared to Competitor 4, which is a self-bathing service only. They are located around 5 miles from the DGS location and have a facility of around 2,000 square feet. They offer boarding services as an integral part of their operation, allocating much space for dog exercise (this space is in addition to the 2,000-square-foot facility square). Our impression is that this organization is first a boarding operation with grooming a cross-sell onto the boarding instead of first and foremost a grooming operation. Given the over 5-mile radius distance from the DGS location, the emphasis on boarding instead of grooming, the expensive self-service option, and the expected high groomer turnover, we do not view this to be a serious competitor to our proposed offering.

Competitor 4

Competitor 4 offers self-service bathing and supplies; professional grooming is offered on an exception basis instead of as a core aspect of their business. They do not offer any boarding services. DGS's self-service bathing prices were set to match those of Competitor 4 to offer incentive to those closer to DGS to use DGS instead of travelling to Competitor 4. We do not expect to win dedicated customers from Competitor 4. The additional grooming services, self-service grooming and bathing, and training offered by DGS will offer adequate value for prospective customers who are closer to DGS to choose DGS over Competitor 4.

Competition Summary

The competition listed are those perceived as the most likely alternate choices for prospective customers who are interested in grooming and bathing services for their pets. DGS pricing has been set as competitive to those offered by others. DGS offers a spacious, modern, easily accessed location that will provide more than a place to groom your pet—it will also offer a community for like-minded pet owners to connect with each other and experts in the field. The combination of self- and full services is unique as well, allowing customers to enter on the services ladder at the level that is right for them. We believe that this combination offers substantial competitive advantage to the existing competition, which will be perceived by customers as a value proposition differential to choose DGS over the competition.

Marketing and Sales Strategy

The DGS target location is situated on a corner of a building in a high-traffic retail mall. One side of the building faces a busy street and also sits on a driveway through which a large percentage of traffic in and out of the overall retail will travel. This wall presents a unique advertising opportunity for DGS in that services, specials, and other promotions can be advertised on a low cost basis through effective use of these windows.

STREET SMARTS

Your plan should cover the marketing and sales aspect of your business in as much detail as possible. Demonstrating your ability to create sales is arguably the most important, and least certain, thing that you have to show in your plan and accomplish in reality. Notice the intent to promote an online community using various social media and website services. These are set up to complement the on-ground networking events, which also help to promote a sense of community.

Immediately after the space is leased, banner posters will be hung in these windows advertising that a "full- and self-service pet grooming and services" business will be opening in 90/60/30 days. As the opening date approaches, we will advertise grand opening specials, such as the first 200 customers will get 10 percent off of all services for one year. We will get permission from the mall to periodically place flyers under the windshields of cars parked for the other stores. We will occasionally groom dogs outside, in front of the store—weather permitting—to attract passers-by.

We intend to create a series of dog bathing and grooming videos that are each less than three minutes in length that will be posted to YouTube. As customers begin using our service, we will post customer testimonial videos to YouTube, which will be linked to our website and Facebook pages. Finally, we will ask local veterinarians to offer testimonials related to the health value of periodic grooming for pets, offering them free publicity in exchange for their comments.

DGS will review veterinarians in the area and set up cooperative promotion and advertising activities with them, given that the services are complementary and not competitive. We will look for several veterinarians in the area who are geographically dispersed and ask to have DGS promotion materials placed at the point of purchase location in exchange for posting their materials near ours. This approach will help foster the perception that DGS is a total-service pet-oriented community organization. Conscious effort will be made to seek out and capitalize on cooperative advertising and promotion opportunities with complementary businesses that cater to DGS's target market. This targeted marketing approach is expected to offer the highest ongoing return for promotion dollars spent.

Customers will have the option of joining our "Frequent Bather/Groomer" club, where they can receive one free bath after any of the bathing or grooming services has been used 15 times. The goal of this program is to stimulate repeat business, create mind share, and increase customer activity, making the free service a worthy investment. A referral program will be implemented whereby DGS customers can receive grooming discounts based on the number of referred customers.

STREET SMARTS

The fundamental approach to DGS promotion is to foster cooperative, community-oriented word-of-mouth advertising. The inclusive approach is intended to not only create awareness about DGS but to also create a friendly, cooperative perception about the organization. Notice also that by getting locally recognized organizations to display DGS materials, we are also receiving a tacit endorsement of sorts. In the month leading up to and for several months after the grand opening, it might be a good idea to do conventional advertising, such as shopper inserts, door hangers, and local area newspaper ads to help people learn that DGS exists. The overall strategy success is predicated on getting people in the door the first time and then keeping them as a repeat customer for the life of their pets. All roads should lead toward promoting this goal.

Customers will be asked to register online or in the store to become a member of our online community. We will offer text and/or phone notification to customers of when their pet is ready for pickup after receiving service. Facebook will be used as the hub of this community, whereby they can communicate with other owners about the services and knowledge related to pet grooming and care. Online members will be invited to periodic special online seminars to be presented by veterinarians, groomers, and other professionals who service pets and their owners. Members will also be asked to sign up for automatic reminders, which will allow them to set the type of service for which they would like to be reminded along with the frequency and type of reminder. People live very busy lives and might lose track of time, not realizing that their dog's nails need clipping or that the dog needs grooming or a bath. The reminder service that DGS will offer will help owners bathe and groom their dogs at the frequency that is right for their pet.

DGS will offer a range of shampoos, conditioners, and other products that are formulated for pets. DGS will also offer specialized products such as shampoos for removing skunk smell, skin irritation treatments, and related products. We will offer bundled pricing that will combine discounts on products in conjunction with associated services. For example, customers who complete a grooming class will receive a 15 percent discount on grooming equipment, such as clippers and scissors. We will offer price discounts on shampoos and specific equipment for customers who use the self-service bathing, also offering to keep their shampoos on site should they choose specialized shampoos over those included with the self-bathing service.

The basic marketing intent is to offer specials to initially get people in the door. Once they have become customers we intend to keep them as customers by creating mind share through service reminders as appropriate for their pet and usage, social media conversations related to pet topics, in-house educational events (which will also be partially social), and seasonal specials such as summer flea and tick treatment, winter paw protection from cold and salt, winter bathing to control pet odor, etc. Educational topics could include protection from poisonous plants, Christmas season safeguards, socialization behavior, and other pertinent topics as appropriate. We will offer a special Christmas or holiday promotion that includes a half-price professional photo of the owners and their pets with a total grooming package.

Operations Plan

DGS will be located in an active retail strip mall with outside access and abundant, lighted parking provided. It will not be within an enclosed mall to ensure that owners can easily and safely park their cars and escort their pets into the store with minimal interaction with the general public. A grassy area will be provided outside so that owners can stop to allow their dogs to relieve themselves when entering or exiting the store. A "Dogs Only" sign with a humorous design will be placed on the grassy area to help promote the pet orientation perception of DGS. DGS personnel will monitor this area regularly during the day to ensure that it is clean. A plastic bag dispenser and trash receptacle will be offered so that owners can pick up after their own pets. Special effort will be made to ensure that this area does not create odors offensive to those walking by. DGS will sell the bag and odor control products used in this area.

The store itself will have several areas dedicated to different functions. These primary areas are for the professional groomers, the professional bathers, the self-service groomers, and the self-service bathers. A common area will be offered for customer waiting which will double as an educational setting for seminar events. A kitchen area is also offered, which will have a coffee bar, to promote the community atmosphere of the store. Vending machines will be sought to offer cold drinks and snacks. Ample area will be provided for crating of animals before and after professional grooming or professional bathing as well as a drying area. A mix of large and small crates will be provided, with the larger crates on the lower level and the smaller crates above, up to a total of three levels.

A laundry area will be included to wash towels and other items needed in the bathing and grooming process. A locked storage room will be included for supplies and retail items. Retail products will be displayed in the front of the store behind a counter.

Windows are used abundantly throughout the shop so that people can be both entertained as well as educated in grooming and bathing techniques. The windows in the front of the shop will allow those walking by to view the dogs being groomed, enticing them to stop in and find out more about the service. Both men's and women's bathrooms will be provided to help foster the community aspect of the shop, which will entice folks to linger a little longer.

STREET SMARTS

This section of the plan should give the reader a clear picture of how the business will operate, with flowcharts, pictures, diagrams, and other visual support tools. Again, include as much detail as possible to show that you understand the daily reality of the business you are starting. You could consider adding more detail about ways in which the kitchen area could be turned into a profit center using vending machines or self-service items. It would also be common to include capacity utilization calculations to indicate the total percentage of possible grooming and bathing appointments needed to reach intended financial goals. This would require the estimation of average time per groom or bath, average drying time, etc. Again, this level of detail adds credibility to your plan in the reader's mind. The plan here is for illustration purposes only.

Adequate space is allowed for the common areas for people to walk past each other, keeping their dogs on a leash, protecting everyone's safety. The layout of the shop is included at the end of this plan as Appendix 3.

Hours of operation will be from 9 A.M. to 9 P.M. Monday through Friday, 8 A.M. to 5 P.M. on Saturday, and noon to 6 P.M. on Sunday. These hours will roughly track the hours of operation of the other stores in the retail mall, allow for morning and afternoon drop-off and pickup of pets by owners who are shopping, while also allowing availability in the evening for working customers.

There is no officially approved grooming license, but all DGS groomers will be required to have a certificate of completion from a reputable grooming school. All DGS personnel will be required to undergo a one-hour grooming training session per month so that their skills improve, allowing them to perhaps assist the groomers during peak periods. This also will allow management to better appreciate the skills levels of the groomers.

DGS will pay its groomers 50 percent of the grooming prices billed. The professional bathers will be paid on an hourly basis of $10 per hour, and they will assist the groomers with rough grooming during slower times and also provide daily cleanup and towel washing services. Bathers must demonstrate proper bathing technique to the satisfaction of the manager, the lead groomer, or one of the professional groomers.

Groomers will not be required to bathe dogs, which will be the responsibility of the professional bathers. For this reason, the bathers will be on duty more hours than the groomers because they will be able to serve more than one groomer at a time.

Management Team

DGS will initially be managed by the owner with the intent of hiring an assistant manager when revenues increase to the required level. Initially the owner will coordinate groomer scheduling and hiring activities with the goal of eventually adding a lead groomer, whose job will partially be to take over these responsibilities as well as perform grooming on a commission basis, just like the other groomers.

Owner, Founder, and Manager

The owner of DGS has over 20 years of working experience in retail sales and also in retail management. His initial experience was working for a major retail auto parts supplier, first as counter help and later as an assistant manager. He then moved to being the assistant manager for a major retail pet supply company. Recent downturn in the economy forced layoffs from the company, which prompted him to want to start this business. He is a lifelong dog owner and has trained and shown his dogs for confirmation. He has an associate of arts degree from an accredited community college.

The owner's sister will initially work as the assistant manager during the first few months that the business is in operation. She has agreed to work for $10 per hour on a part-time basis. She is a stay-at-home mother with two children and she would be able to work during the day when the children are at school, allowing the owner to work the equivalent of second shift. After the business has established an adequate revenue stream, assumed to be in month 4 for purposes of analysis, a lead groomer will be hired who will also serve as assistant manager. This person's compensation will be a combination of nominal salary and grooming commissions, allowing this person to achieve a competitive salary while also offering management experience.

STREET SMARTS

Here is where you present why the founders are the right people to manage this business. Remember that all of the investment sophistication in the world won't save a business from poor management, and this section should show why you are the right person for this business.

We intend to use contractors for professional assistance during the starting phase of the business to avoid unnecessary fixed expenses. Bookkeeping will be done by a contracted accountant using data collected by the point-of-sale system. To minimize the amount of expense related to legal activities, we plan to create drafts of business formation and other documents which we will then pass by a lawyer for final review. The lease agreement, contracting agreements, and others will be run by the lawyer for review as well. We are working with a business consultant who will assist us in the marketing and sales aspects of the company during the first months of operation. We expect the consultant's involvement to decrease to a small retainer after month 6 to assist with growth and other management activities. We currently have a personal banking relationship with the Bank Of Groomland and have already discussed moving our business account to this bank. We have a personal relationship with Mrs. Jones, who is a personal banker. All of these professionals are dog owners and we will look for ways to barter skills for DGS services whenever possible to minimize cash outflow.

Financial Overview and Funding Needs

The financial analysis of the DGS service proposal is included as a revenue analysis (see Appendix 2 at the end) and a cost, break-even, and cumulative cash analysis (see Appendix 4 at the end). Assumed standardized costs for the various services and products are shown in Appendix 1. These are some of the assumptions associated with the analysis:

- A 100 percent markup (50 percent gross margin) was assumed as the cost for all products. The groomers were also assumed to be on a 50 percent commission for services cost purposes.
- Dogs will need some type of recurring services such as nail clipping, bathing, trimming, etc., on a periodic basis, which means that happy customers should become repeat customers using one or more of the various services. This is not a once-in-a-lifetime visit type of business.
- The competition is relatively weak either by breadth of offering or proximity, allowing DGS to gather market share quickly and to a higher level than just a few percent.
- The superb corner location offers excellent advertising space for the cost of sign production, and DGS plans to make full use of the space, social media, and customer allegiance programs to keep marketing costs to a minimum.
- The owner will receive a 20 percent salary increase at the end of the first and second years.
- Annual revenues were assumed to increase 10 percent in each of years 2 and 3 based on increased name awareness and continued success with word-of-mouth advertising.
- The total number of dogs in the target population is calculated from the number of households using the AVMA multiplier presented earlier in this document.
- The penetration estimates are calculated by dividing the number of non-product-related visits per month (services) by the total number of dogs in the area.

- Discussions with dog-grooming shop owners in similarly sized population areas indicated that 400 nongrooming visits per month is common, and DGS management believes that the additional self-grooming services in conjunction with the owner training and community development will enable market penetration beyond that estimated in the proposal. If achieved, the financial estimates presented are assumed conservative and actual performance should be better than presented.
- The build-out estimates were provided by a general contractor familiar with commercial construction in the target area, and all other fixed expenses such as lease rate, utilities, and insurance were based on estimates obtained from established businesses in the area.

It is estimated that DGS will generate revenue across all of its service offerings, with grooming being the primary revenue and gross profit generator. Retail is offered as a convenience to customers and as a way of furthering the total service positioning goal, and contributes nominally to revenue and also occupies a limited yet prominent location in the shop.

STREET SMARTS

Don't expect the financial statements to speak for themselves. Interpret the numbers in this section so that the readers can clearly understand the key assumptions that the calculations used to determine the initial investment amount, how money is being used, when the business hits break-even, how investors harvest their investment, and how sales are expected to grow.

The business breaks even (shows a gross profit equal to fixed expenses) in month 7 and therefore will require approximately $120,000 in cash to fund the business until break-even. The total initial investment is fully recouped in the beginning of year 3, at which time the business should generate around $70,000 in net income annually in addition to the owner's salary (around $60,000). The annual return on investment for the initial $120,000 required to fund the business is far superior to any other investment available from nonentrepreneurial ventures such as the stock market, bonds, or other fixed risk-free alternatives.

It is recommended that DGS acquire in excess of $160,000 in capital to ensure adequate initial funding to weather a slower and more expensive startup phase than estimated. Ideally, $200,000 in capital should be obtained. It is also recommended that the owner have enough cash on hand to cover six months of personal expenses should his spouse lose her job after DGS is started and financial commitments have been made.

Investment Opportunity

DGS founders believe that DGS presents an excellent return on investment opportunity and is offering 45 percent of company ownership in exchange for an investment of $110,000 in cash, valuing the overall company at $245,000 ($110,000 ÷ .45). All owners will recoup their investment in the forms of Sub S-corporation distributions expected to start in year 3, as shown on the financial analysis, and continue for as long as the company is in existence. The founder is investing a combination of $55,000 in cash, foregone salary as opportunity cost, and liability securitization in exchange for keeping 55 percent ownership. Outside investment is sought because the founders do not have sufficient cash on hand to fund the total business and their own personal expenses with adequate excess to cover unforeseen circumstances.

STREET SMARTS

In this section you explain what the investors get for their investment, the amount invested by the owners, and the investment harvest details.

His opportunity cost contribution is based on his alternate employment opportunities. As mentioned earlier, the founder was laid off from his past job and has recently received an employment offer that would earn him an $80,000 annual salary. He is willing to reduce his DGS salary to $48,000 as outlined in the business plan for the first year, costing him $32,000 in opportunity for the first year alone. Adding in the opportunity cost for the second ($22,000) and third years ($11,000), his total opportunity cost contribution is $65,000, considering only the first three years of operation. He will also be securing personally various aspects of DGS and assuming the risk for unknowns that may arise, and this uncertainty coverage is factored in as $15,000, bringing his combined contribution to $135,000 or 55 percent of $245,000.

Investors can expect to recoup their investment as Sub S-corporation distributions starting in year 1 around $8,000 (approximately 45 percent of $17,659), year 2 as $24,000 (approximately 45 percent of $54,969), and recurring after year 3 of $31,000 (approximately 45 percent of $69,070). At the end of year 3, the outside investor is expected to have recouped approximately $60,000 of the initial investment. All of the investment is expected to be recouped by the end of year 5. Annually the DGS will return around $35,000, offering a nearly 30 percent annual return on investment for as long as DGS remains in business and executing in accordance with the presented plan. Naturally, there is no guarantee that the financial performance of DGS will happen as presented, but the return offered for the risk involved is attractive, presenting an excellent investment opportunity.

Summary and Conclusion

Americans have discovered that dog ownership complements their health and quality-of-life improvement goals. Dog owners treat their pets like members of their family and tend to be dog owners for life. Caring for a dog involves various periodic grooming services that are often beyond the skill of the owner, requiring them to pay a third party. Many owners would self-groom and self-bathe their pets if they had the skills and a convenient place to go. Other owners want a full-service salon where they can bring their dog for quality professional care. Dog Grooming Services (DGS) provides the place, the training, and the services needed by dog owners at all levels of the full-service to self-service continuum. The existing competition does not offer these services, presenting DGS with an excellent opportunity to gain market share with its unique offering.

DGS can reach its revenue and profitability goals by gaining less than 3 percent penetration of the target market and requires an initial investment of $110,000 from an outside investor. Investors are projected to begin recouping their investment in year 1 and fully recoup their investment by the end of year 5, offering a 30 percent return annually thereafter.

References

Achooallergy.com (2011) *Pet Care Products.* achooallergy.com/petcare.asp

American Pet Products Association (APPA) americanpetproducts.org/press_industrytrends.asp

American Veterinary Medical Association (2007a) avma.org/reference/marketstats/sourcebook.asp

American Veterinary Medical Association (2007b) avma.org/reference/marketstats/ownership.asp

ASPCA (2011) as downloaded from aspcabehavior.org/articles/44/Bathing-Your-Dog-.aspx

Daniels, S. (2011) "Studies show owners reap physiological benefits from pets." *Chicago Tribune.* http://articles.chicagotribune.com/2011-08-08/news/ct-met-war-dog-psych-benefits-20110808_1_pet-ownership-dog-owners-mcconnell

Grooming Angel Pet Salon (2011) *Recommended Grooming Schedule for Most Breeds* as downloaded from groomingangel.com/id61.html

The Humane Society of America (2011) humanesociety.org/issues/pet_overpopulation/facts/pet_ownership_statistics.html

Patz-dogs.com (2011) *Dog grooming—puppy and adult* as downloaded from patz-dogs.com/doggrooming.html

Ruff Ideas (2008) *How often should I wash my dog?* as downloaded from happytailsspa-blog.com/2008/06/02/how-often-should-i-wash-my-dog/

Appendixes

Appendix 1: Prices and Costs

	DGS	VelvTouch Comp 1	Petsmart Comp 2	Paradise Comp 3	DoItUrSelf Comp 4
Bath/Dry					
Self Service	$ 18			$ 10	$ 18
Full Service	$ 30	$ 30		$ 55	
Owner Training	$ 45				
Nail Trim					
Trim	$ 12	$ 10	$ 9	$ 15	
Grinding	$ 20		$ 12	$ 25	
Owner Training	$ 40				
Total Groom					
Small	$ 45	$ 45	$ 44	$ 40	
Medium	$ 60	$ 60	$ 60	$ 60	
Large	$ 75	$ 75	$ 76	$ 75	
Owner Training	$ 179				
Self Groom	$ 50				
Retail Equipment					
Clippers	$ 145				
Grinders	$ 45				
Scissors	$ 25				
Other	$ 10				
Retail Supplies					
Shampoo	$ 15				
Other	$ 10				
Training Classes	$129				

Competitive Pricing Comparison

GM Rate: 50%

DGS Variable Costs

Bath/Dry		
Self Service	$	2.00
Full Service	$	10.00
Owner Training	$	15.00
Nail Trim		
Trim	$	4.00
Grinding	$	6.00
Owner Training	$	20.00
Total Groom		
Small	$	22.50
Medium	$	30.00
Large	$	37.50
Owner Training	$	95.00
Self Groom	$	5.00
Retail Equipment		
Clippers	$	72.50
Grinders	$	22.50
Scissors	$	12.50
Other	$	5.00
Retail Supplies		
Shampoo	$	7.50
Other	$	5.00

Standardized Costs

Appendix 2: Revenue and Gross Profit Estimates

		Prospective Market Penetration Estimates																					
Household Data		0.01%	0.02%	0.03%	0.04%	0.06%	0.08%	0.10%	0.12%	0.14%	0.16%	0.18%	0.20%	0.22%	0.24%	0.26%	0.28%	0.30%	0.34%	0.38%	0.42%	0.46%	0.50%
Total Households	47000	5	9	14	19	28	38	47	56	66	75	85	94	103	113	122	132	141	160	179	197	216	235
Total Households With Dogs	17484	2	3	5	7	10	14	17	21	24	28	31	35	38	42	45	49	52	59	66	73	80	87
Total With 1 Dog	10490.4	1	2	3	4	6	8	10	13	15	17	19	21	23	25	27	29	31	36	40	44	48	52
Total With 2 Dogs	4895.52	0	1	1	2	3	4	5	6	7	8	9	10	11	12	13	14	15	17	19	21	23	24
Total With 3 Dogs	2098.08	0	0	1	1	1	2	2	3	3	3	4	4	5	5	5	6	6	7	8	9	10	10
Total Dogs	29704																						
						Mo -3			Mo -2			Mo -1			Mo 1			Mo 2			Mo 3		
Service Category	Price Each	VarCost	Gross Profit	% GM	Units	Sales	GP	Units	Sales	GP	Units	Sales	GP	Units	Sales	GP	Units	Sales	GP	Units	Sales	GP	Units
Bath																							
Self Service	$ 18	$ 2.00	$ 16.00	89%	0	$ -	$ -	0	$ -	$ -	0	$ -	$ -	10	$ 180	$ 160	15	$ 270	$ 240	25	$ 450	$ 400	45
Full Service	$ 30	$ 10.00	$ 20.00	67%	0	$ -	$ -	0	$ -	$ -	0	$ -	$ -	5	$ 150	$ 100	7	$ 210	$ 140	15	$ 450	$ 300	30
Owner Training	$ 45	$ 15.00	$ 30.00	67%	0	$ -	$ -	0	$ -	$ -	0	$ -	$ -	0	$ -	$ -	1	$ 45	$ 30	3	$ 135	$ 90	5
														15			23			43			80
Nail Trim																							
Trim	$ 12	$ 4.00	$ 8.00	67%	0	$ -	$ -	0	$ -	$ -	0	$ -	$ -	10	$ 120	$ 80	15	$ 180	$ 120	25	$ 300	$ 200	45
Grinding	$ 20	$ 6.00	$ 14.00	70%	0	$ -	$ -	0	$ -	$ -	0	$ -	$ -	10	$ 200	$ 140	15	$ 300	$ 210	25	$ 500	$ 350	35
Owner Training	$ 40	$ 20.00	$ 20.00	50%	0	$ -	$ -	0	$ -	$ -	0	$ -	$ -	5	$ 200	$ 100	5	$ 200	$ 100	7	$ 280	$ 140	10
														25			35			57			90
Total Groom																							
Small	$ 45	$ 22.50	$ 22.50	50%	0	$ -	$ -	0	$ -	$ -	0	$ -	$ -	5	$ 225	$ 113	10	$ 450	$ 225	20	$ 900	$ 450	35
Medium	$ 60	$ 30.00	$ 30.00	50%	0	$ -	$ -	0	$ -	$ -	0	$ -	$ -	5	$ 300	$ 150	10	$ 600	$ 300	20	$ 1,200	$ 600	35
Large	$ 75	$ 37.50	$ 37.50	50%	0	$ -	$ -	0	$ -	$ -	0	$ -	$ -	5	$ 375	$ 188	10	$ 750	$ 375	20	$ 1,500	$ 750	35
Owner Training	$ 179	$ 95.00	$ 84.00	47%	0	$ -	$ -	0	$ -	$ -	0	$ -	$ -	1	$ 179	$ 84	2	$ 358	$ 168	3	$ 537	$ 252	5
Self Groom	$ 50	$ 5.00	$ 45.00	90%	0	$ -	$ -	0	$ -	$ -	0	$ -	$ -	2	$ 100	$ 90	5	$ 250	$ 225	10	$ 500	$ 450	20
														18			37			73			130
Retail Equipment																							
Clippers	$ 145	$ 72.50	$ 72.50	50%	0	$ -	$ -	0	$ -	$ -	0	$ -	$ -	1	$ 145	$ 73	2	$ 290	$ 145	4	$ 580	$ 290	8
Grinders	$ 45	$ 22.50	$ 22.50	50%	0	$ -	$ -	0	$ -	$ -	0	$ -	$ -	1	$ 45	$ 23	2	$ 90	$ 45	4	$ 180	$ 90	8
Scissors	$ 25	$ 12.50	$ 12.50	50%	0	$ -	$ -	0	$ -	$ -	0	$ -	$ -	1	$ 25	$ 13	2	$ 50	$ 25	4	$ 100	$ 50	8
Other	$ 10	$ 5.00	$ 5.00	50%	0	$ -	$ -	0	$ -	$ -	0	$ -	$ -	1	$ 10	$ 5	2	$ 20	$ 10	4	$ 40	$ 20	8
Retail Supplies																							
Shampoo	$ 15	$ 7.50	$ 7.50	50%	0	$ -	$ -	0	$ -	$ -	0	$ -	$ -	10	$ 150	$ 75	20	$ 300	$ 150	30	$ 450	$ 225	45
Other	$ 10	$ 5.00	$ 5.00	50%	0	$ -	$ -	0	$ -	$ -	0	$ -	$ -	10	$ 100	$ 50	20	$ 200	$ 100	30	$ 300	$ 150	45
Totals															$ 2,504	$ 1,442		$ 4,563	$ 2,608		$ 8,402	$ 4,807	
																58%			57%			57%	
Total Non-Product Visits														58			95			173			300
% Penetration														0.20%			0.32%			0.58%			1.01%

0.60%	0.70%	0.80%	0.90%	1.00%	1.10%	1.20%	1.30%	1.40%	1.50%	1.60%	1.70%	1.80%	1.90%	2.00%	2.10%	2.20%	2.30%	2.40%	2.50%	2.60%	2.70%	2.80%	2.30%	3.00%	
282	329	376	423	470	517	564	611	658	705	752	799	846	893	940	987	1,034	1,081	1,128	1,175	1,222	1,269	1,316	1,363	1,410	
105	122	140	157	175	192	210	227	245	252	280	297	315	332	350	367	385	402	420	437	455	472	490	507	525	
63	73	84	94	105	115	126	136	147	157	168	178	189	199	210	220	231	241	252	262	273	283	294	304	315	
29	34	39	44	49	54	59	64	69	73	78	83	88	93	98	103	108	113	117	122	127	132	137	142	147	
13	15	17	19	21	23	25	27	29	31	34	36	38	40	42	44	46	48	50	52	55	57	59	61	63	
Mo 4			Mo 5			Mo 6			Mo 7			Mo 8			Mo 9			Mo 10			Mo 11			Mo 12	
Sales	GP	Units	Sales	GP	Units	Sales	GP	Units	Sales	GP	Units	Sales	GP	Units	Sales	GP	Units	Sales	GP	Units	Sales	GP	Units	Sales	GP
$ 810	$ 720	60	$ 1,080	$ 960	60	$ 1,080	$ 960	60	$ 1,080	$ 960	60	$ 1,080	$ 960	60	$ 1,080	$ 960	60	$ 1,080	$ 960	60	$ 1,080	$ 960	60	$ 1,080	$ 960
$ 900	$ 600	45	$ 1,350	$ 900	60	$ 1,800	$ 1,200	75	$ 2,250	$ 1,500	90	$ 2,700	$ 1,800	90	$ 2,700	$ 1,800	90	$ 2,700	$ 1,800	90	$ 2,700	$ 1,800	90	$ 2,700	$ 1,800
$ 225	$ 150	8	$ 360	$ 240	12	$ 540	$ 360	15	$ 675	$ 450	15	$ 675	$ 450	15	$ 675	$ 450	15	$ 675	$ 450	15	$ 675	$ 450	15	$ 675	$ 450
		113			132			150			165			165			165			165			165		
$ 540	$ 360	60	$ 720	$ 480	75	$ 900	$ 600	90	$ 1,080	$ 720	90	$ 1,080	$ 720	90	$ 1,080	$ 720	90	$ 1,080	$ 720	90	$ 1,080	$ 720	90	$ 1,080	$ 720
$ 700	$ 490	50	$ 1,000	$ 700	60	$ 1,200	$ 840	75	$ 1,500	$ 1,050	75	$ 1,500	$ 1,050	75	$ 1,500	$ 1,050	75	$ 1,500	$ 1,050	75	$ 1,500	$ 1,050	75	$ 1,500	$ 1,050
$ 400	$ 200	15	$ 600	$ 300	20	$ 800	$ 400	20	$ 800	$ 400	20	$ 800	$ 400	20	$ 800	$ 400	20	$ 800	$ 400	20	$ 800	$ 400	20	$ 800	$ 400
		125			155			185			185			185			185			185			185		
$ 1,575	$ 788	45	$ 2,025	$ 1,013	60	$ 2,700	$ 1,350	75	$ 3,375	$ 1,688	90	$ 4,050	$ 2,025	90	$ 4,050	$ 2,025	90	$ 4,050	$ 2,025	90	$ 4,050	$ 2,025	90	$ 4,050	$ 2,025
$ 2,100	$ 1,050	45	$ 2,700	$ 1,350	60	$ 3,600	$ 1,800	75	$ 4,500	$ 2,250	90	$ 5,400	$ 2,700	90	$ 5,400	$ 2,700	90	$ 5,400	$ 2,700	90	$ 5,400	$ 2,700	90	$ 5,400	$ 2,700
$ 2,625	$ 1,313	45	$ 3,375	$ 1,688	60	$ 4,500	$ 2,250	75	$ 5,625	$ 2,813	90	$ 6,750	$ 3,375	90	$ 6,750	$ 3,375	90	$ 6,750	$ 3,375	90	$ 6,750	$ 3,375	90	$ 6,750	$ 3,375
$ 895	$ 420	8	$ 1,432	$ 672	10	$ 1,790	$ 840	14	$ 2,506	$ 1,176	18	$ 3,222	$ 1,512	18	$ 3,222	$ 1,512	18	$ 3,222	$ 1,512	18	$ 3,222	$ 1,512	18	$ 3,222	$ 1,512
$ 1,800	$ 900	35	$ 1,750	$ 1,575	45	$ 2,250	$ 2,025	55	$ 2,750	$ 2,475	70	$ 3,500	$ 3,150	70	$ 3,500	$ 3,150	70	$ 3,500	$ 3,150	70	$ 3,500	$ 3,150	70	$ 3,500	$ 3,150
		178			235			294			358			358			358			358			358		
$ 1,160	$ 580	8	$ 1,160	$ 580	8	$ 1,160	$ 580	8	$ 1,160	$ 580	8	$ 1,160	$ 580	8	$ 1,160	$ 580	8	$ 1,160	$ 580	8	$ 1,160	$ 580	8	$ 1,160	$ 580
$ 360	$ 180	8	$ 360	$ 180	8	$ 360	$ 180	8	$ 360	$ 180	8	$ 360	$ 180	8	$ 360	$ 180	8	$ 360	$ 180	8	$ 360	$ 180	8	$ 360	$ 180
$ 200	$ 100	8	$ 200	$ 100	8	$ 200	$ 100	8	$ 200	$ 100	8	$ 200	$ 100	8	$ 200	$ 100	8	$ 200	$ 100	8	$ 200	$ 100	8	$ 200	$ 100
$ 80	$ 40	8	$ 80	$ 40	8	$ 80	$ 40	8	$ 80	$ 40	8	$ 80	$ 40	8	$ 80	$ 40	8	$ 80	$ 40	8	$ 80	$ 40	8	$ 80	$ 40
$ 675	$ 338	60	$ 900	$ 450	75	$ 1,125	$ 563	90	$ 1,350	$ 675	90	$ 1,350	$ 675	90	$ 1,350	$ 675	90	$ 1,350	$ 675	90	$ 1,350	$ 675	90	$ 1,350	$ 675
$ 450	$ 225	60	$ 600	$ 300	75	$ 750	$ 375	90	$ 900	$ 450	90	$ 900	$ 450	90	$ 900	$ 450	90	$ 900	$ 450	90	$ 900	$ 450	90	$ 900	$ 450
$ 14,595	$ 8,453		$ 19,692	$ 11,527		$ 24,835	$ 14,463		$ 30,191	$ 17,506		$ 34,807	$ 20,167		$ 34,807	$ 20,167		$ 34,807	$ 20,167		$ 34,807	$ 20,167		$ 34,807	$ 20,167
	58%			59%			58%			58%			58%			58%			58%			58%			58%
		416			522			629			708			708			708			708			708		
		1.40%			1.76%			2.12%			2.38%			2.38%			2.38%			2.38%			2.38%		

Appendix 3: Floor Plan

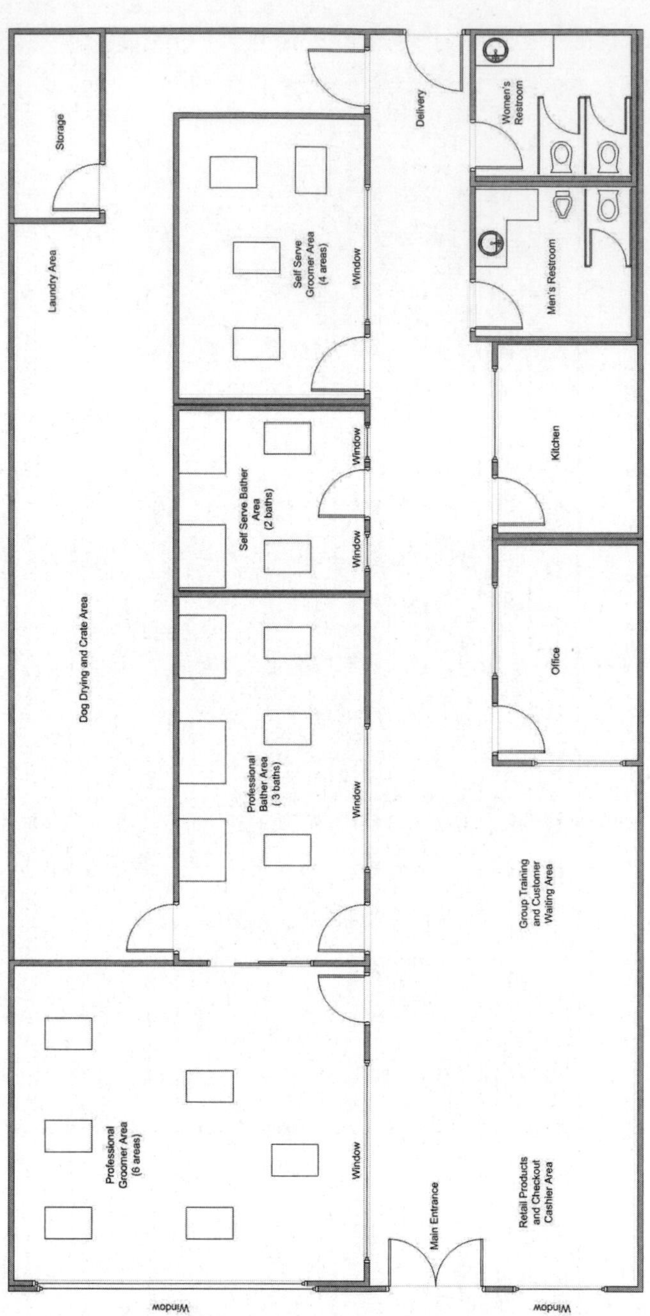

Appendix 4: Break-Even and Cumulative Cash Analysis

	Base Amount	Sign Lease Mo -3	Mo -2	Mo -1	Opening Mo 1	Mo 2	Mo 3	Mo 4	Mo 5	Mo 6	Mo 7	Mo 8	Mo 9	Mo 10	Mo 11	Mo 12	Yr 2	Yr 3
Gross Profit		$ -	$ -	$ -	$ 1,442	$ 2,608	$ 4,807	$ 8,453	$ 11,527	$ 14,463	$ 17,506	$ 20,167	$ 20,167	$ 20,167	$ 20,167	$ 20,167	$ 266,204	$ 292,825
Startup Expenses																		
Buildout		$ 10,000	$ 10,000	$ 20,000														
Business Licenses		$ 3,000	$ 3,000	$ 3,000														
Deposits:																		
Retail Space		$ 9,333																
Misc		$ 1,500	$ 1,600	$ 1,600														
Professional Fees		$ 2,000	$ 2,000	$ 2,000														
Startup Expenses		$ 25,833	$ 16,600	$ 26,600														
Fixed Expenses																		
Rent	$ 4,667	$ 4,667	$ 4,667	$ 4,667	$ 4,667	$ 4,567	$ 4,667	$ 4,667	$ 4,667	$ 4,667	$ 4,667	$ 4,667	$ 4,667	$ 4,667	$ 4,667	$ 4,667	$ 56,000	$ 56,000
Utilities	$ 800	$ 800	$ 800	$ 800	$ 800	$ 800	$ 800	$ 800	$ 800	$ 800	$ 800	$ 800	$ 800	$ 800	$ 800	$ 800	$ 9,600	$ 9,600
Insurance:																		
Business Liability	$ 300	$ 300	$ 300	$ 300	$ 300	$ 300	$ 300	$ 300	$ 300	$ 300	$ 300	$ 300	$ 300	$ 300	$ 300	$ 300	$ 3,600	$ 3,600
Medical/Dental	$ 600	$ 600	$ 600	$ 600	$ 600	$ 600	$ 600	$ 600	$ 600	$ 600	$ 600	$ 600	$ 600	$ 600	$ 600	$ 600	$ 7,200	$ 7,200
Life	$ 300	$ 300	$ 300	$ 300	$ 300	$ 300	$ 300	$ 300	$ 300	$ 300	$ 300	$ 300	$ 300	$ 300	$ 300	$ 300	$ 3,600	$ 3,600
Salaries:																		
Manager/Owner Salary	$ 4,000	$ -	$ -	$ -	$ 4,000	$ 4,000	$ 4,000	$ 4,000	$ 4,000	$ 4,000	$ 4,000	$ 4,000	$ 4,000	$ 4,000	$ 4,000	$ 4,000	$ 57,600	$ 69,120
Lead Groomer Salary	$ 1,500				$ -	$ -	$ -	$ -	$ 1,500	$ 1,500	$ 1,500	$ 1,500	$ 1,500	$ 1,500	$ 1,500	$ 1,500	$ 18,000	$ 18,000
Assistant Manager	$ 1,500			$ 500	$ 1,000	$ 1,000	$ 1,000	$ 1,000	$ -	$ -	$ -	$ -	$ -	$ -	$ -	$ -	$ -	$ -
Marketing		$ 1,500	$ 500	$ 2,500	$ 2,500	$ 2,500	$ 2,500	$ 1,500	$ 1,500	$ 1,000	$ 1,000	$ 500	$ 500	$ 500	$ 500	$ 500	$ 7,200	$ 7,200
Bookkeeping	$ 200			$ 200	$ 200	$ 200	$ 200	$ 200	$ 200	$ 200	$ 200	$ 200	$ 200	$ 200	$ 200	$ 200	$ 2,400	$ 2,400
Legal	$ 300				$ 300	$ 300	$ -	$ -	$ 150	$ -	$ -	$ -	$ -	$ 150	$ -	$ -	$ -	$ -
Consulting	$ 300				$ 300	$ 300	$ 300	$ -	$ -	$ 300	$ -	$ -	$ 300	$ -	$ -	$ 300	$ 1,200	$ 1,200
Repair and Maintenance	$ 200				$ 200	$ 200	$ 200	$ 200	$ 200	$ 200	$ 200	$ 200	$ 200	$ 200	$ 200	$ 200	$ 2,400	$ 2,400
Cleaning Service	$ 300				$ 300	$ 300	$ 300	$ 300	$ 300	$ 300	$ 300	$ 300	$ 300	$ 300	$ 300	$ 300	$ 3,600	$ 3,600
Garbage Removal	$ 150				$ 150	$ 150	$ 150	$ 150	$ 150	$ 150	$ 150	$ 150	$ 150	$ 150	$ 150	$ 150	$ 1,800	$ 1,800
Supplies	$ 200				$ 200	$ 200	$ 200	$ 200	$ 200	$ 200	$ 200	$ 200	$ 200	$ 200	$ 200	$ 200	$ 2,400	$ 2,400
					$ -	$ -	$ -	$ -	$ -	$ -	$ -	$ -	$ -	$ -	$ -	$ -	$ -	$ -
					$ -	$ -	$ -	$ -	$ -	$ -	$ -	$ -	$ -	$ -	$ -	$ -	$ -	$ -
					$ -	$ -	$ -	$ -	$ -	$ -	$ -	$ -	$ -	$ -	$ -	$ -	$ -	$ -
					$ -	$ -	$ -	$ -	$ -	$ -	$ -	$ -	$ -	$ -	$ -	$ -	$ -	$ -
					$ -	$ -	$ -	$ -	$ -	$ -	$ -	$ -	$ -	$ -	$ -	$ -	$ -	$ -
Expenses Total					$ 15,817	$ 15,817	$ 15,517	$ 14,217	$ 14,867	$ 14,517	$ 14,217	$ 13,717	$ 14,017	$ 13,867	$ 13,717	$ 14,017	$ 176,600	$ 188,120
Net Profit Before Tax		$ (25,833)	$ (16,600)	$ (26,600)	$ (14,375)	$ (13,209)	$ (10,710)	$ (5,764)	$ (3,340)	$ (54)	$ 3,289	$ 6,450	$ 6,150	$ 6,300	$ 6,450	$ 6,150	$ 89,604	$ 104,705
Taxes:																		
Federal	25%				$ -	$ -	$ -	$ -	$ -	$ -	$ (822)	$ (1,613)	$ (1,538)	$ (1,575)	$ (1,613)	$ (1,538)	$ (22,401)	$ (26,176)
State	7.5%				$ -	$ -	$ -	$ -	$ -	$ -	$ (247)	$ (484)	$ (461)	$ (473)	$ (484)	$ (461)	$ (6,720)	$ (7,853)
Payroll Taxes	15%				$ (768)	$ (768)	$ (768)	$ (768)	$ (844)	$ (844)	$ (844)	$ (844)	$ (844)	$ (844)	$ (844)	$ (844)	$ (10,131)	$ (10,131)
Uneployment	2%				$ (115)	$ (115)	$ (115)	$ (115)	$ (127)	$ (127)	$ (127)	$ (127)	$ (127)	$ (127)	$ (127)	$ (127)	$ (1,518)	$ (1,518)
Sales	8%																	
Total Tax Paid					$ (883)	$ (883)	$ (883)	$ (883)	$ (971)	$ (971)	$ (2,040)	$ (3,067)	$ (2,970)	$ (3,018)	$ (3,067)	$ (2,970)	$ (35,635)	$ (35,635)
Net Profit (Loss)		$ (25,833)	$ (16,600)	$ (26,600)	$ (15,258)	$ (14,091)	$ (11,592)	$ (6,647)	$ (4,310)	$ (1,025)	$ 1,250	$ 3,383	$ 3,181	$ 3,282	$ 3,383	$ 3,181	$ 53,969	$ 69,070
Cumulative Cash Flow		$ (25,833)	$ (42,433)	$ (69,033)	$ (84,291)	$ (98,332)	$ (109,974)	$ (116,621)	$ (120,931)	$ (121,956)	$ (120,707)	$ (117,324)	$ (114,143)	$ (110,861)	$ (107,478)	$ (104,297)	$ (50,328)	$ 18,742

The Kwik Chek Auto Evaluation Business Plan

Appendix

C

Recommendations for Using This Business Plan

What follows is an actual business plan I wrote a while back for a used car evaluation service business called Kwik Chek. I wrote this plan to determine whether the idea would fly as an independent investment with national franchise potential or whether I should go back to the drawing board and find a new idea. I did not want to actually operate one of the Kwik Chek services myself, which is important to understanding the conclusions. The plan is included as a model to help you get a flavor for what is involved in writing a plan for your own business.

Don't get lazy and try to use this plan as is. It won't work for you or your idea, even if you have the same idea! You will clearly need to do your own research, write your own content, create your own financial analysis, and fill in the sections in a way applicable to your particular business idea.

Although I did not implement the plan, it served its purpose at the time it was written. The plan showed that the idea wasn't right for me since I did not want to be doing the work on the cars myself, and the analysis shows that owner/operator management was the way to go. Notice that the plan did what was expected of it. It told me that this idea did not fit my criteria for a business venture that I wanted to sink my time and money into.

Use this sample plan as a road map for the development of your own plan, and don't take the specific plan content literally. Think of it as a sample shell into which you will pour your own content.

STREET SMARTS

The flow, format, style, analysis process, and presentation are what you should be looking at when you review the plan. Don't get put off by the plan's data being from the 1980s. The analysis process is still valid.

Remember also that your plan should address the questions of the intended readers—this means that sections should be added or deleted as needed. Your levels of detail, section flows, and writing style will likely differ from that presented in the Kwik Chek plan. That is okay. Just make sure that you include an executive summary, the business description, competition, marketing plan, organization personnel, operations, funding requirements, and financial statements sections. The industry analysis, market analysis, and conclusion section contents will vary based on the market familiarity of the intended readers. The more familiar your reader is with the target marketplace and its unique attributes, the less detailed these sections need to be. The less familiar your reader is, the greater the need for detailed explanations in these sections.

These next few points are very important.

1. Write the executive summary after you have completed the plan. This sequence keeps you from writing something that meets your "picture" of how things should be as opposed to how they really are as supported by plan data and analysis.
2. The overall plan contents should support the conclusions outlined in the executive summary.
3. The appendix should support the overall plan contents and add details that were simply too much for the chapters themselves.

No single sample plan can do justice to the numerous business opportunities and entrepreneurial styles that exist. Read this, or any plan, as a guide, and make your business plan your own. Good luck, and start writing.

Cover Sheet

(Do not include this "Cover Sheet" text on your actual cover sheet. They will know it is the cover sheet.)

Plan Number: __________ Presented to: __________ Date: __________

Kwik Chek, Inc.

(A Texas Corporation)

(Corporate Office)
123 Balcones Drive
Austin, TX 78751

Phone: (512) 555-5555
Fax: (512) 555-5556
Web URL: www.kwikchek.com

Primary Contact: John Doe, President and Founder

The management of Kwik Chek has prepared this business plan for the expressed purpose of securing funding from the parties to whom the plan is presented. This business plan and all of its contents, methods, data, procedures, and other proprietary information are company confidential information. No part of this plan may be revealed, copied, or duplicated in any way without the expressed written permission of Kwik Chek management. Copyright 1989 by Kwik Chek. All Rights Reserved.

Table of Contents

(Include page numbers on your final plan.)

Executive Summary

This plan presents Kwik Chek, a mobile used automobile inspection service, to determine whether it is a profitable business venture to pursue as either an investor or owner/operator. The report begins with a brief description of the service concept and then proceeds with an in-depth look at the services proposed, an in-depth look at the used car market for purchasing characteristics, an operational analysis of the requirements for providing the service, and a financial analysis of the cash flows expected over the first three years of operation.

The results of the study show that Kwik Chek, when treated as an absentee owner investment only, requires over $100,000 in cash to accommodate negative cash flows in the first year of operation and shows a positive return on investment in Year 3 of operation.

Further analysis shows that Kwik Chek, when treated as an owner/operator business, still requires $70,000+ in cash, but it shows a positive return on investment in less than two years instead of three and shows a substantial positive cash flow in Year 3 and beyond. The return on investment time period is reduced by one year.

There is already competition in the used automobile inspection area, but there is substantial market share to be had by each entrant. The Kwik Chek analysis assumes that only 20 percent market penetration is achieved by Kwik Chek to achieve the goals outlined—this is reasonable given the anticipated competitive environment.

It is not recommended that an absentee owner pursue Kwik Chek as strictly an investment because the return on investment period is over three years and the longer-term positive cash flows are nominal. It is, however, recommended as an investment for an owner/operator who can serve as both owner and inspection technician with another family member working as dispatcher. This scenario provides the family with an opportunity to generate in excess of $100,000 in household income by the end of Year 2.

A Description of the Proposed Kwik Chek Service

Kwik Chek is a user vehicle inspection service designed to provide prospective buyers with objective information about the mechanical condition of the vehicle that they intend to purchase. The inspection is performed at the vehicle's location, and a complete report of the mechanical and electrical condition of the car is provided. Kwik Chek inspects automobiles and light trucks.

To schedule an appointment, the customer telephones a local Kwik Chek office and schedules a time and location for the inspection. This provides a major benefit in that the customer does not have to "borrow" the car to bring it to a mechanic and the vehicle seller does not run the risk of someone unknown driving the car around town. When the inspection is completed, the customer is provided with a sheet detailing the condition of the vehicle. In total, approximately 90 points are inspected. The customer can be assured that the major vehicle components will be inspected and that any major defects will surface during the inspection.

STREET SMARTS

Notice that this description not only provides details about the service being provided but also presents the major customer benefits derived from using the service. The reader not only knows what Kwik Chek is about but also why someone would be interested in using the service. Notice that everyone has experience with buying or selling a car, so you can assume a certain level of familiarity with the need for this type of service. Gauge your description to your reader's experience level with respect to your industry. The detailed listing of inspected vehicle components simply adds credibility to your story by showing that you have thought out the details.

A detailed listing of the inspections performed during a Kwik Chek inspection is included in the next section.

The inspection time takes around 40 minutes once the mechanic is set up. Each Kwik Chek technician is an experienced mechanic. The equipment in the Kwik Chek van is designed to streamline the inspection process as much as possible. (See Exhibit X for a detailed listing of van equipment.)

The primary benefit being purchased by the user is the peace of mind associated with an objective, informed, third-party opinion of the used car purchase. Most people want to know what they are buying and not be surprised by major defects later when the vehicle is theirs. The Kwik Chek information can also be used by both buyer and seller as a negotiating tool to achieve a more equitable price for the vehicle.

In summary, the benefits associated with the Kwik Chek service are peace of mind and convenience. The major marketing questions are how many people are willing to pay for the service, and at what price? The Market and Industry Revenue Potential Analysis section addresses these important marketing-related issues.

Kwik Chek Tests Performed

Engine Diagnostics

Compression

Rotor

Cap

Capacitor (as required)

Points (as required)

Electronic ignition

Oil leakage

Spark plug fouling

Spark plug wires

Belts

Exhaust for age and leaks

Oil consumption/burning

Suspension and Steering

Tire wear

Shock absorbers

Alignment (from tire wear in front)

Torsion bars tightness

Cracked leaf springs

Spare tire condition

Brakes

Check pads/shoes for wear

Check one rotor/drum for wear

Check for pulling when braking

Check emergency brake

Accessories

AM/FM radio/cassette

Power windows

Power locks

Power seats

Air conditioning

Heater and fan speeds

Gauges

Speedometer/odometers

Cigarette lighter

Windshield washer

Windshield wiper operation and blade condition

Transmission

All speeds

Clutch slip and adjust (manual)

Reverse

Lights

Headlights (low/high)

Turn signals

Hazard lights

Backup lights

License plate lights

Dome lights

Instrument cluster lights

Outside lights

Fluid Levels and Condition

Oil

Transmission

Differential

Clutch

Brake

Coolant plus hoses for leaks

Battery

Washer fluid

Steering

Hydrometer test of coolant for antifreeze

Electrical

Alternator charging

Battery load test

Slow leak test

Body

Undercoating

Accident repairs

Rust

Fading/peeling paint

Proper closure of doors and windows

Mirrors (inside and out)

Trailer hitch hook-up residuals

The Market and Industry Analysis

The automobile marketplace has been in a state of transition since the beginning of the 1980s. There has been a trend in recent years away from purchasing new automobiles and toward purchasing an automobile on the used car market.

It has recently become common knowledge to the general public that a new car purchased from a dealer loses a tremendous amount of its resale value almost immediately. This amount of initial loss is generally financed and paid for by the owner over a three- to five-year period and consequently does not get amortized as quickly as the car loses its value. A used car, on the other hand, does not lose value as quickly after purchase because the bulk of the "new car" depreciation has already occurred by the time of purchase.

STREET SMARTS

This section presents the big-picture case for the service. It helps the reader understand the nuances related to the marketplace and its trends over the past decade or so. In this way, the reader learns that this is not a temporary opportunity but one indicative of a longer-lasting nature.

Data from the 1988 Motor Vehicle Manufacturers Association Facts and Figures, as shown in the following table, shows that the total number of registered vehicles on the road today has increased steadily from 1980 to 1988, and the mean and median ages have also increased.

Registrations and Vehicle Ages

	1980	1988
Registered vehicles	150 million	180 million
Mean age of vehicles	6.6 years	7.6 years
Median age of vehicles	6.0 years	6.8 years

There are many possible reasons for this recent trend. The increased need for fuel-efficient cars, combined with difficult financial times for the public at large, have made people more cautious about how they spend their money. They are tending to treat an automobile purchase as an investment decision, rather than an impulse buy.

The major problem with a used automobile is that the buyer generally purchases the vehicle in "as-is" condition. The buyer is typically unaware of the mechanical condition of the vehicle and consequently purchases the vehicle on faith that it does not have major mechanical or electrical problems that will substantially increase the overall cost of ownership.

The current alternative to buying on faith is to take the car to a mechanic for a complete mechanical review. This action takes time and money on the part of the buyer, and trust by the seller. In addition, the scheduling of the mechanical inspection is typically done during the day when the buyer is at work. In essence, it is a hassle at best and prohibitive for many. Consequently, even though everyone agrees that an independent inspection is a good idea, few people actually have the inspection done.

From the seller's perspective, it is valuable to have an independent inspection report of the mechanical condition of the vehicle to assure potential buyers that there are no hidden defects in the vehicle.

This procedure is similar to that done when a person buys a house and arranges an inspection of the physical condition of the house. In some states, it is a legal requirement to have a house inspection before the house can be sold. Because a house and a car are typically the two largest purchases the average person makes in a lifetime, it stands to reason that they should both be treated with the same level of care.

It makes intuitive sense that a service that offers reliable mechanical inspection of vehicles in a convenient way and for a reasonable price would be well received by the used-vehicle buying public.

Market Opportunity Estimate

It is assumed that the Kwik Chek service proposed would be most applicable to used car purchases because new car purchases come with a warranty, providing the purchaser with post-purchase security. This report concentrates on the used car market as the potential opportunity for Kwik Chek. It initially looks to verify the business concept in the Austin, Texas area (the founder's home town) and then expand it across the country if shown viable.

STREET SMARTS

Notice that this section so far helps the reader understand not only the total number of used cars that will be purchased in Austin over the next 12 months, but also that 67 percent of these cars will be purchased on the open market, with the remaining 33 percent being purchased from dealers. Also note that the reader is clearly made aware that 67 percent/33 percent national average ratio being applied to the Austin market is a clearly stated "assumption" on my part. They may not agree, but there is also no sleight of hand here.

The Scarborough Report on Austin Automobile Purchases for 1988 shows that 31 percent of all adults in Austin are planning to purchase an automobile, and 47 percent of those are planning a used car purchase. This implies that 14 percent (47 percent of 31 percent = 14 percent) of all adults in Austin are planning a used car purchase within the next year. (See Exhibit I.)

There are 569,000 adults in the Austin SMSA according to the most recent Census data. Fourteen percent of this number (those estimated to be looking to purchase a used vehicle) indicates that it can be estimated that 81,190 (569,000 × 0.14) used cars will be purchased each year. (See Exhibit I.)

The Scarborough report also shows that, on a national basis, 23,386,400 used cars were purchased in 1988. Of these, 7,607,172 (33 percent) were purchased from dealers according to the Wards report. It is then assumed that the remaining 15,779,228 (67 percent) were purchased on the open market. (See Exhibit I.)

For purposes of analysis, it is assumed that the 33 percent dealer/67 percent open market ratio outlined in the previous paragraph of used car purchases is indicative of the entire nation, including Austin, in determining the number of used cars purchased from dealers or on the open market.

Referring to Exhibit II, it can be seen that Austin should be purchasing more used automobiles than indicated in Exhibit I because the total purchases divided by the total registrations indicates a holding period of 4.6 years per purchased vehicle. This is more than the 3 to 4 years indicated by the *Medical Economics Journal*, February 6, 1989, page 174.

STREET SMARTS

These last two paragraphs provide justification to the reader that I am not being too aggressive with my estimates. In fact, I make the case that, if anything, the number of used cars that could use the Kwik Chek service is actually larger than that estimated here. This is always good news to investors who want you to have more people to sell to instead of fewer. Makes sense to me.

The estimated new car purchases are assumed accurate because they come from manufacturer data. An increase in the total number of used cars purchased would decrease the holding period for vehicles and indicate a larger turnover than estimated for this analysis. A larger turnover would decrease the holding period and make it closer to the 3 to 4 years estimated. Consequently, it is assumed that this analysis is conservative and reflects a slightly pessimistic case for analysis.

These unit market potential estimates will be tied in with the pricing and other pertinent data to present Kwik Chek's projected financial performance.

Pricing of Kwik Chek Inspections

Exhibit III reflects the price demand curve for the Kwik Chek service at different prices. The curve is derived from data obtained from a survey of prospective purchasers of the service. The curve indicates that only 70 percent of used car purchasers would use the service at any price and that none would use it if priced at more than $110. The curve is most flat in the $40 to $60 range, with most people saying that $49 sounded "about right." It should also be noted that some mentioned a tendency to price the evaluation service at a percentage of the purchase price of the vehicle in question.

Verification of the $49 price came from the Credit Union National Association *Guide to Buying and Selling a Used Car.* The guide indicates that "If you think this is a car you want, hire a mechanic or car care center to evaluate the car. You can usually do so for $40 or less."

Based on the added convenience of performing the evaluation on site instead of having to take it to a mechanic as is assumed in the Credit Union guide, a $49.95 price seems reasonable and justifiable. A graph of Exhibit III data indicates that with a price of $49.95, the available market of potential users of the Kwik Chek service becomes 37.5 percent of the total number of used car purchasers.

STREET SMARTS

Notice that this pricing discussion is based on "real world" feedback in the form of personal interviews and then verified with a reality that already exists in the marketplace. This type of confirmation helps to add credibility to your estimates and assumptions. It accepts a mid-range price as a way of getting more customers and selling more inspections.

In summary, Kwik Chek proposes to offer its service to the general public for $49.95 and expects that 37.5 percent of all possible used car purchasers are viable prospects for using the service at that price.

STREET SMARTS

Notice that the plan has now laid the foundation for a total revenue potential analysis. The assumptions related to the total number of unit sales are presented, as are the dealer and open market pricing estimates. It is now time to do the math and see where the national and Austin revenue potential winds up. These estimates are shown in the next section.

It should also be noted that national purchases are somewhat seasonal in nature, as indicated from the Scarborough report data shown in Exhibit IV. The peak buying season appears to be March (9.6 percent of purchases) through August, with the end of the year and the beginning of the year relatively slow (6.98 percent of purchases according to Exhibit IV). It is recommended that Kwik Chek be introduced to the buying public in January to allow familiarity with the concept in time for the March to August buying peak. The moderate Austin climate may reduce some of this seasonality, but it should be assumed highly pertinent in areas that experience cold winters.

As mentioned previously, 33 percent of all used cars are purchased from dealers. Kwik Chek can provide a similar service to the dealers as it intends to provide on the open market. The dealers will probably want a discount of 20 to 25 percent off the retail price, based upon past experience of Kwik Chek management. Kwik Chek can justify this discount because of the ease of inspection of many vehicles in the same location, instead of many locations all over the city. The reduced travel time reduces time and travel expenses, which enables the lower dealer price. The dealers will use Kwik Chek so that their mechanics can be working on more expensive and complicated repairs.

It is assumed that there will be two classes of service: (1) the dealer service at $39 per inspection, and (2) the open market at $49.95 per inspection.

Market Sales Potential

Exhibit V indicates that at the $49.95 price, and with an estimated 37.5 percent of the used car buyers as potential customers, the total U.S. revenue potential is $438M. This exhibit also shows that if 20 percent of national potential customers use the Kwik Chek service, $87.6M in sales will be generated. It is assumed by management that Kwik Chek cannot obtain more than 20 percent penetration due to competition. Note that this exhibit and Exhibit VI do not include a breakdown for dealer/open market inspections. This breakdown is presented in Exhibits VII and VIII.

STREET SMARTS

We now have total possible revenue projections for the Austin marketplace and for the nation. These projections are based on market conditions, *not* what I "think" should be true, other than the assumptions that are intrinsic to the analysis. It is now time to determine if Kwik Chek, its owners, and investors can financially survive with these revenue projections and to assess its competitive challenges.

Exhibit VI indicates that the Austin market alone has a total potential market of $1.5M at the $49.95 price, and that a 20 percent penetration of that market will generate $304,000 in annual revenues.

Exhibit VII indicates that the national potential revenues with 20 percent penetration of both the dealer and open markets is $76M, down from the previous $87M estimate but still a substantial number.

Exhibit VIII outlines the same breakdown as mentioned in the previous paragraph, but for the Austin area. It is seen that Austin can be expected to generate $282,000 in revenues and perform 6,090 inspections per year with 20 percent potential market penetration.

Competition

Kwik Chek already has two competitors in the Austin area: Auto Chek and No Lemons. In addition, a potential competitor named CheckOut may be about to launch a national franchise.

Auto Chek

Auto Chek has been in business for almost one year. The president is a successful entrepreneur who recently sold another company and started Auto Chek a short time afterward.

The president has every intention of making Auto Chek a national franchise and has already sold the franchise rights to organizations in Dallas and San Antonio.

Auto Chek wants an initial franchise fee of $25,000 and an 8 percent royalty on sales. It has advertised widely in Austin, but an informal survey of people regarding the service showed that there is awareness of the service but not the name of the company. There is a potential free rider opportunity available to Kwik Chek.

Auto Chek charges $49.50 for its services and checks 90 points on each car, making it comparable with the Kwik Chek offering.

No Lemons

No Lemons has come onto the market in the past month. It charges $59.50 for its service and claims to inspect 120 points, but it inflates the number a little (by treating each tire as an inspection point, wipers as two inspection points instead of one, and so on).

Rumor around town is that many dealers are shying away from doing business with No Lemons. We intend to find out more about what these problems may be between No Lemons and the dealerships to determine if there is an opportunity here for Kwik Chek. It is definitely in the market and already out there with a van and providing the service. No Lemons is planning to franchise nationally. Fees and royalty information were not available.

CheckOut

CheckOut is an inspection company in New Jersey that has been providing services for over five years but is confined primarily to the New Jersey/New York area. It charges $59 for its service and checks around 90 points.

CheckOut is rumored to have started a national franchise, but to date, I haven't found evidence of that being the case.

Marketing and Sales Strategy

The most powerful tool for promoting Kwik Chek's success is positive word of mouth where one satisfied user tells several friends about the value received from using the service. This applies equally well for the dealer and open market segments, with the dealer segment involving a much smaller number of people. The most difficult initial problem is increasing the public's awareness about the service availability and benefits. A special referral reward system should be established where a person can earn a free inspection for recommending 10 people for the service. Vouchers can be used to track the referrals.

A monthly marketing expense of $2,500 is assumed, and it should be spent in the following areas:

Monthly Yellow Pages advertising	½ page ad at $1,200 per month = $1,200
Direct-mail pieces to dealers	200 pieces at $1 each = $200
Direct-mail pieces to households	$400 as an insert in a bulk mailing pack
Commissions for part-time sales	$700 per month at 10 percent of partial revenues

It is also assumed that around $10,000 will be spent during the first few months on radio and newspaper advertising. In addition, special promotions should be set up with the dealers around town in conjunction with radio simulcasts where free used car inspections are provided if you bring your car in for inspection while the radio station is broadcasting and on-site.

STREET SMARTS

Notice that this plan not only presents details with respect to advertising and sales activities in the first few months of operation, but also provides a rationale as to why this approach is taken.

Given the more ready access to the dealer market and its decision makers, a special sales push will be applied to the dealer segment during the first few months of operation. The special emphasis to the dealer will be that using Kwik Chek to inspect the cars is less expensive than them paying their own mechanics to perform the check. This is justified by the assumption that the dealer pays around $70 per mechanic hour, including overhead and benefits, and a 40-minute inspection would cost the dealership $47 and revenue lost by that mechanic not being able to repair a dealership customer's car. At $39 per inspection, Kwik Chek should be attractive to the dealership.

Operations Plan

Exhibit IX outlines the logistical analysis used to determine the total number of vans that would be required to address Austin at the 20 percent penetration rate. Twenty percent was used to determine the state of the company when working at its peak efficiency.

It is assumed that inspections are provided 11 hours per day, 7 days per week. Dealer inspections will occur during the week, and open market inspection will occur additionally on the weekends and evenings. Initially one person may try covering this number of hours and, if successful, a second person should be added to reduce hours to a normal work week for both.

It is assumed that a dealer inspection will constitute 33 percent of inspections. Using the estimated 40-minute inspection time per vehicle, dealer inspection of each vehicle is expected to take 0.67 hours (40/60 minutes). The open market inspections cannot be scheduled in closer than 1.5-hour (90-minute) intervals due to 45 minutes of assumed travel time between appointments and other unforeseen circumstances.

STREET SMARTS

Notice the level of detail included with this operational assessment. There is a quantifiable justification for the analysis and its findings, which is substantially different from just projecting hunches. With these numeric estimates, the reader can make his or her own determination as to the validity of the analysis, and you have something concrete and specific to discuss in coming to agreement. Notice the comment related to adding another driver to cover part of the 77 hour work week. This is a decision usually made on the fly, but at least you start with some concrete idea of requirements.

Based on these assumptions—and the 33 percent dealer/67 percent open market split mentioned previously—a maximum of 272 inspections can be performed by one van in one month. The chart indicates that at the 20 percent penetration rate, an average of 1.9 vans will be needed to meet estimated maximum demand in Austin.

It is recommended to start out with one van with Mr. Doe performing the inspections and then add a technician along with progression to a second van when the number of inspections warrants the addition, sometime in Year 2 of operation when the total number of monthly inspections approaches the maximum per van of 272 indicated in Exhibit IX. (See Exhibit XI and XII for inspection rampup details.)

The initial plan is for the Kwik Chek office to operate out of Mr. Doe's home, which is assumed acceptable since customers will never have to visit the office. All inspections take place at the customer's location and not at the Kwik Chek office.

The van driver/mechanic will carry a cellular phone and also have a two-way radio so that scheduled appointments can be passed to the driver on a real-time basis. It is important that drivers and the dispatcher/office telephone operator be in regular communication with each other to ensure that customer schedules are kept and delays are immediately acted upon and relayed to the customer.

The Management Team

John Doe is the author of this plan and the president of the new company. He has worked as a mechanic for over 10 years and has experience repairing both domestic and imported automobiles. He has served as the shop foreman for the local Ford dealership for the past two years. His foreman duties also include profit and loss projections for the service segment of the local dealership's operation. Mr. Doe will be the initial inspection technician, with others hired as business grows.

His wife, Judy, intends to work as the secretary/dispatcher to make the initial Austin, Texas, operation a success and to improve their income from the business. She has experience as both a switchboard operator for a large corporation and as an executive secretary.

Mr. Doe has a wide network of mechanic colleagues who are interested in working with Kwik Chek once the idea proves successful.

Financial Analysis

This section presents a detailed financial analysis of the Kwik Chek business idea. It first looks at the variable and fixed costs associated with the business operation. This section includes a profit analysis for each van, determines the break-even number of inspections needed to support the van and its driver, and then ties the pieces together into a complete profit and loss analysis over a three-year period.

Fixed- and Variable-Cost Analysis

Exhibit X outlines the fixed and variable costs associated with the operation of Kwik Chek.

It can be seen that the van with its equipment has a cost of $24,140. If financed over a three-year period at 10 percent interest rate, this becomes a payment of $779 per month. It is also assumed that a technician/mechanic is dedicated to the van with a salary of $1,800 per month, which is initially paid to Mr. Doe. Adding in paging, service, and maintenance, the fixed costs associated with operating a van are expected to be $2,925 per month.

The general overhead cost is outlined in Exhibit X to be $7,191 per month. This number assumes that most equipment such as computers, copiers, and so on will be financed over a three-year period at 10 percent for a monthly payment of $336. It also assumes a secretary who doubles as an appointment scheduler and earns $1,500 per month and $2,500 in monthly marketing expenses. The general overhead number also includes a $417 monthly amortization of a franchise fee of $15,000 that is equally divided over 36 months. All appointments for inspection are scheduled through the main office operator/dispatcher. This $7,191 figure includes 20 percent margin for error to allow for things that were not initially anticipated, so it should reflect a maximum amount.

Exhibit X also shows that the variable costs associated with dealer inspection is $10, and it is $11 for the open market inspection because gas mileage is involved. Included in this cost is a $5 incentive to the mechanic for each inspection performed and paid for by the customer. This is to keep the drivers motivated to complete as many inspections as possible while assuring quality work.

It can be seen from Exhibit X that total contribution to overhead for operations when at 20 percent (and working with 2 vans) is $16,475 per month. The total overhead (fixed cost) is expected to be $13,040 (2 × $6,520), which leaves the net profit before taxes at $3,435. Up to this point, there has not been any allowance for owner income other than the income earned by Mr. Doe as the test technician. At this point, it appears that the maximum before-tax income to the owner of the Austin Kwik Chek franchise would be $3,435 per month or $41,220 per year. If the franchise were owned as a subchapter S-corporation, the owner would still need to pay taxes on this amount.

STREET SMARTS

Notice also the level of detail included in this analysis. There is a lot of information here, and a case can be made for it being a reasonable projection of the future. The break-even numbers provide initial operational goals to shoot for so that, at a minimum, the business is paying for itself with Mr. Doe at least taking home some salary.

It is also seen from Exhibit X that the inspection break-even for the entire operation with 2 vans is 402 inspections and that the incremental costs associated with another van are covered with 90 inspections.

Overall Financial Analysis

Exhibit XI shows the financial results expected from Kwik Chek operation when the owner is not involved with the inspections. Exhibit XII shows the expected financial results when the owner actually performs inspections from one of the vans. The owner/operator actually makes the $20,000 allocated to the van operator and retains whatever profits are left over at the end of the year.

STREET SMARTS

Look at how important that cumulative cash flow number is to the total attractiveness assessment of this business venture. Notice also that the company hits its break-even point somewhere between Month 12 and the end of Year 2. If the break-even quantity is reached earlier than in Month 12, then the amount of cash required to open the business is reduced and the return on investment improves accordingly.

It is assumed that Kwik Chek acquires 1 percent additional market share for each month it is in operation. At the end of the second year, Kwik Chek is assumed to be at the 20 percent penetration target.

The chart also indicates that there is a substantial negative cumulative cash flow during the first year. The peak negative value is $102,026 for absentee owners and $72,000 for the owner/operator. The profits derived by the second year of operation begin to erode the negative cumulative cash situation. Kwik Chek is still in a negative cumulative cash flow situation by the end of Year 3 for the absentee investors but shows a positive turn for owner/operators. Absentee owner/investors begin to show a return on their investment beginning in Year 4.

The chart shows that the company operates with a negative net operating income over the first year of existence for absentee investors and turns slightly positive for the owner/operator and turns positive for both scenarios in Year 2. The owner/operator stands to make substantial money after the first year should business plan projections be accurate.

An additional van is required during the second year to meet market demands. When included in the expenses of the second and ongoing years, Kwik Chek can be expected to yield a net profit before tax of $41,208 for absentee owners and $89,808 for owner/operators.

Anyone who invests in a Kwik Chek franchise must be willing to risk between $70,000 and $100,000 in cash and wait between 2 and 4 years for a positive return on that investment.

Summary and Conclusion

It can be seen from the previous discussion that the investment potential of a Kwik Chek franchise is not a viable option for a person who treats it exclusively as an investment.

Exhibit XII shows what happens to the financials of the project if the owner is also the mechanic for the first van. This creates a saving on two counts: (1) The $5 incentive per inspection is not needed to motivate the mechanic because the mechanic is the owner, and (2) there is an $18,000 savings per year in the salary paid to the mechanic.

It can be seen from Exhibit XII that there is still a substantial negative cumulative cash flow for the first year, but, for the investor scenario, the cash flow drain reverses direction in Month 11 as opposed to some time in Year 2. We see that the project becomes a positive cumulative cash flow project by the end of Year 2 and becomes a generator of substantial cumulative cash, $107,841, in Year 3.

It still requires $75,000 (plus living expenses) to ensure minimum cash reserves for the business. If the marketing penetration rampup is greater than expected, then the business will generate cash faster.

It is thus concluded that Kwik Chek is not a viable investment for someone who does not intend to operate the business himself, performing inspections in one of the vans. It does not generate a positive return on investment until Year 3 and requires over $100,000 in cash reserves to start. This time frame is simply too long for most investors.

If a person wants to invest his own time in the project and operate one of the vans, then there is substantial future revenue-earning potential from Year 3 onward. There is still over $75,000 in cash required to fund the business, but the long-term prospects for return are much improved over treating the project as only an investment.

Kwik Chek should be started in Austin by a mechanic who wants to start his or her own business. If it begins to show the returns expected, then the project should be set up for national franchising to mechanic/investor groups who want to provide the service. At that time, additional funding can be obtained based upon the company's successful track record.

Exhibits

Exhibit I: Scarborough Report on Automobile Purchases

From the Scarborough Report on Austin automobile purchases (1988)

Percent of adults planning to purchase a car:	31%
(This fact implies that people change cars every 3.2 years)	
Percent of adults planning a used car purchase:	14%
Total number of Austin SMSA adults:	569,355
Percent of women adults buying used cars:	69%
Total number of planned used car purchases:	81,190
Women planning to buy a used car:	56,021
Men planning to buy a used car:	25,169

Notes:

1) The median price range for women's purchases is $6,900
2) The median price range for men's purchases is $10,300
3) The bulk of those buying used cars have median incomes of $27,000
4) The total number of licensed drivers in the U.S.= 164,000,000

There are	Number of male drivers=	85,000,000
	Number of female drivers=	79,000,000

Assuming the Austin ratios for adults purchasing used cars is valid for the the entire U.S., then we can assume that the total number of used car purchases in a year are:

Total number of drivers:	164,000,000	
Percent buying used cars:	14%	
Percent buying new cars:	16%	
Total used car purchases:	23,386,400	
Cars purchased by women:	16,136,616	
Cars purchased by men:	7,249,784	
Cars purchased from dealers:	7,607,172	[from Wards, p. 166]
Cars purchased on open market:	15,779,228	

Exhibit II: Validation of Conservative Estimates

To determine whether Austin is representative of the U.S. in general, we can compare the new car purchases nationally to those expected in Austin. Austin is expecting new car percentage purchases of 15.5%.

New car information:

1988 new vehicle purchases:	15,245,843
Percent of licensed drivers:	9%

This information indicates that the national average of used car purchases may actually be higher than that seen in Austin.

Total new car purchases:	15,245,843
Used car purchases:	23,386,400

Total annual purchases:	38,632,243
Total registered vehicles:	179,000,000
Percent purchases to registration:	22%
Average holding period:	5

The national average for holding a car is 3-4 years. These numbers indicate that the numbers used for analysis are conservative and that more used cars are probably sold annually than predicted.

Sources:
Motor Vehicles Manufacturers Association Facts and Figures (1988)
Wards Automotive Yearbook, 1989

Exhibit III: Price Demand Curve

Price ($)	Demand	Tot Rev ($)
0	100	0
20	70	1,400
40	50	2,000
50	38	1,875
60	25	1,500
110	0	0

Exhibit IV: Seasonality of Buyer Purchasing Habits (1987-1988)

Month	1987	% of total	Cumulative %	1988	% of total	Cumulative %
1	1,001,879	5.99%	5.99%	1,211,704	6.98%	6.98%
2	1,249,911	7.48%	13.47%	1,412,058	8.14%	15.12%
3	1,527,827	9.14%	22.62%	1,667,601	9.61%	24.73%
4	1,554,248	9.30%	31.92%	1,493,641	8.61%	33.34%
5	1,464,754	8.76%	40.68%	1,629,931	9.39%	42.74%
6	1,584,114	9.48%	50.16%	1,634,003	9.42%	52.16%
7	1,478,519	8.85%	59.01%	1,426,720	8.22%	60.38%
8	1,522,813	9.11%	68.12%	1,446,218	8.34%	68.72%
9	1,413,512	8.46%	76.58%	1,339,803	7.72%	76.44%
10	1,330,895	7.96%	84.54%	1,381,685	7.96%	84.40%
11	1,231,478	7.37%	91.91%	1,313,526	7.57%	91.97%
12	1,352,231	8.09%	100.00%	1,392,945	8.03%	100.00%
	16,712,181			17,350,435		

Exhibit V: National Potential Sales in Units and Dollars at 5, 10,& 20% Penetration

Month	1988 Percent	Used Car Sales (Units)	Total Kwik Chek Market @ $49.95 (Units)	Total Kwik Chek Revenues @ $49.95 (Dollars)	At a 5% Penetration of Total Market (Units)	At a 5% Penetration of Total Market (Dollars)	At a 10% Penetration of Total Market (Units)	At a 10% Penetration of Total Market (Dollars)	At a 20% Penetration of Total Market (Units)	At a 20% Penetration of Total Market (Dollars)
January	6.98%	1,633,238	612,464	$30,592,594	30,623	$1,529,630	61,246	$3,059,259	122,493	$6,118,519
February	8.14%	1,903,293	713,735	$35,651,048	35,687	$1,782,552	71,373	$3,565,105	142,747	$7,130,210
March	9.61%	2,247,735	842,901	$42,102,891	42,145	$2,105,145	84,290	$4,210,289	168,580	$8,420,578
April	8.61%	2,013,257	754,971	$37,710,821	37,749	$1,886,541	75,497	$3,771,082	150,994	$7,542,164
May	9.39%	2,196,960	823,860	$41,151,814	41,193	$2,057,591	82,386	$4,115,181	164,772	$8,230,363
June	9.42%	2,203,258	826,222	$41,269,771	41,311	$2,063,489	82,622	$4,126,977	165,244	$8,253,954
July	8.22%	1,923,055	721,146	$36,021,228	36,057	$1,801,061	72,115	$3,602,123	144,229	$7,204,246
August	8.34%	1,949,336	731,001	$36,513,505	36,550	$1,825,675	73,100	$3,651,351	146,200	$7,302,701
September	7.72%	1,805,901	677,213	$33,826,784	33,861	$1,691,339	67,721	$3,382,678	135,443	$6,765,357
October	7.96%	1,862,353	698,382	$34,884,203	34,919	$1,744,210	69,838	$3,488,420	139,676	$6,976,841
November	7.57%	1,770,483	663,931	$33,163,353	33,197	$1,658,168	66,393	$3,316,335	132,786	$6,632,671
December	8.03%	1,877,530	704,074	$35,168,491	35,204	$1,758,425	70,407	$3,516,849	140,815	$7,033,698
		23,386,400	8,769,900	$438,056,505	438,495	$21,902,825	876,990	$43,805,651	1,753,980	$87,611,301

Notes:

1) 1988 percentages taken from Exhibit IV: Seasonality of Buyer Purchasing Habits
2) Used car sales derived from data in Exhibit II for total national used car purchases
3) Total Kwik Chek market derived from Exhibit III. 37.5% demand expected at $50 pricing
4) 20% penetration is the maximum expected due to future entrants and other competition

Exhibit VI: Austin Potential Sales in Units and Dollars at 5, 10 & 20% Penetration

Month	1988 Percent	Used Car Sales (Units)	Total Kwik Chek Market @ $49.95 (Units)	Total Kwik Chek Revenues @ $49.95 (Dollars)	At a 5% Penetration of Total Market (Units)	At a 5% Penetration of Total Market (Dollars)	At a 10% Penetration of Total Market (Units)	At a 10% Penetration of Total Market (Dollars)	At a 20% Penetration of Total Market (Units)	At a 20% Penetration of Total Market (Dollars)
January	6.98%	5,670	2,126	$106,208	106	$5,310	213	$10,621	425	$21,242
February	8.14%	6,608	2,478	$123,769	124	$6,188	248	$12,377	496	$24,754
March	9.61%	7,803	2,926	$146,168	146	$7,308	293	$14,617	585	$29,234
April	8.61%	6,989	2,621	$130,920	131	$6,546	262	$13,092	524	$26,184
May	9.39%	7,627	2,860	$142,866	143	$7,143	286	$14,287	572	$28,573
June	9.42%	7,649	2,868	$143,275	143	$7,164	287	$14,328	574	$28,655
July	8.22%	6,676	2,504	$125,054	125	$6,253	250	$12,505	501	$25,011
August	8.34%	6,767	2,538	$126,763	127	$6,338	254	$12,676	508	$25,353
September	7.72%	6,270	2,351	$117,436	118	$5,872	235	$11,744	470	$23,487
October	7.96%	6,465	2,425	$121,107	121	$6,055	242	$12,111	485	$24,221
November	7.57%	6,147	2,305	$115,132	115	$5,757	230	$11,513	461	$23,026
December	8.03%	6,518	2,444	$122,094	122	$6,105	244	$12,209	489	$24,419
		81,190	30,446	$1,520,790	1,522	$76,040	3,045	$152,079	6,089	$304,158

Notes:
1) 1988 percentages taken from Exhibit IV: Seasonality of Buyer Purchasing Habits
2) Used car sales derived from data in Exhibit I for total Austin used car purchases
3) Total Kwik Chek market derived from Exhibit III. 37.5% demand expected at $50 pricing
4) 20% penetration is the maximum expected due to future entrants and other competition

Exhibit VII: National Dealer/Open Market Potential Sales in Units and Dollars at 10 & 20% Penetration

Dealer Percentage: 33%
Open Market Percentage: 67%

Month	1988 Percent	Used Car Sales (Units)	Total Kwik Chek Market @ 37.5% (Units)	Potential Dealer Sales @ 33% (Units)	Dealer Revenues @ 10% Penetrat. of Dealer Potential & $39 Price (Dollars)	Dealer Revenues @ 20% Penetrat. of Dealer Potential & $39 Price (Dollars)	Potential Open Market Sales @ 67% (Units)	Open Market Revenues @ 10% Penetrat. of Open Mrkt. Potential & $49 Price (Dollars)	Open Market Revenues @ 20% Penetrat. of Open Mrkt. Potential & $49 Price (Dollars)
January	8.14%	1,903,293	713,735	232,165	$905,443	$1,810,887	481,570	$2,405,441	$4,810,882
February	9.61%	2,247,735	842,901	274,180	$1,069,303	$2,138,607	568,720	$2,840,758	$5,681,517
March	8.61%	2,013,257	754,971	245,579	$957,756	$1,915,512	509,393	$2,544,417	$5,088,835
April	9.39%	2,196,960	823,860	267,987	$1,045,148	$2,090,297	555,873	$2,776,587	$5,553,175
May	9.42%	2,203,258	826,222	268,755	$1,048,144	$2,096,288	557,467	$2,784,546	$5,569,093
June	8.22%	1,923,055	721,146	234,576	$914,845	$1,829,690	486,570	$2,430,418	$4,860,835
July	8.34%	1,949,336	731,001	237,781	$927,348	$1,854,695	493,220	$2,463,632	$4,927,265
August	7.72%	1,805,901	677,213	220,285	$859,112	$1,718,224	456,928	$2,282,354	$4,564,709
September	7.96%	1,862,353	698,382	227,171	$885,967	$1,771,935	471,211	$2,353,700	$4,707,401
October	7.57%	1,770,483	663,931	215,965	$842,262	$1,684,525	447,966	$2,237,592	$4,475,183
November	8.03%	1,877,530	704,074	229,022	$893,188	$1,786,375	475,051	$2,372,882	$4,745,764
December		0	0	0	$0	$0	0	$0	$0
		23,386,400	8,157,436	2,653,466	$10,348,517	$20,697,034	5,503,970	$27,492,329	$54,984,657

Notes:
1) 1988 percentages taken from Exhibit IV: Seasonality of Buyer Purchasing Habits
2) Used car sales derived from data in Exhibit II for total national used car purchases
3) Total Kwik Chek market derived from Exhibit III. 37.5% demand expected at $50 pricing
4) 20% penetration is the maximum expected due to future entrants and other competition
5) It is assumed that dealers will want a 20% discount off of retail to use the service
6) The breakdown of dealer to open market sales percentages is taken from Exhibit I

Exhibit VIII: Austin Dealer/Open Market Potential Sales in Units and Dollars at 10 & 20% Penetration

Dealer Percentage: 33%
Open Market Percentage: 67%

Month	1988 Percent	Used Car Sales (Units)	Total Kwik Chek Market @ 37.5% (Units)	Potential Dealer Sales @ 33% (Units)	Dealer Revenues @ 10% Penetrat. of Dealer Potential & $39 Price (Dollars)	(Units)	Dealer Revenues @ 20% Penetrat. of Dealer Potential & $39 Price (Dollars)	(Units)	Potential Open Market Sales @ 67% (Units)	10% Penetrat. of Open Mrkt. Potential & $49 Price (Dollars)	(Units)	Open Market Revenues @ 20% Penetrat. of Open Mrkt. Potential & $49 Price (Dollars)	(Units)
January	6.98%	5,670	2,126	692	$2,697	69	$5,395	138	1,435	$7,166	143	$14,332	287
February	8.14%	6,608	2,478	806	$3,143	81	$6,287	161	1,672	$8,351	167	$16,702	334
March	9.61%	7,803	2,926	952	$3,712	95	$7,425	190	1,974	$9,862	197	$19,724	395
April	8.61%	6,989	2,621	853	$3,325	85	$6,650	171	1,768	$8,833	177	$17,667	354
May	9.39%	7,627	2,860	930	$3,628	93	$7,257	186	1,930	$9,639	193	$19,279	386
June	9.42%	7,649	2,868	933	$3,639	93	$7,278	187	1,935	$9,667	194	$19,334	387
July	8.22%	6,676	2,504	814	$3,176	81	$6,352	163	1,689	$8,438	169	$16,875	338
August	8.34%	6,767	2,538	825	$3,219	83	$6,439	165	1,712	$8,553	171	$17,106	342
September	7.72%	6,270	2,351	765	$2,983	76	$5,965	153	1,586	$7,924	159	$15,847	317
October	7.96%	6,465	2,425	789	$3,076	79	$6,152	158	1,636	$8,171	164	$16,343	327
November	7.57%	6,147	2,305	750	$2,924	75	$5,848	150	1,555	$7,768	156	$15,536	311
December	8.03%	6,518	2,444	795	$3,101	80	$6,202	159	1,649	$8,238	165	$16,476	330
		81,190	30,446	9,904	$38,624	990	$77,248	1,981	20,543	$102,610	2,054	$205,221	4,109

Notes:

1) 1988 percentages taken from Exhibit IV: Seasonality of Buyer Purchasing Habits
2) Used car sales derived from data in Exhibit II for total national used car purchases
3) Total Kwik Chek market derived from Exhibit III. 37.5% demand expected at $50 pricing
4) 20% penetration is the maximum expected due to future entrants and other competition
5) It is assumed that dealers will want a 20% discount off of retail to use the service
6) The breakdown of dealer to open market sales percentages is taken from Exhibit I

Exhibit IX: Operations Breakdown for Austin to Determine the Number of Vans Required

Dealer Price:	$39.00
Open Market Price:	$49.95
Number of inspection hours per day:	11
Number of days per week:	7
Inspection hours per week:	77
Inspection hours per year:	4,004
Average inspection hours per month:	334
Maximum inspections per van/month:	272
(Assuming 33%-67% dealer-open market split)	
Inspect time (Hrs.):	1.50 (Open market inspection time including 30 minutes travel)
Inspect time (Hrs.):	0.67 (Dealer inspection time of 40 minutes)

Month	20% Penetrat. of Dealer Potential & $39 Price (Dollars)	(Units)	Inspection Hours Required	20% Penetrat. of Open Mrkt. Potential & $49 Price (Dollars)	(Units)	Inspection Hours Required	Total Num. Inspt.	Total Van Hours Needed	Total Vans Needed
January	$5,395	138	92	$14,332	287	430	425	523	1.6
February	$6,287	161	107	$16,702	334	502	496	609	1.8
March	$7,425	190	127	$19,724	395	592	585	719	2.2
April	$6,650	171	114	$17,667	354	531	524	644	1.9
May	$7,257	186	124	$19,279	386	579	572	703	2.1
June	$7,278	187	124	$19,334	387	581	574	705	2.1
July	$6,352	163	109	$16,875	338	507	501	615	1.8
August	$6,439	165	110	$17,106	342	514	508	624	1.9
September	$5,965	153	102	$15,847	317	476	470	578	1.7
October	$6,152	158	105	$16,343	327	491	485	596	1.8
November	$5,848	150	100	$15,536	311	467	461	567	1.7
December	$6,202	159	106	$16,476	330	495	489	601	1.8
	$77,248	1,981	1,320	$205,221	4,109	6,163	6,089	7,483	1.9

Exhibit X: Fixed and Variable Cost Breakdown per Van and Inspection

Van Equipment		Cost	
The van		$15,000	
Test equipment:		$290	
Compression		$50	
Calipers		$50	
Depth gauge		$50	
VOM		$125	
Hydrometer		$15	
Scope and analyzers		$3,500	
Portable personal computer		$3,000	
Other equipment:		$1,350	
Generator		$200	
Hydraulic jack		$200	
Jack stands		$150	
Scooter		$50	
Misc hand tools		$750	
Van Customization		$1,000	
Total Van Cost:		$24,140	
Van Fixed Costs:		$2,925	
Monthly payment		$779	(Finance over 3 years at 10%)
Technician wages		$1,800	($20k per year + benefits)
Paging service		$25	
Insurance		$220	
Maintenance (@ 5%)		$101	
General Overhead Costs:		$7,191	(Including 20% buffer for error)
Office rent		$450	
Postage		$150	
Marketing		$2,500	
Insurance/benefits		$500	
Franchise fee ($15K)		$417	(Divided over 36 months)
Telephone		$140	
Secretary/appointment		$1,500	(Includes appointment scheduling)
Office equipment:		$336	(Finance over 3 years at 10%)
Computer	$5,000		
FAX	$900		
Copier	$1,500		
Furniture	$1,500		
Telephone	$500		
Misc	$1,000		
Total	$10,400		

Fixed Cost per Van Assuming Two Vans Are in Operation:			$6,520
Van fixed cost	$2,925		
Office overhead (pro-rated)	$3,595		
Fixed Cost per Van-Hour of Operation (The Scarce Item):			$20
Pro-rated cost per dealer inspection	$13		
Pro-rated cost per open market inspection	$29		
Variable costs per Inspection:			$11
Gasoline	$1	(Assume 10 miles/call @ 10mpg & $1/gal.)	
Misc consumables	$5		
Incentive to tech	$5		

Profit Margin Analysis for Dealer and Open Market Inspections

	Open Market	Dealer	
Revenue	$49.95	$39.00	
7% franchise fee	($3.50)	($2.73)	
Variable cost	($11.00)	($10.00)	(No gas for dealer insp.)
Contribution	$35.45	$26.27	
Inspections per month:	342	165	
Segment contribution:	$12,138	$4,336	
Monthly expected total contribution:		$16,475	
Less: total fixed cost		($13,040)	
Net total profit before tax:		$3,435	

Assuming a 33% Dealer/67% Open Market Breakdown in Inspections:		
Break-even monthly inspections quantity:		402
Total 2-van fixed cost:	$13,040	
Dealer inspections:	133	
Open market inspections:	269	

Break-even Quantity for Justifying Another Van Purchase:		
Van break-even for 33%/67% split:		90
Van incremental fixed cost:	$2,925	

Exhibit XI: Summary Financial Analysis for Kwik Chek in Austin

	Start	Mo. 1	Mo. 2	Mo. 3	Mo. 4	Mo. 5
Market share	0%	1%	2%	2%	3%	3%
Dealer inspections	0	8	17	17	25	25
Open market inspections	0	17	34	34	51	51
Total inspections	0	25	51	51	76	76
Number of vans needed	1	1	1	1	1	1
INCOME FROM PRODUCTION ACTIVITIES						
Dealer sales ($)	0	322	644	644	966	966
Open mkt sales ($)	0	855	1,710	1,710	2,565	2,565
Less: cost of good sold						
Variable costs	0	(271)	(542)	(542)	(813)	(813)
Franchise royalty	0	(82)	(165)	(165)	(247)	(247)
Gross margin	0	824	1,647	1,647	2,471	2,471
OPERATING EXPENSES						
General fixed costs	(7,191)	(7,191)	(7,191)	(7,191)	(7,191)	(7,191)
Van fixed costs	(2,925)	(2,925)	(2,925)	(2,925)	(2,925)	(2,925)
Net operating income	(10,116)	(9,292)	(8,469)	(8,469)	(7,645)	(7,645)
ADDITIONAL EXPENSES						
Promotion cost	(10,000) [Initial advertising, public relations, etc.]					
Misc. startup cost	(5,000)					
Net profit before tax	(25,116)	(9,292)	(8,469)	(8,469)	(7,645)	(7,645)
CUMULATIVE CASH FLOW	(25,116)	(34,408)	(42,877)	(51,345)	(58,990)	(66,635)

Assumptions:

1) There is a 33%/67% quantity split between dealers and open market inspections
2) Dealer inspections cost $39.00 and open market inspections cost $49.95
3) The maximum number of inspections per van is 272 per month
4) Office fixed expenses can handle up to 4 vans without expansion
5) Demand will never exceed 37.5% of all used car purchases
6) Kwik Chek can achieve a 20% share of the demand within 2 years
7) More than 20% share may not be possible due to competition
8) Available market for dealers and open market inspections in units is:

Dealers: 9,904 (From Exhibit VIII)
Open Mkt: 20,543 (From Exhibit VIII)

Mo. 6	Mo. 7	Mo. 8	Mo. 9	Mo. 10	Mo. 11	Mo. 12	Year 2	Year 3
4%	4%	5%	6%	7%	8%	9%	20%	20%
33	33	41	50	58	66	74	1,981	1,981
68	68	86	103	120	137	154	4,109	4,109
101	101	127	152	178	203	228	6,089	6,089
1	1	1	1	1	1	1	2	2
1,288	1,288	1,609	1,931	2,253	2,575	2,897	77,251	77,251
3,420	3,420	4,276	5,131	5,986	6,841	7,696	205,225	205,225
(1,083)	(1,083)	(1,354)	(1,625)	(1,896)	(2,167)	(2,438)	(65,003)	(65,003)
(330)	(330)	(412)	(494)	(577)	(659)	(741)	(19,773)	(19,773)
3,295	3,295	4,119	4,942	5,766	6,590	7,414	197,700	197,700
(7,191)	(7,191)	(7,191)	(7,191)	(7,191)	(7,191)	(7,191)	(86,292)	(86,292)
(2,925)	(2,925)	(2,925)	(2,925)	(2,925)	(2,925)	(2,925)	(70,200)	(70,200)
(6,821)	(6,821)	(5,997)	(5,174)	(4,350)	(3,526)	(2,702)	41,208	41,208
(6,821)	(6,821)	(5,997)	(5,174)	(4,350)	(3,526)	(2,702)	41,208	41,208
(73,456)	(80,277)	(86,274)	(91,448)	(95,797)	(99,323)	(102,026)	(60,818)	(19,610)

Exhibit XII: Owner/Mechanic Summary Financial Analysis for Kwik Chek in Austin

	Start	Mo. 1	Mo. 2	Mo. 3	Mo. 4	Mo. 5
Market share	0%	1%	2%	2%	3%	3%
Dealer inspections	0	8	17	17	25	25
Open market inspections	0	17	34	34	51	51
Total inspections	0	25	51	51	76	76
Number of vans needed	1	1	1	1	1	1
INCOME FROM PRODUCTION ACTIVITIES						
Dealer sales ($)	0	322	644	644	966	966
Open mkt sales ($)	0	855	1,710	1,710	2,565	2,565
Less: cost of good sold						
Variable costs	0	(144)	(288)	(288)	(432)	(432)
Franchise royalty	0	(82)	(165)	(165)	(247)	(247)
Gross margin	0	951	1,901	1,901	2,852	2,852
OPERATING EXPENSES						
General fixed costs	(7,191)	(7,191)	(7,191)	(7,191)	(7,191)	(7,191)
Van fixed costs	(1,125)	(1,125)	(1,125)	(1,125)	(1,125)	(1,125)
Net operating income	(8,316)	(7,365)	(6,415)	(6,415)	(5,464)	(5,464)
ADDITIONAL EXPENSES						
Promotion cost	(10,000) [Initial advertising, public relations, etc.]					
Misc. startup cost	(5,000)					
Net profit before tax	(23,316)	(7,365)	(6,415)	(6,415)	(5,464)	(5,464)
CUMULATIVE CASH FLOW	(23,316)	(30,681)	(37,096)	(43,511)	(48,975)	(54,439)

Assumptions:

1) There is a 33%/67% quantity split between dealers and open market inspections
2) Dealer inspections cost $39.00 and open market inspections cost $49.95
3) The maximum number of inspections per van is 272 per month
4) Office fixed expenses can handle up to 4 vans without expansion
5) Demand will never exceed 37.5% of all used car purchases
6) Kwik Chek can achieve a 20% share of the demand within 2 years
7) More than 20% share may not be possible due to competition
8) Available market for dealers and open market inspections in units is:

Dealers: 9,904 (From Exhibit VIII)

Open Mkt: 20,543 (From Exhibit VIII)

Mo. 6	Mo. 7	Mo. 8	Mo. 9	Mo. 10	Mo. 11	Mo. 12	Year 2	Year 3
4%	4%	5%	6%	7%	8%	9%	20%	20%
33	33	41	50	58	66	74	1,981	1,981
68	68	86	103	120	137	154	4,109	4,109
101	101	127	152	178	203	228	6,089	6,089
1	1	1	1	1	1	1	2	2
1,288	1,288	1,609	1,931	2,253	2,575	2,897	77,251	77,251
3,420	3,420	4,276	5,131	5,986	6,841	7,696	205,225	205,225
(576)	(576)	(720)	(864)	(1,008)	(1,152)	(1,296)	(65,003)	(65,003)
(330)	(330)	(412)	(494)	(577)	(659)	(741)	(19,773)	(19,773)
3,802	3,802	4,753	5,704	6,654	7,605	8,556	197,700	197,700
(7,191)	(7,191)	(7,191)	(7,191)	(7,191)	(7,191)	(7,191)	(86,292)	(86,292)
(1,125)	(1,125)	(1,125)	(1,125)	(1,125)	(1,125)	(1,125)	(21,600)	(21,600)
(4,514)	(4,514)	(3,563)	(2,612)	(1,662)	(711)	240	89,808	89,808
(4,514)	(4,514)	(3,563)	(2,612)	(1,662)	(711)	240	89,808	89,808
(58,953)	(63,466)	(67,029)	(69,642)	(71,303)	(72,014)	(71,775)	18,033	107,841

Legal Considerations

The primary legal issues that should be considered in establishing Kwik Chek as a national franchise are (1) franchiser liability for franchisee actions, and (2) termination of franchise agreement by either the franchiser or the franchisee.

The principal way that the franchiser can be held liable for the actions of a franchisee is if the franchisee represents itself as an agent of the parent company. To avoid this agency issue, all collateral literature published by the franchiser should indicate that all Kwik Chek operations are independently owned and operated. In this way, there can be no mistake on the part of the customer that the local franchisee is working their own business and on their own behalf.

A clear definition of the agency relationship will protect the franchiser from liability related to injury or accidents resulting from improper inspection and also from any financial liabilities that the franchisee may incur.

To address the termination of franchise agreement issue, it should be clearly delineated in the franchise agreement what the required payment procedures and time frames should be from the franchisee to the franchiser. In addition, the level of support that the franchisee can reasonably expect from the franchiser should also be clearly defined. In this way, there is less likelihood of misunderstanding by either party, and the franchiser is protected from having a franchisee that is not performing up to expectations bring down the rest of the organization.

In addition, if the franchiser has agreed to supply credit to the franchisee to start the business, then the franchiser should protect the investment by having strict reporting procedures as to the actions being taken by the franchisee to meet the required revenue goals.

Franchising agreements are being treated more as "relational contracts" that extend over a longer period of time than as individual contracts that have a clearly defined duration and outcome. Many courts are treating franchise agreements as a sort of marriage, and many of the precedents established for divorce law in community property states are being incorporated into termination of franchise agreements. The relationship is treated as a type of partnership, and the parties involved are compensated for their "expected" returns from the venture should it be terminated.

In this way, it should be clearly understood by the franchisee that should the franchisee lose the right to operate under the Kwik Chek name, the business is returned to the franchiser. An equitable settlement for the return can be established at the time of transfer.

Resources and Bibliography

Appendix

D

The following offers you extra resources on a variety of business and entrepreneurial subjects. I included website addresses where possible.

Small Business—General

American Chamber of Commerce Executives
4875 Eisenhower Avenue, Suite 250
Alexandria, VA 22304
703-998-0072
acce.org

The American Institute for Small Business
Educational Materials for Small Business and Entrepreneurship
426 Second Street
Excelsior, MN 55331
800-328-2906
aisb.biz

American Success Institute
5 North Main Street
Natick, MA 01760
508-651-3303
success.org

Business Owner's Toolkit
toolkit.com

Business Resource Center
morebusiness.com

IRS Small Business/Self-Employed Resource
irs.gov/businesses/small

The National Association for the Self-Employed
PO Box 612067
DFW Airport
Dallas, TX 75261-2067
800-232-6273
nase.org

National Business Incubation Association
20 East Circle Drive, #37198
Athens, OH 45701-3571
740-593-4331
nbia.org

Saint Louis University, eWeb: Education for Entrepreneurship
eweb.slu.edu

Service Core of Retired Executives (SCORE)
score.org

Small Business Development Centers (SBDC)
sba.gov/content/small-business-development-centers-sbdcs

SmartBiz.com General Business Information
smartbiz.com

U.S. Business Advisor (Sponsored by the SBA)
business.gov

U.S. Chamber of Commerce
1615 H Street NW
Washington, DC 20062-2000
800-638-6582
uschamber.com

U.S. Small Business Administration (SBA)
409 3rd Street SW
Washington, DC 20416
800-U-ASK-SBA
sba.gov

Special Topics

The following are specialized resources that may be of use to you in your business.

Census Information

U.S. Bureau of the Census
4700 Silver Hill Road
Washington, DC 20233-0001
301-763-4636
census.gov

Financing

American Express Home Page
americanexpress.com

General and Comprehensive Business Loan Information Link Page
smallbusinesscenter.com

LendingTree.com Commercial Loan Center
lendingtree.com/stm/sblc

Moneycafe.com
nfsn.com

SBA Finance Website
sba.gov/financing

Visa Home Page
usa.visa.com

Franchises

allBusiness.com, a D&B Company
allbusiness.com

American Association of Franchisees & Dealers
PO Box 81887
San Diego, CA 92138-1887
800-733-9858
aafd.org

Bison.com Franchise Opportunity Web Page
bison.com

Franchise Solutions
franchisesolutions.com/resource

Import Export Help General Links Web Page
importexporthelp.com

International Business
Business Network International
545 College Commerce Way
Upland, CA 91786
800-825-8286 (outside Southern California)
909-608-7575 (in Southern California)
bni.com

International Chamber of Commerce
1212 Avenue of the Americas
New York, NY 10036-1689
212-703-5060
iccwbo.org

International Franchise Association
1501 K Street NW, Suite 350
Washington, DC 20005
202-628-8000
franchise.org

Michigan State University GlobalEdge.com Web Page
globaledge.msu.edu

Nettizen.com Franchise Resource
nettizen.com

U.S. Agency for International Development (USAID)
Public Inquiries Information Center
U.S. Agency for International Development
Ronald Reagan Building
Washington, DC 20523-1000
202-712-0000
usaid.gov

U.S. Council for International Business
1212 Avenue of the Americas
New York, NY 10036
212-354-4480
uscib.org

Marketing—General

Marketing Resource Center
Concept Marketing Group, Inc.
8655 East Via de Ventura, Suite G-200
Scottsdale, AZ 85258
800-575-5369
marketingsource.com

Software Marketing General Resource Web Page
softwaremarketingresource.com

Market Research

General Internet Trends and Statistics
clickz.com/stats

InfoTrac General Business Information Source
infotrac.com

Specialized Market Research Reports
newsletters.com

The Wall Street Journal
wsj.com

Minorities in Business

General Entrepreneurship Information for the Black Community
einfonews.com

Hispanic Business Magazine Website
hispanicbusiness.com

Minority Business Entrepreneur Magazine Website
mbemag.com

National Minority Business Council
25 West 45th Street, Suite 301
New York, NY 10036
212-997-4753
nmbc.org

National Minority Supplier Development Council
1040 Avenue of the Americas, 2nd Floor
New York, NY 10018
212-944-2430
nmsdcus.org

U.S. Department of Commerce
Minority Business Development Agency
1401 Constitution Avenue NW
Washington, DC 20230
888-324-1551
mbda.gov

Patents

U.S. Patent and Trademark Office
PO Box 1450
Alexandria, VA 22313-1450
800-786-9199
uspto.gov

General Patent Information:

Oppedahl & Larson LLP
patents.com

General Intellectual Property Information:

University of New Hampshire Law School
piercelaw.edu/tfield/ipbasics.htm

Professional Associations

American Bar Association
321 North Clark Street
Chicago, IL 60654-7598
americanbar.org

American Chiropractic Association
1701 Clarendon Boulevard
Arlington, VA 22209
703-276-8800
acatoday.org

American Dental Association
211 East Chicago Avenue
Chicago, IL 60611-2678
312-440-2500
ada.org

American Institute of Architects
1735 New York Avenue NW
Washington, DC 20006-5292
202-626-7300
aia.org

American Medical Association
515 North State Street
Chicago, IL 60654
800-621-8335
ama-assn.org

National Society of Accountants
1010 North Fairfax Street
Alexandria, VA 22314
800-966-6679
nsacct.org

National Society of Professional Engineers
1420 King Street
Alexandria, VA 22314
703-684-2800
nspe.org

Women in Business

Center for Women's Business Research
1411 K Street NW, Suite 1350
Washington, DC 20005-3407
202-638-3060
nfwbo.org

National Association of Women Business Owners
8405 Greensboro Drive, Suite 800
McLean, VA 22102
703-506-3268
nawbo.org

U.S. Small Business Administration Office of Women's Business Ownership
409 Third Street SW
Washington, DC 20416
202-205-6673
sba.gov/about-offices-content/1/2895

Women's Business Enterprise National Council
1120 Connecticut Avenue NW, Suite 1000
Washington, DC 20036
202-872-5515, ext.10
wbenc.org

Bibliography

We can all learn from each other, and books are a great way to expand what you know. What follows is a listing of books that I have found valuable in my own work. Keep reading and keep learning.

General Small Business

Carlock, Randel, and John Ward. *Strategic Planning for the Family Business: Parallel Planning to Unify the Family and Business.* New York: Palgrave Macmillan, 2001.

———. *When Family Businesses Are Best: The Parallel Planning Process for Family Harmony and Business Success.* New York: Palgrave Macmillan, 2010.

Cushway, Barry. *The Employer's Handbook 2010–11: An Essential Guide to Employment Law, Personnel Policies, and Procedures, Seventh Edition.* Philadelphia: Kogan Page, 2010.

Entrepreneur Magazine. Starting an Import/Export Business. New York: John Wiley and Sons, Inc., 1995.

McQuown, Judith H. *Inc Yourself: How to Profit by Setting Up Your Own Corporation.* Franklin Lakes, NJ: Career Press, Inc., 2004.

McWhirter, Darien. *The Personnel Policy Handbook for Growing Companies.* Holbrook, MA: Bob Adams, Inc., 1994.

Paulson, Ed. *The Complete Idiot's Guide to Buying and Selling a Business.* Indianapolis: Alpha Books, 1999.

Sutton, Garrett, Ann Blackman, and Robert T. Kiyosaki. *Own Your Own Corporation: Why the Rich Own Their Own Companies and Everyone Else Works for Them.* New York: Warner Books, 2001.

Technology, Websites, and Social Networking

Barreca, Hugo. *Business Owner's Guide to the Internet: How to Build a Strong Web Presence for Your Business (Quick Start Your Business), 2nd Edition.* Naperville, IL: Sphinx Publishing, 2008.

Barreca, Hugo, and Julia O'Neill. *The Entrepreneur's Internet Handbook: Your Legal and Practical Guide to Starting a Business Website.* Naperville, IL: Sphinx Publishing, 2002.

Comm, Joel. *Twitter Power.* New York: John Wiley & Sons, Inc., 2009.

Gillan, Paul. *Secrets of Social Media Marketing.* Fresno, CA: Quill Driver Books, 2009.

Siegel, Carolyn. *Internet Marketing: Foundations and Applications, 2nd Edition.* Boston: Houghton Mifflin Company, 2006.

Tapscott, Don, David Ticoll, and Alex Lowy. *Digital Capital: Harnessing the Power of Business Webs.* Boston: Harvard Business School Press, 2000.

Collections, Accounting, Finance, and Taxes

Carter, Gary. *J. K. Lasser's Taxes Made Easy for Your Home Based Business.* New York: John Wiley & Sons, 2005.

Lasser, J. K. *Your Income Tax.* New York: John Wiley & Sons, updated and published annually.

Magos, Alice. *Small Business Financing: How and Where to Get It, 2nd Edition.* Riverwoods, IL: Commerce Clearing House, 2002.

Paulson, Ed. *The Complete Idiot's Guide to Personal Finance with Quicken.* Indianapolis, IN: Alpha Books, 1998.

Placencia, Jose, Bruce Weige, and Don Oliver. *Business Owner's Guide to Accounting and Bookkeeping.* Central Point, OR: PSI Research-Oasis Press, 1997.

Troy, Leo. *Almanac of Business and Industrial Financial Ratios, 2006 Edition.* Gaithersburg, MD: Aspen Publishers, Inc., 2006.

Warner, Ralph E. *Everybody's Guide to Small Claims Court, 8th Edition.* Berkeley, CA: Nolo Press, 2005.

Weltman, Barbara. *J. K. Lasser's Small Business Taxes 2006: Your Complete Guide to a Better Bottom Line.* New York: John Wiley & Sons, 2006.

Wilber, W. Kelsea. *Getting Paid in Full.* Naperville, IL: Sourcebooks Inc., 1994.

Marketing, Sales, and Promotion

Barban, Arnold, Steven Cristol, and Frank Kopec. *Essentials of Media Planning, 3rd Edition.* New York: McGraw Hill Trade, 1993.

Green, Charles. *Trust-Based Selling: Using Customer Focus and Collaboration to Build Long-Term Relationships.* New York: McGraw Hill, 2006.

Hopkins, Tom. *How to Master the Art of Selling.* New York: Business Plus, 2005.

Levinson, Jay Conrad. *Guerrilla Marketing: Secrets for Making Big Profits from Your Small Business, 3rd Edition.* New York: Mariner Books, 1998.

Additional Reading

Block, Peter. *Flawless Consulting: A Guide to Getting Your Expertise Used.* New York: Pfeiffer, 2011.

Carew, Rene. *The Complete Idiot's Guide to Discovering Your Perfect Career.* Indianapolis: Alpha Books, 2005.

Covey, Stephen. *The 7 Habits of Highly Effective People.* New York: Fireside/Simon & Schuster, 1989.

Johnson, Spencer. *One Minute for Myself.* New York: Avon, 1991.

Patsula, Peter J. *Successful Business Planning in 30 Days: A Step-By-Step Guide for Writing a Business Plan and Starting Your Own Business.* Mansfield, OH: Patsula Media, 2004.

Stewart, Thomas. *Intellectual Capital: The New Wealth of Organizations.* New York: Doubleday, 1997.

Especially for Women

Moore, Dorothy. *Careerpreneurs: Lessons from Leading Women Entrepreneurs on Building a Career Without Boundaries.* Palo Alto, CA: Davies-Black Publishing, 2000.

Moore, Dorothy, and Holly Buttner. *Women Entrepreneurs Moving Beyond the Glass Ceiling.* Thousand Oaks, CA: Sage Publications, 1997.

Pollak, Jane. *Soul Proprietor: 100 Lessons from a Lifestyle Entrepreneur.* Berkeley, CA: Publishers Group West, 2001.

Popcorn, Faith, and Lys Marigold. *EVEolution: The Eight Truths of Marketing to Women.* New York: Hyperion, 2000.

Shirk, Martha, and Anna Wadia. *Kitchen Table Entrepreneurs: How Eleven Women Escaped Poverty and Became Their Own Bosses.* Boulder, CO: Westview Press, 2004.

Silver, A. David. *Enterprising Women: Lessons from 100 of the Greatest Entrepreneurs of Our Day.* New York: Amacom Books, 1994.

International

Friedman, Thomas. *The World Is Flat 3.0: A Brief History of the Twenty-First Century.* New York: Picador, 2007.

McGregor, James. *One Billion Customers: Lessons from the Front Lines of Doing Business in China.* New York: Free Press, 2005.

Index

A

B

C

D

E

F

G-H

I-J-K

L

M

N-O

P

Q

R

S

T

U–V

W-X-Y-Z